HISTORICAL DICTIONARIES OF INTERNATIONAL ORGANIZATIONS SERIES
Jon Woronoff, Series Editor

European Organizations, by Derek W. Urwin. 1994
International Tribunals, by Boleslaw Adam Boczek. 1994
Aid and Development Organizations, by Guy Arnold. 1996
World Bank, by Anne C. M. Salda. 1997
United Nations Educational, Scientific and Cultural Organization (UNESCO), by Seth Spaulding and Lin Lin. 1997
Inter-American Organizations, by Larman C. Wilson and David W. Dent. 1997
World Health Organization, by Kelley Lee. 1998
International Monetary Fund, Second Edition, by Norman K. Humphreys. 1999
Refugee and Disaster Relief Organizations, Second Edition, by Robert F. Gorman. 2000
Arab and Islamic Organizations, by Frank A. Clements. 2001
International Organizations in Asia and the Pacific, by Derek McDougall. 2002
International Organizations in Sub-Saharan Africa, Second Edition, by Terry M. Mays and Mark W. DeLancey. 2002
League of Nations, by Anique H.M. van Ginneken. 2006
European Union, by Joaquín Roy and Aimee Kanner. 2006
United Nations, by Jacques Fomerand. 2007
Human Rights and Humanitarian Organizations, Second Edition, by Robert F. Gorman and Edward S. Mihalkanin. 2007
NATO and Other International Security Organizations, by Marco Rimanelli. 2008
International Organizations, by Michael G. Schechter. 2010
Multinational Peacekeeping, Third Edition, by Terry Mays. 2011
International Monetary Fund, Third Edition, by Sarah Tenney and Norman K. Humphreys. 2011.

Historical Dictionary of the International Monetary Fund

Third Edition

Sarah Tenney
Norman K. Humphreys

The Scarecrow Press, Inc.
Lanham • Toronto • Plymouth, UK
2011

Published by Scarecrow Press, Inc.
A wholly owned subsidiary of The Rowman & Littlefield Publishing Group, Inc.
4501 Forbes Boulevard, Suite 200, Lanham, Maryland 20706
http://www.scarecrowpress.com

Estover Road, Plymouth PL6 7PY, United Kingdom

British Library Cataloguing in Publication Information Available

Library of Congress Cataloging-in-Publication Data

Tenney, Sarah, 1960-
Historical dictionary of the International Monetary Fund / Sarah Tenney, Norman K. Humphreys. — 3rd ed.
p. cm. — (Historical dictionaries of international organizations series)
Prev. ed. entered under Norman K. Humphreys.
Includes bibliographical references.
ISBN 978-0-8108-6790-1 (cloth : alk. paper) — ISBN 978-0-8108-7531-9 (ebook)
1. International Monetary Fund—History—Dictionaries. 2. International finance—Dictionaries. 3. International Monetary Fund—History. I. Humphreys, Norman K., 1924- II. Humphreys, Norman K., 1924- Historical dictionary of the International Monetary Fund. III. Title.
HG3881.5.I58H86 2011
332.1'52--dc22

2010049348

∞™ The paper used in this publication meets the minimum requirements of American National Standard for Information Sciences—Permanence of Paper for Printed Library Materials, ANSI/NISO Z39.48-1992.

Printed in the United States of America

Contents

Editor's Foreword

Once a relatively obscure organization, known mainly to bankers and academics, over the past few decades the International Monetary Fund (IMF) has become better known than it would perhaps wish. It is talked up by some as a "central bank's central bank" and main savior in the event of serious financial crises. By others it is decried as a villain imposing its will on developing countries and possibly even causing some of the crises. This debate is far from resolved; if anything it has been fueled by recent events. But what is actually more important than whether the praise and criticism, the hopes and fears are justified today is whether the IMF will be better tomorrow once it has implemented yet another series of reforms. In studying its history, since it was founded in 1945, the growth and changes are impressive. And it is clear that the IMF does learn from its mistakes and is improved and reinforced by crises.

One can see this in the third edition of the *Historical Dictionary of the International Monetary Fund*, remarkably different from the second edition a decade back and the first edition two decades ago. While not strictly a history, it does present the IMF as it is today and also shows what it was like at earlier stages in its evolution while mentioning proposals for the future. It first traces the IMF's evolution in the chronology and then offers a broad general survey in the introduction. The list of acronyms helps readers through the maze of related organizations. But the dictionary section as always is the core of the book, with hundreds of entries on the IMF's constituent bodies; its policies, programs, and rules; its action in crucial member countries; those who have played an important role in managing it; and many of the problems and crises it has gone through. For those who want more information, further reading is provided in the bibliography, which includes both publications of the Fund itself and other independent works on it by observers with different views and conclusions.

This third edition was written by Sarah Tenney, building on the first two editions by Norman K. Humphreys. Mr. Humphreys is a graduate of the London School of Economics and Political Science and became a banker and freelance contributor to various financial journals in the city of London for a dozen years, with a stint of two years as economic and financial correspondent in Brazil. He joined the staff of the IMF in 1964 and, during a career of 23 years with the Fund, he served as its chief editor for more than a decade. Dr. Tenney studied at the University of Kent at Canterbury and received her PhD from the University of Mississippi. From 1987–2003 she was a special assistant to the director at the IMF and she is presently an assistant professor of political science and criminal justice at The Citadel. Over the years she has focused on international financial cooperation and coauthored "The Social Dimensions of the Work of the IMF" and is writing a book on surveillance. Most of the operations of the IMF are technical and hard for outsiders to follow, but this partly inside–partly outside view will do much to explain the activities and achievements of an organization that is, whether we realize it or not, one of the most important in the world.

Jon Woronoff
Series Editor

Acknowledgments

In updating and preparing the manuscript of this third edition of the *Historical Dictionary of the International Monetary Fund*, we have again drawn extensively on the published work of others, particularly on the publications of the Fund. Much of the basic material contained herein appeared in the first two editions. In this respect, the work of Norman K. Humphreys in preparing the second edition, published in 1998, is paramount.

As he noted at that time, a significant amount of the material has been drawn from published histories of the Fund prepared by its historians, J. Keith Horsefield, Margaret Garritsen de Vries, and James Boughton. The dictionary also draws heavily on IMF official documents. For the sake of accuracy, the language follows as closely as possible that of the originals. These documents include the Fund's Articles of Agreement, Annual Reports of the IMF, Executive Board decisions, IMF Factsheets published on the Fund's official website, and Chairmen's summings up of Board deliberations, as well as staff reports, pamphlets, and other IMF staff publications. All of these documents are available to the public and many can be accessed through the Fund's official external website.

It should be noted that, like the previous editions, this third edition of the *Historical Dictionary of the International Monetary Fund* can be seen as only a snapshot of the institution taken at the time of publication. As the history clearly shows, the Fund has evolved over time largely in response to the demands of an increasingly integrated global economy and its expanding membership. These persistent forces of change will likely continue to determine the direction of the institution for the foreseeable future.

Of course, it remains to be noted that although the factual material for this volume has been drawn mainly from "official" sources, responsibility for its accuracy and interpretation rests solely with the authors.

Norman K. Humphreys and Sarah Tenney

Acronyms and Abbreviations

It is the convention to refer to institutions and organizations, particularly international bodies, by their abbreviations and acronyms. This volume has tried to avoid the resultant "alphabet soup," but the abbreviations and acronyms in common use for many of these organizations, as well as the facilities, accounts, and organs of the Fund, are listed below.

ACB	Africa Capacity-Building Initiative
ACBF	African Capacity-Building Foundation
ADB	Asian Development Bank
AFRITAC	African Regional Technical Assistance Center
AMF	African Monetary Fund
AML/CFT	Anti-Money Laundering and Combating the Financing of Terrorism
AREAER	Annual Report on Exchange Arrangements and Exchange Restrictions
ASEAN	Association of Southeast Asian Nations
BCEAO	Banque Centrale des Etats de l'Afrique de l'Ouest
BEAC	Banque des Etats de l'Afrique Centrale
BIS	Bank for International Settlements
BRSA	Borrowed Resources Suspense Account
BSFF	buffer stock financing facility
CAC	Collective Action Clause
CARTAC	Caribbean Regional Technical Assistance Center
CCFF	compensatory and contingency financing facility
CCL	Contingent Credit Lines
CEMAC	Central African Economic and Monetary Community
CFF	compensatory financing facility
CMCG	Capital Markets Consultative Group
CRU	collective reserve unit
CSF	Currency Stabilization Fund
DC	Development Committee
DDSR	debt and debt-service reduction
DQAF	Data Quality Assessment Framework
DSA	Debt Sustainability Assessment

DSBB	Data Standards Bulletin Board
DSF	Debt Sustainability Framework
EAP	Enlarged Access Policy
EBRD	European Bank for Reconstruction and Development
EC	European Community
ECB	European Central Bank
ECCB	Eastern Caribbean Central Bank
ECCU	Eastern Caribbean Currency Union
ECOFIN	Council of Economic and Finance Ministers
ECU	European currency unit
EFF	Extended Fund facility
EFM	Emergency Financing Mechanism
EMS	European Monetary System
EMU	Economic and Monetary Union
ENDA	Emergency Natural Disaster Assistance
EPCA	Emergency Post-Conflict Assistance
ESAF	Enhanced structural adjustment facility
ESF	Exogenous shocks facility
EU	European Union
EURIBOR	Euro Interbank Offered Rate
FAA	Framework Administered Account for Technical Assistance Activities
FATF	Financial Action Task Force
FCC	Forward Commitment Capacity
FCL	Flexible Credit Line
FSAP	Financial Sector Assessment Program
FSI	Financial Soundness Indicator
FSLC	Bank-Fund Financial Sector Liaison Committee
FSSA	Financial System Stability Assessment
FSU	Former Soviet Union
GAB	General Arrangements to Borrow
GATT	General Agreement on Tariffs and Trade
GCC	Gulf Cooperation Council
GDDS	General Data Dissemination System
GDP	Gross domestic product
GFSR	Global Financial Stability Report
GMR	Global Monitoring Report
GNP	Gross national product
GRA	General Resources Account
HIPC	heavily indebted poor countries
IBRD	International Bank for Reconstruction and Development (World Bank)
IC	Interim Committee

ICSID	International Center for the Settlement of Investment Disputes
IDA	International Development Association
IDB	Inter-American Development Bank
IEO	Independent Evaluation Office
IFC	International Finance Corporation
IIF	Institute for International Finance
IMF	International Monetary Fund
IMFC	International Monetary and Financial Committee
INS	IMF Institute
I-PRSP	Interim Poverty Reduction Strategy Paper
ISDB	Islamic Development Bank
ITO	International Trade Organization
JIC	Joint IMF/World Bank Implementation Committee
JSA	Joint Staff Assessments
JSAN	Joint Staff Advisory Note
LIBOR	London Interbank Offered Rate
LOI	Letter of Intent
MCM	Monetary and Capital Markets Department
MD	Managing Director
MDG	Millennium Development Goals
MDRI	Multilateral Debt Relief Initiative
MEFP	Memorandum on Economic and Financial Policies
MERM	Multilateral exchange rate model
METAC	Middle Eastern Regional Technical Assistance Center
MFG	Manila Framework Group
MIGA	Multilateral Investment Guarantee Agency
MTS	Medium Term Strategy
NAB	New Arrangements to Borrow
NEPAD	New Partnership for Africa's Development
NGA	Nongovernmental agencies
NGO	Nongovernmental organization
ODA	Official development assistance
OECD	Organization for Economic Cooperation and Development
OFC	Offshore Financial Center
OIA	Office of Internal Audit
OPEC	Organization of Petroleum Exporting Countries
PACT	Partnership for Capacity Building in Africa
PFTAC	Pacific Financial Technical Assistance Center
PIN	Press/Public Information Notices
PPM	Post-Program Monitoring
PRGF	Poverty reduction and growth facility
PRGT	Poverty Reduction and Growth Trust

PRS	Poverty Reduction Strategy
PRSP	Poverty Reduction Strategy Paper
PSI	Policy Support Instrument
PSIA	Poverty and Social Impact Analysis
RAP	Rights accumulation program
ROSC	Report on the Observance of Standards and Codes
RTAC	Regional Technical Assistance Center
SAF	Structural adjustment facility
SBA	Stand-by arrangement
SCA	Special Contingent Account
SDA	Special Disbursement Account
SDDS	Special Data Dissemination Standard
SDR	Special Drawing Right
SFF	Supplementary financing facility
SMP	Staff-Monitored Program
SRF	Supplemental reserve facility
SRP	Staff Retirement Plan
SSN	Social Safety Net
STF	Systemic transformation facility
TIM	Trade Integration Mechanism
TMU	Technical Memorandum of Understanding
TPRM	Trade Policy Review Mechanism
UN	United Nations
UNCTAD	United Nations Conference on Trade and Development
UNDP	United Nations Development Programme
UNEP	United Nations Environmental Programme
USSR	Union of Soviet Socialist Republics
VAT	Value-added tax
WAEMU	West African Economic and Monetary Union
WEMD	World Economic and Market Developments
WEO	*World Economic Outlook*
WTO	World Trade Organization

Chronology

1944 1–22 July: The International Monetary and Financial Conference was held at Bretton Woods, New Hampshire, attended by representatives from 44 countries. The Articles of Agreement of the International Monetary Fund (IMF) and the World Bank were put in final form.

1945 27 December: The Fund's Articles of Agreement entered into force with the signatures of 29 governments, accounting for 80 percent of the original quotas.

1946 8–18 March: The inaugural meeting of the Board of Governors was held in Savannah, Georgia. It was decided that the Fund's headquarters would be in Washington, D.C., the by-laws were adopted, and the first Executive Directors were elected. **6 May:** The Executive Board held its inaugural meeting, consisting of 12 Executive Directors, five appointed by each of the five members having the largest quotas in the Fund, and seven elected by groups of members. Camille Gutt, of Belgium, became the first Managing Director of the Fund. **27 September:** The first annual meetings of the Boards of Governors of the Fund and the World Bank opened in Washington, D.C. **18 December:** Initial par values were agreed upon for most members and their nonmetropolitan areas.

1947 1 March: The Fund opened its doors for financial operations. **8 May:** The first drawing on the Fund was made by France, for $25 million. **18 December:** The Fund circulated a letter to all members, setting out its policies on multiple currency practices.

1948 25 January: The Fund first exercised its authority over members' exchange rates by objecting to a proposed change in the par value of the French franc on the grounds that it involved the introduction of a multiple currency practice. **19 September:** The pound sterling was devalued, a move that was followed in the next few days by similar devaluations by a number of other members.

1950 **1 March:** The first issue of the *Annual Report on Exchange Restrictions* was published (renamed the *Annual Report on Exchange Arrangement and Exchange Restrictions* after the par value system collapsed in the 1970s).

1951 **3 August:** Ivar Rooth, of Sweden, became the second Managing Director of the Fund.

1952 **13 February:** The Fund codified its policies on the use of its resources, establishing the tranche policies. Members were allowed virtually automatic use of their gold tranche. A period of three to five years was established for repayments to the Fund. In addition, a general framework was agreed upon for use of the Fund's resources under what later came to be known as "stand-by arrangements." **1 March:** In accordance with its Articles, the Fund began annual consultations with members who were maintaining exchange restrictions under Article XIV five years after the Fund began financial operations. **19 June:** The Fund entered into its first stand-by arrangement, with Belgium.

1956 **17 October:** The Fund approved drawings and stand-by arrangements for France and the United Kingdom, prompted in part by the loss of revenue from the closing of the Suez Canal. These drawings were the first major use made of the Fund's resources by advanced industrial countries and served to signal that the Fund would be a significant player in the international financial community. **21 November:** Per Jacobsson, of Sweden, became the third Managing Director of the Fund.

1958 **29 December:** Fourteen Western European countries made their currencies externally convertible for current transactions. Nonresidents were able to freely transfer holdings of one currency into any other currency. It was the first major step toward the multilateral trading system envisioned in the Articles of Agreement.

1959 **9 September:** The first general increase in Fund quotas became effective, raising total quotas from $9.2 billion to $14 billion.

1961 **15 February:** Nine Western European countries accepted the obligations of Article VIII, thereby making all major currencies convertible.

1962 **24 October:** The General Arrangements to Borrow went into effect, whereby the 10 largest industrial members agreed to be on call to lend the Fund the equivalent of $6 billion if needed to prevent a disruption of the international payments system. The participants were Belgium, Canada, France, Germany, Italy, Japan, the Netherlands, Sweden, the United Kingdom, and the United States. The arrangements were the beginning of the so-called Group of Ten.

1963 27 February: The compensatory financing facility was established. Under the facility, members experiencing temporary shortfalls in their export earnings could draw on the Fund. It was the first of the facilities established to finance a particular element in a country's balance of payments, rather than dealing with the balance of payments as a whole. Other later facilities were the oil facilities, the buffer stock financing facility, the emergency assistance facility, the structural adjustment facility, and the systemic transformation facility. **5 May:** Per Jacobsson, the Fund's Managing Director, died in office. **1 September:** Pierre-Paul Schweitzer, of France, became the fourth Managing Director. **27 September:** The Managing Director announced in his opening address to the annual meetings that the question of international liquidity was the business of the Fund and that the Fund would be intensifying its studies on the problem. The announcement was a contradiction of the Group of Ten's efforts to make international liquidity a matter of concern only to the industrial countries and to limit any scheme for reserve creation to those countries.

1965 15 October: The Executive Board agreed to a four-year renewal of the General Arrangements to Borrow. The terms of the arrangements were left unchanged, providing for the Fund to borrow up to the equivalent of $6 billion from 10 members.

1966 23 February: A second general increase of 25 percent in quotas was agreed to, along with special increases for 16 members. Total quotas in the Fund rose, as a result, from $16 billion to $21 billion. **3 March:** The Managing Director proposed to the Executive Board, and then to the Group of Ten, an approach to reserve creation through the Fund that would include distribution of any new reserve assets to all members. It was an approach that would culminate in the Special Drawing Rights (SDRs) scheme three years later. **20 September:** The compensatory financing facility, introduced in 1963, was extended and liberalized. **23 November:** It was agreed that Executive Directors of the Fund, representing all Fund members, would hold a series of meetings with Deputies of the Group of Ten to discuss reserve creation schemes. These meetings, in effect, brought representatives of Third World countries face to face with their counterparts from the industrial countries for the first time in discussing problems of international liquidity. **28–30 November:** The first joint meeting of the Executive Directors and Deputies of the Group of Ten, held in Washington, D.C., was a further step toward a universal reserve creation scheme.

1967 25–26 January: A second meeting of the Executive Directors and the Deputies of the Group of Ten, held in London, began to consider seriously a plan to establish SDRs. **25–26 April:** The Executive Directors and Deputies of the Group of Ten met for a third time, in Washington, D.C. **19–21**

June: The Executive Directors and Deputies of the Group of Ten met for the fourth time, in London. The SDR scheme began to take final shape. **26 August:** The ministers and governors of the Group of Ten met in London and agreed on voting majorities and reconstitution provisions for an SDR facility. **29 September:** At the annual meetings held in Rio de Janeiro the Board of Governors adopted a resolution, to which was attached an *Outline of a Facility Based on Special Drawing Rights in the Fund*, requesting the Executive Board to begin drafting appropriate amendments to the Articles of Agreement, incorporating the new facility and other, mostly minor, reforms into the Articles. **19–29 November:** The United Kingdom devalued the pound sterling from $2.80 to $2.40 per pound. The Fund approved a stand-by arrangement for the United Kingdom in the amount of $1.4 billion.

1968 16 March: A two-tier market for gold was established as a result of a decision by the central banks from seven industrial member countries to buy and sell gold at the official price of $35 an ounce only in transactions with monetary authorities. The price at which private transactions in gold were transacted was thus left to be determined by supply and demand. **29–30 March:** The ministers and governors of the Group of Ten met in Stockholm, Sweden, to resolve several issues in the proposed first amendment to the Articles of Agreement that were being drafted by the Executive Directors. **16 April:** The Executive Board completed its work on the amendment to the Articles and submitted its report to the Board of Governors. **31 May:** The Board of Governors approved the proposed first amendment, which was then submitted to members for acceptance and ratification. **4–19 June:** Heavy use was made of the Fund's financial resources when France drew $645 million and the United Kingdom drew $1.4 billion under stand-by arrangements approved in November 1967. **20 September:** Prompted by what they considered to be the favorable terms of the stand-by arrangement approved for the United Kingdom in 1967, Executive Directors representing the developing countries successfully pressed for the adoption of guidelines that would ensure uniform and equitable treatment for all members in the use of the Fund's financial resources.

1969 20 June: A new stand-by arrangement, in the amount of $1 billion, was approved for the United Kingdom. **25 June:** The buffer stock financing facility was established. **28 June:** The first amendment to the Articles of Agreement entered into force, authorizing the establishment of the SDR facility and introducing a number of minor operational reforms. **6 August:** The Special Drawing Account was established, setting the stage for a distribution of SDRs in the years 1970–1972. **10 August:** France devalued the franc by 11.1 percent. **19 September:** A stand-by arrangement, for $985 million, was approved for France. **29 September:** In the face of persistent surpluses in its balance of payments, the Federal Republic of Germany allowed the rate for the deutsche mark to float. **3 October:** The Board of Governors approved the Managing Director's proposal to make an allocation of SDRs, amounting to SDR 9.3 billion over a basic period of three years, beginning 1 January 1970. This was the first allocation of SDRs. **17 October:** The Executive Board approved a second renewal of the General Arrangements to Borrow, under which the Fund could borrow up to the equivalent of $6 billion from its 10 largest industrial members. The renewal was for five years, to begin 24 October 1970. **28 October:** The Federal Republic of Germany ended the floating of its currency by revaluing the deutsche mark by 8.39 percent.

1970 1 January: The first allocation of SDRs was made, for SDR 3.5 billion, distributed among 104 participants, with the largest participant, the United States, receiving SDR 867 million and the participant with the smallest quota, Botswana, receiving SDR 504,000. **9 February:** A third general increase in Fund quotas was approved by the Board of Governors, raising total quotas from $21.3 billion to $28.9 billion, an increase of 36 percent. **25 November:** The International Tin Agreement became the first commodity agreement for which use of the buffer stock financing facility was authorized.

1971 1 January: The second allocation of SDRs was for SDR 2.9 billion, distributed among 109 participants. **9–11 May:** In the face of heavy capital movements, the Federal Republic of Germany and the Netherlands allowed the rates for their currencies to float. Austria revalued its currency, and Belgium-Luxembourg enlarged their free market for capital transactions. **16 July:** The first purchases under the buffer stock financing facility were made by Bolivia and Indonesia. **15 August:** The United States announced that it would no longer freely buy and sell gold for the settlement of international transactions, thus suspending the convertibility of the dollar held by official institutions. The announcement, in effect, brought to an end the Bretton Woods system, although there was an attempt to maintain a fixed-rate (i.e., central rate) exchange rate system for another 18 months, before the Bretton Woods system finally collapsed and generalized floating became the norm. **16 August:** For the next four months, exchange rates were in total disarray, with Fund members introducing various exchange rate arrangements, including floating currencies by some members. **17–18 December:** The Group of Ten concluded the Smithsonian agreement, providing for the realignment of the major currencies and an increase in the official price of gold from $35 to $38 an ounce. It was the first time that exchange rates had been negotiated in a multinational conference. **18 December:** The Fund formally established a temporary regime of central rates and wider margins, set at 2.25 percent either side of an established central rate, thereby providing for an overall margin of 4.5 percent.

1972 1 January: The third and final allocation of SDRs, amounting to SDR 2.95 billion, was made for the first basic period. **20 March:** The Board of Governors authorized the Fund to express its accounts in terms of the SDR instead of U.S. dollars. **24 April:** The European Community's (EC's) narrow margins agreement went into effect for six currencies, limiting margins to 2.25 percent, half the margin established under the Fund's temporary regime of central rates. **8 May:** A new par value for the U.S. dollar was established, based on the new price of gold of $38 an ounce agreed at the Smithsonian Institution in December 1971. **23 June:** The British authorities announced that the pound sterling would float. This action was the first break in the pattern of rates established by the Smithsonian agreement. **26 July:** The Committee of Twenty (formally known as the *Committee of the Board of Governors on Reform of the International Monetary System and Related Issues*) was established to negotiate a reformed international monetary system. **6 September:** The Executive Board published a report, *Reform of the International Monetary System*, establishing a base for further study and discussion. **28 September:** The Committee of Twenty held its inaugural meeting, setting a target of two years to complete its work.

1973 1 January: A second basic period began, in which no SDRs were allocated. **22–23 January:** Italy introduced a free market for capital transactions and Switzerland floated the Swiss franc, further undermining the Smithsonian agreement. **19 March:** The EC countries introduced a joint float for their currencies against the U.S. dollar. This marked the beginning of generalized floating and the end of the attempt to maintain an international system of fixed rates. **22–27 March:** In view of the final breakdown of a regulated system, the Deputies of the Committee of Twenty embarked with urgency on the drafting of an outline of a reformed system. The Committee, reflecting the desire of the international financial community, reiterated its preference for a new exchange rate regime based on "stable but adjustable par values." **21 May–31 July:** The Deputies of the Committee of Twenty drafted an *Outline of Reform*, and the Committee of Twenty held its third meeting. **1 September:** H. Johannes Witteveen, of the Netherlands, became the fifth Managing Director of the Fund. **5–24 September:** The Deputies of the Committee of Twenty met in Paris and failed to agree on arrangements for a reformed international monetary system. Later, at a meeting of the Committee of Twenty, held in Nairobi in conjunction with the annual meeting of the Board of Governors, it became clear that there would be no early agreement on reforming the system. **10–17 October:** Six members of the Organization of Petroleum

Exporting Countries (OPEC), meeting alone, increased prices for crude oil by about 70 percent. The meeting was a forerunner of future crude oil price increases that would disrupt the world economy throughout the 1970s. **23 December:** Six oil exporting countries again announced increases in the prices of crude oil, thus nearly quadrupling prices that had come into effect three months earlier.

1974 3 January: The Managing Director of the Fund proposed the establishment of a temporary facility in the Fund to finance members' balance of payments deficits caused by the additional costs of oil imports. **17–18 January:** The Committee of Twenty, meeting in Rome, suspended efforts for a full-scale reform of the international monetary system. The Fund staff presented the Committee with its estimate that in 1974 the aggregate balance of payments deficit of developing countries would be of an unprecedented magnitude. **7–9 May:** The Deputies of the Committee of Twenty completed a draft of a revised *Outline of Reform* and discussed the immediate steps required to move existing arrangements forward. **10–11 June:** The Deputies of the Committee of Twenty held a final meeting and completed their recommendations. **12–13 June:** At its final meeting, the Committee of Twenty agreed on a number of immediate steps to help the international monetary system evolve and on an *Outline of Reform* that the international monetary authorities should endeavor to work out and implement in the future. The immediate steps included the establishment of an Interim Committee, with advisory powers; the adoption of a method of valuing the SDR based on a basket of 16 currencies; establishment of guidelines for the management of floating exchange rates; establishment of an oil facility in the Fund; provision for members to pledge, on a voluntary basis, not to intensify restrictions; early adoption of an extended facility in the Fund, whereby developing countries could use Fund financing on terms of up to 10 years to address structural changes in their economies; and the establishment of a committee to study the question of the transfer of real resources to developing countries. **1 July:** The Fund introduced a new method of valuing the SDR, based on a basket of the 16 currencies most used in world trade instead of gold. **22 August:** First use was made of the oil facility. **13 September:** An extended facility was established in the Fund to give medium-term assistance to developing member countries. **30 September:** The Managing Director proposed that another larger oil facility be established for 1975. **2 October:** The Interim Committee of the Fund's Board of Governors on the International Monetary System was established, as was the Joint Ministerial Committee of the Boards of Governors of the Bank and Fund on the Transfer of Real Resources to Developing Countries (the Development Committee). **23 October:** The General Arrangements to Borrow were renewed for the third time, until October 1980.

1975 15–16 January: The Interim Committee recommended the establishment of an oil facility for 1975 and a Subsidy Account to help the most seriously affected developing countries defray the interest cost of using the facility. It was also agreed that under the sixth general review, total quotas should be increased from SDR 29.2 billion to SDR 39 billion, with the quotas of oil exporting members as a group being doubled. **14 March:** An oil facility for 1975 was established. **1 August:** A Subsidy Account was established to assist the Fund's most seriously affected members to meet the cost of using the 1975 oil facility. **31 August:** The Interim Committee agreed upon the sale of one-sixth of the Fund's gold (25 million ounces) for the benefit of developing members, the establishment of a Trust Fund, and the restitution of one-sixth of the Fund's gold to all members. **15–17 November:** The first economic summit meeting was held by six industrial nations in Rambouillet, France. The U.S. and French monetary authorities settled their differences on the exchange rate system that was to be incorporated in the amended Articles of Agreement of the Fund. **24 December:** The compensatory financing facility, which had been established in 1963 and liberalized in 1966, was further liberalized. The changes included a technical change in the method of calculating export shortfalls so that the shortfalls could be larger than under the previous procedure, and that drawings under the facility would be allowed up to a larger proportion of a member's quota. **31 December:** The United Kingdom drew SDR 1 billion under the 1975 oil facility and the Fund approved a one-year stand-by arrangement for SDR 700 million, in the first credit tranche.

1976 7–8 January: Meeting in Jamaica, the Interim Committee agreed on an interim reform of the international monetary system, to be legalized in a second amendment to the Articles of Agreement. The Committee's conclusions included agreement on exchange arrangements, the treatment of gold, establishment of the trust fund for developing countries, and the distribution of quota increases among individual members. The quota increases were subject to the second amendment coming into effect, but until that time the Committee agreed to a temporary enlargement of members' access to the Fund's resources under existing quotas. **19 January:** Following the recommendation by the Interim Committee, the Executive Board extended the size of each credit tranche by 45 percent, enabling members to increase their potential for drawing on the Fund's regular resources by that amount, pending the coming into effect of the sixth general review of quotas. **30 April:** The Board of Governors approved the proposed second amendment to the Articles of Agreement, which was then submitted to member governments for acceptance and ratification. **5 May:** The Fund announced a program to dispose of one-third of its gold holdings, one-sixth to be sold by auction over a two-year period and one-sixth to be restituted to members. The trust fund was established.

3 November: Participants in the General Arrangements to Borrow agreed that Japan should almost quadruple its commitment under the arrangements, thereby raising the total amount available to about SDR 6.2 billion.

1977 3 January: The Executive Board approved a two-year stand-by arrangement for the United Kingdom for SDR 3.36 billion, the largest amount ever approved. **25 January:** The Fund made the first loans to 12 members from the trust fund. **23 February:** The Fund completed the first of four annual restitutions of gold to its members, amounting to six million ounces, sold at the official price of SDR 35 an ounce to 112 members in proportion to their quotas. **29 April:** The Executive Board took its first decision on how "firm surveillance" of members' exchange rate policies would be implemented after the second amendment became effective. It agreed on three broad principles: members should avoid manipulating exchange rates to gain unfair advantage; members should intervene in exchange markets to counter disorderly conditions; and members should take into account in their intervention policies the interests of other members. **6 August:** The Managing Director invited 14 potential lenders to the Fund to meet in Paris to discuss the amounts and terms on which they would lend to the Fund to establish a supplementary financing facility in the Fund. The borrowed resources would be used to supplement the Fund's regular resources, enabling members to draw resources from the Fund in excess of their credit tranches, with longer repayment terms. **29 August:** The supplementary financing facility was established, to become effective when loan commitments totaling not less than SDR 7.75 billion were in effect.

1978 13 March: The quota increases resulting from the sixth general review went into effect. **1 April:** The second amendment to the Articles of Agreement went into effect, after three-fifths of the membership representing four-fifths of total voting power had accepted the increases. The relevant resolution had been submitted to the membership on 30 April 1976, and its acceptance by the requisite number of members and votes had taken nearly two years. **29–30 April:** The Interim Committee, meeting in Mexico City, agreed on a coordinated strategy to regenerate growth in a stagnant world economy. **17 June:** Jacques de Larosière, of France, succeeded Witteveen as the sixth Managing Director of the Fund. **24 September:** The Interim Committee recommended an increase of 50 percent in the overall size of members' quotas under the seventh general review, raising total quotas from SDR 39 billion to SDR 59.5 billion. The Committee also agreed on an allocation of SDRs of SDR 4 billion in each of the three years 1979, 1980, and 1981, the third basic period. **4–5 December:** The European Council agreed to introduce the European Monetary System (EMS) on 1 January 1979.

1979 **1 January:** SDR 4 billion were allocated to 137 Fund members as the first of three annual allocations in the basic period 1979–1981. **23 February:** The supplementary financing facility became operative after lending commitments had reached SDR 7.5 billion. **2 March:** The Executive Board completed a comprehensive review of conditionality attached to the use of the Fund's financial resources, the first such review since 1968. The review codified and clarified existing guidelines on the use of the Fund's general resources (i.e., resources not borrowed or held by the trust fund). **7 March:** The Interim Committee, meeting in Washington, D.C., asked the Executive Board to set up a substitution account that would accept deposits in foreign exchange from members on a voluntary basis in exchange for an equivalent amount of SDR-denominated claims. Such an account had been discussed extensively by the Committee of Twenty and other bodies as part of the reform of the international monetary system. The Interim Committee's proposal did not come to fruition. **13 March:** The EMS came into existence. **12 April:** The Tokyo Round of Multilateral Trade Negotiations was concluded. **28 June:** The OPEC announced an increase of 24 percent in the price of crude oil. This large increase, which followed smaller increases announced a few months earlier, raised the "marker" price of oil by 42 percent over its 1978 level (i.e., from $12.70 to $18 a barrel). **2 August:** The compensatory financing facility was further liberalized by, among other things, premitting receipts from travel and from workers' remittances to be taken into account in calculating shortfalls. **24 August:** The General Arrangements to Borrow were renewed, for the fourth time, for another five years, until 23 October 1985. **3 December:** The maximum repayment period under the extended facility was increased from 8 to 10 years.

1980 **1 January:** The Fund allocated SDR 4 billion to 139 members, the second of three annual allocations to be made in the third basic period. **17 April:** The People's Republic of China was recognized as a member of the Fund. **25 April:** The Interim Committee, meeting in Hamburg, agreed that the Fund should play a growing role in the adjustment and financing of payment imbalances and the recycling of funds of surplus balance of payments countries to members in balance of payments deficit. It was recognized that further Fund borrowing and longer terms of repayment for members in balance of payments deficit were needed. The Committee, reversing a position that it had taken earlier, concluded that agreement on a substitution account was unlikely in the foreseeable future. **7 May:** The gold sales program agreed in August 1975 was completed. Under the program, 25 million ounces of gold had been sold (restituted) to countries that were members of the Fund on 31 August 1975 at the official price of SDR 35 an ounce. In addition, 25 million ounces of gold had been auctioned over a four-year period, raising a total of SDR 4.6 billion, of which $1.3 billion had been distributed directly to 104 developing members and the balance, together with income from investments, had been made available for concessionary loans by the trust fund to 62 eligible members. **8 September:** China's quota in the Fund, which had remained at SDR 550 million set in the original Articles, was increased to SDR 1.2 billion. **17 September:** The Executive Board took a number of decisions to enhance the attractiveness of the SDR, the most important of which were reducing the basket from 16 to 5 currencies (U.S. dollar, deutsche mark, French franc, pound sterling, and Japanese yen) and raising the rate of interest on the SDR to the market rate. **27 September:** The Interim Committee, meeting in Washington, D.C., recommended that potential Fund assistance to members be enlarged to 200 percent of quota over a three-year period, up to a total of 600 percent, excluding use of the compensatory financing facility and the buffer stock financing facility. **29 November:** The increase in quotas under the seventh general review became effective, raising the Fund's general resources from SDR 39.8 billion to SDR 60 billion. **17 December:** A subsidy account for the supplementary financing facility was established.

1981 1 January: The third and final allocation of SDRs, amounting to SDR 4 billion, was made to 141 members for the third basic period. **11 March:** In accordance with the Interim Committee's earlier recommendation, the Executive Board introduced a policy of "enlarged access." Under the new policy, the Fund could approve stand-by or extended arrangements for up to 150 percent of a member's new quota each year, for a period of three years, with a cumulative limit of 600 percent of quota. **31 March:** The final loan disbursement from the trust fund, which was established in May 1976, brought total disbursements from the Trust to SDR 3 billion. **6–7 May:** After the Executive Board had authorized the Managing Director to borrow from the Saudi Arabian Monetary Agency, the Fund concluded an agreement under which the Agency would lend the Fund SDR 4 billion in the first year of the commitment period and up to SDR 8 billion in the second year of a six-year commitment period. These commitments enabled the enlarged access policy to become operative. **13 May:** The compensatory financing facility was again amended to cover financing to members that encountered balance of payments difficulties caused by an excessive rise in the cost of cereal imports that were largely beyond the control of the member. The amendment was expected to be of particular benefit to low-income countries. **21 May:** The Interim Committee, meeting in Gabon, emphasized the need for effective adjustment policies among members and urged the Executive Board to work on the eighth general review of quotas. **31 May:** The quota for Saudi Arabia was increased from SDR 1 billion to SDR 2.1 billion, in view of its enlarged role in the world economy resulting from the oil price increases in the 1970s. **9 June:** As required under the Articles, the Managing Director consulted with participants in the SDR facility and found no consensus in favor of allocations for the fourth basic period, to begin on 1 January 1982. **4 August:** The Fund reached agreement with the Bank for International Settlements (BIS) and with the central banks or monetary agencies of 16 industrial countries to lend the Fund the equivalent of SDR 1.3 billion over a period of two years. **27 September:** The Interim Committee, after a two-day meeting in Washington, D.C., again urged industrial countries to reduce inflation and noted concern about the problems of adjustment and financing in non-oil-developing countries. While agreeing that the Fund should continue its borrowing efforts, the Committee stressed that the Fund should rely on quota increases as the basic source for its funds and urged that the eighth general review of quotas be expedited.

1982 **13 January:** The Executive Board established guidelines for borrowing by the Fund, stipulating that total outstanding borrowing, plus unused credit lines, should not exceed 50 to 60 percent of total quotas. **12–13 May:** The Interim Committee, meeting in Helsinki, called for quotas to be the primary source of the Fund's resources, a commitment to complete the eighth general review of quotas, and effective surveillance of exchange rates for all members. **13 August:** Mexico closed its foreign exchange market in the face of serious difficulty in servicing its foreign debt. This marked the onset of the debt crisis that was to affect many developing countries in the ensuing years. **23 December:** The Fund approved a three-year extended arrangement for Mexico of SDR 3.6 billion to support a medium-term adjustment program.

1983 **1 January:** The year opened with a general recognition by the world's monetary authorities that a major and widespread debt crisis among developing countries was at hand. The Chairman of the Interim Committee called for an early meeting of the Interim Committee. **18 January:** The Group of Ten agreed to a major enlargement of the General Arrangements to Borrow, from SDR 6.4 billion to SDR 17 billion, with additional lenders and revisions in its terms to allow the arrangements to be used for drawings from the Fund by all members. **24 January:** The Fund approved a stand-by arrangement and compensatory financing drawing for Argentina totaling SDR 2 billion. **10–11 February:** The Interim Committee, meeting in Washington, D.C., recommended an increase in quotas under the eighth general review that would enlarge total quotas from SDR 61 billion to SDR 90 billion. **28 February:** The Fund approved an extended arrangement for Brazil for SDR 5 billion. **20 May:** A borrowing arrangement with Saudi Arabia, associated with the General Arrangements to Borrow, was approved by the Executive Board in the maximum amount of the equivalent of SDR 1.5 billion. **25 September:** The Interim Committee, meeting in Washington, D.C., endorsed the Managing Director's strategy of adjustment and financing for dealing with the debt problems of developing countries and agreed that the temporary enlarged access policy on Fund resources should be continued and that there should be new access limits under that policy. **30 November:** The increased quotas under the eighth general review went into effect.

1984 **6 January:** The policy on enlarged access was extended until the end of the year, but access limits were set in terms of the new quotas established under the eighth general review. Thus, annual limits were set at 102 or 125 percent of quota, three-year limits at 306 or 375 percent, and cumulative limits at 408 or 500 percent, depending on the seriousness of the member's balance of payments need and the strength of its adjustment efforts. Similarly, the limits under the compensatory financing facility were reduced, as were those set for the buffer stock financing facility. **24 April:** The Fund concluded four new short-term borrowing agreements, totaling SDR 6 billion, with the Saudi Arabian Monetary Agency, the BIS, Japan, and the National Bank of Belgium. **16 November:** The policy of enlarged access was extended to the end of 1985 and access limits were reduced in accordance with the request of the Interim Committee. The new annual limits were set at 95 or 115 percent of quota (instead of 102 or 125 percent), three-year limits at 280 or 345 percent (instead of 306 or 375 percent), and cumulative limits at 408 or 450 percent (instead of 408 or 500 percent), depending on the severity of the member's balance of payments difficulties and the strength of the adjustment effort. **28 December:** The Fund approved a drawing of SDR 1.7 billion for Argentina under a stand-by arrangement and the compensatory financing facility.

1985 **25 March:** In its review of surveillance procedures, the Executive Board stressed the need for "evenhandedness" of surveillance of all members and put forward suggestions for improving the surveillance procedures by the Fund. **17–19 April:** The Interim Committee, meeting in Washington, D.C., reiterated that adjustment in economic policies of members was essential and unavoidable to correct external imbalances and called for improvements in the effectiveness of surveillance over policies of members. **3 May:** The Executive Board extended for four years, until May 1989, the coverage of the compensatory financing facility to cereal imports. **25 September:** Members of the Group of Five met in New York and agreed to pursue a policy of coordinated intervention in the foreign exchange markets to reduce the value of the dollar. **6–7 October:** The Interim Committee, meeting in Seoul, stressed the need for noninflationary growth policies for industrial countries, for renewed growth in developing countries, and for adequate financing support of developing countries in their adjustment efforts.

1986 26 March: The structural adjustment facility was established with funds that accumulated in the Special Disbursement Account, and the low-income countries eligible to use the facility were listed. **25 July:** The Fund established the principle of "burden sharing," whereby the rate of charge was increased on the use of the Fund's resources and the rate of remuneration was reduced on creditor positions in order to strengthen the Fund's reserve position. A special contingency account was established to supplement the Fund's general reserve.

1987 16 January: Michel Camdessus, of France, became the seventh Managing Director of the Fund. **23 November:** The General Arrangements to Borrow were renewed for a period of five years from 26 December 1988. **18 December:** The enhanced structural adjustment facility (ESAF) was established.

1988 20 April: The initial maximum limit on access of each eligible member to the enhanced facility was set at 250 percent of quota, with a provision that this limit could be increased to 350 percent of quota in exceptional cases. The interest rate on loans was set at 0.5 percent. **6 June:** The mix of ordinary and borrowed resources for purchases under the enlarged access policy was set at the ratio of two to one in the first credit tranche and one to two in the next three credit tranches. Thereafter, purchases were to be made with borrowed resources. Purchases under extended arrangements were to be made with ordinary resources up to 140 percent of quota, and thereafter with borrowed funds.

1989 19 May: The compensatory and contingency financing facility (CCFF) was established, extending the Fund's financing to members in balance of payments difficulties for temporary export shortfalls; adverse external contingencies; excess cost of cereal imports; and, temporarily, for excess cost of oil imports.

1990 16 March: The Managing Director outlined the timetable for dealing with members having overdue obligations to the Fund, leading to compulsory withdrawal from the Fund up to two years after the emergence of arrears. **20 June:** The Executive Board adopted the "rights" approach to overdue obligations. A member in arrears to the Fund would be able to earn rights, conditioned on a satisfactory performance under an adjustment program monitored by the Fund, toward a disbursement by the Fund once the member's overdue obligations had been cleared and upon approval of a successor arrangement by the Fund. **28 June:** The Board of Governors adopted a resolution that increased by 50 percent the quotas of members under the ninth general review of quotas; no increase was to become effective until members having not less than either 85 percent or 70 percent (depending on whether the determination was made before or after 30 December 1991) of total quotas had consented to the increase and not before the effective date of the third amendment of the Articles. The proposed third amendment to the Articles of Agreement was also adopted by the Board of Governors on this date. **5 October:** The Executive Board reviewed the currencies and their weights making up the SDR basket and determined that the list of currencies and their weights should be as follows: the U.S. dollar (with a weight of 40), the deutsche mark (21), Japanese yen (17), French franc (11), and pound sterling (11). **5 December:** In view of the Middle East crisis, the Executive Board took a number of decisions to help members face unexpected economic difficulties. The measures included suspending until the end of 1991 the lower annual, three-year, and cumulative borrowing limits under the enlarged access policy; increasing the financing under the enhanced structural adjustment policies at the time of midyear reviews for such arrangements and, where necessary, adding a fourth year to those programs due to be completed before November 1992; adding an oil import element to the CCFF; and providing for a contingency mechanism to be attached to current Fund arrangements at the time that they come up for review.

1991 1 March: The Fund published a joint study of the Soviet economy by the Fund, World Bank, Organization for Economic Cooperation and Development, and European Bank for Reconstruction and Development. **14 October:** Michel Camdessus, of France, was reappointed Managing Director of the Fund for a term of five years.

1992 4 May: The Board of Governors approved membership resolutions for Russia and 14 other states of the former Soviet Union. **9 November:** The Executive Board announced new access limits on the amounts of financing available to members that would apply once the 50-percent increase in quotas under the ninth general review of quotas went into effect. It terminated the enlarged access policy in effect since 1981, under which the Fund supplemented its quota resources with borrowed funds. The new limits, expressed in terms of the new quotas, were intended to maintain members' access to the Fund's resources. **11 November:** The quota increases under the ninth general review of quotas entered into force, providing for an increase in a member's quota of nearly 50 percent and for total quotas in the Fund to rise from SDR 97.4 billion to about SDR 145 billion ($200 billion). At the same time, the third amendment to the Articles of Agreement became effective, providing for the removal of voting and other rights of "ineligible" members.

1993 16 April: The Executive Board approved the creation of the systemic transformation facility—to assist countries facing balance of payments difficulties arising from transformation from a planned to a market economy—to be in place through 1994. **27 April:** Tajikistan was the fifteenth and the last of the countries of the former Soviet Union to join the Fund. **30 June:** The Fund approved a drawing by Russia amounting to SDR 1.1 billion ($1.5 billion) under the systemic transformation facility.

1994 12 January: The African Financial Community (CFA) franc was devalued. The CFA franc zone consisted of seven members of the West African Economic and Monetary Union (EMU), six members of the Banque des états de l'Afrique Centrale, and the Comoros. The devaluations were followed in the ensuing weeks by Fund arrangements for 13 of the countries. **23 February:** The Executive Board initiated operations under the renewed and enlarged ESAF. **6 June:** The Fund announced the creation of three Deputy Managing Director posts. **2 October:** The Interim Committee adopted the Madrid Declaration calling on industrial countries to sustain growth, reduce unemployment, and prevent a resurgence of inflation; on developing countries to extend growth; and on transition economies to pursue bold stabilization and reform efforts.

1995 1 February: The Executive Board approved a stand-by arrangement of SDR 12.1 billion for Mexico, the largest financial commitment in the Fund's history. **12 September:** Emergency financing mechanism approved by the Executive Board.

1996 26 March: The Executive Board approved an SDR 6.9 billion extended Fund facility (EFF) for Russia—the largest EFF in the Fund's history. **16 April:** The Fund established a voluntary special data dissemination standard for member countries having or seeking access to international capital markets. A general data dissemination system would be implemented later. **29 September:** The Interim and Development Committees endorsed a joint initiative for heavily indebted poor countries (HIPCs).

1997 27 January: The Executive Board approved New Arrangements to Borrow (NAB) as the first and principal recourse in the event of a need to provide supplementary resources to the Fund. **25 April:** The Executive Board approved the issuance of Press/Public Information Notices (PINs) following the conclusion of members' Article IV consultations with the Fund—at the request of members—to make the Fund's views known to the public. **May:** The Fund reclassified, for statistical purposes, several newly industrialized economies in Asia (Hong Kong Special Administrative Region [SAR], Singapore, and Taiwan Province of China), as well as Israel, in the group of countries classified as *industrial countries* and renamed this expanded group of countries *advanced economies*. The reclassification reflected the advanced stage of development in these economies and the characteristics that they now shared with the industrial countries. **19 May:** The Fund issued its first PIN after concluding its Article IV consultation with the Kingdom of the Netherlands: Aruba. Two additional PINs followed on June 5 for Belize and Tunisia. **2 July:** Thailand introduced a managed float for its currency, the baht, followed by a prompt depreciation of the currency of about 20 percent. **11 July:** Following increased pressure on its reserves, accentuated by the float of the baht a few days earlier, the Philippine authorities allowed the peso to float. **4 August:** The Executive Board adopted guidelines covering the role of the Fund on the issue of governance. **1 September:** The Fund opened its Regional Office for Asia and the Pacific in Tokyo. **25 September:** The Board of Governors adopted a Resolution approving a special, onetime SDR equity allocation of SDR 21.4 billion that would equalize all members' ratio of SDRs to quotas at 29.3 percent, and it also agreed on a 45-percent increase in members' quotas. **11 October:** Indonesia adopted the first of its economic programs to cope with the Asian economic and financial crisis. **5 November:** The Fund approved an SDR 10 billion three-year stand-by arrangement for Indonesia. **4 December:** The Executive Board approved an SDR 21 billion stand-by credit for Korea. Fund assistance was requested by Korea on 21 November, and negotiation of the arrangement was concluded with unprecedented speed. **17 December:** The Executive Board approved the establishment of the supplemental reserve facility to provide financial assistance to a member country experiencing balance of payments difficulties due to a short-term financing need resulting from a sudden and disruptive loss of market confidence reflected in capital flight.

1998 **15 January:** Indonesia adopted a reinforced Fund-supported reform program after its financial markets declined sharply in response to doubts over the country's commitment to reform. **6 February:** The Board of Governors adopted a Resolution proposing an increase of 45 percent in the total Fund quotas to approximately SDR 212 billion (about $288 billion). The increase would only become effective when members having not less than 85 percent of total quotas have consented to the increase in their quotas. **19 February:** The Fund and Russia agreed to extend the current SDR 10 billion EFF credit for an additional year and to augment the Fund's financial assistance under the program. **24 March:** Malaysia introduced a package of measures to strengthen its financial sector and rebalance its macroeconomic policies. **27 April:** The Interim Committee adopted a Code of Good Practices on fiscal transparency. **4 May:** The Fund-Singapore Regional Training Institute was opened. **24 June:** The Indonesian government and the Fund signed a new agreement aimed at halting the deterioration in the Indonesian economy and paving the way for a resumption of international trade. **25 June:** The Executive Board completed the seventh review of Russia's economic and financial program and added a further $670 million to the financial package, bringing the total disbursements under the program to $5.8 billion, out of a total credit of $10.1 billion. **13 July:** The Managing Director of the Fund and the Russian authorities agreed on a major strengthening of Russia's economic program with additional financial support from the Fund amounting to SDR 8.5 billion (about $11.2 billion) in 1998, bringing total Fund financing available for Russia in the year to SDR 9.5 billion ($12.5 billion). The new financing was subject to the Russian legislature enacting required reforms and to the approval of the Executive Board. **20 July:** The General Arrangements to Borrow were activated for the first time for a nonparticipant and for the first time for 20 years to finance the SDR 6.3 billion augmentation of the extended arrangement for Russia. **30 September:** The Fund announced that after the launch of the EMU in Europe on 1 January 1999, the euro would replace the current currency amounts of the deutsche mark and the French franc in the SDR valuation basket. **30 October:** The Fund announced in Moscow that after a 10-day meeting with the Russian authorities, a number of points in the formulation of Russia's new economic program had been clarified, but necessary measures in important areas needed to be agreed upon, particularly the budget for 1999, before the financial program agreed to in July could be resumed. **2 December:** The Executive Board approved a three-year stand-by arrangement for Brazil, with a total financial package from the Fund, other international financial organizations, and bilateral lenders amounting to about $41 billion. The NAB was activated for the first time. **22 December:** The Fund announced that, effective 1 January 1999, the euro would replace the deutsche mark and the French franc in the basket of currencies making up the value of the SDR.

1999 1 January: Eleven European member countries adopted a new common currency, the euro. The European Central Bank (ECB), which manages monetary policy for the euro area, was granted observer status in the Fund. **22 January:** Increases in member quotas agreed on under the eleventh general review came into effect. This resulted in an increase of total quotas to SDR 212 billion. **23 April:** The Executive Board expanded the special reserve facility to provide for contingent credit lines that could be made available for members with strong economic policies that might be affected by financial contagion from other countries. **30 September:** The Board of Governors approved a proposal to transform the Interim Committee into the International Monetary and Financial Committee (IMFC). **30 September:** The Executive Board adopted a resolution to conduct, as a onetime, exceptional operation, off-market gold sales of up to 14 million ounces to allow the Fund to finance its share of the enhanced HIPC initiative. **22 November:** The ESAF was renamed the *poverty reduction and growth facility (PRGF).* The main objectives of the new facility were to foster durable growth in order to raise living standards and reduce poverty. **10 December:** Uganda become the first country to receive assistance under the new PRGF.

2000 14 January: The Executive Board agreed to eliminate the buffer stock financing facility and the contingency element of the CCFF in order to streamline and simplify its facilities. **16 March:** As part of a broad review of Fund Financing Facilities, the Executive Board agreed to eliminate Currency Stabilization Funds and Debt-Service-Reduction Operations. **4 April:** The Executive Board adopted plans to monitor the use of Fund resources by member countries more closely. Toward this end, beginning in July 2000, it required the central banks of borrowing countries to publish annual financial statements audited to international standards by outside experts and to provide more economic information to the Fund. **5 April:** The Fund completed the last of seven off-market gold transactions with Brazil and Mexico conducted over the period since December 1999. Under these transactions, 12.944 million troy ounces of gold were sold and accepted back immediately at the same price in settlement of these members' obligations to the Fund. The Fund retained the book value of the gold (about $47 per troy ounce) and invested the remainder of the proceeds to help finance its contribution to debt relief and financial support for the world's poorest countries. **10 April:** The Executive Board agreed to establish an Independent Evaluation Office (IEO) to assess the Fund's operations and policies. **1 May:** Horst Köhler took office as Managing Director. **22 May:** The General Data Dissemination System entered into operation. **19 July**: The IMF launched publication on its website of quarterly reports on developments in the Special Data Dissemination Standard, with a view to chronicling progress and giving the initiative more prominence. **1 August:** Sudan's voting rights were restored, after having been suspended since August 1993.

2001 8 January: Managing Director Horst Köhler and World Bank President James Wolfensohn announced that 22 countries, including 18 African states, qualified for debt relief under the HIPC Initiative. This relief represented a two-thirds reduction, on average, of these countries' foreign debt. **2 February:** The Fund approved an increase in the quota of the People's Republic of China to SDR 6,369.2 million from SDR 4,687.2 million to reflect China's growing position in the world economy after resuming sovereignty over Hong Kong SAR. **1 March:** The International Capital Markets Department was established to enhance surveillance, crisis prevention, and crisis management. **7 March:** Following a review of Fund conditionality, the Executive Board agreed to move toward a more streamlined and focused approach. **27 April:** The Fund and Brazil agreed to establish a Joint Regional Training Center for Latin America located in Brasilia. **8 May:** Deputy Managing Director Stanley Fischer announced his intention to resign his post. **7 June:** The Managing Director announced the appointment of Anne O. Krueger as First Deputy Managing Director and the appointments of Gerd Hausler as Counsellor and Director of the new International Capital Markets Department. He also appointed Kenneth Rogoff as Economic Counsellor and Director of the Research Department and Timothy Geithner as Director of the Policy Development and Review Department. **17 September:** In the wake of the events of 11 September 2001, the Managing Director issued a joint statement with the President of the World Bank to announce that the joint annual meetings of the Boards of Governors would not take place in Washington, D.C., as originally planned. The meetings of the IMFC and the Development Committee took place in Ottawa, Canada, on 17–18 November 2001. **26 November:** First Deputy Managing Director Anne Krueger proposed a plan under which countries with unsustainable debts would be protected from their creditors while they conducted negotiations with them.

2002 **1 January:** In the final step in European Monetary Union, euro notes and coins were introduced in the 12 countries of the euro area. **16 January:** The Executive Board agreed to a one-year extension of Argentina's $933 million repayment under the supplemental reserve facility. **4 February:** The Executive Board approved a three-year, $16 billion loan for Turkey, the largest finance arrangement extended by the Fund to that date. **25 February:** Anoop Singh, a national of India, was appointed to the newly created position of Director for Special Operations. **10 July:** The Managing Director appointed an advisory panel for Argentina. **6 September:** The Fund approved a new stand-by arrangement for Brazil of up to $30.4 billion, the largest in the institution's history. **6 September:** The Executive Board agreed to tighten the standards for approving financial support to members in excess of the normal access limits set in relation to members' quotas. **25 September:** The first report by the IEO on the prolonged use of Fund resources was issued. In response, the Managing Director established a task force to implement the IEO's recommendations aimed at strengthening the effectiveness of Fund-supported programs. **26 September:** New conditionality guidelines aimed at promoting national ownership of policy reforms and streamlining and focusing conditionality were adopted. **24 October:** The East Africa Regional Technical Assistance Center (AFRITAC) in Dar es Salaam, Tanzania, was opened as part of the Fund's response to Africa's request for help in strengthening institutions and in designing and implementing better policies. **22 November:**

A 12-month pilot project, aimed at supporting international efforts to prevent money laundering and the financing of terrorism, was approved.

2003 **24 January:** The Executive Board approved financial support enabling Argentina to defer $6.6 billion in repayments to the institution. **4 February:** The Twelfth General Review of Quotas was concluded without a proposal to increase quotas, which remained unchanged at SDR 212.7 billion ($287 billion). **12 April:** The International Financial and Monetary Committee decided against a proposal on the establishment of a statutory sovereign debt restructuring mechanism and asked the Fund to focus on finding other methods for the orderly resolution of financial crises. **13 April:** The Development Committee endorsed a joint Fund–World Bank project to monitor the policies and actions needed for the achievement of the Millennium Development Goals by 2015.

2004 **4 March:** The Managing Director announced his resignation upon his nomination for the position of President of the Federal Republic of Germany. The First Deputy Managing Director, Anne O. Krueger, became Acting Managing Director pending the selection of a new Managing Director. **2 April:** The Trade Integration Mechanism (TIM) was established to help developing countries overcome temporary balance of payments difficulties related to increased trade liberalization. **7 June:** Rodrigo de Rato began his five-year term as Managing Director. **7 June:** The new Managing Director initiated a broad review of the Fund's medium-term strategic direction on the occasion of the sixtieth anniversary of the Bretton Woods institutions. **28 July:** Bangladesh became the first country to benefit from assistance under the TIM, through augmented access to financing under the PRGF. **25 October:** The Middle East Technical Assistance Center was established in Beirut, Lebanon, to promote capacity building and training in the region. **18 November:** The Fund and the World Bank launched the quarterly external debt statistics database (QEDS) containing quarterly external debt statistics for 41 countries.

2005 **31 January:** The Russian Federation completed the early repayment of its outstanding obligations to the Fund, amounting to SDR 2.19 billion (about $3.33 billion). The loans, which had been approved by the Executive Board in March 1996, were originally scheduled to be paid off in 2008. **25 September:** The IMFC and the Development Committee reached agreement on a Group of Eight proposal to provide 100-percent debt relief on all debt incurred by the world's HIPCs to the Fund, the World Bank, and the African Development Fund. **5 October:** The Fund adopted the Policy Support Instrument for member countries that did not want or need financial assistance, but sought the Fund's assessment and endorsement of their policies. **23 November:** The exogenous shocks facility (ESF) was established within the PRGF

Trust to provide concessional financial support for low-income member countries facing exogenous shocks, such as from adverse commodity price swings, natural disasters, or conflicts and crises in neighboring countries. **13 December:** Brazil announced its intention to make an early repayment of its entire outstanding obligations to the Fund, amounting to $15.46 billion. **15 December:** Argentina announced its intention to make an early repayment of its outstanding obligations to the Fund, amounting to $9.9 billion. **21 December:** The Fund approved 100-percent debt relief in the amount of $3.3 billion under the Multilateral Debt Relief Initiative for 19 countries: Benin, Bolivia, Burkina Faso, Cambodia, Ethiopia, Ghana, Guyana, Honduras, Madagascar, Mali, Mozambique, Nicaragua, Niger, Rwanda, Senegal, Tajikistan, Tanzania, Uganda, and Zambia.

2006 **1 February:** The Managing Director announced the merger of existing departments into the International Capital Markets Department and the Monetary and Financial Systems Department to integrate and bolster the institution's financial, capital market, and monetary work. **4 May:** The Fund announced the creation of an $8.7 billion investment account to address a projected income shortfall in the 2007 fiscal year. **18 May:** The Managing Director announced the appointment of a committee of eminent persons, led by Andrew Crockett of JP Morgan Chase International, to provide an independent view of the options available to finance the Fund's operating costs over the long term. **5 June:** The Fund announced the first of its proposed multilateral consultations on issues of systemic or regional importance that would focus on global imbalances, with China, the euro area, Japan, Saudi Arabia, and the United States participating. **1 September:** John Lipsky succeeded Anne Krueger as the First Deputy Managing Director. **18 September:** The Board of Governors adopted a package of reforms aimed at more closely aligning members' quota shares with their relative positions in the world economy and enhancing the participation and voice of low-income countries. **5 October:** Indonesia announced its intention to make an early repayment of its outstanding obligations to the Fund, amounting to $3.2 billion.

2007 **9 January:** The AFRITAC was opened in Libreville, Gabon. **24 January:** The Joint India–IMF Training Program was inaugurated in Pune, India. The ITP became the seventh training program to be established by the IMF Institute outside of its headquarters in Washington, D.C. The other programs are located in Abu Dhabi, Austria, Brazil, China, Singapore, and Tunisia. **31 January:** The Committee of Eminent Persons submitted its report on a new income model for the Fund, recommending that the Fund increase its income base in order to reduce its reliance on lending to finance public goods, such as surveillance and technical assistance. **27 February:** The Managing Director and the World Bank President released a statement welcoming a report by the External Review Committee on IMF–World Bank collaboration, headed by Pedro Malan, aimed at better clarifying the roles of the two institutions. **14 April:** The IMFC called for a new quota formula that would be simple and transparent, and appropriately capture the relative positions of members in the global economy. **21 June:** The Executive Board concluded a year-long review of the 1977 Decision on Surveillance over Exchange Rate Policies, and adopted the New Framework for Surveillance aimed at improving the quality, evenhandedness, and effectiveness of Fund surveillance. **1 November:** Dominique Strauss-Kahn, a French national, assumed office as the Managing Director, succeeding Rodrigo de Rato.

2008 4 January: The Executive Board submitted a report to the Board of Governors recommending that the Thirteenth General Review of Quotas be concluded without an increase in members' quotas. **14 January:** The PRGF–HIPC Trust Instrument was amended to provide for staff-monitored programs. **29 February:** The Fund and the World Bank released new enhanced versions of the QEDS and the joint external debt hub. **14 March:** The Executive Board approved a range of measures to enable Liberia to fully normalize its financial relations and voting and related rights in the Fund after more than two decades of protracted arrears to the institution. **7 April:** The Executive Board proposed a new and sustainable income and expenditure framework for the Fund. **29 April:** The Board of Governors adopted a resolution on reforms of the institution's governance, including changes to the quota and voting share structure to enhance the participation and voice of emerging market and developing countries as well as a realignment of members' shares with their relative positions in the global economy. **5 May:** The Board of Governors adopted a resolution broadening the Fund's investment authority that would enable the institution to generate revenues from a variety of sources. **30 May:** The Executive Board agreed to integrate the offshore financial center assessment program with the financial sector assessment program. **9 June:** The Managing Director made a statement urging policy makers around the world to seek a cooperative approach to the global challenges stemming from the rise in food and fuel prices and spillover effects from the U.S. financial crisis. **4 September:** The Managing Director announced the appointment of a committee of eminent persons to assess the adequacy of the Fund's framework for decision making and advise on any modifications that might enable the institution to fulfill its global mandate more effectively. **19 September:** The Executive Board approved modifications to its ESF. **25 October:** The Executive Board concluded an inquiry into the conduct of Managing Director, Dominique Strauss-Kahn, finding no abuse of authority on his part. **29 October:** The short-term liquidity facility was established to provide quick-disbursing finance for countries with strong economic policies faced with temporary liquidity problems in the global capital markets. **15 November:** At the conclusion of a Group of Twenty (G-20) Summit on Financial Markets and the World Economy, G-20 leaders issued a statement setting forth their commitment to act together to meet global macroeconomic challenges, using both monetary and fiscal policy. They also agreed to strengthen the Fund's resources and its mandate for macroeconomic surveillance, lending to member countries in need, and providing assistance to build capacity in emerging market and developing countries.

2009 12 January: The Fund and the European Commission signed a Framework Agreement on a technical assistance partnership. **24 March:** The Executive Board approved comprehensive reforms to strengthen the institution's capacity to prevent and resolve crises, in particular by improving the effectiveness of its nonconcessional lending facilities, modernizing conditionality, increasing access limits, and reforming the pricing of high and precautionary access to nonconcessional lending. **1 April:** The Fund launched a donor-supported trust fund to finance technical assistance in anti-money laundering and combating the financing of terrorism. **23 April:** The Executive Board agreed to double the borrowing limits of the poorest countries under the PRGF and ESF. **13 May:** The BIS, the ECB, and the IMF jointly released the first part of the *Handbook on Securities Statistics.* **18 June:** The U.S. Congress passed the domestic legislation needed to agree to an increase in Fund quotas, a reform of governance in the Fund, an expansion of the NAB by up to $100 billion, a one-time allocation of SDRs, limited gold sales, and expanded investment authority for the institution. **1 July:** The Executive Board approved the issuance of IMF notes to member countries and their central banks. **20 July:** The Executive Board submitted to the Board of Governors a proposed resolution calling for an allocation of SDRs equivalent to about $250 billion, of which nearly $100 billion would be for emerging markets and developing countries and about $18 billion would for low-income countries. **23 July:** The Executive Board established the Poverty Reduction and Growth Trust to replace and expand the PRGF-ESF Trust. **28 July:** For the first time, the Fund used resources made available by members under bilateral borrowing agreements to supplement its quota resources, drawing on agreements as follows: Japan (SDR 1.287 billion), Canada (SDR 128.7 million), and Norges Bank (SDR 59.4 million). **29 July:** The Executive Board approved unprecedented measures to sharply increase the resources—including from the sale of IMF gold—available to low-income countries in the wake of the global financial crisis. It also agreed to zero interest payments on outstanding concessional loans through the end of 2011. **30 July:** The *State of Public Finances: A Cross-Country Fiscal Monitor* was launched. **7 August:**

The Board of Governors approved a general allocation of SDRs equivalent to $250 billion to provide liquidity to the global economic system. **31 August:** The Executive Board adopted revised guidelines for establishing debt limits in Fund-supported programs. **2 September:** China made the first purchase agreement for IMF notes of up to SDR 32 billion (about $50 billion). **18 September:** The Executive Board approved limited gold sales of up to 403.3 metric tons as part of the new income model. **24 November:** The NAB was expanded to include 13 potential new participants and credit arrangements of to up to $600 billion. **10 December:** The Fund and the European Investment Bank signed a Letter of Understanding to enhance cooperation in capacity building in sub-Saharan African countries.

Introduction

In its more than 65 years of existence, the International Monetary Fund (IMF) has evolved from a small, obscure international agency, with new and uncertain responsibilities, into a powerful institution that today has assumed center stage in the international monetary system. This evolution has occurred even though 36 years ago, when the Bretton Woods system collapsed, the Fund seemed to have lost the central purpose of its existence. It is a remarkable story of how an institution has developed and adapted itself to an evolving world and a changing membership in ways that perhaps no other international agency has been forced or able to do. Moreover, this transformation has taken place despite bouts of criticism from industrial and developing countries alike, frequent exploitation by national politicians as a convenient way of deflecting criticism from their own disastrous national policies, serious controversy and criticism in the academic community, general suspicion in the trade union movement, antagonism from nongovernmental organizations (e.g., charity, church, and relief organizations), and a widespread lack of interest or understanding on the part of the general public with respect to an institution that has such a remote and technical role.

Along the way, the Fund has developed new financing facilities; extended and enlarged the financial assistance available to its members; taken on new and wide-ranging responsibilities in the area of international surveillance of member countries' economic and financial policies; developed programs of reform in the areas of fiscal, monetary, structural (i.e., aspects of banking, corporations, and contract law), governance, and social policy; and broadened and intensified its technical assistance and training programs. At the same time, the Fund has moved from an inward-looking and rather secretive bureaucracy, to become an institution anxious to explain itself to the public, although still mindful of its confidential relations with its members. It now has a very large publications program; covering country economic reports; comprehensive and authoritative reports on the world economy; international capital markets; economic and financial statistics; and, with the agreement of the member involved, a website (www.imf.org) that reproduces the results of the Fund's Article IV consultations with member countries, as well as letters of intent and memoranda on the programs that it supports in those countries.

In urging greater transparency on its members, the Fund in its own operations has now gone a long way in putting into practice what it preaches.

GROWING THROUGH CRISES

Several developments and international crises have given the Fund the opportunity to be an important international player. Its first significant appearance on the international stage was in 1956, when all four combatants in the Suez Canal military adventure sought the Fund's financial assistance, for an amount that far exceeded the total amount of funds disbursed in the preceding nine years. In 1974 and 1975, when the par value system crumbled, the Fund created the oil facilities, which played an important role in acting as a conduit for recycling petrodollars from the suddenly rich oil-producing countries, caused by the action of the Organization of Petroleum Exporting Countries (OPEC) in tripling international oil prices, to the poorer, hard-hit oil-consuming countries. In 1982, when Mexico abruptly announced that it could no longer service its loans and was on the brink of default, the Fund took a major role in persuading the international banking community not to run for cover but to reschedule old loans and provide new money in support of Mexico, predicating the Fund's own financial assistance on the condition that the banks come up with a sufficient financial package to give Mexico time to implement corrective policies. *Concerted lending*, as it was called, was the pattern of the financial packages that was used for the rest of the decade in providing assistance to heavily indebted countries. During the 1980s, when many countries were strapped with high indebtedness, the Fund introduced the structural adjustment facility (SAF) and the enhanced structural adjustment facility (ESAF) to provide expanded and concessional assistance to poorer countries, as well as the enlarged access policy (EAP) for other countries.

In the three years following the collapse of the Soviet Union in 1991, the Fund membership increased from 152 countries to 172, making it a nearly universal institution. During this period, the Fund was called on to take a leading role in helping the Baltic states, the Russian Federation, and other states of the former Soviet Union weather the collapse of central planning and the transition to market-driven economies. This kind of economic transformation had never before been attempted, and these countries worked closely with the Fund for most of the 1990s. For this new group of members, a special temporary facility, the systemic transformation facility, was established. In addition, the Fund provided intensive and widespread technical assistance and training in spearheading the effort to establish the basic infrastructure, legal environment, and social policies necessary to bring about market economies. By 2004, most of the economies in transition had successfully graduated to market economy status after several years of intense reforms and some have since joined the European Union.

In order to meet its enlarged responsibilities in the 1990s, the size of the Fund's staff increased by nearly 30 percent, and the Executive Board was expanded from 22 seats to 24 to accommodate representatives from Switzerland, which joined the Fund in May 1992; the Russian Federation; and other states of the former Soviet bloc.

The Fund's role as crisis manager emerged fully in 1994, when Mexico was struck by a resurgence of investors' fears and the country again turned to the Fund for assistance. When the U.S. Congress refused the Administration's request to provide $40 billion in loan guarantees, the Fund stepped in (with the support of the U.S. administration) and increased its financing package from an initial $7.8 billion to $17.8 billion. In addition, the U.S. administration provided $20 billion from the Exchange Stabilization Fund (a resource that did not require congressional approval). Investors' confidence was thereby very shortly restored, Mexico was able to repay its credits ahead of schedule, and a wider conflagration was avoided. All told, as many as 20 countries were involved in a crisis, which up to that point was considered one of the most serious in the postwar world.

In 1997–1998, the Fund's role as crisis manager as demonstrated in 1982 and 1994 was again put to a test as the Asian economic and financial crisis broke. Using the emergency financing facility introduced after the 1992 Mexican crisis, the Fund put together massive financing packages, including multilateral and bilateral financing, in support of macroeconomic and structural reform programs in the countries involved—mainly Korea, Indonesia, the Philippines, and Thailand—and counseled other countries to which the contagion had spread, such as the Hong Kong Special Administrative Region (SAR), Malaysia, and Singapore. Outside the Asian area, other countries, principally Russia but also several countries in Latin America, also suffered from the resurgence of investors' fears, requiring many billions of dollars in emergency financing.

This experience highlighted the need to pay much more attention than in the past to weaknesses in individual countries' banking sectors and to the effects of those weaknesses on domestic macroeconomic stability as well as possible spillover effects for others. In 1999, the IMF together with the World Bank launched the Financial Sector Assessment Program and began conducting national assessments on a voluntary basis. Greater attention was also geared toward identifying the institutional prerequisites for successful capital account liberalization as well as the appropriate timing and sequencing of reform.

The financial assistance required during the Asian crisis resulted in severe pressure on the Fund's resources, both in terms of manpower and finances. Although a general increase of 45 percent in quotas had been approved by the Board of Governors early in 1998, the reluctance of the U.S. Congress to authorize payment of its subscription brought about a general slowdown in the payment of all subscriptions, thereby delaying a much-needed reinforcement of the Fund's financial resources. Similarly, the New Arrangements to Borrow (NAB), which were approved by the Executive Board in January 1997, became linked to the quota increase and suffered a corresponding delay in becoming effective. Neither the quota increase nor the NAB could become effective without payment of the subscription by the United States, since it alone holds 18 percent of the total voting power and both measures require members totaling 85 percent of the Fund's total voting strength to enact all necessary legislation and make the relevant payments to the Fund. In August 1998, therefore, with the Fund's liquidity at a historically low level, it became necessary to activate the General Arrangements to Borrow (GAB) to replenish the Fund's resources—the first time that the GAB had been activated since 1978. Subsequently, the NAB became effective in November 1998 and the quota increase shortly thereafter.

The Fund's role in the prevention and management of international crises is being solidified in the midst of the current global financial crisis, which began with the collapse of mortgage lending in the United States in 2007. After U.S. giant, Lehman Brothers Holdings, Inc., filed for bankruptcy in September 2008, the meltdown spread rapidly through trade and financial linkages to other countries and regions. In an environment characterized by the burgeoning of trade and cross-border financial flows—which had increased ninefold in less than two decades—the crisis culminated in widespread wealth destruction, deep recession, and high unemployment across the globe. The large-scale fiscal stimulus measures initiated by many states, especially in Europe and the emerging markets of central Asia, in the initial aftermath of the crisis—combined with lower revenues caused by the recession—gave rise to a secondary sovereign debt crisis and further calls for greater international coordination of policies.

These events have clearly placed the Fund on the front lines of lending to countries to help boost the global economy as it suffers from the deepest recession since the Great Depression. With broad support from its membership, the Fund's lending capacity is being tripled in order to meet a burgeoning demand for stand-by arrangements and other forms of financial and policy support. It is closely monitoring global economic and financial developments to provide policy advice to countries and regions, in particular on how best to regulate banks and other financial institutions, effectively address risk, and strengthen economic cooperation. The crisis also marks a watershed in the institution's evolution as founding principles are being reshaped to "fix" the international financial markets and streamline and modernize the system of international regulation and governance.

It is visionary to see the IMF progressing to become the world's central bank, but the movement to "one world" is not to be denied. The establishment toward the end of 1998 of a powerful regional central bank, the European Central Bank, serving 11 advanced industrial countries, is an interesting precursor of wider international developments. The Fund has already clearly become the world's lender of last resort—an important attribute of a central bank. It has also demonstrated that it has the experience, expertise, and staff to take the lead in a crisis. The Fund's attempt to create the Special Drawing Right (SDR) in the late 1960s, in order to be able to regulate the level of international liquidity in accordance with the world's needs (i.e., a role parallel to a national central bank's role in controlling the domestic money supply), was resisted, largely owing to the integration of the international capital markets. Nevertheless, the rapid, and unbalanced, increase in the flow of capital across borders, rising to $7.2 trillion, or roughly 15 percent of world GDP over the period 1995 to 2006, proved to be a source of underlying fragility, leading to the current global crisis. Hence, the special allocation of SDRs, equivalent to about $34 billion that came into effect under the Fourth Amendment of the Articles on 10 August 2009 and the general SDR allocation equivalent to about $250 billion that became effective on 28 August 2009 will bolster the Fund's ability to provide liquidity to the global economic system by supplementing members' foreign exchange reserves.

On the broader question of coordinating national economic and financial policies, the Fund has worked diligently and with increasing sophistication in carrying out and expanding its responsibilities of surveillance over members' economic and financial policies. Its analysis carries great weight in international financial organizations, summit meetings of the industrial countries, regional gatherings, and other fora, but so far it has had less impact in national capitals. It has, therefore, yet to realize its goal of being able to coordinate the policies of its member countries and thus to place the world economy on a secure and stable footing. This is the test that it now faces, and it is the test that its members also face in becoming fully cooperative participants in the international monetary system, and thereby furthering the goals of the Fund's founders.

THE GOLD AND GOLD EXCHANGE STANDARDS

The IMF was born out of the experience of the interwar years. During the last half of the nineteenth century and up to the outbreak of World War I, the world's monetary and exchange rate system was based on gold, as was the domestic money supply in most countries. The gold standard system was, in theory, self-regulating; a deficit in a country's balance of payments would result in an outflow of gold, followed by a reduction of money in circulation, deflation, and thus a correction in the external balance. The gold standard was accepted as the natural order of things, and although it may not have been ordained by God, it was a religion that central bankers could believe in. While industrial countries competed on an equal footing and the rules of the game were adhered to, the system worked well. The center of the monetary universe was London, and the Bank of England was the fulcrum on which the system was balanced. The London bank rate was the signal for monetary retrenchment or expansion, as the case might be, and the rest of the trading world watched and acted accordingly. Adjustments tended to be made in unison, with each economy in lockstep with the others. The exchange rate, that is, the value of a currency in terms of gold, was "a given," and was immutable. There were signs, however, even before World War I that cracks were appearing in the edifice. Reserve currencies were becoming a growing part of countries' reserves, and the impact of gold movements was being neutralized. World War I brought the system temporarily to an end.

The outbreak of World War I led to currency inconvertibility, blocked balances, and the imposition of exchange controls. After the war ended, repair of the system was neither easy nor immediately possible. Exchange controls persisted, currencies remained inconvertible, and central banks intervened in exchange markets to manipulate the rates. The war and its aftermath had been accompanied by a vastly uneven increase in the general price levels among countries and a profound redistribution of gold, away from London. Nevertheless, sentiment for a return to the gold standard remained strong, and the pound sterling returned to gold in 1925 at its prewar parity. At that rate, the pound was substantially overvalued, and the cost at home was severe unemployment. The move to gold, moreover, did not restore stability to the world's exchange rate system; the pound began to lose its primacy to the U.S. dollar, and reserve currencies were increasingly being held as major components of international reserves alongside gold. The world, in fact, had moved to a gold exchange standard, a system in which gold bullion was the only ultimate means of settlement among nations, and one in which gold specie rarely circulated. The link between the balance of payments and domestic money supply had been broken, and national economic policies began to be set mainly to achieve domestic objectives rather than to uphold the gold content of currencies. Confidence in the system was severely weakened, and it became subject to increasing speculative attacks.

The pound sterling was forced off gold in 1931, followed two years later by the U.S. dollar and the currencies of most other industrial countries. The collapse of the gold exchange standard ushered in a period of near chaos in international financial relations. Discriminatory currency blocs, bilateral trade and exchange agreements, multiple currency practices, trade quotas, and other stratagies to gain national advantage were pursued at the expense of the common good. It was the "beggar-thy-neighbor" decade. The Great Depression, the breakdown of the international financial system, and the growth of economic nationalism all fed on each other, resulting in a startling contraction in international trade. The Tripartite Agreement of 1936, between France, the United Kingdom, and the United States was an early and notable attempt to bring some measure of stability among exchange rates. Of more importance, perhaps, it indicated to future policy makers a way to go forward.

ESTABLISHMENT OF THE FUND

World War II saw a repeat of the economic disruption that had accompanied World War I—exchange controls, blocked balances, and bilateral arrangements in external dealings, and physical controls and suppressed inflation at home. The lessons of the interwar years, however, were there for all to see. Men on both sides of the Atlantic, with vision and expertise—notably John Maynard Keynes in Great Britain and Harry Dexter White in the United States—almost simultaneously and independently of each other, began to assemble a blueprint for the international monetary system of the postwar world. Each produced a plan for a new international organization, the one called for an *International Currency* (or *Clearing*) *Union* and the other a *Stabilization Fund*, and though each came to the task from a different perspective and with somewhat different national interests in mind, there was a remarkable overlap in their proposals. These two plans, drawn up late in 1942 in the midst of war, were joined over the following two years by other plans and proposals from several other countries, officials (including those of governments in exile), economists, and other individuals. The final texts of two international agreements—the Articles of Agreement of the IMF and the Articles of Agreement of the International Bank for Reconstruction and Development—were hammered out at the International Monetary and Financial Conference held at Bretton Woods, New Hampshire, during 1–22 July 1944. Delegates from 44 countries, plus a representative from Denmark, were present, as well as observers from several international organizations.

The aim in setting up the IMF was clear and simple. It was to establish a new world order based on an open exchange and trading system that would operate under international scrutiny and control. In particular, exchange rates were recognized as being matters of international concern. Currencies would have internationally approved par values in an exchange rate system that aimed at stability without rigidity, discriminatory and unfair practices would be outlawed, and a new spirit of enlightened self-interest would be fostered. The establishment and maintenance of such a system would be the responsibility of the IMF, an organization whose membership, open to all countries, would entail both obligations and privileges. The Fund would enunciate a code of conduct to be observed by all its members. Members would subscribe to and have available to them a pool of currencies that they could draw upon in times of external payments difficulties. Within this unique framework, which included regulatory functions, financial operations, multilateral consultations, and technical assistance, the Fund would bring into existence a new comity of nations. The Fund was to be firefighter, policeman, and counselor simultaneously.

PAR VALUES AND EXCHANGE RESTRICTIONS

The inaugural meeting of the Board of Governors was held in Savannah, Georgia, in May 1946, and the Fund opened its doors for business in Washington, D.C., in March 1947. Its first order of business was to invite its members to propose par values for their currencies, to be established in terms of gold as a common denominator or in terms of the U.S. dollar of the weight and fineness in effect on 1 July 1944. Apart from a cumulative initial change of 10 percent, par values could be changed only on a proposal by the member and subject to a finding by the Fund that the member's balance of payments was in fundamental disequilibrium. Among a number of general obligations included in the Articles of Agreement, each member was to avoid restrictions on current payments, abstain from discriminatory currency practices, and establish convertibility for foreign-held currency balances (Article VIII). Recognizing the uncertain conditions brought about by the war, however, the Articles also provided (Article XIV) for a transitional period, in which members could maintain and adapt to changing circumstances the restrictions on payments and transfers for current transactions.

In the event, all but a handful of members availed themselves of the transitional arrangements under Article XIV, and it was not until 1961 that most industrial countries had formally established convertibility for their currencies and had undertaken to perform the obligations of Article VIII. Informal convertibility had, in fact, been established two or three years earlier, and by 1960 the preponderance of international trade and payments was being conducted on an open, nondiscriminatory basis. One of the major goals of the Bretton Woods system had thus largely been attained. Despite the disruption of the Bretton Woods exchange rate system in the early 1970s, the drive to an open trading system has been maintained, and the number of members accepting the obligations of Article VIII has increased steadily over the years. At the beginning of December 2009, 187 members, including all the major trading countries, had accepted the obligations of Article VIII, while 19 other countries are still availing themselves of the transitional arrangements.

THE RISE AND FALL OF THE BRETTON WOODS SYSTEMS

The 1960s proved to be an expansive decade. The value of world trade increased by about 135 percent, world economic growth averaged nearly 6 percent a year, and inflation, though increasing, remained moderate until the end of the decade, especially compared with developments that were to occur in the 1970s. The revolution in communications and transportation, together with open exchange and trade arrangements over much of the world, unleashed capital movements, encouraged the formation of multinational and transnational corporations, and began the transformation of the world economy into what was later to be called "the global village."

But disquieting trends began to surface. Economic growth was uneven among countries, as were rates of inflation, and the system began to lose its center as Europe started competing with the United States, both economically and politically. The system came under stress. The United States, increasingly involved in the Vietnam War, found it politically difficult to adopt corrective domestic economic policies and continued to run balance of payments deficits. Externally, the U.S. authorities felt that their hands were tied. On the one hand, they believed that the United States was unable to change the value of the dollar against other currencies by raising the price of gold, because they were convinced that devaluation would have prompted offsetting moves by other countries. On the other hand, they were unwilling to raise the price of gold, partly because of the political implications of benefiting South Africa and the Union of Soviet Socialist Republics (USSR), the world's main gold producers. Other countries, too, were unable or unwilling to devalue or appreciate their currencies against the dollar, resulting in a general stickiness in the exchange rate system. The continued growth of foreign-held dollar balances intensified the pressure on the dollar, and the almost riskless cost of speculating against a fixed-rate currency invited periodic bouts of speculation against the weaker currencies. The Bretton Woods par value system came to an end on 15 August 1971, when the United States suspended the convertibility of official holdings of dollar balances into gold.

A brief attempt to restore the fixed-rate system was made in December 1971, when finance ministers of the Group of Ten countries held a meeting, the first of its kind, at the Smithsonian Institution in Washington, D.C., to negotiate a new pattern of rates for their currencies, including a devalued rate for the dollar and the creation of central rates, with wider margins and a less formal procedure for exchange rate changes. One by one, however, the major industrial countries abandoned fixed rates for their currencies and let them float. By March 1973, all the major currencies were floating against each other, marking the end of the exchange rate system established at Bretton Woods.

After the breakdown of the Bretton Woods system, several difficult years for the Fund followed. The main currencies floated against each other, either as a managed float or floating freely according to demand and supply (referred to at the time as "dirty" or "clean" floating), depending on the degree or absence of official intervention. Other members adopted a variety of exchange arrangements. Some preferred to let their currencies float, some opted to peg the value of their currencies to one of the major currencies, some to a trade-weighted composite of currencies, and a few to the SDR, the new reserve asset created in the Fund in 1968. In 1974, the SDR itself was revalued by the Fund in terms of a basket of 16 currencies, reduced to a basket of 5 currencies seven years later. The link between gold and currency values having been broken, national monetary authorities were no longer able to maintain an official price for gold. Nonmonetary gold transactions (i.e., private sales and purchases) took place at three or four times the nominal official price. All these developments were, of course, contrary to the legal obligations that members had assumed under the Articles of Agreement.

Despite its loss of control over the value of its members' exchange rates, the Fund continued to exercise what authority remained to it. It requested members to provide the Fund with full details of their exchange arrangements, continued to hold members bound by their undertakings on exchange restrictions, lent heavily on the obligation that each member had undertaken to "collaborate with the Fund to promote exchange stability, to maintain orderly exchange arrangements with other members, and to avoid competitive exchange alterations," and promulgated a set of guidelines to be observed by members engaged in managed floating. Furthermore, following a recommendation by the Committee of Twenty, the Fund circulated a declaration on trade to all members, asking them to voluntarily pledge that they would not introduce or intensify trade or other current account measures without a finding by the Fund that there was a balance of payments justification for such measures.

REFORM OF THE INTERNATIONAL MONETARY SYSTEM

While these attempts were being made by the Fund to continue exercising some control over international monetary relations, it was also focusing intensively on a reform of the system. Early in 1972, the Executive Directors had submitted a report to the Board of Governors, entitled *Reform of the International Monetary System*, which, among other things, suggested further study on a number of issues on which the Executive Directors had not been able to agree. Publication of the report was followed by the establishment of the Committee of Twenty and its Deputies, charged with the task of putting together a draft of a reformed system. The Committee worked for two years, produced many interesting and useful technical studies, but, citing the highly uncertain economic conditions then prevailing in the world economy, admitted that it had been unable to reach agreement on a comprehensive reform. It settled instead on an *Outline of Reform*, indicating the general direction in which the Committee believed the international monetary system could evolve, and proposing a list of immediate measures that could assist in the evolution of the system. Among these immediate measures was a recommendation to establish an Interim Committee to advise the Board of Governors on the supervision, management, and adaptation of the monetary system.

The task of negotiating a reformed system had thus reverted to the Fund. After two years of intensive work within the Fund, along with several referrals to the Interim Committee and bilateral negotiations on a number of key points, agreement was reached on a full-scale reform of the international monetary system in 1976. The new system came into effect in April 1978. Its main themes, spelled out in the second amendment to the Articles of Agreement, were that each member could adopt the exchange arrangement of its choice; a system of par values could be introduced if 85 percent of the total voting power of the membership agreed; exchange arrangements would be subject at all times to firm surveillance by the Fund; the role of gold would be reduced, including the disposition of the Fund's own gold holdings, to be effected by the elimination of gold as a common denominator of the par value system, the abolition of its official price, the abrogation of obligatory gold payments to the Fund, and a requirement that the Fund complete the disposition of 50 million ounces of its gold holdings, as well as authorization to dispose of the remainder of its holdings; the introduction of changes in the characteristics of the SDR, so as to assist it to become the principal reserve asset of the international monetary system; simplification and expansion of the types of the Fund's financial operations and transactions; provisions to establish a Council as a new organ of the Fund, its establishment to be subject to an 85-percent majority of the total voting power; certain improvements in the organizational aspects of the Fund, principally involving the composition of the Executive Board and the election of Executive Directors; and a reduction in the categories of special majorities to 70 percent and 85 percent, but with a considerable expansion in the number of decisions of the Executive Board or the Board of Governors subject to these special majorities; all other decisions would be taken by a majority of the votes cast.

SURVEILLANCE OVER EXCHANGE RATE POLICIES

Although the second amendment to the Articles was comprehensive, with ramifications throughout the operations of the Fund, the fundamental change that overshadowed all others related to the exchange rate system, under which a member could adopt the exchange arrangement of its choice and no longer had to declare the value of its currency to the Fund or gain approval for a change in its value. Instead of having the responsibility of approving currency values and their changes, the Fund was charged with a less specific but broader, and more important, responsibility of exercising firm surveillance over members' exchange rate policies. Firm surveillance was a new, crucial provision of the reformed system, and in order for it to become effective the Fund needed the continuous cooperation of its members, particularly the major industrial countries, in areas of national policy that had not hitherto been under compelling continuous scrutiny. To be effective, surveillance would have to apply not only to exchange rate policies, as such, but also to the broader national monetary and financial policies that were being pursued by national monetary authorities, whether they used the Fund's resources or not. The major industrial countries had always sought to maintain their independence of the Fund under the Bretton Woods system, and even when they had altered the par values of their currencies, they had notified the Fund of the change at the last minute, rather than following the impractical procedure of seeking its approval, thereby complying with the obligations of the Articles in form rather than in substance. It was unlikely, therefore, that an important advance in policy coordination could be developed suddenly, particularly in the light of the difficult economic circumstances of the 1980s.

Surveillance did, indeed, become gradually more sophisticated and effective over the ensuing decades, but, nonetheless, it proved to be a difficult area for the Fund and for the major industrial countries, which were loath to cede any of their sovereignty over economic policy to an international forum. The analysis conducted in the Fund, the probing of national economic policies, and the regular examination by the Fund of exchange rate movements and their underlying causes gradually gained weight and influence, particularly in the more restricted fora outside the Fund, such as in the economic summit meetings of the leaders of the Group of Seven industrial countries and other multinational fora. These meetings proved to be a more intimate forum in which the major powers could be open with each other. Since the Plaza Hotel meeting in New York in September 1985, the major industrial countries have sought, still with only partial success, to bring some measure of harmony to their national economic policies and to cooperate—sometimes with success—in exchange rate management.

In 1977, the Executive Board established three broad principles for the guidance of members' exchange rate policies. These were (1) a member should avoid manipulating exchange rates or the international monetary system in order to prevent balance of payments adjustment or to gain an unfair competitive advantage, (2) a member should intervene in the exchange markets to counter disorderly conditions, (3) and members should take into account in their intervention policies the interests of other members. The Board also established a number of other criteria that would be taken into account in judging the application of these principles, such as protracted large-scale intervention in one direction, an unsustainable level of borrowing for balance of payments purposes, the pursuit for balance of payments purposes of monetary and financial policies that provide abnormal encouragement or discouragement to capital flows, and the behavior of the exchange rate in a manner that would appear to be unrelated to the underlying economic and financial conditions.

The Fund's surveillance procedures include analyzing the economic and financial conditions in member countries and focusing on the international issues that are of concern to all members. Regular consultations are held, normally each year, with each member country to assess the appropriateness of its domestic macroeconomic and structural policies and the impact of these policies on exchange rates. The Fund also conducts a multilateral surveillance procedure twice a year through the Executive Board, aimed at assessing the world economic outlook, the interaction of members' economic policies, and the presentation of alternative policy options, together with related projections of various international scenarios. These reviews by the Executive Board are supplemented by regular discussions on exchange rate developments and on the conditions of the financial markets. The Managing Director's attendance at the meetings of the Group of Seven industrial countries brings to those meetings a broad and knowledgeable international perspective, based on the Fund's surveillance procedures.

INTERNATIONAL LIQUIDITY

In the 1960s, a new and major problem began to emerge, that of international liquidity, a subject that had been discussed but not actively engaged at the Bretton Woods Conference of 1944. The dilemma was that as world trade and other international transactions expanded, and the potential magnitude of external imbalances increased, the need for international liquidity would rise. Unconditional liquidity (i.e., owned reserves) consisted of gold, reserve currencies (mainly U.S. dollars), and reserve positions in the Fund (the reserve tranche). Of these three components, only U.S. dollar reserves were capable of expansion, since both the world's stock of monetary gold and reserve positions in the Fund were fixed, at least in the short and medium term. The continued growth of the U.S. dollar in international reserves itself involved a paradox. On the one hand, dollar holdings by foreign national monetary authorities could expand only if the United States continued to run a balance of payments deficit, thereby expanding claims by foreigners on the United States, and on its stock of gold. On the other hand, the viability of the U.S. dollar required that foreign national authorities (and private foreigners) continue to have confidence in it as a stable unit of value and in its convertibility into gold. These were two contradictory lines of development that, at some point in time, were bound to bring the system into crisis.

The discussions involved issues of whether the need was for better adjustment policies or increased international liquidity; whether the potential need should be met through increased conditional liquidity (such as drawings on the Fund) or through increased unconditional liquidity (i.e., owned reserves); whether a scheme for reserve creation should be confined to a group of industrial countries or be a universal one; and whether such a scheme should be linked to the needs of developing countries by establishing a mechanism for promoting the growth of development finance, the so-called link. An overriding issue was to what extent any new provisions should be mandated or be left to voluntary compliance. Many proposals were put forward, including special reserve balances in the Fund, multicurrency reserve schemes, various forms of a substitution account, and several schemes for the creation of reserve units. The debate ended in a compromise, with the establishment of the SDR facility in the Fund, brought into effect by the first amendment of the Articles of Agreement (1969).

THE SDR FACILITY AND GOLD

The chief characteristics of the SDR facility were that it was a universal scheme open to all members of the Fund, although participation in it was voluntary; allocations and cancelations of SDRs would seek to meet long-term global needs as a supplement to existing reserve assets; allocations and cancellations would be made to all participants in the facility as a percentage of each member's quota; SDRs would be created on the books of the Fund, backed by an international agreement (the Fund's Articles of Agreement); use of the SDR would rest on two legal foundations: the obligation of the Fund to designate a transferee of SDRs if requested by a participant, and the obligation of the designated transferee to provide freely usable currency in exchange for SDRs; SDRs would be for use through the Fund by national monetary authorities and a limited number of other official holders, and would not be available for use in private markets; decisions on allocations and cancellations of SDRs would be made for basic periods of five years (although the Fund was authorized to vary the length of the period) and be subject to a cautionary procedure that subjected the final decision to an 85-percent majority vote of the Fund's Board of Governors; and the value of the SDR, originally defined in terms of gold, was to be determined by a basket of currencies.

The international community, eager to test its fledgling reserve-creating mechanism, authorized allocations of SDRs during the first basic period of three years (1970–1972) amounting to SDR 9.3 billion. Thereafter, however, the new system of floating exchange rates and the availability of petrodollars for recycling purposes fundamentally changed the world's liquidity position. No further allocations of SDRs were made until the third basic period (1978–1981), when SDR 12.1 billion was allocated, partly, one can surmise, to be in accord with the second amendment to the Articles (1978), which called for the SDR to be the principal reserve asset of the international monetary system. The assumption then was presumably that a virtually nonexistent reserve asset could hardly be a principal asset.

In mid-1998, however, the Executive Board drew up a proposed fourth amendment to the Articles of Agreement that would provide for a onetime allocation of SDRs. The amendment was aimed at correcting a perceived inequity, insofar as members that had joined the Fund since 1981 had not received any allocations of SDRs, and many that had joined before that year had received only partial allocations. That allocation came into effect finally on 10 August 2009, when the United States joined 133 other members in supporting the Amendment, thus meeting the requirement of acceptance by three-fifths of the membership having 85 percent of the total voting power. This special allocation was implemented on 9 September 2009, increasing members' cumulative SDR allocations by SDR 21.5 billion. Another general allocation of SDR 161.2 billion was approved on 7 August 2009 and took place on 28 August 2009. With these two allocations, the *total amount of SDRs in circulation increased from SDR 21.4 billion to SDR 204.1 billion (about $324 billion).*

Despite the fact that measures have been taken to make the SDR more attractive (e.g., its valuation in terms of a basket of five currencies, its market related interest rate, and a broadening of its uses), the SDR has remained very far from being a principal reserve asset.

In an article posted in late March 2009, Zhou Xiaochuan, the governor of the People's Bank of China proposed using the SDR as a worldwide reserve currency as a way to cope with problems associated with use of the U.S. dollar and the euro. However, the SDR is unlikely to emerge as an alternative reserve currency in the foreseeable future.

Indeed, measured by the extent of its use, the SDR remains small in relative importance, with exchanges of SDRs for freely usable currencies averaging about SDR 2.2 billion per annum. Even following the recent allocations, projections under various scenarios suggest that total transfers of SDRs will likely reach a level of SDR10–30 billion. This compares with a record level of SDR 27.4 billion in the year ended 30 April 1996. Similarly, SDRs have been a declining and insignificant proportion of international reserves, accounting in 2009 for about 3 percent of global reserves, about one-third of a percent of global GDP, and about 3.5 percent of global cross-border capital flows.

Through the decade leading up to 2007, international liquidity was not a focus of attention. Instead, the most immediate concern was the integration of the world's capital markets. Although bringing undoubted long-term benefits, the sharp rise in international capital flows has posed significant problems, in particular owing to the volatile character of capital movements that move in and out of immature and vulnerable private banking sectors in developing, and even some advanced, economies.

The second amendment to the Articles of Agreement eliminated gold from the operations of the Fund and required the Fund to sell 50 million ounces of its gold holdings. Accordingly, in the period from 1976 to 1980, the Fund sold (restituted) half of this amount (25 million ounces) to its members at the official price of SDR 35 an ounce and sold by auction a further 25 million ounces at prices several times higher than the official price of gold, placing the profits on these sales in a trust fund for the benefit of low-income countries. Again, in December 1999, the Executive Board authorized off-market transactions in gold of up to 14 million ounces to help finance the Fund's participation in the heavily indebted poor countries (HIPC) initiative.

As part of the Fund's new income model designed in the wake of the current global financial crisis, the Executive Board has agreed to further limited gold sales of up to 403.3 metric tons, or roughly one-eighth of the Fund's total gold holdings, in order to bolster the institution's lending capacity and to help put its finances on a sound long-term footing. A central component of the new income model is the establishment of an endowment funded by the profits from the sale of gold acquired by the Fund after the Second Amendment of the Articles.

CONDITIONALITY

One of the purposes of the Fund is to "give confidence to members by making the general resources of the Fund temporarily available to them under adequate safeguards," as stated in Article I of its charter. In putting forward a request to use the Fund's financial resources, a member must represent that it has a need to make the purchase "because of its balance of payments or its reserve position or developments in its reserves." It is these conditions—the requirement of a balance of payments need, temporary use, and adequate safeguards—that have distinguished the Fund's financial operations from its sister institution, the World Bank, facing it across the street in Washington, D.C. Whereas the World Bank primarily deals in long-term finance for development purposes, such as agricultural, irrigation, and transport projects or for sectoral development, and is concerned, among other matters, with the viability of the particular project being financed and the credit status of its loan recipients, the Fund provides short- to medium-term finance for general balance of payments support and is concerned primarily with a member's macroeconomic policies (i.e., monetary and fiscal policies, and related structural improvements) and the ability of the member to repay the Fund within a specified period. It should be noted, however, that the character of the Bank's lending is also changing, with project financing accounting for a declining proportion of the total, while sectoral lending is increasing.

In the very early days of its operations, the Fund settled on a pragmatic and flexible set of policies and procedures, known as "conditionality," which established the terms that would govern the use of the Fund's financing.

First, members' drawing (purchasing) privileges were divided into tranches, each amounting to 25 percent of a member's quota. The first 25 percent of quota, known as the *reserve tranche* (formerly the *gold tranche*), could be drawn (purchased) without challenge. Requests for drawings in the second 25 percent of quota, known as the *first credit tranche*, could be made subject only to moderate conditionality. Use of a member's second, third, and fourth credit tranches, known as the *upper credit tranches*, required substantial justification and agreement by the Fund on a sound corrective program. Second, it was determined that "temporary" use of resources should mean that repayments (repurchases) should be made in three to five years. Third, use of the Fund's resources in the upper credit tranches would be made available under what was then a new instrument of international finance, the stand-by arrangement. With the introduction of the stand-by arrangement, which was normally for a period of one year (although members often entered into successive one-year arrangements), came two other precautionary measures—the quarterly phasing of members' drawings under the arrangement and the setting of performance criteria to assess the progress of programs.

The character, range, severity, and efficacy of the conditionality required by the Fund have been much discussed over the years, both inside and outside the organization. In particular, Fund conditionality has been criticized as being too harsh, too insensitive to social conditions, and heedless of programs of economic growth. In fact, Fund-supported adjustment programs have had mixed success, with failures stemming mainly from a lack of internal political will or exogenous and unforeseen factors. More rarely, the fault has lain with an ill-designed program. Certainly, the membership must be assured that a Fund-supported program will consist of policies that will result in a sustained balance in a country's external payments and provide the basis for further economic growth. However, in the final analysis, the individual elements of a program and the timing of their implementation rest with the national authorities of the country concerned.

Against this background, in March 2009, the Executive Board of the Fund agreed to a major overhaul of its financing facilities to modernize and strengthen its lending framework while enabling the institution to respond more quickly and effectively to systemic crises. Toward this end, the Fund will shift more toward the use of qualification criteria (ex-ante conditionality) rather than on traditional (ex-post) conditionality. It will also monitor the implementation of structural policies in the context of program reviews, rather than through the use of formal structural performance criteria. To increase flexibility, the Fund also introduced the flexible credit line (FCL) for countries with very strong fundamentals, policies, and track records of policy implementation. This credit line will be made available for crisis prevention purposes with access determined on a case-by-case basis. Disbursements under the FCL will not be phased or conditioned on policy understandings as in the case of traditional Fund-supported stand-by and extended arrangements.

RESOURCES OF THE FUND

The resources of the Fund consist of its ordinary resources and its borrowed resources. Ordinary resources consist of gold, SDRs, and currencies of members' paid to the Fund in accordance with their quota subscriptions, and the undistributed net income from the use of those resources. The value of these resources is determined in terms of SDRs, the Fund's unit of account.

A member's quota establishes its basic relationship with the Fund. First, it determines a member's subscription to the institution. Second, it determines its voting power. Third, it determines the member's maximum potential access to the Fund's financial resources. Finally, it determines a participant's share in the allocation of SDRs. After the second amendment of the Articles (1978), gold was eliminated from the Fund's operations, and the part of the quota subscription that used to be paid in gold (up to a maximum of 25 percent of quota) is now paid in SDRs or usable currencies, and this amount establishes the reserve tranche.

Quotas are determined through the application of uniform formulas established to assess each member's relative economic strength in the international community. For this purpose, the original formula used at Bretton Woods (1944) included a range of basic economic variables, such as the value of annual average imports and exports, gold holdings and dollar balances, and national income. Since then, beginning in the early 1960s, that formula has been supplemented by four other formulas containing the same basic variables but with different weights. These five formulas were run with alternative sets of data, roughly measuring the same economic characteristics but using somewhat different concepts. The resulting 10 formulas were used, in the period up to 1980, to determine the initial quotas of new members and to adjust existing members' quotas under the periodic general quota reviews. Subsequently, the number of formulas was reduced to five, but further changes were made to the weights and in the data. The proliferation of formulas and the conceptual changes made in the data suggest correctly that a member's calculated quota is not a definitive determination of its final quota. In the last analysis, a member's quota is determined by the Executive Board's recommendation to the Board of Governors, guided by the use of formulas.

On 28 April 2008, following two years of deliberation, the Board of Governors adopted far-reaching reforms of the institution's governance. This reform effort includes changes to the quota and voting share structure that will enhance the participation and voice of emerging market and developing countries, and realign members' quota with their relative weight and role in the global economy. The reform builds on an initial step agreed on in September

2006 to make ad hoc adjustments in the quotas of four countries—China, Korea, Mexico, and Turkey—that had experienced rapid economic growth in recent years. The April 2008 reform package, which applies to the membership as a whole, included the adoption of a new quota formula, ad hoc quota increases for 54 countries that were underrepresented according to the new quota formula, a tripling in the number of basic votes to increase the voice of low-income countries, a measure to protect the relative share of the basic votes in total voting power going forward, provisions for an additional Alternate Executive Director for the two African chairs in the Executive Board, and measures for realigning quota and voting shares every five years. For this package of reforms to become effective, it will need to be accepted by 112 member countries representing at least 85 percent of the total voting power. As of 19 August 2010, 85 members had accepted the Amendment.

The Fund is required by its Articles of Agreement to conduct a general review of quotas at intervals of not more than five years. However, the last two such general reviews completed in 2003 and 2008 were approved without an increase. The Fourteenth General Review of Quotas is currently underway and is expected to be completed by January 2011. In view of the length of time that it can take for the Fund to increase its ordinary resources through a quota increase, whereas payments imbalances may appear suddenly and may be the result of temporary factors such as occurred in the 1970s through the oil shocks, the Fund has resorted to borrowing to tide it over periods in which members have an enlarged need for its financing. From 1962, the Fund entered into the GAB with members of the Group of Ten for the purpose of having available access to borrowed funds in the event of a major disruption to the world balance of payments. These arrangements were enlarged in the 1980s. Since its establishment in 1962, the GAB has been renewed 10 times, most recently in November 2007 for a five-year period from December 2008.

In January 1997, the Executive Board further strengthened the Fund's financial resources by approving the NAB. Under these arrangements, 25 participating countries and institutions stand ready to lend the Fund additional resources when needed, on terms similar to the GAB, in a total amount of SDR 34 billion (about $47 billion). On 2 April 2009, the Group of Twenty (G-20) industrialized and emerging market economies agreed to a further increase in the Fund's ability to borrow resources by up to $500 billion. This increase will entail two steps. First, the Fund will be given immediate access to bilateral financing from member countries. Second, this financing will be incorporated into an expanded and more flexible NAB. As of December 2009, six countries had signed bilateral loan agreements with the Fund worth $169 billion. The NAB do not replace the GAB, but they will be the facility of first recourse.

Other borrowing arrangements have been entered into over the years, such as those in 1974 and 1975 with the OPEC to finance the oil facilities (a total of SDR 5.7 billion); in 1979 for the supplementary financing facility (SDR 7.8 billion); and in 1981–1984 for the EAP (SDR 18.3 billion).

The Fund also receives income from investments and from charges levied on its financing operations. From such income, the Fund covers its administrative budget and pays remuneration to members with creditor positions in the Fund. Net income is placed to the general and special reserve accounts.

SPECIAL FACILITIES

Both the volume and the types of loans provided by the Fund have fluctuated significantly over time. The oil shock of the 1970s and the debt crisis of the 1980s were followed by sharp increases in lending. In the 1990s, the transition process in central and eastern Europe and the crises in emerging market economies also led to surges of the demand for Fund resources. This demand rose again in the late 1990s and early 2002, owing to the widespread crises in Asia and Latin America, although these loans were repaid rapidly as conditions improved. Fund lending rose again starting in late 2008 in the wake of the current global financial crisis.

Throughout its history, most of the Fund's financing has been provided on condition that corrective policy actions will be taken to bring about an appropriate adjustment to a member's domestic economy, thus ensuring that the Fund will be repaid. However, the Fund also provides financing when members encounter balance of payments difficulties that are transitory or reversible, where no corrective policies may be required.

The first of these facilities was the compensatory financing facility, under which members could draw on the Fund to offset export shortfalls caused by factors largely beyond their control. Use of this facility was based on the assumption that the shortfall was temporary (such as a crop failure) and that export earnings would recover over the short- to medium-term. Drawings were not only subject to a low level of conditionality (such as merely an obligation to collaborate with the Fund), but also floating, allowing members to draw on it independently of, and in addition to, drawings under the regular tranche policies. Another special facility was originally designed to help members finance international buffer stocks. Later, the compensatory financing facility was expanded to include variations in expatriate workers' remittances and cereal import costs. Accordingly, it was renamed the *compensatory and contingency financing facility (CCFF).*

As part of the reform of the global financial system underway since 2000, the Executive Board has conducted a wide-ranging review of the Fund's facilities, with a view to determining whether and how they need to be modified. This review has resulted in the elimination of several facilities that were little used or had become obsolete, including the policies on currency stabilization funds (CSF), support for commercial bank debt and debt-service reduction (DDSR), the buffer stock financing facility, and the CCFF.

For low-income countries, these facilities largely have been replaced by the exogenous shocks facility (ESF), which is designed to provide support to countries hit by sudden events that can have a significant negative impact on the economy and that are beyond the control of the government. This could include commodity price changes (including oil and food), natural disasters, and conflicts or crises in neighboring countries that disrupt trade. In such cases, the ESF is designed to provide the assistance needed quickly. The conditionality associated with the ESF is specifically tailored to the particular needs and circumstances of the member concerned and is often focused on policies to address the shock.

In addition, a FCL has been established for countries with very strong fundamentals, policies, and track records of policy implementation. It is particularly for crisis prevention purposes, with a term of six months or one year (with a mid-term review). Access to the FCL is determined on a case-by-case basis, rather than being subject to the normal access limits, and is available in a single up-front disbursement rather than phased. Because disbursements under the FCL are not conditioned on implementation of specific policy understandings, members have the ability to draw on the credit line at the time it is approved or to treat it as precautionary.

The Fund has also established an emergency assistance policy to provide loans to members confronted with natural disasters and conflicts, in some cases at concessional interest rates.

ENLARGED USE OF THE FUND'S RESOURCES

The decade of the 1970s experienced the oil price shocks, worldwide recession, and persistent high levels of inflation. The quadrupling of international oil prices led the Fund to establish in 1974, and again in 1975, the so-called oil facilities to help countries meet the higher cost of their oil imports. Drawings under the facilities, which were financed by borrowings from members of OPEC, were repayable over seven years (an extension over the three to five years that had normally been in force up to then), carried light conditionality, and were additional to the availability of normal tranche drawing.

The reasoning behind the extended repayment terms was that whereas the balance of payments deficits were spread among nearly all developing countries, many with relatively large economies and sizable populations, the balance of payments surpluses were concentrated among a few oil-producing countries, mostly undeveloped economies with sparse populations. In these circumstances, it was clear that the oil-producing countries would not be able to absorb quickly their new wealth through increased imports, while attempts by non-oil-producing countries to correct their external imbalances would mainly impact each other, and thus run the risk of causing a further general contraction in international trade and world economic growth. Accordingly, the facility was designed to finance the deficits rather than to promote adjustment. Drawings under the facility did not affect the amount that members could purchase under the credit tranche policies.

Nevertheless, despite the evident rationale behind the Fund's approach to the worldwide oil-price difficulties of the 1970s, some critics have maintained that the failure of the developing countries to adjust to the new circumstances sowed the seeds for the debt problems of the 1980s. Certainly, the payments problems experienced by many member countries in the late 1970s and early 1980s called for a different approach from that adopted for the oil facilities. For one thing, the balance of payments for a number of countries had not only worsened, but had been superimposed on long-standing imbalances. For another, the causes of the imbalances had become deep-seated and of a structural character that would take longer to correct and require larger resources than those available under the Fund's normal financing facilities.

To meet these new conditions, a new facility, providing for extended arrangements over a three-year period, was introduced in 1974 to focus on structural adjustments and provide members with access to the Fund's financing in amounts larger and with longer repayment terms than had hitherto been available under the Fund's regular tranche policies. In 1979, the extended facility was complemented by the supplementary financing facility, again established with borrowed funds, to provide further enlarged access to the Fund's financing, up to 300 percent of a member's quota in exceptional cases.

Within two years, the resources of the supplementary facility were exhausted and the facility was replaced by the enlarged access policy, involving similar high levels of conditionality and access to Fund resources, and financed by another round of borrowing.

FACILITIES FOR LOW-INCOME COUNTRIES

The mounting difficulties of developing countries, particularly the low-income countries, during the 1970s and 1980s made these countries increasingly restive against what they considered to be the Fund's traditional approach to balance of payments problems, contending that the adjustment policies and the extent and duration of the financing available from the Fund did not take into account the special character of their problems. In response to these needs, the Fund introduced financing programs specifically for low-income countries. As noted previously, the Fund had been authorized to sell at auction 25 million ounces of its gold holdings, which yielded a profit (over the former official price of SDR 35 an ounce) of $4.6 billion. Of this amount, $1.3 billion was distributed directly to 104 developing countries in proportion to their quotas, and the remainder, after meeting expenses, was placed in a trust fund. The resources of the trust fund, established in May 1976, were to be used exclusively for the specific purpose of providing loans to poorer developing countries. The conditions governing use of the Fund's ordinary resources did not apply to the trust fund, which made loans, as distinct from providing financing through purchasing operations. The loans were subject to very light conditionality, carried a highly concessional rate of interest of 0.5 percent per annum, and had a maturity of 10 years. The trust fund made its final disbursement in March 1981, when its business was terminated and the interest payments and loan repayments were transferred to the Special Disbursement Account (SDA) (i.e., an account within the main body of the Fund). These interest payments and loan repayments that began to accumulate in the SDA provided the resources for the establishment of another similar facility, the SAF.

The SAF, established in 1986 to replicate the aims of the preceding trust fund, provided assistance on concessional terms to low-income member countries facing protracted balance of payments problems. Conditionality under the new facility was tightened and, in view of the modest resources available in the facility, it was hoped that its loans would act as a catalyst in encouraging the provision of additional resources to members from other international organizations and member countries. Programs supported by the loans were to be explicitly directed toward the elimination of structural imbalances and rigidities. Annual programs were to be put forward within the context of a three-year policy framework paper, prepared in collaboration with the staffs of the Fund and the World Bank, setting out the objectives, the priorities, and the broad thrust of macroeconomic and structural adjustment policies, and referencing the likely requirements and sources of the external financing envisaged under the program. Loan disbursements were made in three annual installments, bore an interest rate of 0.5 percent per annum, and were repayable in 5.5 years to 10 years.

To supplement the funds available under the SAF, the ESAF was established as a trust fund in the following year, to operate concurrently with the

SAF. Finance for the ESAF was to be derived in part from the SDA and in part from contributions in the form of loans and grants from aid agencies of member countries. Members eligible to use the ESAF and the terms of its loan were similar to those of the SAF. In 1996, the Fund and the World Bank jointly initiated a new facility for HIPCs that, linked to the ESAF, was aimed at bringing a country's debt burden down to sustainable levels through a combination of internal economic policy reforms and the renegotiation of external debts in an orderly and comprehensive program through the Paris Club and other multinational groupings.

The combination of the EAP and the establishment of the SAF and ESAF brought a dramatic rise in the use of the Fund's resources by low-income countries. Total loans and credits outstanding from the Fund rose to over SDR 37 billion by the end of 1984 and climbed again in the 1990s to a record SDR 56 billion ($75.4 billion) on 30 April 1998, reflecting in large part the extraordinary drawings made as a result of the Asian crisis. While the use of Fund resources by all countries gradually diminished during the early part of the 2000s, reaching a low in credit outstanding of only SDR 1.3 million for eight countries in 2008, the current global financial crisis has forced many members to resort to the use of the Fund resources. By the end of August 2010, 60 members had arrangements totaling more than SDR 132.4 billion.

THE DEBT CRISIS

In August 1982, at the Fund–World Bank annual meetings in Toronto, Mexico announced it was unable to service its debts, thereby initiating a debt crisis that would persist for the next decade or so. The origins of the debt crisis, sparked by the deep world recession of 1982–1983 lay in the two oil shocks of the 1970s, the resurgence of inflation toward the end of the decade, the easy availability of credit from the commercial banks at low or even negative rates of real interest that had persisted since the early 1970s, and the failure of many developing countries to adjust to evolving economic conditions. By 1982, the aggregate debt of non-oil-developing countries amounted to about $600 billion, of which about half was from commercial sources and one-fifth was of a short-term character.

In response to the Mexican announcement, the Fund took the initiative and drew up an adjustment program in conjunction with the Mexican government that embraced spending and pricing policies, investment priorities, monetary policy, and flexible exchange rates over a three-year period, and approved the use of SDR 3.6 billion of its resources in support of the program. Even with the Fund's financial support, however, there was still a financing gap of about

$7 billion, of which about $2 billion was to be sought from official institutions and the remainder from commercial banks. The Managing Director took the initiative and, instead of waiting for other potential creditors to come forward in their own time after the Fund had committed its resources, he insisted that they reach agreement on rescheduling existing loans, adjusting interest rates, and extending new loans to fill the financing gap before the Fund itself committed resources. In the end, financing of $5 billion was arranged with as many as 530 commercial banks. The Fund's response to the Mexican crisis was to set the pattern for a number of similar "rescue" operations, such as for Argentina, Brazil, and the Philippines, in the years to follow.

The Fund, however, was beginning to feel the effects of the debt crisis on its own operations. More and more developing countries ran into debt-servicing difficulties and began to default on their obligations to the Fund. From 1985 onward, a growing number of members that had overdue obligations to the Fund of six months or more were declared ineligible to use the Fund's resources. Ineligibility is the initial step in a procedure in which the Fund endeavors to enlist the member in a cooperative program, without further Fund financing, aimed at restoring the member to good standing. In the event that the member is judged not to be cooperating with the Fund, and not paying off, or even freezing, its arrears, a series of further steps can eventually lead to the compulsory withdrawal of the member from the organization. On 30 April 1992, overdue obligations had risen to a peak of SDR 3.5 billion, and eight members remained ineligible to use the Fund's resources. As of end-June 2005, the number of members with protracted overdue financial obligations to the Fund had fallen to four—Liberia, Somalia, Sudan, and Zimbabwe. The three members with arrears dating back to the mid-1980s—Liberia, Somalia, and Sudan—accounted for 90 percent of total arrears to the Fund, and Sudan alone accounted for 53 percent. Liberia cleared its arrears to the Fund in 2008. Zimbabwe, which became a protracted arrears case on 14 August 2001, settled its remaining overdue obligations to the General Resources Account on 15 February 2006, but it still had substantial arrears to the poverty reduction and growth facility (PRGF). As of December 2009, total overdue obligations amounted to SDR 1.3 billion.

In dealing with the problem of overdue obligations, the Fund adopted a three-prong strategy—prevention, deterrence, and intensified collaboration. Prevention consisted of designing adjustment programs that would analyze and take special account of risks attached to the program, thereby ensuring that any member using the Fund's resources would be able to meet its obligation to the Fund. Deterrence comprised a procedure that would lead, successively, to a declaration of ineligibility, a declaration of noncooperation, suspension of the member's voting rights and representation in the Fund, and ultimately the member's compulsory withdrawal from the Fund. In a related move, the Fund proposed a third amendment to its Articles of Agreement, which became effective in November 1992, under which the Executive Board could, by a 70-percent voting majority, suspend the voting and related rights of those members in arrears in their repayments to the Fund. The third aspect gave ineligible members an opportunity to implement, in conjunction with consultants or major creditors, a Fund-monitored "shadow" program, allowing a member to accumulate "rights" to future drawings on the Fund under a successor program, once the member had paid off its arrears. The Fund also adopted guidelines providing for a proportion of the resources committed under a stand-by or extended arrangement to be set aside to finance operations involving a reduction in the stock of debt (through buybacks, debt conversion, and other debt-reducing mechanisms), as well as providing for additional access to its resources to be made available to a member to facilitate DDSR and to catalyze other financial resources.

To place its financing on a sound footing, the Fund also adopted a burden-sharing strategy, setting up two special contingency accounts, one to cover outstanding overdue charges and repurchases, and the other to safeguard purchases made by members under a successor arrangement after a "rights" accumulation program has been successfully completed. The reserve accounts were funded in accordance with a burden-sharing formula, which increased the charges on the use of the Fund's resources and reduced the rate of remuneration on creditor positions in the Fund.

SERVICES

The Fund has provided its members, and particularly developing member countries, with a growing array of training and technical assistance, in accordance with the provisions of Article V, Section 2*(b)* of its Articles of Agreement. Indeed, in recent years, the needs of many new developing member countries and of new members in eastern Europe and the former Soviet Union have required a major expansion in the Fund's technical assistance and training services. The IMF Institute, founded in 1964, provides courses in macroeconomics, fiscal affairs, statistics, and balance of payments at the Fund's headquarters in Washington, D.C., for officials of member countries. The Institute also provides lecturers for overseas seminars and courses related to the work of the Fund. Several other technical assistance programs have increased their reach in recent years, covering a wide range of areas, such as central banking, monetary and exchange rate policy, tax policy and administration, and official statistics. The IMF has also given advice to countries that have had to reestablish government institutions following severe civil unrest or war. Technical assistance is provided in a variety of forms, through technical assistance missions, resident advisors, or secondment of outside experts to key positions in institutions of member countries.

Beginning at the end of the 1980s, membership of the former communist countries in eastern Europe and the Russian Federation, with their desperate need to reshape their economic systems, added a new dimension and urgency to the provision of Fund technical assistance. In addition to expanding its training in Washington, D.C., the Fund opened, in conjunction with five other international organizations, an institute in Vienna to present courses in macroeconomics and statistics to officials of the former Soviet Union and countries in Eastern Europe. In May 1998, the Fund inaugurated the IMF–Singapore Regional Training Institute, which was established in cooperation with the Singapore authorities to hold seminars and training courses for officials in the Asia and Pacific areas. It also has a network of regional training institutes, including the Joint Africa Institute (in Tunisia), the Joint China–IMF Training Program (in Dalian, China), the Joint IMF–Arab Monetary Fund Regional Training Program (in the United Arab Emirates), the Joint India–IMF Training Program (in Pune, India), and the Joint Regional Training Center for Latin America (in Brazil). In addition, a Central America, Panama and Dominican Republic Technical Assistance Center began operations in May 2009 in Guatemala, and three new regional technical assistance centers—one in Central Asia and two in Africa—are expected to be opened in the near future.

The Fund issues a variety of periodicals dealing with the work of the Fund and related matters. These include the *World Economic Outlook* and related studies (twice a year); the *Global Financial Stability Report* and related materials (twice year); the *IMF Survey* (twice a month); *Finance & Development* (quarterly); *International Financial Statistics* (monthly); IMF *Staff Papers* (quarterly); the *Balance of Payments Statistics Newsletter* (twice a year), as well as the *Annual Report of the Executive Board* and *Summary Proceedings* of the annual meetings (annually). In addition, the Fund has an extensive publishing program, which includes pamphlets, Occasional Papers, working papers, books, country reports, as well as online periodicals, videos, and press material (*see* the bibliography).

MEMBERSHIP

Representatives from 45 countries attended the International Monetary and Financial Conference of the United and Associated Nations at Bretton Woods in July 1944, and the Fund came into existence when 29 of those countries had completed ratification of the agreement and their representatives had attended a formal signing ceremony on 27 December 1945. All the other members, except one, that had attended the Bretton Woods Conference joined the Fund in the following years, although New Zealand did not do so until 1961 and Liberia not until 1962. The USSR, the one exception, had been an active participant at the conference and had been given a quota of $1.2 billion (then the third largest quota in the Fund, after the United States and the United Kingdom), but it did not take up the ratification procedure. It was not until the communist system collapsed and the Soviet Union broke up into 15 sovereign countries that all of its former members joined the Fund, completing the relevant membership procedures in the period from June 1992 to April 1993.

Three founding members withdrew from the Fund: Poland in 1950, alleging that the Fund had failed to fulfill the expectations of its founders; Czechoslovakia in 1955, in a dispute as to whether it was required to provide data to the Fund; and Cuba in 1964, after protracted negotiations on overdue payments to the Fund. Both Poland and Czechoslovakia rejoined in 1986 and 1990, respectively. Germany and Japan joined the Fund in 1952; mainland China's request for the ouster of the Chinese National Government was rejected in 1950, but accepted 30 years later. Switzerland, after maintaining a long association with the Fund as a nonmember, became a member in 1992. By the end of August 2010, membership in the Fund had climbed to 187 members, and only Cuba, North Korea, and a few scattered ministates remained outside the Fund.

STRUCTURE OF THE FUND

The highest authority of the Fund is the Board of Governors, which consists of a Governor and an Alternate appointed by each member country. The Governors are usually ministers of finance, central bank governors, or officials of comparable rank. Under the Articles of Agreement, the Board of Governors has a number of specific powers, as well as all powers under the Articles not expressly conferred on the Executive Board or the Managing Director. The specific powers, which cover such matters as the admission of new members, the determination of quotas, and the allocation of SDRs, can be exercised only by the Board of Governors. All other powers can be, and have been, delegated by the Board of Governors to the Executive Board.

The Executive Board consists of 24 Executive Directors, in addition to the Managing Director, who is Chairman. Each Executive Director appoints an Alternate, who can participate in meetings but can vote only when the Executive

Director is absent. Members having the five largest quotas in the Fund (the United States, Germany, Japan, France, and the United Kingdom) each appoint one member to serve until his or her successor is appointed. Of the remaining Executive Directors, 18 are elected for two-year terms, in elections that take place every even-numbered year at the time of the annual meetings.

Of the 19 elected Directors, three countries (China, Russia, and Saudi Arabia) have chosen to elect their own Director, and have large enough quotas and sufficient votes to do so. The remaining 16 Directors are elected by groups of countries, with some Directors having over 20 countries in their constituencies. In order to cope with the business of so many countries, it has become the practice for an Executive Director representing a large constituency to appoint one or more Advisors to help in the day-to-day business and to take a seat at Executive Board meetings when the Executive Director and the Alternate are both absent.

The size and composition of the Executive Board have changed radically since the Board was first formed in 1946. Originally, it consisted of 12 members, but as the Fund's membership increased, so too was the Board enlarged, although not proportionately to the growth in membership. Thus, whereas the 45 countries participating in the Bretton Woods Conference in 1944 were to be represented by 12 Executive Directors, by 1998 the number of members had quadrupled, but the number of Executive Directors had only doubled, to 24. There have also been important changes in the rankings of the five members with the largest quotas; Germany replaced China (Taiwan) in 1960 and Japan took the place of India in 1972. Within the group of members having the five largest quotas, Japan and Germany have moved up to second and third places, respectively, while France and the United Kingdom, with equal quotas, have moved into the fourth and fifth places.

The personalities on the Board have also undergone a marked change. At the Bretton Woods Conference, Lord Keynes and several other delegates had argued for an Executive Board composed of high-level officials who would meet only periodically to settle substantive policy matters. Although that proposal was overruled in favor of having the Board in "continuous session," in the early years a number of the Directors were high-level officials and did not stay in Washington, D.C., to attend all Board meetings. Inevitably, the evangelical spirit and determination of the pioneers to make the organization a success faded over the years. Executive Directors tend to be younger, from less senior positions in their home governments, and Board meetings have become more frequent, longer, and more demanding in time and effort.

The trend toward less senior representation was, in part, encouraged by the introduction of the Interim Committee, which succeeded the Committee of Twenty and met at least twice a year to discuss and advise on major policy issues. The structure of the Interim Committee replicated that of the Executive Board, but its members were ministers of finance, central bank governors, or officials of comparable rank. As an advisory body, the Interim Committee did not possess the authority to take decisions. It was called *Interim*, because the second amendment to the Articles of Agreement provided for the establishment of a Council, as an organ of the Fund, that would have decision-making power. The Council, to be structured along the same lines as the Interim Committee, would require an 85-percent majority vote by the Board of Governors for it to come into existence. So far, there have been no signs that such a Council will be established in the near future.

In September 1999, the Board of Governors strengthened and transformed the Interim Committee into the International Monetary and Financial Committee (IMFC), to enhance the effectiveness of members' oversight of the Fund from a political perspective. The IMFC remains an advisory body. It monitors developments in global liquidity and the transfer of resources to developing countries, considers proposals by the Executive Board to amend the Articles of Agreement, and deals with unfolding events that may disrupt the global financial system.

Like the Interim Committee, the members of the IMFC are governors of the Fund, Ministers, or others of comparable rank. Each member that appoints an Executive Director and each member or group of members that elects an Executive Director also appoints one member of the IMFC and up to seven associates. Thus the IMFC has the same number of members and the same constituency groupings as the Executive Board of the Fund, although the IMFC member is not always from the same country as the Executive Director.

In practice, the IMFC selects a Chair from among its members, who serves for such period as the IMFC determines. Members of the IMFC, their associates, and Executive Directors or their alternates are entitled to attend the meetings of the IMFC, unless the IMFC decides to hold a more restricted session. The IMFC may also invite observers to its meetings. The Managing Director participates in all IMFC meetings and may be accompanied by up to two staff members. The Secretary of the Fund serves as the Secretary of the IMFC.

Also, like the former Interim Committee, the IMFC ordinarily meets twice a year, in April and at the time of the annual meetings of the Board of Governors, but ad hoc meetings may be requested at any time by any member of the Committee. In addition, the meetings of the IMFC are normally preceded by a preparatory meeting of "Deputies," or representatives of IMFC members. The IMFC Chair calls meetings of Deputies in consultation with other IMFC members.

The IMFC issues a communiqué after each meeting summarizing the outcome of its discussions and giving strategic direction to the Fund's policy work for the near to medium term. On the basis of the communiqué, the Managing Director draws up a work program for the institution covering the following 6–12 month period. After discussion by the Executive Board, and amended as necessary, the work program forms the basis for the Board's calendar of meetings.

The Development Committee is a joint committee made up of Governors of the World Bank, Governors of the Fund, ministers, or others of comparable rank. The Committee was set up to continue the work of the Committee of Twenty to study issues related to economic development and to make recommendations on the transfer of real resources to developing countries. The IMFC and the Development Committee normally meet twice a year (in April and September) and in the same place, with sessions of the IMFC being followed by those of the Development Committee, or vice versa.

The Articles of Agreement specify that the principal office of the Fund shall be located in the territory of the member having the largest quota. Accordingly, the headquarters of the Fund is located in the United States, in Washington, D.C., where its staff is stationed, apart from five small liaison offices outside the United States, in Guatemala City, New York, Paris, Tokyo, and Warsaw. The organization consists of five area departments; seven functional and special services departments; and five information, liaison, and support departments.

The Managing Director, selected by the Executive Board, is Chairman of the Board and chief of the operating staff. The Articles of Agreement specify that he or she shall not be a Governor or Executive Director. In June 1994, the number of Deputy Managing Directors was increased from one to three, the first major structural change in management since the Fund's inception. The Managing Director and the staff owe their duty entirely to the Fund, and to no other authority. Unlike the United Nations, the Fund is not bound by a national quota system for recruiting staff members. The Fund's Articles of Agreement states, "In appointing staff the Managing Director shall, subject to the paramount importance of securing the highest standards of efficiency and of technical competence, pay due regard to the importance of recruiting personnel on as wide a geographical basis as possible." This language has enabled the Fund, in recruiting staff, to avoid purely political nominations from member countries.

On 30 April 2009, the Fund had 1,862 professional and managerial staff and 616 staff at other levels, recruited from 143 countries.

VOTING

The Fund has a system of weighted voting power. Each member has a basic allotment of 250 votes and, in addition, has one vote for each portion of its quota equivalent to SDR 100,000. This formula has not changed over the years (except SDRs have replaced U.S. dollars). Consequently, in 1944, at the Bretton Woods Conference, basic votes of the 44 prospective members amounted to 11.3 percent of total votes, whereas in 1998 the basic votes for the 182 members accounted for just over 2 percent of total votes. As quotas are based on a number of economic variables, the relative size of a member's quota can be adjusted over time, reflecting changes in its economic position among members. Moreover, as the Fund's overall membership has grown, each individual member has suffered a corresponding reduction in its proportionate voting strength.

Thus, when the last increase in quotas under the eleventh general review of quotas came into effect on 22 January 1998, the U.S. voting strength (the largest in the Fund) fell from 29.6 percent of the total under the 1944 Bretton Woods schedule to 17.5, the United Kingdom from 14.25 percent to 5.1 percent, the Netherlands from 3.2 percent to 2.4 percent, and Panama from 0.27 percent to 0.097 percent.

On 28 April 2008, the Board of Governors approved a large-scale quota and voice reform aimed at making quotas more responsive to economic realities by increasing the representation of fast-growing economies and giving low-income countries more say in the Fund's decision making. The reform includes a tripling of the number of basic votes as well as measures to protect the share of basic votes in total voting power in the future. This reform will become effective when the reform package is accepted by 111 member countries representing at least 85 percent of the total voting power. As of early March 2010, 65 members representing about 70 percent of total voting power had accepted.

Major policy decisions taken by the Board of Governors, such as approval of a quota increase, provisions for general exchange arrangements, or establishment of the Council, require a high majority vote of 85 percent of the total. The United States alone, or the members of the European Union or the developing countries when voting together, can veto proposals subject to a high majority. The high majority requirement applies to 22 types of decisions, but they pertain to important structural and operational aspects of the Fund that rarely come up for decision. In addition to these issues, another 21 types of decisions require a voting majority of 70 percent. All other decisions, and these are by far the majority of those taken, require only a simple majority vote.

The Board of Governors meets once a year at the annual meeting, but apart from the votes that may be taken on those occasions, all votes are normally conducted by mail. The Executive Board, which has a tradition of decision making by consensus, rarely votes. Instead, it tries to reach decisions by capturing a sense of the meeting. These consensus decisions, however, usually reflect the voting power of Executive Directors.

In retrospect, the last two decades will be seen as a critical turning point in the progression toward a truly international economy. The most recent period has encompassed not only a revolution in communication and a further breakdown of barriers to trade, but also the nearly complete integration of world capital markets. Spurred by rapid growth in emerging market economies, the transformation of formerly communist countries, and the further incorporation of developing countries into the world economy, the flow of capital across borders more than tripled over the period 1995 to 2007, totaling about $7.2 trillion or 15 percent of world GDP. While the most rapid increase in cross-border capital flows was experienced in the advanced economies, the emerging markets and developing countries have also become far more financially integrated than ever before.

The rapid globalization of capital markets represents a major transformation of the international monetary and financial system and a watershed in the history of the Fund. Assuming that private capital flows would never again play the role they did in the late 19th century, the founders at Bretton Woods set up the Fund to monitor exchange arrangements and assist members facing current account difficulties. In that context, the focus of the Fund's work has traditionally focused on policies and prospects affecting the current account of the balance of payments.

This underlying assumption proved to be obsolete in the aftermath of the Asian financial crisis, when the Fund, attempting to apply the lessons taken from the experiences of Indonesia, Korea, Thailand, and others, intensified its surveillance over members' financial policies, established standards for the timely and accurate dissemination of economic data, urged a strengthening of members' financial and banking sectors, and advocated greater transparency in government. It also introduced significant changes in its lending policies to meet sudden demands on its resources. It sought a substantial strengthening of its resources through an increase in quotas and new borrowing arrangements.

These measures, however, proved to be insufficient to head off the current Great Recession, which represents the most significant global downturn since that Great Depression that preceeded the Bretton Woods Conference in 1944. Likened to "the perfect storm" by the Fund's Managing Director, Dominique Strauss-Kahn, the crisis emerged in an environment characterized by a prolonged period of strong global growth, increased capital flows, low interest rates, and a breakdown of financial regulation and supervision. In this environment, and fueled by the U.S. housing bubble, financial institutions and other market participants lowered their lending standards in search of higher yields. At the same time, weak underwriting standards, unsound risk management practices, increasingly complex and opaque financial products, and consequent excessive leverage combined to create a series of vulnerabilities in the system. The collapse of the global housing bubble, which peaked in 2006, caused the values of securities tied to real estate to plummet. The storm took shape in the United States when the investment bank, Lehman Brothers, folded and the U.S. government intervened to rescue the world's largest insurance company (American International Group).

Although the so-called storm originated as a problem in the U.S. financial sector, it quickly became a macroeconomic crisis as concerns about bank solvency and credit availability swept the U.S. economy, eroding consumer confidence. It became an international problem when global stock markets began to hemorrhage, giving rise to unprecedented losses. Banks in Western Europe and elsewhere faced large write downs, and some of the most reputable names in international finance came into question. As deleveraging cascaded across the global financial system, liquid assets were devalued, credit lines were slashed, and equity prices sank rapidly. Even emerging markets and developing countries that had only limited exposure to the U.S. subprime mortgage market were devastated as a result of falling commodity prices, weak export demand, dwindling flows of bank-related financing, and volatile exchange markets. Worldwide industrial production and merchandise trade fell sharply in late 2008 and early 2009, as a result of a global credit crunch.

Despite the efforts of governments and central banks to respond rapidly with unprecedented fiscal stimulus packages, monetary policy expansion, and institutional bailouts, global GDP declined by 6.25 percent in the last quarter of 2008, and the trend continued into 2009. The affects of the crisis were particularly severe for countries, primarily in eastern Europe and central Asia, with relatively more leveraged domestic financial systems and pegged exchange rate regimes. For example, Latvia experienced a decline in GDP of about 18 percent combined with unemployment of more than 22 percent in 2009.

In Greece, an increase in overall public debt to well over 100 percent of GDP—following increased fiscal spending on wages and social programs in 2008—gave way to a secondary "sovereign debt crisis," as sharply rising spreads on Greek bonds eroded market sentiment concerning the large and growing external debt of several leading industrial countries.

In November 2008, the G-20 held its first leaders meeting—attended by heads of state and government of the members along with the Secretary-General of the United Nations, the President of the World Bank, the Managing Director of the Fund, and the Chair of the Financial Stability Forum (later reconstituted at the London Summit as the Financial Stability Board)—in Washington, D.C., to formulate a response to the global economic crisis. This plan was reviewed and revised at two subsequent meetings held in London in April 2009 and Pittsburg in September 2009. In the context of these meetings, members of the G-20 agreed to coordinate policies aimed at strengthening transparency and accountability, enhancing sound regulation, promoting integrity in financial markets, reinforcing international cooperation, and reforming the international financial institutions. In this context, members of the G-20 endorsed a substantial increase in the financial resources available to the Fund, including a new increase in quotas and an expansion of the NAB by up to $600 billion, and a strengthening of its role in crisis prevention.

At its meeting in October 2009, the IMFC welcomed the work of the G-20, in particular its commitment to articulating policies for strong, sustained, and balanced growth in the global economy. In light of its central role in bilateral and multilateral surveillance, the Committee called on the Fund to assist the G-20 by developing a forward-looking analysis of whether policies are collectively consistent with more sustainable and balanced trajectories for the global economy. It highlighted the need to remain vigilant to prevent financial sector excesses and the reaccumulation of unsustainable global imbalances. To this end, the Committee noted, all countries needed to reinvigorate their structural reform agendas supported by sound fiscal, monetary, exchange rate, and financial sector policies.

The decisions taken by the Fund membership as a whole at the October 2009 annual meetings in Turkey—the "Istanbul Decisions"—called for wide-ranging reforms in the Fund, particularly in four areas—aligning its mandate with the realities of the modern global financial system, improving financing instruments to increase the Fund's crisis-prevention capabilities, strengthening surveillance, and improving quota shares by giving a greater voice to underrepresented, dynamic emerging economy members.

By the time the 2009 annual meetings took place, the world economy was showing early signs of recovery, led by strong performance of the Asian economies and a rebound in manufacturing. Global growth was projected to reach 3 percent in 2010 and average just above 4 percent over the period 2010–2014. Nevertheless, the pace of recovery was expected to be slow and uneven, as financial and corporate restructuring would continue to suppress economic activity and the need for both countries and households to rebuild savings would likely continue to dampen demand. In this context, Committee members highlighted the need to maintain supportive fiscal, monetary, and financial sector policies until a durable recovery was secured and the need to stand ready to take further action if needed to revive credit, recover lost jobs, and reverse setbacks in poverty reduction. They called for agreed financial sector and regulatory reforms to be completed without delay. Committee members also emphasized the collective responsibility to avoid protectionism in all its forms and to work together in articulating and implementing credible and coordinated exit strategies as the recovery takes hold.

More broadly, the Great Recession and the response to it has brought the membership of the Fund to a turning point in the governance of the international economic and financial system. The events of the past two decades have clearly highlighted the linkages that exist not only between the financial sector and the real economy, but also between individual economies and the global system. This has led to a growing recognition that multilateral collaboration is essential not only to prevent and respond to systemic crises, but also to work toward shared goals aimed at the achievement of sustainable and balanced growth in an orderly international environment. This is perhaps more apparent now than it has been since the Fund was established in the aftermath of World War II.

A

ACCESS LIMITS. A member's access to the Fund's financial resources is determined in individual cases based on a set of criteria agreed on in 1983 and on a system of access limits, which are subject to periodic review, usually every two years, by the **Executive Board**, taking into account the Fund's **liquidity** position, and the demand for its **resources** by members. The access limits, expressed as a percentage of members' **quotas** that may be exceeded in exceptional cases, in effect as of the end of November 2009 were as follows:

Stand-by and Extended Arrangement

Annual	200
Cumulative	600

Special Facilities

Emergency Assistance	25–50

Exogenous Shocks Facility

Rapid access	50
High access	150
Flexible Credit Line	none

Poverty Reduction and Growth Facility

Three-year access	
Maximum	280
Exception maximum	370

The actual amount of access in individual cases is determined by taking into account several criteria, including the member's need for Fund resources, its capacity to service its indebtedness to the Fund, its outstanding use of Fund resources, and its record of using Fund resources in the past. In cases involving exception access, the Executive Board is also guided by the extent to which the member suffers exceptional balance of payments pressures, its **debt sustainability analysis**, an expectation of reentry to capital markets, and strong program design and implementation prospects.

ACCOUNTING UNIT. The Fund's unit of account in which its books and financial records are maintained is the **Special Drawing Right (SDR)**, an **international reserve** asset created by the Fund in 1968. The value of the SDR is determined daily based on the four **currencies** issued by Fund members, or by monetary unions that include Fund members, whose exports of goods and services during the five-year period ending 12 months before the effective date of the revision had the largest value and which have been determined by the Fund to be freely usable currencies. These currencies currently include the **euro**, Japanese yen, pound sterling, and the U.S. dollar. The U.S. dollar-value of the SDR is posted daily on the IMF's website. It is calculated as the sum of specific amounts of the four currencies valued in U.S. dollars, on the basis of exchange rates quoted at noon each day in the London market.

The composition of the basket, and the weight of each currency in the basket, are reviewed every five years. At the most recent review in November 2005, the weights of the currencies in the SDR basket were revised based on the value of the exports of goods and services and the amount of reserves denominated in the respective currencies held by other members. These changes became effective on 1 January 2006. The next review is scheduled to take place in late 2010.

When the Fund's current income model was adopted by the **Executive Board** in April 2008, the gold value assumed for the purpose of making medium-term income projections was $850 per ounce, based on current and historical developments in gold prices at that time.

ACCOUNTS OF THE FUND. The Fund's accounts fall into three categories: the **General Department**, the **Special Drawing Rights (SDRs) Department**, and the Administered Accounts. All three accounts are operated and maintained in the Treasurer's Department, and the account names refer to accounting entities, rather than structural departments.

The General Department is the main source of finance available to members. It consists of (1) the **General Resources Account**, which is the basic account of the Fund, consisting of ordinary resources made up chiefly of **quota** subscriptions paid to the Fund by members and borrowed resources; (2) the **Special Disbursement Account**, with resources that come from the profits on past **gold** sales by the Fund, interest on loans made by the **trust fund**, income from **investments by the Fund**, and other transfers and interest payments; (3) the **Investment Account**; and (4) the **Borrowed Resources**

Suspense Account, which authorized the Fund to invest in SDR-denominated deposits and borrowings made under agreements for the **enlarged access policy (EAP)**.

The SDR Department records all transactions and operations in SDRs. SDRs are an interest-bearing asset allocated by the Fund to each member that is a participant in the SDR Department. SDRs may be used by participating members to settle accounts between themselves and in **transactions** with the Fund.

Administered Accounts include various accounts administered by the Fund, principally the **poverty reduction and growth facility (PRGF)** trust and in the context of the **heavily indebted poor country (HIPC)** initiative through the **PRGF–HIPC** trust, as well as accounts-holding grants, concessional loans, and other loans contributed by members to provide technical and other assistance to members. These activities are undertaken separately from the Fund's regular lending operations, with resources provided voluntarily by members independent of their capital subscriptions, and in part from the Fund's own resources. The Administered Accounts, which play a critical role in financing concessional lending and debt relief, are funded through a cooperative effort currently involving 94 countries.

ADJUSTMENT PROGRAM. *See* BALANCE OF PAYMENTS ADJUSTMENT; CREDIT CONTROLS; FINANCIAL PROGRAMMING; STABILIZATION PROGRAMS.

ADMINISTRATIVE AND CAPITAL BUDGETS OF THE FUND. The budget is prepared annually by the staff of the Office of Budget and Planning, which in 1992 was transferred from the Administration Department to the Office of the **Managing Director**. The budget is subject to the approval of the **Executive Board**. Unlike the United Nations, which requires annual budgetary subscriptions from its members, the Fund is self-financing, deriving income from its financial operations with members. In setting its budgetary target, the Fund aims to cover its administrative expenses and to be able to allocate prudent amounts to its reserve after meeting remuneration and interest payments to members. The Fund's financial year begins on 1 May and ends on 30 April.

The Administrative Budget for the financial year ended 30 April 2010, provided for total net administrative expenditures of $880 million as well as an appropriation of $45 million for capital projects. It also included a carryover of up to 6 percent, or $52 million of unused resources from the 2009 administrative budget.

The underrun from 2009 occurred as a result of an ambitious program of reforms incorporated in the 2009–2011 **medium-term** budget aimed at reshaping the Fund with a view toward achieving a leaner, more modern institution, with expenditures permanently cut by $100 million in real terms, and **staff** positions reduced by 380. The streamlining exercise had been front-loaded, with the bulk of the adjustment implemented in 2009.

The staff reduction envisaged for the 2009–2011 period was largely accomplished, as the number of staff volunteering to separate from the Fund had been greater than targeted. This reduction in the workforce, as well as other factors including declines in travel, building, and other administrative expenditures, resulted in a significant undershooting of the 2009 administrative budget. However, the Fund had been called upon to respond vigorously to the **global financial crisis** by shifting its work program during the course of the year. Because the crisis broke out in the midst of the Fund's restructuring exercise, the heavy workload was borne chiefly by the staff as uncompensated overtime and, to a lesser extent, by volunteers who delayed their departure dates.

Against this backdrop, the Fund had been forced to set its budget strategy for 2010–2012 in a very uncertain environment. Its main goal would be to respond fully to the increased demands for country programs and enhanced **surveillance**. Moreover, as the Fund took on added responsibilities under a new global financial architecture, the longer-term work program stemming from the global financial crisis would likely place a further burden on the existing staff.

The capital budget in the year ended 30 April 2010, was set at $45 million to finance investment projects supporting the Fund's response to the global crisis with significantly reduced staffing and to deliver efficiency dividends. In this vein, and relative to the previous three-year plan, the 2010–2012 capital plan entailed a phased reallocation of capital resources from improvement and maintenance of building facilities to information technology.

AFRICA CAPACITY BUILDING (ACB) INITIATIVE. In response to calls by African leaders, including under the New Partnership for Africa's Development, the Fund launched the ACB in May 2002 to strengthen economic governance and the capacity of governments to design and implement poverty-reduction strategies. The initiative was also aimed at improving the coordination of capacity building technical assistance in the **Poverty Reduction Strategy Paper** process, including through increased Fund **technical assistance**.

As part of the initiative, the Fund established three **African Regional Technical Assistance Centers (AFRITACs)**: East AFRITAC in Dar es Salaam; West AFRITAC in Bamako, Mali; and Central AFRITAC in Libreville, Gabon.

AFRICAN CAPACITY BUILDING FOUNDATION (ACBF). The ACBF is the implementation agency for the Partnership for Capacity Building in Africa. The Fund launched the ACBF in May 2002. It works closely with the ACBF on capacity building–related training activities and strengthening knowledge networking in Africa.

AFRICAN FRANC ZONE. On 12 January 1994, the African Financial Community (CFA) franc and the Comorian franc (CF) were devalued, the CFA franc to 100 per French franc and the CF to 75 per French franc. These devaluations were accompanied by major fiscal, monetary, wage, and structural policy measures and were followed by Fund **stand-by** or **enhanced structural adjustment facility** programs in seven of the CFA franc countries. The CFA franc zone had experienced some 30 years of strong growth and low inflation compared with other sub-Saharan African countries, but in the years 1986–1993 growth had begun to weaken in the face of a sharp deterioration in the zone's terms of trade. At the same time, fiscal imbalances and the external public debt had increased substantially and had been accompanied by the emergence of sizable domestic and external payments arrears and a major weakening of the soundness and financial position of the banking systems in the CFA franc zone.

The CFA franc zone currently consists of two separate groups of sub-Saharan African countries. The first group includes the seven members of the West African Economic and Monetary Union (WAEMU)—Benin, Burkina Faso, Côte d'Ivoire, Mali, Niger, Senegal, and Togo. The second group includes the six members of the **Central African Economic and Monetary Union (CAEMC)**—Cameroon, the Central African Republic, Chad, the Congo, Equatorial Guinea, and Gabon. These countries share a common currency, the CFA franc; CFA stands for Communauté Financière Africaine in the WAEMU and for Coopération Financière en Afrique Centrale in the CAEMC.

Since 1 January 1999, when the **euro** replaced the French franc at the rate of 6.55957 francs for 1 euro, the CFA franc has been pegged to the euro at 100 CFA francs = 0.152449 euro or 1 euro = 655.957 CFA francs. Although central African CFA francs and west African CFA francs have the same monetary value against other currencies, the west African currency is not accepted in countries using central African CFA francs and vice versa.

AFRICAN REGIONAL TECHNICAL ASSISTANCE CENTER (AFRITAC). *See* AFRICA CAPACITY BUILDING INITIATIVE (ACB).

ALTERNATE EXECUTIVE DIRECTOR. Each **Executive Director** appoints an Alternate, with full power to act in his or her absence. When Executive Directors who appointed them are present, Alternates may participate in **Executive Board** meetings but may not vote.

ANINAT, EDUARDO (1948–). Eduardo Aninat served as **Deputy Managing Director** of the Fund from December 1999 to June 2003. Prior to his service at the Fund, Mr. Aninat taught Public Finance and Economic Development at the Pontificia Universidad Católica de Chile and was an assistant professor of economics at Boston University. Mr. Aninat was the Finance Minister of Chile from March 1994 to December 1999. He was the Chairman of the Board of Governors of the Fund and World Bank in 1995–1996, and served three years as a member of the Development Committee of the World Bank and the Fund, representing Chile, Argentina, Bolivia, Peru, Uruguay, and Paraguay.

Mr. Aninat served in a range of economic positions in the Chilean Government; these included chief senior negotiator for the bilateral Canada–Chile trade agreement, and chief debt negotiator and senior advisor of the Central Bank of Chile and the Ministry of Finance. He has a PhD in economics from Harvard University.

ANNUAL MEETINGS. Annual meetings of the **Board of Governors** are held jointly with the Governors of the **World Bank** Group. The inaugural meeting was held in Savannah, Georgia, in March 1946. The first meeting of the Board was held in Washington, D.C., in September and October 1946; the second meeting, in London, England, in September 1947; the third, fourth, fifth, and sixth annual meetings were held in Washington, D.C., in September 1948, 1949, 1950, and 1951, respectively. The seventh meeting was held in Mexico City in September 1952, and thereafter it became the convention to hold consecutive meetings in Washington, D.C., and every third meeting in a member country other than the United States. Insofar as it is physically feasible, it is the practice to rotate the meetings held outside the United States among the world's geographical regions. Thus, the meeting was held in Istanbul, Turkey, in 1955; Delhi, India, in 1958; Vienna, Austria, in 1961; Tokyo, Japan, in 1964; Rio de Janeiro, Brazil, in 1967; Copenhagen, Denmark, in 1970; Nairobi, Kenya, in 1973; Manila, the Philippines, in 1976; Belgrade, Yugoslavia, in 1979; Toronto, Canada, in 1982; Seoul, Korea, in 1985; Berlin, Germany, in 1988; Bangkok, Thailand, in 1991; Madrid, Spain, in 1994; Hong Kong SAR, China, in 1997; Dubai, United Arab Emirates, in 2003; Singapore in 2006; and Istanbul, Turkey, in 2009.

Although traditionally little official business is accomplished, the annual meetings provide an important and rare opportunity for a face-to-face exchange of views by members. The meetings have assumed increasingly informal importance over the years as the largest international conference at which the world's financial officials, private financiers, and economists, journalists, and special guests are present. The Joint Fund–World Bank meetings are regularly preceded by meetings of the **Group of Ten**, the **Group of Twenty-Four**, the **International Monetary and Financial Committee**, and the **Development Committee**. All told, the meetings are attended by several thousand participants, observers, and journalists, forming a unique confluence of official and private interests in the world of finance.

ANNUAL REPORT OF THE EXECUTIVE BOARD. Prepared for the financial year by the **Executive Directors** and submitted by the Chairman of the **Executive Board** to the Chairman of the **Board of Governors**. The *Report* briefly reviews international financial and economic developments during the previous financial year, reports on the Fund's operations during that period, and discusses and explains the policies adopted or applied during the year. The *Report* is the major item for discussion on the agenda of the **annual meetings** and is usually submitted to the Governors approximately one month before the date of the meetings.

During the 1950s and 1960s, the *Annual Report* was the primary source of information on the Fund's activities and policies; it was in the *Report* that the Fund's assessment of the world economy first appeared and where its major policy decisions, such as its reserve and **credit tranche** policies and its views on **conditionality** and **international liquidity**, were given publicity. In the 1970s, however, the *Report* lost its primacy, partly because of the publication of the staff's ***World Economic Outlook*** and other publications such as the *IMF Survey* and *Finance & Development*, which were able to give more timely attention to the world economic situation, and partly due to the establishment of the **Interim Committee**, which raised and discussed most major policy questions in advance of the publication of the *Report*. The *Annual Report* continues to be an important document of record and chronicles the activities and policies of the Fund, together with an account of the evolution of the world economy, over the past 65 years.

ANNUAL REPORT ON EXCHANGE ARRANGEMENTS AND EXCHANGE RESTRICTIONS (AREAER). Provides an overview of the **foreign exchange** restrictions prevailing in the **international monetary system**, and describes the exchange rate system in effect in each member country.

The authority for publishing the *Report* is derived from the Fund's original **Articles of Agreement**, which envisioned the establishment of a multilateral system of payments, free of restrictions on current transactions. The Articles recognized, however, that in the exceptional conditions of the postwar years, it would not be possible to establish a freely operating system immediately, and thus provided for a transitional period in which members would be able to maintain restrictions and adapt them to changing circumstances. But after a transitional period of three years, the Fund was required to report on any restrictions remaining in force, and after five years and each year thereafter, members retaining such restrictions had to consult with the Fund to determine whether retention of the restrictions was inconsistent with members' obligations under the Articles. The transitional provisions in the Articles have been maintained through all subsequent amendments to the Articles.

The *Report* fulfills the Fund's obligation to report on the restrictions in effect in each country and includes a detailed description of each country's exchange arrangements.

ANTI-MONEY LAUNDERING AND COMBATING THE FINANCING OF TERRORISM (AML/CFT). Following the events of 11 September 2001, the Fund intensified its AML activities and extended them to include CFT. It also launched a donor-supported trust fund to finance technical assistance in these areas. *Money laundering* refers to the processes by which the actual source of assets obtained or generated by criminal activity are concealed in order to obscure the link between the funds and the original criminal activity. Terrorist activities are often financed by the proceeds of illegal activities. Perpetrators of these activities constantly seek new ways to launder money to avoid drawing the attention of country authorities to the source of the funds and links with underlying crimes. The Fund began expanding its work in the area of AML in 2000.

ARCHIVES OF FUND OPENED. For nearly 50 years, since its inception, the Fund maintained that its archives should not be made available to the public and was one of the few international or national institutions to keep its records private. In January 1996, however, the **Executive Board** decided that outside persons would be allowed access to archived material in the Fund that is over 30 years old, provided that access to Fund documents originally classified as "Secret" or "Strictly Confidential" would be granted only upon the **Managing Director's** consent to their declassification. The Board added that it was understood that this consent would be granted in all instances except those in which, despite the passage of time, the material remained highly confidential or sensitive.

It was agreed that access to the following would not be granted: (1) legal documents and records maintained by the Legal Department that are protected by attorney–client privilege; (2) documentary material furnished to the Fund by external parties, including member countries, their instrumentalities and agencies and central banks, that bear confidential markings, unless such external parties consent to their declassification; (3) personnel files and medical and other records pertaining to individuals; and (4) documents and proceedings of the Grievance Committee

ARGENTINA. Argentina has made frequent use of the Fund's financial **resources** since it became a member in 1956. For several decades after the end of World War II, economic policies were heavily interventionist, with high tariffs to protect local industry, government boards to regulate all aspects of commerce, and political decisions taking precedence over the marketplace.

The transformation of the economy began at the end of the 1980s under President Carlos Menem, when a start was made on privatization, a reduction in government expenditures, a drastic reduction in import tariffs, and a transformation of the central bank into a currency board arrangement, with the peso backed by gold or **foreign exchange**.

The transformation was assisted first by a 17-month **stand-by arrangement** in November 1989, amounting to Special Drawing Right (SDR) 1,104 million (about $1,500 million), and by a nine-month stand-by arrangement in July 1991, amounting to SDR 780 million (about $1,120 million), which was replaced in March 1992 by a program supported under the **extended Fund facility** authorizing **drawings** up to SDR 2,483 million (about $3.6 billion). During this period Argentina also benefited from drawings under the **compensatory financing facility** and from the use of Fund financing in support of a reduction in its debt- and debt-service-support operations, covering an estimated total of $29.2 million of debt and debt servicing and reducing its obligations by about $980 million a year for the rest of the decade. All told, the financial assistance available to Argentina at this time amounted to about $3.8 billion.

During 1991–1993, the authorities reinforced fiscal adjustment and structural reforms. A key feature of the reform program was the Convertibility Law, enacted in March 1991, which provided for the convertibility of the peso at a fixed parity to the U.S. dollar. It established the backing of the monetary base with the central bank's gross **international reserves** and prohibited the indexation of domestic-currency contracts. In the area of public finance, the authorities eliminated the fiscal deficit, streamlined the tax system, rationalized government spending, expanded privatization, and restored Argentina's creditworthiness. Other measures included structural reforms, such as deregulation and trade liberalization, and a start on reforming the financial markets, the social security system, and provincial government finance.

This bold economic program produced remarkable results. Real investment recovered strongly and real consumption expanded rapidly, with real average GDP growth averaging 7 percent a year in 1991–1993. Consumer price inflation fell abruptly to 80 percent during 1991 (down from 1,300 percent the year before) and then moved down to industrial-country levels in 1993 and thereafter. A tripling of imports (led by capital goods) moved the external current account into deficits, averaging more than $8 billion a year in 1992–1993 (3.5 percent of GDP) from a surplus of $2 billion in 1990. Capital inflows, however, more than covered the current account deficit, thereby raising the central bank's gross international reserves to over $15 billion (about 10 months of imports).

The contagion (dubbed *Tequila*) effect of the **Mexican financial crisis** at the end of 1994 triggered a slump in investor confidence, and Argentina experienced a large outflow of capital. By April 1995, reserves had fallen by one-third. Argentina introduced a strong package of fiscal measures to stabilize the financial situation, including a temporary increase in the value-added tax, increases in import duties, a broadening of the tax base, reform of the wealth tax, and improvements in the tax administration, aimed at restoring liquidity to the financial sector, raising domestic saving, and reestablishing confidence in the government's ability to defend the fixed exchange rate that is at the heart of the Convertibility Plan. Structural policies included further steps toward privatization, labor market reform, and a bankruptcy law. The program was supported by an extension of the extended facility for a further year and an increase of SDR 1,537 million (about $2 billion) in the available financing. As confidence gradually strengthened, deposits reflowed into the country, interest rates declined, and access to foreign borrowing was restored. While real GDP contracted by 4.4 percent, inflation declined to 1.6 percent in 1995, the lowest level in 50 years. The external current account deficit was halved in 1995, mainly due to an increase in exports.

In April 1996, the Fund approved a **stand-by arrangement** authorizing drawings up to the equivalent of SDR 720 million (about $1.0 billion) over the following 21 months in support of an economic program for 1996–1997. Its aim was to restore economic growth under conditions of low inflation and external viability, based on the strategy of maintaining fiscal and monetary discipline in the context of the Convertibility Law. Structural reforms were centered on the restructuring of the federal and provincial governments, as well as merging or eliminating a number of public institutions. At the end of the program period, real GDP had risen from 4.2 percent in 1996 to 8.1 percent in 1998; consumer prices remained flat; the overall fiscal balance declined from a deficit of 2.2 percent of GDP to a deficit of 1.4 percent; and, although the external current account balance had increased from 1.9 percent to 3.8 percent, the authorities had no difficulty in financing the deficit through favorable capital movements despite the turbulence that affected international capital markets in the latter part of the year.

In February 1998, the Fund approved another three-year credit for Argentina, equivalent to SDR 2.08 billion (about $2.8 billion) under its extended Fund facility, to support the government's medium-term economic program for 1998–2000. In requesting the credit, it was the government's intention to regard the credit as precautionary and to draw on it only if adverse external circumstances made it necessary.

The medium-term program for 1988–2000 basically envisaged the same policies that had been implemented in the previous six or seven years. It included further reforms in the labor market, in the tax system, and in budgetary procedures; the conclusion of the privatization process; and reforms in the health and judicial systems; thus completing a decade of economic, financial, and social reform. Although buffeted during the year by the effects of the **Asian financial crisis** in September 1998, the Fund announced at the conclusion of its first review of the extended arrangement that all applicable performance criteria had been met and that substantial progress had been made in the implementation of structural reforms.

On 10 March 2000, the Fund approved a three-year stand-by credit for Argentina in an amount equivalent to SDR 5,398.61 million (about $7.2 billion) to support the government's 2000–2002 economic program. The Argentine authorities have indicated that they intend to treat the credit as precautionary. However, in 2001–2002, Argentina experienced one of the worst economic crises in its history. Output, which had begun to contract in 1999, fell by about 20 percent in the three years ending December 2002, inflation reignited, the government defaulted on its debt, the banking system became largely paralyzed, and the Argentine peso, which was then pegged at par to the U.S. dollar, reached lows of Arg$3.90 per U.S. dollar (in mid-2002).

At the outset of the crisis in January 2001, the Fund provided an augmentation of Argentina's stand-by arrangement to SDR 10.6 billion (about $14 billion) provided under the **supplemental reserve facility**. This augmentation was part of a financial support package totaling about $39.7 billion from official and private sources, including the Inter-American Development Bank, the **World Bank**, and Spain. The overall financing package was aimed at helping Argentina maintain access to capital markets as the government put in place a comprehensive and ambitious program aimed at promoting economic growth and regaining sustainability with respect to its fiscal and external financial situations. The program contained measures to promote investment, including the elimination of tax disincentives; the creation of a private sector infrastructure fund; and an increase in public investment. It also included important structural reforms intended to ensure fiscal sustainability and reduce the public debt burden over the medium term. Key structural reforms included a new fiscal pact with the provinces, reform to the social security system, and measures to improve tax enforcement. The Fund-supported stand-by arrangement was further augmented to SDR 16.94 billion (about $21.57 billion) in September 2001.

At a review of experience in Argentina held on 24 March 2004, the Executive Board considered that the crisis had been brought about by the interaction of several sources of vulnerability that had lingered in the background during the boom years of the 1990s: the deteriorating public debt dynamics—driven to a sizable extent by off-budget spending; the constraint on monetary policy imposed by the currency board; and continued structural and institutional weaknesses, some of which had plagued Argentina for a long time. Despite these ongoing vulnerabilities, the private financial community had continued to finance Argentina's growing borrowing requirements—a factor that had further exacerbated the buildup of weaknesses. The underlying economic vulnerabilities in Argentina had become evident with the onset of the economic slump in 1998 in a context of heightened political uncertainty and exogenous financial shocks. This combination of weaknesses, especially the public debt dynamics, had limited the authorities' room to provide fiscal stimulus while the currency board limited the scope for active monetary policy.

During the latter part of the 1990s, the Fund—like other observers—had erred in its assessment of the Argentine economy by overestimating its growth potential and underestimating its weaknesses. These overly optimistic projections had resulted in Fund-supported programs that were insufficiently ambitious and excessively accommodative of slippages. Although the authorities had received warnings from the Fund at least by early 1998 stressing the need for further fiscal adjustment and structural reform, the Fund had continued to provide support on the basis of a policy package that was ultimately inadequate. In retrospect, it was clear that the successive Fund-supported programs put in place in the 1990s had included insufficient structural content and conditionality.

Noting that the level of debt relative to the size of the economy, at least at face value, had not been alarming prior to the crises, the Executive Board emphasized the need for rigorous **debt sustainability assessments**—along with strengthened analysis of balance-sheet weaknesses, notably currency mismatches—taking into account country-specific constraints, including foreign currency constraints. They also called for measures to "stress test" projections on economic growth and other key variables underlying sustainability assessments.

ARREARS IN PAYMENTS. Payment arrears were defined by the Fund in the early 1970s as undue delay in making **foreign exchange** available for international transactions, and were regarded as a payments restriction. The emergence of payment arrears was, of course, also a symptom of **balance of payments** difficulties, and the Fund was, therefore, often involved with members in payment arrears. **Adjustment programs** supported by the Fund have always given high priority to setting macroeconomic targets that would allow accumulated arrears to be cleared.

ARTICLE VIII. Within the context of Article IV consultations, the Fund also reviews the elimination or retention of exchange restrictions under **Articles VIII** and **XIV**. These so-called Article VIII and Article XIV consultations are "comprehended" by the Article IV consultation, but they are legally different from the Fund's regular surveillance activities and serve different purposes.

Article VIII, Sections 2, 3, and 4, provides the legal basis for the obligation of member countries to maintain **currency convertibility** and exchange regimes free of restrictions or discriminatory practices, and to provide adequate information to the Fund regarding their exchange practices. In particular, Section 2 prohibits members from imposing restrictions on the making of payments and transfers for current international transactions without the approval of the Fund. The Fund will approve restrictions only for **balance of payments** purposes, and then only if their use will be temporary and nondiscriminatory, while the member is seeking to eliminate the need for them. Section 3 prohibits members from engaging in any discriminatory currency arrangements or multiple currency practices except as authorized under the **Articles of Agreement** or approved by the Fund. Members maintaining such arrangements or practices are expected to consult with the Fund as to their progressive removal, unless they are maintained or imposed under the Article XIV, Section 2. Finally, Section 4 requires members to maintain the convertibility of their currency, by buying balances of their currency held by other members when requested by these other members.

ARTICLE XIV. Article XIV provides **transitional arrangements** for countries that have not yet accepted the obligations under **Article VIII**. Section 1 requires members to notify the Fund upon joining of whether they intend to avail themselves of the transitional arrangements contained in Section 2 of this Article, or whether they are prepared to accept the obligations of Article VIII, Sections 2, 3, and 4. Section 2 permits members to maintain and adapt to changing circumstances the restrictions on payments and transfers for current international transactions that were in effect on the date on which they became members. However, members are expected to withdraw restrictions maintained under this Section, and to accept the obligations under Article VIII, Sections 2, 3, and 4, as soon as **balance of payments** conditions permit. Section 3 stipulates that the Fund shall make annual reports on the restrictions in force under Section 2 of this Article. Any member retaining any restrictions inconsistent with Article VIII, Sections 2, 3, and 4, is required to consult annually with the Fund as to their further retention.

ARTICLES OF AGREEMENT. The original Articles of Agreement of the International Monetary Fund were agreed upon at the International Monetary and Financial Conference of the United and Associated Nations convened at **Bretton Woods**, New Hampshire, on 1 July 1944. The Conference was attended by delegates from 44 members of the United and Associated Nations and by a representative of Denmark, as well as delegates from several international organizations. The Final Act, embodying the Articles of Agreement of the International Monetary Fund and of the **International Bank for Reconstruction and Development** (the **World Bank**), was signed by all delegates on 22 July 1944.

The original Articles were based on the concept of a multilateral trade and payments system, operating with convertible currencies and free of payment restrictions on transfers relating to current transactions. They envisaged an exchange rate system that, contrary to the rigidity of the old gold exchange standard, would be stable, but flexible. The Fund was given authority to approve initial **par values** (i.e., to accept an exchange rate value declared by a member), and members could change these initial exchange rates (beyond an accumulated 10 percent) only with the concurrence of the Fund. Members were to subscribe to a pool of **gold** and **currencies** that could be drawn upon temporarily by members to help them finance their balance of payments disequilibria.

The first amendment to the Articles became effective on 28 July 1969. Its main purpose was to establish the **Special Drawing Rights Department** and to provide for the creation of **Special Drawing Rights (SDRs)**, a new **international reserve** asset to be issued by the Fund to supplement existing international reserve assets.

The second amendment to the Articles of Agreement became effective on 1 April 1978. This was a comprehensive reform of the Articles, recognizing that the old Bretton Woods par value system had collapsed. In the place of par values, the new Articles allowed a member to establish the exchange arrangement of its choice, although the Articles continued to require members to foster orderly economic growth with reasonable price stability, promote stability through orderly underlying economic and financial conditions, and avoid the manipulation of **exchange rates** or the **international monetary system** to gain unfair competitive advantage over other members. The second amendment also introduced the concept of firm **surveillance over the exchange rate** policies of members by the Fund and required the cooperation of members in this endeavor. Thus, the Fund had lost the authority given to it under the original Articles to approve members' initial par values and subsequent changes in them, but had gained a wider, although perhaps a more nebulous, authority, that of firm surveillance over members' exchange arrangements. The effective exercise of this new authority proved to be a critical but difficult challenge for international monetary cooperation in succeeding years.

A third amendment to the Articles of Agreement was approved by the **Board of Governors** in 1990 and became effective in November 1992. This amendment, the principal feature of which was the suspension of voting and related rights of those members in arrears in their repayments to the Fund, was also linked to an increase in members' **quotas** in the Fund, in accordance with the ninth general review of quotas.

A fourth amendment to the Articles was being prepared by the **Executive Board** in 1998 to give the Fund jurisdiction over capital account movements and to provide for a onetime equity allocation of SDRs, as requested by the **Interim Committee** at its meeting in Hong Kong SAR in September 1997. The fourth amendment became effective on 13 August 2009 in the midst of the **global financial crisis**, following a call by **Group of Twenty** leaders at their April summit to boost global liquidity.

In April 2008, the Fund Board of Governors approved a Resolution proposing an amendment of the Fund's Articles of Agreement on reform of quota and voice that included targeted quota increases for emerging market and developing countries in order to increase their representation based on a new quota formula. The Resolution was part of a larger effort to reform the Fund's governance structure, by ensuring voting weights better reflect members' relative positions in the world economy and to take into account changes in the global economy. The proposed amendment also provided for a tripling of basic votes and an additional **Alternate Executive Director** for large constituencies, in particular the two sub-Saharan chairs on the **Executive Board**. The effect of an increase in basic votes is to strengthen the representation of smaller economies, and the amendment would also protect the share of basic votes going forward.

On 5 May 2008, the Board of Governors overwhelmingly approved a Resolution proposing another amendment of the Articles to broaden the Fund's investment authority, a key element of the proposed new income model for the Fund. The amendment will enable the institution to generate revenues from a variety of sources, including limited gold sales. It also authorizes the Fund to create an endowment, based on gold sales, to be invested with a view to generating income while preserving the long-term real value of these resources.

The Proposed Amendments will enter into force for all members once three-fifths of the members (111), holding 85 percent of the total voting power, have accepted them. As of 19 November 2009, 44 members had accepted the Amendment on Voice and Participation, and 41 members had accepted the Amendment to Expand the Fund's Investment Authority.

In order to become a member, the Fund's Articles of Agreement must be ratified under the legislative procedure mandated for an international agreement in the member country, and **membership** does not become effective until the country has paid its **subscription** to the Fund and deposited with the designated depository, which is currently the government of the United States, an instrument setting forth that it has accepted the agreement in accordance with its law and has taken all the steps necessary to enable it to carry out all of its obligations under the agreement. *See* OBLIGATIONS UNDER ARTICLE VIII; TRANSITIONAL ARRANGEMENTS.

ASIAN FINANCIAL CRISIS. The Asian financial crisis that erupted in July 1997 in **Thailand** prompted a record level of Fund lending in 1997–1998, adding immediacy to the need to strengthen the financial resources of the institution to enable it to continue playing a fully effective role in the globalized world economy. The crisis also led to the creation of a new lending facility, the **supplemental reserve facility**; to stepped-up work on strengthening the conduct of **surveillance**; and, more generally, to the elaboration of a framework for strengthening the architecture of the international monetary system.

The crisis emerged suddenly in 1997 when the financial and exchange markets in Thailand, after a decade of rapid economic development, came under acute pressure. The erosion of Thailand's international competitiveness and a dramatic fall in the value of the baht following the attempt by authorities to adopt a managed float for the **currency** led to an abrupt loss of confidence by domestic and international investors alike. The crisis in Thailand quickly spread to other Asian economies, including **Indonesia**, **Korea**, **Hong Kong SAR**, **Malaysia**, the **Philippines**, and Singapore. Precipitous declines in currency values and stock markets were widespread throughout the region.

In 1997–1998, the member countries directly affected by the crisis drew SDR 19 billion ($25.6 billion) from the **General Resources Account** in the credit tranches—nearly four times the level of the previous year. The Fund approved nine new **stand-by arrangements**, with total commitments of SDR 27.3 billion, and four new Extended Arrangements, with total commitments of SDR 2.8 billion. The largest stand-by arrangements were for Korea (which also made use of the new supplemental reserve facility), Indonesia, and Thailand; the largest Extended Arrangement was for Argentina. In addition, the Fund approved eight new arrangements under the **enhanced structural adjustment facility (ESAF)** with commitments totaling SDR 1.7 billion. Total Fund credit outstanding rose to a record SDR 56 billion ($75.4 billion) as of 30 April 1998, compared with SDR 40.5 billion ($55.3 billion) a year earlier. The Asian financial crisis occurred after several decades of outstanding and unprecedented economic performance. Annual GDP growth in five countries of the Association of Southeast Asian Nations—Indonesia, Malaysia, the Philippines, Singapore, and Thailand—averaged close to 8 percent over the previous decade, and during the 30 years preceding the crisis per capita income levels had increased tenfold in Korea, fivefold in Thailand, and fourfold in Malaysia. Per capita income levels in Hong Kong SAR and Singapore had climbed to be in excess of those in some industrial countries. Until the crisis, Asia had attracted almost half of total capital flows to developing countries—nearly $100 billion in 1996. In the decade preceding the crisis, the share of developing countries and emerging market economies of Asia in world exports had nearly doubled, to almost one fifth of the total. Thus, they had been considered the "tiger" economies of the age.

The very success of these economies ironically also contributed to their undoing. Intoxicated by the success of their growth policies, the authorities in several of the countries had brushed off warnings from the Fund and other organizations that their economies were overheating and had serious structural weaknesses, particularly in the financial sectors. Hong Kong SAR, Malaysia, and Singapore, after the initial impact of the crisis, quickly took corrective action in raising interest rates and undertaking fiscal reforms to stabilize their currencies and stock prices without resorting to Fund resources, while Thailand, Korea, and Indonesia appealed for and received very large amounts of assistance from the Fund and other international institutions.

The Asian countries affected by the crises had different degrees of financial and structural problems, notably in current account positions and fiscal situations, but they also had a number of fundamental structural weaknesses in common. The Fund's first priority was to restore confidence in the region through massive injections of financial resources and the correction of excessively low interest rates. Beyond that, however, the Fund's challenge was not so much to devise corrective macroeconomic policies, as to lay out a series of structural reforms. To this end, the IMF-supported adjustment programs had many of the following common features:

- The introduction of flexibility to exchange rates where it did not exist already
- A temporary tightening of monetary policy to stem pressures on the **balance of payments** and staunch the outflow of reserves
- Immediate action to correct obvious weaknesses in the financial system
- Structural reforms to remove features of the economy that had become impediments to growth, such as monopolies, trade barriers, and preferential practices among corporations
- Assistance in reopening or maintaining lines of external financing
- The maintenance of a sound fiscal policy, taking into account the budgetary cost of restructuring the financial sector and the need to protect social spending

The heart of all the programs was structural reform, in contrast to many of the Fund-supported programs of the past, where the focus had most often been on macroeconomic policies to rectify monetary, fiscal, and external imbalances. Moreover, because financial sector problems were the major cause of the crises, the centerpiece of the Asian programs was a comprehensive reform of the financial systems. Such reforms included closure of financial institutions that were not viable, with an associated write-down of shareholders' capital; the recapitalization of undercapitalized institutions; close supervision of weak institutions; and increased foreign participation in the domestic financial system.

Greater transparency and efficiency in government was addressed through measures designed to improve the effectiveness of markets, break the close links between business and governments, and prudently liberalize capital markets. Improvements in data collection and dissemination were also addressed, not only for the economy (particularly for external reserves and liabilities), but also for the fiscal, corporate, and banking sectors. These efforts were coordinated with the **World Bank**, with its focus on structural and sectoral issues, and with the Asian Development Bank, with its regional specialization.

Although the overall situation remained volatile, a financial turnaround in most of the countries affected by the Asian financial crisis countries began in the first quarter of 1998, with both the Thai baht and the Korean won strengthening by about 18 percent and ending the quarter worth about 38 percent less in terms of U.S. dollars than they were before the crisis. Similar gains were made in the stock markets of both countries. More moderate gains, but still positive ones, were made in the markets of Malaysia and the Philippines.

The course of recovery suffered a severe setback, however, when Indonesia failed to follow through on its program with the Fund. Ironically, Indonesia had called for Fund assistance at a far earlier stage of the crisis than others in the region, but had delayed the implementation of corrective measures, particularly those requiring the closure of nonviable banks and government enterprises (some of which were owned or operated by members of the president's family). It was not until April 1998 that a further renegotiation of the Indonesia program was completed and full support for it had been pledged by President Suharto. By that time, however, the Indonesia rupiah had lost 70 percent of its value since the middle of 1997 and 35 percent since the beginning of 1998. The delay in implementing corrective measures proved extreme costly; the austerity program, seen against a political regime that was perceived to be corrupt and marked by cronyism and nepotism, aroused widespread opposition from vulnerable groups of the population. On 20 May, in the face of mounting pressure, violence in the streets, and demands for his resignation, President Suharto announced his withdrawal from the presidency. The vice president, B. J. Habibie, was immediately sworn in as head of state and the Fund began the negotiations for a new recovery program. But it was not until July 1998 that a far tougher program was completed—12 months after the first signs of the crisis had appeared. Meanwhile, the mounting stress in Indonesia was enough to disrupt an already extremely fragile situation in the rest of Asia, and progress of the recovery slowed and was even reversed in some countries. With the confidence of international investors shattered, the crisis rapidly spread to other parts of the world economy, notably **Russia** and countries in Latin America. For Russia, which in 1997 had finally produced a small but positive growth of GDP and appeared to be set for continued progress, the Fund entered into a massive multinational financial aid program, linked to a broad range of macroeconomic policies and structural reforms. However, political instability inside Russia and the continuing incapacity of its president severely damaged the government's ability to carry through the program, and disbursements from the Fund were halted. The government announced a default on its foreign debts and floated the ruble, which fell from 6 to 15 to the U.S. dollar by the end of the month.

From Russia, which, although of strategic importance, was not of major economic significance, the battle line moved to Latin America, where both **Argentina** and **Brazil** were suffering stress. Argentina had entered into a three-year arrangement with the Fund in 1997 and, despite some loss of reserves and rising interest rates, succeeded in riding out the storm. At its first annual review of the arrangement in September 1998, the Fund found that Argentina had met all the performance criteria under the program and was making satisfactory progress in implementing structural reforms. In Brazil, where a presidential election was due early in October, **international reserves**, the exchange rate, and the stock market were all under pressure, but the government was reluctant to enter into an arrangement with the Fund until after the elections. On 13 November 1998, the Fund and Brazil were able to announce a major economic adjustment program, supported by a financing package totaling $41 billion over the following three years, in which the Fund, the World Bank, the Inter-American Development Bank, and the **Bank for International Settlements**, as well as many industrial countries, were all participants. The financing program was accompanied by a three-year economic program, under which the Brazilian authorities undertook to implement a comprehensive set of revenue-raising and expenditure-saving measures to achieve a major fiscal adjustment by the year 2001.

Toward the end of 1998, the crisis seemed to have reached rock bottom, and was beginning to recover. The volatility of the Asian financial markets had eased, and many currencies had stabilized and even strengthened. Interest rates in the crisis countries had come down and foreign exchange reserves were rising. Even in Indonesia, there were first signs of improvement. Nevertheless, the efforts of the Fund to cope with the Asian financial crisis had been greeted on all sides by criticism. The programs were too tough, they were too soft, they addressed the wrong problems, the measures proposed were inappropriate, they rewarded bad behavior, and even that the Fund had caused the whole crisis by its intervention in the first place. At one extreme were those who wanted to abolish the Fund and leave events to the free market. At the other were those who wanted to erect a new institution to operate alongside the Fund to control international financial movements. In between these two extremes were the Fund's management and probably most officials and professionals advocating a steady further evolution of the existing system.

Throughout the entire period of the crisis, the Fund strenuously refuted the main charges, but did admit that its initial insistence on retrenchment was probably too tough in view of the depth and weaknesses of the economies in question—an underestimate shared by others and promptly rectified when the depth of the crisis became apparent. It launched an unusually large-scale media effort to combat criticism. The **Managing Director** and the **Deputy Managing Directors** spoke in numerous fora explaining the Fund's programs; its mission chiefs appeared on television and before the press in the countries involved to answer questions; the programs themselves were published (with the permission of the countries concerned); and a mass of information, including letters of intent, news briefs, country studies, and economic data, was made available on the Fund's website.

The lessons of the Asian financial crisis led to an intensification of the Fund's work on surveillance, particularly in recognition that promoting good governance, making budgets more transparent, improving data collection and disclosure, and strengthening financial sectors are increasingly important if countries are to establish and maintain private sector confidence and lay the groundwork for sustained growth.

In a preliminary review in March 1998 of the implication for Fund surveillance of the Asian financial crisis, the Executive Board drew five lessons:

1. Effective surveillance depends critically on the timely availability of accurate information.
2. The focus of surveillance has to extend beyond short-term macroeconomic issues, yet remain appropriately selective.
3. Surveillance at the country level should pay more explicit attention to policy interdependence and the risks of contagion.
4. The crucial role of credibility in restoring market confidence underscores the importance of transparency.
5. Effective surveillance depends fundamentally on the willingness of members to take the Fund's advice.

More generally, the challenges posed by the ongoing globalization of financial markets highlighted the need for further efforts to strengthen the Fund's surveillance functions. In its continuing discussions of additional initiatives to strengthen the architecture of the international monetary system, the **Executive Board** in 1997–1998 identified the following imperatives:

- Improving international and domestic financial systems
- Strengthening Fund surveillance
- Promoting the wider availability and greater transparency of information on economic data and policies
- Reinforcing the central role of the Fund in crisis management
- Introducing more effective procedures for involving the private sector in resolving financial crises.

ASSET SETTLEMENT. A proposal made by the **staff of the Fund** in connection with discussions on the **reform of the international monetary system** after the breakdown of the **par value system** early in the 1970s. The idea was to replace the **currency convertibility** provisions of the original **Articles of Agreement** and eliminate or reduce the role of **reserve currencies**

by requiring the issuers of such currencies to prevent the further buildup of liabilities in their currencies and to reduce existing holdings by using reserve assets—**gold**, **Special Drawing Rights**, or reserve positions in the Fund. Thus, the proposal would have required reserve currency centers, such as the United States, to move toward settling their **balance of payments** deficits on a current basis and would have eliminated the privileges that accrue to a currency issuer.

Asset settlement was one of the proposals examined by the **Committee of Twenty** in an attempt to reach agreement on a comprehensive reform of the international monetary system. The serious disagreement over the various issues, together with the sharp increase in world oil prices toward the end of 1973, led the Committee of Twenty to abandon its efforts to reach agreement on a comprehensive and immediate reform, including the asset settlement proposal.

ASSETS OF THE FUND. *See Resources of the Fund; Subscriptions to the Fund.*

B

BALANCE OF PAYMENTS. The concept of a country's balance of payments and the ability to determine to what extent a country is under pressure on its external payments account is of critical importance in the operations of the Fund, since a member may not use the Fund's financial resources unless it has a balance of payments need. Under the **Bretton Woods system**, indeed, a member could, in general, change its **par value** only when its balance of payments was in "**fundamental disequilibrium**." The term itself was never defined by the Fund, but was identified and applied on a case-by-case basis.

In an accounting sense, the balance of payments must always balance, since it is a systematic record of all economic transactions between residents of one country and residents of other countries, presented in the form of double-entry bookkeeping. Debit and credit entries in such a statement must show an overall balance, since net differences in any one item in the statement—merchandise trade, services, and capital flows—must be offset by other entries, including monetary movements (i.e., changes in assets and liabilities). Similarly, since exports by one country correspond to the imports of other countries, and payments by one country must be received by others, globally the sums of all payments and receipts should balance. Unfortunately, this is not so, because all kinds of discrepancies arise from errors, omissions, timing, and asymmetries in reported payments data, primarily on trade in services and on portfolio investment. These discrepancies on a global basis can be substantial, involving many billions of dollars a year, and can fluctuate unpredictably as the pattern of international payments changes.

The framework of the overall balance of payments comprises the current account (merchandise trade, services, and official transfers), and the capital account (long-term and short-term capital movements); any net difference in these accounts will be reflected in the movement in monetary assets and liabilities. Within the overall balance of payments statement, it can be useful to examine particular components, or a combination of particular components, to analyze the position of countries, groups of countries, or worldwide trends in payments. The decision on where to draw the line in a balance of payments statement reflects a judgment as to which set of transactions best indicates the need for **balance of payments adjustment**. No unambiguous criteria exist for making such a judgment and the ultimate decision rests on a subjective assessment of the situation. It is not surprising, therefore, that several balance of payments concepts have developed.

The narrowest definition of payments imbalance relates to the trade balance—the difference between exports and imports. A somewhat broader and more informative representation of a country's transactions is the current account. It covers transactions in goods, services, and income, and may or may not include private or all unrequited transfers, again depending on the judgment of the classifier. The basic balance attempts to indicate a longer-run balance of payments position by including long-term capital flows in addition to the current account items. A variant of the basic balance is the liquidity balance, which includes short-term, domestically held claims on nonresidents among the components making up the balance. Finally, there is the overall balance, which includes in the balance everything except the **reserve assets** and liabilities that automatically change to accommodate the payments imbalance of the rest of the items.

For most developing countries, the current account captures the essential picture of their external accounts, although as these countries develop and benefit from capital inflows, the overall balance and reserve movements assume greater importance. In addition, for countries such as the United States that act as a **reserve currency** center and whose currency is widely used in international transactions, the traditional concept of a balance may not be appropriate and may send a wrong signal in terms of balance of payments adjustment. Reserve centers perform the role of financial intermediaries, such as a commercial bank, by lending on a long-term basis and providing short-term investments to foreign monetary authorities. Partly for this reason, the United States ceased publishing official balances on the grounds that they might be positively misleading, although it does show balances as memorandum items in the accounts.

The choice of a balance of payments measurement depends, therefore, on the purpose of the exercise and the structure of a country's overseas payments, as well as the very practical consideration of the reliability of the statistical records in question. Use of the Fund's financial **resources** by a member is dependent, in the first instance, on a requirement that the financing is needed for balance of payments purposes, or, as stated in Article I, "to give confidence to members by making the general resources of the Fund temporarily available to them under adequate safeguards, thus providing them with opportunity to correct maladjustments in their balance of payments without resorting to measures destructive of national or international prosperity." Under the current **Articles**, in order to use the Fund's financial resources, a member must represent "that it has a need to make the purchase because of its balance of payments or its reserve position or developments in its reserves." In practice, developments in a country's **reserve position** become a critical factor and one that can be more easily identified and verified.

BALANCE OF PAYMENTS ADJUSTMENT. Adjustment of a country's **balance of payments** is at the center of the use of the Fund's financial **resources** by its members. Members can avail themselves of those resources only when there is a balance of payments need (i.e., an adverse disequilibrium in a country's external accounts, reflected in a pressure on reserves). Moreover, use of the resources must be only temporary, and thus the member is required to repay the Fund under a normal **stand-by arrangement** within three to five years and under other arrangements up to ten years. The borrowing member, therefore, is under an obligation to introduce corrective economic and financial policies to improve the productivity of the economy and bring about a sustainable balance in its foreign trade and capital flows. In making its financial resources temporarily available to a member, the Fund cooperates with it in working out and agreeing on an adjustment program that will strengthen the economy and enable the member to repay the Fund. The severity of the adjustment program and the terms of the repayment to the Fund will depend on the nature and the extent of the disequilibria to be remedied.

An adjustment program must be tailored to the particular requirements of the country in question, but in general it is aimed at restraining domestic absorption (i.e., domestic consumption, investment, and imports), raising national savings to allow higher productive investment, and using resources more effectively. Such a program will require supporting macroeconomic policies, such as fiscal and monetary measures to correct underlying imbalances, exchange rate policies to improve competitiveness and strengthen the supply side of the economy, and interest rate and pricing policies to increase domestic savings and promote efficient resource allocation and investment. In addition, adjustment programs require adequate financing, not only of the type available from the Fund, but also, if possible, other financial resources from international banks, governments, and in the form of direct private investment. Finally, experience shows that, internally, there must be a political will and cohesion to carry the program through and, externally, a favorable environment of positive terms of trade, buoyant and open markets, and favorable interest rates.

BALANCE OF PAYMENTS MANUAL. First issued in 1948, this manual has been updated several times since, taking into account changes in the international financial situation as new financial instruments and markets have been developed. It contains an internationally agreed-to exposition of **balance of payments** methodology, along with detailed instructions as to how members should report their balance of payments data to the Fund.

BALANCE OF PAYMENTS STATISTICS YEARBOOK. First issued in 1949, the *Yearbook* provides annual and, when available, quarterly **balance of payments** statements for member countries, as well as presentations by regions and by category of payments. The statements, drawn up in a uniform and internationally comparable format, are comprehensive, covering trade and invisibles, as well as short-term and long-term **capital movements**.

BANCOR. Under the **Keynes Plan**, first put forward by **Lord John Maynard Keynes** in 1941, it was proposed to establish a currency union, designated as an International Clearing Union, based on international bank money, which Keynes called *Bancor*, with a fixed (but not unalterable) value in terms of **gold** and to be accepted as the equivalent of gold by all members of the Clearing Union for the purpose of settling international balances. Each member would subscribe a **quota** in gold and **currency**, the amount to be adjusted annually, and would be allowed to draw 25 percent of its quota from the Union annually in the form of an overdraft. A key feature of the plan envisaged that the burden of **balance of payments adjustment** should be shouldered by both surplus and deficit countries. Exchange rates could only be changed with permission of the governing body, and growing balances, either debit or credit, would require the adoption of specific economic and financial policies, including changes in exchange rates. The plan also foresaw a transitional period after the end of World War II in which members would be able to adjust their exchange and trading systems to their evolving situations.

The Keynes Plan and other plans, principally that proposed by **Harry Dexter White** in the United States, became the basis for drawing up the **Articles of Agreement** of the Fund at the **Bretton Woods Conference** in 1944. The idea of deliberately creating a new form of international reserve money did not then survive, but 25 years later a conceptually very different form of international money came into being with the birth of **Special Drawing Rights**.

BANK FOR INTERNATIONAL SETTLEMENTS (BIS). The BIS was established in Basel, Switzerland, in 1930 to handle the payment of reparations by Germany after World War I and to promote cooperation among the central banks of the principal industrial countries. It developed into a center for economic and monetary research and consultation, and became responsible for the execution of certain specific multicountry agreements. Although liquidation of the Bank was recommended at the **Bretton Woods**

Conference following the establishment of the Fund and the **World Bank**, it continued in existence and has played an active role in facilitating cooperation among central banks in Europe, North America, and Japan.

It holds regular monthly meetings attended by the central bank governors of member countries and the Fund's **Managing Director**, or his representative. In addition, the staffs of the BIS and the Fund maintain continuous informal contacts. The BIS was the agent for the Organization for European Economic Cooperation, serving the European Monetary Union. In 1973, it became the agent of the European Monetary Cooperation Fund, set up by the European Community.

The Bank tends to be regarded by the developing countries as an exclusive club for rich countries, but it has a prestigious reputation among central bankers. It has proven to be a convenient institution to take on various ad hoc arrangements and responsibilities in areas that, although not genuinely international in character, are of concern to its multinational membership.

BANK-FUND FINANCIAL SECTOR LIAISON COMMITTEE (FSLC). Established in September 1998, the FSLC is composed of senior staff from the Fund and the World Bank. Its main objective is to facilitate coordination between the two institutions in three areas: (1) work programs in countries facing important financial sector issues, (2) the development of guidelines and procedures for sharing documents and confidential information, and (3) work on standards and sound practices regarding financial sector issues. The **Financial Sector Assessment Program** was initiated in April 1999 as a principal instrument for Bank-Fund collaboration in their financial sector work.

The role of the FSLC has evolved since it was established in 1998. In particular, the international community has continued to urge the Fund and the Bank to take on additional tasks, such as encouraging greater observance of a broadening range of international standards and codes, assessing supervisory cooperation and information exchange between supervisors in offshore financial centers and their counterparts in major countries, and helping to reduce the scope for money laundering. The FSLC has thus become a forum not only for enhancing coordination of the financial sector work programs of the Bank and the Fund, but also and more broadly for helping to integrate the various tasks assigned to the two institutions into a coherent joint work program, and facilitating coordination with the work programs of other institutions.

BASEL AGREEMENT. Following the approval of a **stand-by arrangement** for the United Kingdom in January 1977, agreement was reached in Basel by the United Kingdom and the other nine countries in the **Group of Ten** and Switzerland, meeting under the auspices of the **Bank for**

International Settlements (BIS), affecting the future role of the pound sterling as a **reserve currency**. Under the agreement, $3 billion was made available by several participating central banks and the BIS in support of the pound sterling. The resources, available over a two-year period, were furnished on the understanding that there would be an orderly reduction in the use of the pound sterling as a reserve currency. The **Managing Director** of the Fund was offered and accepted the central role of monitoring the implementation of the agreement.

BASEL COMMITTEE ON BANKING SUPERVISION. Set up in 1974 by the **Governors** of the **Group of Ten** industrial countries, the purpose of the Committee was to coordinate the supervisory efforts of individual countries at the international level over banks and other financial institutions that were increasingly engaging in banking activities. Originally seen as confining its activities to the industrial countries, it soon became apparent that as the financial sectors of emerging and transitional economies assumed greater importance, with expanding cross-border operations, the Basel Committee's standards for capitalization and broad guidelines for sound banking had a wider application. In its **adjustment programs**, the Fund is guided by the Committee's standards in its recommendations on the restructuring that may be required in the financial sectors of its member countries. In furthering this work, the Fund has cosponsored workshops and held seminars on banking supervision, seeking to provide operational guidance on bank licensing; off-site supervision of banks; loan portfolio analysis, classification, and provisioning; and supervisory responses and procedures for intervening with problem banks.

BERNE UNION. The popular name for the *Union d'Assureurs des Crédits Internationaux*, comprising a large group of government and related public agencies that guarantee or insure export credits, including short-term trade credits. Members of the group exchange information on their operations, with particular emphasis on countries that might be overextended in their external credit position.

BERNSTEIN, EDWARD (1910–1996). Deputy to **Harry Dexter White** when the latter was Assistant Secretary in the U.S. Treasury, Edward Bernstein played a leading role in the early negotiations with British officials on the conception of the Fund and in the detailed negotiations on the **Articles of Agreement** at the 1944 **Bretton Woods Conference**. He was the first Director of the Fund's Research Department, from 1948–1958, and in that position was responsible for developing much of the policy and operational approaches adopted by the Fund in those important and formative years. After he left the Fund, he established a private consultancy and remained active in speaking on the Fund and on developments in the **international monetary system** until his death.

BILATERAL SURVEILLANCE. Article IV consultations are the principal tool of bilateral surveillance. These consultations represent bilateral discussions between the Fund and individual member countries. Each consultation begins with a visit from a mission of Fund staff to the country to gather information and conduct discussions with country officials. Missions normally last two to three weeks, and discussions are held primarily with government officials. The **staff** mission often also tries to meet with representatives from the private sector, labor unions, nongovernment organizations, regional organizations, or academia. The objective is for the staff to gain as wide a perspective as possible on the country's economic situation and vulnerabilities. At the end of the mission, final discussions are held with the authorities to present the mission's preliminary findings on developments, vulnerabilities, outlooks, and recommendations. A member of the **Executive Director's** office normally attends these discussions. The staff mission team may also leave with the authorities a statement summarizing its findings.

Upon its return to Fund headquarters, the staff prepares a report, setting out recent developments, a summary of the policy discussions, the short- and medium-term outlook, and the staff's appraisal of the country's economic situation. This report, along with a "buff" statement by the Executive Director, explaining the country authorities' perspective on the issues involved, forms the basis for a discussion by the Fund's **Executive Board** on the country concerned. The Executive Board discussion normally takes within place 65 days of the mission's return to headquarters (or within three months for members eligible for the **poverty reduction and growth facility**).

The Executive Director representing the country takes an important part in the Board discussion, clarifying points about the country's economy and its policies as necessary. Key members of the staff also attend. The **Managing Director**, serving as Chairman of the Board, prepares a summing up of the Board discussion to highlight the key findings and areas of consensus reached by Executive Directors. This summing up is transmitted to the country's authorities and, if the authorities agree, is published in a **Public Information Notice**.

In June 2007, the policy framework concerning the conduct of bilateral surveillance received the first major update since the 1970s, with the adoption of the Decision on Bilateral Surveillance over Members' Policies. The Decision specified that bilateral surveillance focus primarily on assessing whether countries' policies promote external stability. This means that the staff's examination should mainly focus on monetary, fiscal, financial, and exchange rate policies and assess risks and vulnerabilities. It provides guidance to members on how to conduct exchange rate policies in a way that is consistent with the objective of promoting stability and avoiding manipulation. The Decision also emphasizes that surveillance should be collaborative, candid, evenhanded, and forward looking, adopting a multilateral perspective while taking into account individual countries' specific circumstances. *See also* SURVEILLANCE OVER EXCHANGE RATES.

BOARD OF GOVERNORS. The senior decision-making body in the Fund consists of one Governor and Alternate Governor appointed by each member of the Fund. The Governor is chosen by the member and is usually the minister of finance, the governor of the central bank, or an official of similar rank.

Under the **Articles of Agreement**, the Board of Governors has a number of specific powers, as well as all powers under the Articles not expressly conferred on the **Executive Board** or the **Managing Director**. These specific powers, which cover such matters as the admission of new members, the determination of **quotas**, and the allocation of **Special Drawing Rights**, can be exercised only by the Board of Governors. All other powers can be—and, in fact, have been—delegated by the Board of Governors to the Executive Board. Of the specific powers conferred on the Board of Governors, 45 types of decisions require special voting majorities of 70 percent or 85 percent, but these relate to **membership** and quota resolutions or to issues that only rarely arise, and most decisions taken by the Board require a simple majority. In accordance with the Articles, weighted voting is in effect, with each Governor able to cast the number of votes held by the member that appointed him (*see* Voting Provisions).

The Board of Governors is required to meet whenever called upon to do so by at least 15 members or by members having at least one-fourth of the Board's total voting power. A quorum for a meeting exists when a majority of the Governors having at least two-thirds of the total voting power of the Fund's membership are present. The Board normally meets only at the **annual meetings**, which are held jointly with the **World Bank**. The governing boards of these two institutions have established the convention of holding the annual meetings in consecutive years in Washington, D.C., and every third year in a member country other than the United States. The Board may vote on a specific question without meeting, and most votes taken by the Board of Governors are in fact taken by mail.

The second amendment to the Articles provides for the establishment of a Council, to come into being only when a decision to do so has been approved by 85 percent of the total voting power of the Board of Governors. The Council has never been voted into existence, but in 1974 the Board established an **Interim Committee** to serve as an advisory body. The Interim Committee was replaced by the **International Monetary and Financial Committee** in 1999.

BORROWED RESOURCES SUSPENSE ACCOUNT (BRSA). Established in 1981, the Borrowed Resources Suspense Account was set up in the **General Department** to hold and invest borrowed funds pending their use by members. **Investment** of borrowed funds is made in short-term Special Drawing Rights–denominated deposits with an official national institution of those members whose **currencies** are freely usable or with the **Bank for International Settlements**.

BORROWING BY THE FUND. Although **quota** subscriptions by its members are the basic source of resources for financing the Fund's operations, under its **Articles of Agreement**, the Fund is authorized to borrow currencies from its members and others in order to accommodate the financing of a large and temporary payments imbalance. Although the authority to borrow does not preclude borrowing from private sources, so far the Fund has borrowed only from official institutions. From time to time, such borrowing has provided an important supplement to the Fund's subscribed resources.

The first borrowing arrangements entered into by the Fund were the **General Arrangements to Borrow (GAB)**, which became effective in 1962. Under these arrangements, the Fund may borrow, in certain circumstances, specified amounts from 11 industrial countries, including 10 members (the **Group of Ten**) or their central banks (Belgium, Canada, France, Germany, Italy, Japan, Netherlands, Sweden, United Kingdom, and the United States) and Switzerland (which became a member in 1992). The arrangements call upon the main industrial countries to stand ready to lend the Fund up to specified amounts of their currencies when such resources are needed to forestall or cope with an impairment of the **international monetary system (IMF)**. Originally the arrangements provided for credit lines amounting to a total of the equivalent of $6 billion, but in 1983 the total lines of credit were raised to Special Drawing Rights (SDR) 17 billion, with an additional arrangement with Saudi Arabia amounting to SDR 1.5 billion.

Since its establishment in 1962, the GAB has been renewed ten times, most recently in November 2007 for a five-year period from December 2008. In response to the growing pressures on the Fund's resources caused by the emergence of the debt crisis in Latin America in 1982, a broad review was undertaken in 1983. It resulted in a substantial increase in the credit lines, from about SDR 6 billion to SDR 17 billion. Other major amendments to earlier GAB provisions permit the IMF to use it to finance lending to non-participants in the GAB, if the Fund faces a situation where it has inadequate resources of its own. The earlier GAB carried a rate of interest below market rates; this rate was raised at the time of the GAB enlargement and made equal to the SDR interest rate.

To further enhance the Fund's ability to safeguard the international monetary system, the Fund entered into **New Arrangements to Borrow (NAB)** in January 1997. Under these new arrangements, 25 participant countries and institutions stand ready to lend the Fund additional resources—up to SDR 34 billion—to supplement its regular quota resources if needed to forestall or cope with an impairment of the international monetary system or deal with an exceptional situation that threatens the stability of the system. The NAB do not replace the credit lines available under the GAB, but the NAB is the facility of first recourse. The NAB have been renewed twice, most recently in November 2007 for a period of five years from November 2008.

In the wake of the **global financial crisis**, the **Group of Twenty** (G-20) industrial and emerging market economies agreed on 2 April 2009 to further increase the resources available to the Fund by up to $500 billion (which would triple the total precrisis lending resources of about $250 billion) to support growth in emerging market and developing countries. This broad goal was endorsed by the **International Monetary and Financial Committee** in its 25 April 2009 communiqué. This resource increase is to be made in two steps: first through immediate bilateral financing from member countries, and second by subsequently incorporating this financing into an expanded and more flexible NAB increased by up to $500 billion. On 25 September 2009, the G-20 announced it had delivered on its promise to contribute over $500 billion to a renewed and expanded NAB.

As of November 2009, six countries had signed bilateral loan agreements with the Fund worth $169 billion. China had also signed a $50 billion bilateral note purchase agreement.

BRAZIL. For nearly 40 years in the post-World War II era, the Brazilian authorities, like most others in the region, relied on government intervention to promote economic growth, such as price controls, subsidies, import substitution, trade barriers, and forced industrialization through state ownership of many of the basic industries and services, such as steel, oil, aviation, banks, communications, utilities, and other services. Although Brazil went further than any other country in the region in establishing the basic infrastructure of a developing industrial economy, the result was an array of state enterprises kept afloat by the government at the expense of continued high inflation and even hyperinflation.

In 1994, under President Cardoso, the country changed course and embarked on the *Real* Plan, a program whose central theme was stabilization, deregulation, and an open economy based on market forces, both to those at home and to those from abroad. With the introduction of the Plan, the Brazilian economy achieved a remarkable and sustained reduction in inflation, from an annual rate in excess of 2,500 percent in 1993 to less than 3 percent by September 1998—a rate that Brazil had not experienced for over 50 years. This low inflation was achieved without significant loss in economic activity or income. Real GDP grew at an average annual rate of 4.1 percent and real GDP per capita at an annual rate of 2.7 percent, in sharp contrast to the stagnation of real income and high inflation of the 1980s and early 1990s.

This progress in financial stability was accompanied by substantial structural reform, which included a further opening of the economy through the liberalization of trade and capital flows, a large privatization program, demonopolization and deregulation of key sectors of the economy, and a fundamental strengthening of the banking system (including state banks). Investment rose from 15 percent of GDP in 1994 to 18 percent of GDP in 1998, and foreign direct investment from $2 billion to $23 billion over the same period.

Despite the *Real* Plan's successes in macroeconomic stabilization and structural reform, and despite the federal government's efforts to restrain federal spending, modernize the tax system, strengthen its administration, and promote fiscal discipline at the state level, Brazil was not able to stabilize the financing of the nonfinancial public sector. This weakness resulted in a significant deterioration in public finances, persistent, substantial overall deficits in the public sector, in the range of 5 to 7 percent of GDP, and a steady climb in the ratio of public debt to GDP.

This imbalance in the finances of the public sector led to a growing resort to external savings in order to finance the rise in domestic investment, with the result that the deficit in the current account of the **balance of payments** rose to over 4 percent of GDP in 1997. Foreign direct investment covered nearly 50 percent of this deficit, but by mid-1998 gross external debt had risen to $228 billion, or over 28 percent of GDP. With the dramatic worsening of the **Asian financial crisis** in the last quarter of 1997, the exchange rate came under substantial pressure. The central bank responded promptly, however, doubling its basic lending rate to 43 percent and raising revenue by about 2 percent of GDP. These timely measures succeeded in rebuilding confidence and allowing a gradual return of interest rates to their precrisis levels, but not without cost in terms of lower economic activity and higher unemployment.

In February 1998, at the time of Brazil's Article VI consultation with the Fund, the Executive Directors commended the authorities on their quick and decisive policy response to the pressure on the *real* in the foreign exchange market, adding that the higher interest rates and the strong fiscal package had played an important role in limiting the impact of the Asian turmoil on Brazil and the rest of Latin America. Executive Directors at that time, however, also noted a number of vulnerabilities in the debt structure, and the federal and state fiscal situations, but commended the authorities on their actions in many other areas, such as privatization, the proposed constitutional reforms concerning social security and public administration, the strengthening of bank supervision, and the restructuring that had taken place in the banking sector. They urged the authorities to remove the remaining **exchange restrictions** (and move quickly to accept the obligations of Article IV, Sections 2, 3, and 4. They encouraged the Brazilian authorities to take further steps to improve the comprehensiveness of the financial sector and external debt statistics and also to take steps to increase their transparency by subscribing to the Fund's **Special Data Dissemination Standards**.

In August 1998, the capital account again came under serious pressure in the wake of the crisis in Russia. A tightening of fiscal policy by further cuts in public expenditures and cuts in investment expenditures of federal enterprises, together with successive increases in interest rates (with overnight interest rates reaching 42 percent in late October), succeeded in moderating the outflow of **reserves** but did not halt it. International reserves, which had amounted to $70.2 billion at the end of July 1998, declined to $45.8 billion at the end of September and to $42.6 billion at the end of October. It became clear that a speeding up of the pace of change in policy and reforms was needed. President Cardoso, 11 days before the presidential elections, stressed in an important campaign speech that a major fiscal adjustment and reform effort would be the cornerstone of a second mandate for his government.

By the third quarter of 1998, it was not at all clear what course the contagion from the Asian financial crisis would take. The Russian situation had deteriorated and financial markets in North America and Europe were in a nervous state. In this context, the management of the Fund felt that it was crucial to stop the contagion from spreading to Brazil, fearing that otherwise the whole of Latin America would be affected, and eventually the U.S. economy too, thus creating the real possibility of a worldwide recession. In the ensuing weeks, the Fund worked with the Brazilian authorities to put together the parameters of a comprehensive reform plan. On 13 November 1998, the Fund and Brazil were able to announce a major economic adjustment program, supported by a financing package totaling $41 billion over the following three years, in which the Fund, the **World Bank**, the Inter-American Development

Bank, and the **Bank for International Settlements (BIS)**, as well as many industrial countries, were all participants.

Drawings on the Fund are specified in **Special Drawing Rights**, so actual U.S. dollar amounts may vary somewhat, depending on the conversion rate for the U.S. dollar. Bearing this qualification in mind, of the total package of $41 billion, about $18 billion (or 600 percent of **quota**) would come from the Fund, of which $5.5 billion (180 percent of quota) would be under a three-year **stand-by arrangement** and $12.5 billion (420 percent of quota) from the **supplementary reserve facility**. The World Bank and the Inter-American Development Bank each committed $4.5 billion, and the BIS a further $14.5 billion, which included contributions from a large number of industrial countries.

Innovations in the financing program included precautionary elements, including an effort to round up more financing than was thought to be necessary and provisions under which a large part of financing package would become available almost immediately in the form of a first tranche and a second tranche drawings, if needed. Drawings from the Fund would bring about a proportionate use of the bilateral loans from the industrial countries through the BIS, thereby making part of this financing also available immediately. This strong front-loading of the program would have enabled Brazil, in certain circumstances, to draw up to $37 billion in the first year of the program. Furthermore, it was hoped that the design of the program would enable Brazil to approach its creditors in the private sector and negotiate a voluntary restructuring of its external credits (i.e., to "bail in" the private sector).

Under its three-year economic program, the Brazilian authorities undertook to bring about a comprehensive set of revenue-raising and expenditure-saving measures in order to achieve a major fiscal adjustment by the year 2001. These measures included reform of social security, public administration, and public expenditure management; a thorough-going reform of the tax system, both direct and indirect, as well as a series of increased taxation in a number of areas, such as financial transactions and corporate turnovers; and, of some importance, stricter control over bond offerings and bank loans to finance state expenditures.

The Brazilian authorities were also committed to opening up the economy and to ensuring firm monetary discipline and macroeconomic stability. The current exchange rate regime was to be maintained, with an annual slide or crawl of about 7.5 percent, together with a gradual broadening of the band around the central rate. On privatization, the government's program had already encompassed industries as diverse as telecommunications, energy, ports, railways, mining, steel, urban transport, and financial institutions under what has been called one of the largest privatization programs in the world.

In the next three years the continuing privatization program would focus on utilities, most of which were state owned, such as power generation and distribution, a few remaining state banks, and a number of water, gas, and sewerage public utilities.

The financial and economic program was approved by the Executive Board early in December 1998, and a first disbursement, amounting to $5.3 billion, was immediately made available under the stand-by arrangement. Further drawings from the Fund were subject to key provisions of the program being enacted by the Brazilian Congress. To assist in the financing of the package, the **New Arrangements to Borrow**, which had come into effect only a week or two earlier, were activated for the first time.

However, congressional delay in implementing fiscal reform measures, together with the announced opposition of some States to a readjustment of their financial situation, led to a weakening of confidence in the exchange rate and to increased pressure on Brazil's foreign exchange reserves. On 15 January 1999, the announcement by the Brazilian authorities that henceforth the exchange rate would be determined by market forces was followed by a rapid depreciation of the *real,* which by early February had fallen 40 percent below its predevaluation level.

Agreement on a new Brazilian economic program was announced on 8 March, based on the financial package negotiated in November 1998 by the Fund, other international financial organizations, and the BIS. The new program was basically a recommitment to the original reform program, but with stricter financial discipline and tighter monetary policy to counter the deterioration in the fiscal situation brought about by the devaluation of the *real.* It envisaged a decline in GDP of 3–4 percent in 1999, a decline in the rate of inflation to 5–7 percent by the end of the year, and, as a result of the new competitiveness brought about by the devaluation of the *real*, a favorable trade balance of $11 billion in 1999, compared with a deficit of $6.4 billion in the previous year.

Soon after the program was approved, the exchange rate came under renewed pressure following setbacks in securing congressional approval for some of the fiscal measures included in the program. Interest rates were also eased, despite the Fund's misgivings and contrary to an understanding that there would be consultation with the Fund on interest rate policy.

In mid-January 1999, the Central Bank Governor, who had been adamantly opposed to any change in the exchange rate regime, was replaced by a new Governor, who then introduced a complex exchange rate system incorporating a wider exchange rate band in an attempt at a smooth exit from the crawling peg. The Fund's management was informed of this decision the night before the action was to take place, and its efforts to dissuade the authorities were unsuccessful. After losing about $14 billion of reserves in two days, Brazil moved to a de facto floating exchange rate regime on 15 January 1999. The collapse of the peg signaled that the original program had clearly failed in its central objective.

The revised program of March 1999 was unexpectedly successful in terms of its impact on the price level and output. A takeoff in inflation, which was greatly feared following the depreciation, was averted, and consumer price inflation was held at 9 percent during 1999. Stronger-than-expected external financing, particularly larger inflows of foreign direct investment, facilitated a smoother external adjustment. In contrast to pessimistic projections of a decline in GDP of 3.8 percent in 1999, real output grew by 0.8 percent. The financial sector weathered the crisis well, in part owing to the extensive hedge against depreciation provided by the public sector, which also bore the brunt of temporarily increased interest rates. However, the program did not achieve its primary objective of reducing the ratio of net public debt to GDP, in large part owing to the greater-than-expected depreciation of the currency. There was also unexpected slowdown in growth in 2001, because of an electricity crisis. The financial support package was largely repaid ahead of schedule, and the arrangement was treated as precautionary from March 2000.

Before the program could be completed, however, concerns over the external environment, including developments in Argentina, led the authorities to draw again on the arrangement and to request a further stand-by arrangement. The arrangement was canceled in mid-2002, and replaced by a new arrangement, as worries over the continuity of policy following the approaching elections led to a large increase in spreads on Brazil's external debt and exchange rate depreciation. These factors in turn contributed to renewed concerns over the sustainability of Brazil's public debt burden.

While the public image of the December 1998 program is largely colored by its failure to defend the crawling peg, the Fund's overall strategy was successful in many respects. In particular, the adverse impact of the crisis on output and prices was limited and Brazil made a transition to a more disciplined fiscal regime and a new monetary regime based on inflation targeting. One aspect of the December program, however, proved to be a source of later vulnerabilities: it facilitated a large transfer of exchange rate risk from the private to the public sector. Also, the central declared objective of fiscal adjustment—to reduce the ratio of public debt to GDP—was undermined by the large fiscal cost—amounting to as much as 10 percent of GDP—of providing this hedge and defending the crawling peg.

BRETTON WOODS AGREEMENT. *See* ARTICLES OF AGREEMENT.

BRETTON WOODS CONFERENCE. The International Monetary and Financial Conference of the United and Associated Nations (known more generally as the *Bretton Woods Conference*) was convened at the Mount Washington Hotel, Bretton Woods, New Hampshire, on 1 July 1944. The Conference was attended by delegates from 44 members of the United and Associated Nations, by a representative from Denmark, and by delegations from the International Labour Office, the United Nations Relief and Rehabilitation Administration, the Economic Section of the League of Nations, and the United Nations Interim Commission on Food and Agriculture. The Conference lasted longer than was expected, but closed on 22 July 1944, having negotiated, often with some difficulty, an agreement on a Final Act, signed by all delegations, embodying the **Articles of Agreement** of the Fund and of the **World Bank**.

BRETTON WOODS SYSTEM. Envisioned the establishment of a multilateral world trade and payments system that was free of restrictions and a stable system of exchange rates that could not be unfairly manipulated by one country to achieve advantage over others. Discriminatory exchange practices and multiple exchange rates were outlawed. The value of each member's **currency** was to be fixed by declaring to the Fund an initial **par value** in terms of **gold**. Thereafter, apart from initial adjustments up to a cumulative total of 10 percent, the Fund had to concur in any change in the par value proposed by the member. Changes in the value of a currency could be justified only for **balance of payments** reasons; more specifically, the Fund had to find that there was a "**fundamental disequilibrium**" in the member's balance of payments position. Thus, the Bretton Woods system sought to reestablish the stability of the gold standard, but with a degree of flexibility that allowed needed changes in exchange rates to be made under international supervision.

It was the first time that sovereign countries voluntarily agreed to give up part of their sovereignty by recognizing that exchange rates, the single most important price for any economy, were matters of international concern and should be brought under some degree of international control. This fixed, but adjustable, system of exchange rates arose directly from the experiences of the interwar years. The rigidity of the gold exchange standard was believed to have contributed to the onset of the Great Depression, and, after it had broken down, much of the subsequent chaos in international financial relations was attributable to the absence of a worldwide system to bring order and discipline to international trade and payments.

BUFFER STOCK FINANCING FACILITY (BSFF). This facility, established in June 1969, provides resources to help finance members' contributions to buffer stocks established under approved international commodity price stabilization arrangements. Since its inception, the Fund has authorized the use of its **resources** under the facility in connection with buffer stocks established under international agreements for tin, sugar, and natural rubber. Access limits under the BSFF were set in November 1992 at 35 percent of a member's quota. The Executive Board agreed to eliminate this facility in January 2000.

BURDEN SHARING. As the number of Fund members with **overdue obligations to the Fund** grew in the late 1980s and early 1990s, the Fund adopted a series of policies designed to share the burden of financing these overdue obligations among all members. These policies included a buildup in the Fund's **reserves** through the establishment of **special contingency accounts**. Contributions to the accounts would be made in accordance with an agreed-to formula that shared the cost of the overdue obligations among both debtor and creditor countries by reducing the rate of **remuneration** paid on credit balances and raising **charges on the use of the Fund's financial resources**.

BURKINA FASO. Burkina Faso, located in Western Africa, is one of the world's poorest countries. It is landlocked, and has a population and a per capita income estimated in 1996 at 10.8 million and $740, respectively. It has a high population density, a high birth rate, few natural resources, and a fragile soil, subject to a highly variable rainfall. It is estimated that 80 percent of the population is engaged in subsistence agriculture.

The country's sustained adjustment effort has been supported by the Fund under successive programs since 1991. The first of these programs was under the **structural adjustment facility**, followed in March 1993 by a three-year **enhanced structural adjustment facility (ESAF)**. A second ESAF arrangement was approved in June 1996. Under programs supported by these arrangements, Burkina Faso has implemented a broad range of macroeconomic and structural reforms, which have succeeded in redirecting the economy away from a centralized economy to one with market orientation. These programs have brought results in a number of areas, notably in rising per capita GDP and a reduction in the country's internal and external balances. In September and October 1997, the Fund and the **World Bank** approved the country's eligibility under the **heavily indebted poor countries (HIPC)** initiative, under which external debt would be reduced by April 2000 to the equivalent of 205 percent of exports in net present value terms.

In 1997, economic and financial performance continued to be encouraging, with GDP growth estimated to have reached 5.5 percent, slightly below the 6-percent level in the previous year, reflecting erratic rainfall that affected cereal production, but well above the performances of earlier years of 1.2 percent in 1994 and 4 percent in 1995. At the same time, inflation has been brought down from 29 percent in 1994 to a negligible figure in 1997. Although the deficit on current account in terms of GDP remains high, at 13 percent, the capital account improved sharply in 1997, mitigating the fall in gross external reserves, which remained sufficient for over six months' imports.

In 1997 and early 1998, the Burkinabé authorities implemented structural reforms in a number of areas, completing the first phase of the program to restructure and privatize public enterprises—involving 20 out of the 80 existing public enterprises—and made significant progress in implementing the second phase, involving 19 companies. Actions were also taken to strengthen the banking system, including the liquidation of the development bank, the privatization of a commercial bank, and the licensing of two new private banks. In the area of civil service, legislation was enacted in April 1998 to introduce enhanced flexibility into personnel policies.

On 10 September 1999, the Executive Board approved a three-year program supported by the ESAF, which was later replaced by the **poverty reduction and growth facility (PRGF),** in an amount equivalent to Special Drawing Rights (SDR) 39.12 million to support a medium-term strategy aimed at achieving higher growth rates by improving the economy's overall competitiveness, expanding the export base, and tackling remaining structural reforms.

Significant progress was achieved under this program, and, by April 2002, Burkina Faso had fulfilled the conditions for reaching the completion point under the enhanced HIPC initiative. Nevertheless, the economy remained fragile, with a large external current account deficit, and heavy dependence on external assistance and a few export commodities, notably cotton. Poverty remained widespread, and poor infrastructure and limited administrative capacity continued to hinder the implementation of reform measures. Moreover, continued growth in the landlocked Burkina Faso economy was suffering owing to the effects of a crisis in neighboring Côte d'Ivoire, its major regional trading partner.

On 11 June 2003, the Executive Board approved another three-year, SDR 24.08 million (about US$34 million) arrangement under the PRGF for Burkina Faso, which would provide continued support for the government's economic reform program. On 24 April 2007, it approved another three-year PRGF arrangement in the amount of SDR 6.02 million (about US$9.2 million) to support the government's economic reform program for 2007–2010.

At the fourth review of Burkina Faso's PRGF arrangement on 22 June 2009, the Executive Board noted that the authorities were maintaining satisfactory progress under the program. Economic growth had risen to an estimated 5 percent in 2008, thanks to a rebound in agricultural production. However, growth was expected to drop to 3.5 percent in 2009, owing to the effects of the **global financial crisis**, including lower world cotton prices. Although inflation had peaked at 15.1 percent in June 2008, it had since fallen as a result of lower commodity prices and the authorities continued prudent macroeconomic policies.

BY-LAWS OF THE FUND. The by-laws complement the **Articles of Agreement** and are subordinate to them. They are drawn up by the **Executive Directors** and approved by the **Board of Governors**. The **Rules and Regulations** are intended to supplement the Articles of Agreement and the by-laws and are subordinate to both. They are drawn up and amended by the **Executive Board**, but are subject to review by the Board of Governors.

Both the by-laws and the Rules and Regulations have been amended many times since their original formulation in 1946. The by-laws, to the extent consistent with the Articles of Agreement, address the organization of the Fund and policy matters falling within the sphere of the Executive Board. The Rules and Regulations deal with the more day-to-day business of the Fund, including its operating rules, procedures, regulations, and interpretations.

C

CAMDESSUS, MICHEL (1936–). Michel Camdessus, a French national, was the seventh **Managing Director** of the Fund, serving from 16 January 1987 until 14 February 2000. Initially appointed in January 1987, he was reappointed in January 1992 and again in 1997. He is the only Managing Director to have been selected to serve three consecutive five-year terms.

Before his appointment as Managing Director, Michel Camdessus had been Governor of the Bank of France (1984–1987), Director of the French Treasury (1982–1984), Chairman of the Paris Club (1978–1984), and Chairman of the Monetary Committee of the European Community (1982–1984). He was named Alternate **Governor** of the Fund for France in 1983 and Governor of the Fund for France in 1984. He was educated at the University of Paris and earned postgraduate degrees in economics at the Institute of Political Studies in Paris and France's National School of Administration.

After retiring from the Fund in 2000, Mr. Camdessus took up a position as President of the Semaines Sociales de France. He also serves as a member of the pontifical Commission for Justice and Peace and as a member of the Commission for Africa.

CAPITAL BUDGET. *See* ADMINISTRATIVE AND CAPITAL BUDGETS OF THE FUND.

CAPITAL MARKETS CONSULTATIVE GROUP (CMCG). The CMCG was established in July 2000 to provide a forum for informal dialogue between the Fund and participants in international capital markets. At regular meetings of the CMCG, the Fund is represented by its management and members of the senior staff. The CMCG is chaired by the **Managing Director** and includes individuals from institutions that play important roles in international capital markets and financial flows. The membership of the Group is broadly representative in terms of regions and sectors. It meets periodically to discuss matters of common interest and contributes to the Fund's broader effort to enhance constructive engagement with the private sector.

CAPITAL MOVEMENTS. The Fund's original **Articles of Agreement** and those in force through subsequent amendments drew a distinction between current and capital transactions. The Articles stipulated that a member may not use the Fund's **general resources** to meet a large and sustained outflow of capital, and authorized the Fund to request a member to exercise controls to prevent such use of its resources. Contrary to the code of conduct prevailing for current transactions, the Articles expressly permitted members to regulate international capital movements, even going so far as to state that a member failing to exercise appropriate controls could be declared ineligible to use the Fund's resources. The actual wording of Article VI, Section 1*(a)* of the Fund's Articles of Agreement, as drafted at **Bretton Woods** and left substantially unchanged until a projected change in them was formulated in 1998, stated,

> [A] member may not use the Fund's resources to meet a large or sustained outflow of capital as provided in Section 2 of this Article, and the Fund may request a member to exercise controls to prevent such use of the resources of the Fund. If, after receiving such a request, a member fails to exercise appropriate controls, the Fund may declare the member ineligible to use the resources of the Fund.

The Articles attempted to refine the distinctions between the two kinds of transactions, however, by stating that members may use the Fund's resources for capital transactions of a reasonable amount required for the expansion of exports or in the ordinary course of trade, banking, or other business. In practice, the terms *large*, *sustained*, and *reasonable* were never defined for operational purposes, nor was it easy to ascertain when capital movements were not connected to exports or to the ordinary course of trade, banking, or other business. In the past, a number of members had imposed forms of capital controls while still fulfilling their obligations to maintain current transactions free of restrictions, but the obvious existence of capital flows, and their role in aggravating the **balance of payments** position of a member, were never found to be an impediment to the use of the Fund's resources, or to have been seriously considered as such.

Thus, no country was ever declared ineligible to use the Fund's resources on grounds of its failure to control capital movements. Nevertheless, the distinction between capital and trade flows became increasingly difficult to maintain, particularly as capital markets became open and international capital flows underwent a sea change. For many countries, capital movements became a key factor in the balance of payments. Average annual net capital flows to developing countries, for example, exceeded $150 billion in

1990–1996, and although the **Mexican financial crisis** provoked a slowdown in 1995, in the following year the pace quickened again, to a net total of $235 billion. The **Asian financial crisis** produced a similar slowdown in 1997, but there seemed to be no reason to believe that in a global economy the pace of the inflow would not recover once the crisis had been contained.

In these circumstances, Article VI of the Fund's Articles of Agreement was seen to be increasingly anachronistic, particularly as the Fund was being called on to assist in the financing of balance of payments imbalances in which capital movements, both inward and outward, were playing a significant role. The belief spread that it was, indeed, time for capital movements to be subject to international oversight, similar to the treatment afforded current account transactions under the original Articles of Agreement.

At the Fund–Bank annual meetings in Hong Kong SAR in 1997, the **Interim Committee** of the Fund's **Board of Governors** agreed that it was "time to write a new chapter to the Bretton Woods agreement," and invited the **Executive Board** to work on a proposed amendment of the Fund's Articles of Agreement to make the liberalization of capital movements one of the purposes of the Fund and extend its jurisdiction over capital movements.

At its meeting in Washington, D.C., in April 1998, the Interim Committee's communiqué issued after the meeting reaffirmed the view expressed at its Hong Kong SAR meeting, stating that the crisis in Asia had given heightened attention to the role of capital flows in economic development. It noted the work that the Executive Board had already completed on that part of the amendment dealing with the Fund's purposes and requested the Board to pursue with "determination" its work on other aspects, with the aim of submitting an appropriate amendment of the Articles for the Committee's consideration as soon as possible.

CARIBBEAN REGIONAL TECHNICAL ASSISTANCE CENTER (CARTAC). The CARTAC was established in Bridgetown, Barbados, in 2001, to serve 21 Caribbean island countries and dependencies, including Anguilla, Antigua, Bahamas, Barbados, Belize, Bermuda, British Virgin Islands, Cayman Islands, Dominica, Dominican Republic, Grenada, Guyana, Haiti, Jamaica, Montserrat, St. Kitts and Nevis, St. Lucia, St. Vincent and the Grenadines, Suriname, Trinidad and Tobago, and Turks and Caicos. The center is funded by the Canadian International Development Agency, the Inter-American Development Bank, Ireland, the United Kingdom, the United Nations Development Programme, the United States, the European Union, the **World Bank**, the Caribbean Development Bank, and other donors, as well as by the Fund.

CARSTENS, AGUSTÍN (1958–). Agustín Carstens, a Mexican national, served as **Deputy Managing Director** of the Fund from August 2003 until October 2006. Prior to taking up his position as Deputy Managing Director, Mr. Carstens was Mexico's Deputy Secretary of Finance. From 1999–2000, he served as an Executive Director at the Fund for Costa Rica, El Salvador, Guatemala, Honduras, Mexico, Nicaragua, Spain, and Venezuela. Before coming to the Fund, he served at the Banco de México, where his positions included those of Director General, Economic Research, and Chief of Staff in the Governor's office. In addition, he was an organizer of the United Nations Conference on Financing for Development in Monterrey and of meetings of the **Group of Twenty**. He also served as Alternate Governor for Mexico at the Inter-American Development Bank and the World Bank.

Mr. Carstens has a PhD in Economics from the University of Chicago. He has a BA in Economics from Tecnológico Autónomo de México (1982). After leaving the Fund, Mr. Carstens became the Secretary of Finance of Mexico. On 15 December 2009, he was appointed the new Governor of the Bank of Mexico.

CENTRAL AFRICAN ECONOMIC AND MONETARY COMMUNITY (CEMAC). The CEMAC is a monetary union established in June 1999 by Cameroon, Central African Republic, Chad, Congo, Equatorial Guinea, and Gabon to promote economic integration among former members of the CFA franc zone. The CEMAC's objectives are the promotion of trade, the institution of a genuine common market, and greater solidarity among peoples and towards underprivileged countries and regions. CEMAC countries share a common financial, regulatory, and legal structure, and maintain a common external tariff on imports from non-CEMAC countries. The Fund began conducting regular Article IV consultations with the CEMAC in 2006. At that time, the common currency, the CFA franc, was pegged to the euro at CFAF 656 per €1. All members of the CEMAC accepted the obligations of **Article VIII** in June and July 1996.

CENTRAL RATES. The concept of *central rates* came into being after the United States suspended the **convertibility** of U.S. dollars into **gold**, signaling the end of the **par value system** agreed upon at the **Bretton Woods Conference** in 1944. Members of the **Group of Ten**, meeting in Washington, D.C., in December 1971, agreed on a realignment of exchange rates (the so-called **Smithsonian Agreement**). Following that agreement, the Fund adopted a decision authorizing the establishment of central rates.

Central rates were defined in terms of gold, but they were not to be subject to the formal procedure for their establishment and change pertaining to par values under the **Articles of Agreement**. The margins within which central rates were allowed to fluctuate were widened from 1 percent under the par value system to 4.5 percent under the central rate system. The measures were intended to install an interim system with the object of promoting stability in the international exchange rate system, pending the negotiation of amendments to the Articles of Agreement bringing about a fundamental reform of that system.

CHARGES ON THE USE OF THE FUND'S RESOURCES. The Fund aims to be self-financing, and thus the objective is to cover expenses from revenue, mainly from charges on the use of the Fund's **resources** by members. Despite the rise in the scale of charges through the 1970s and 1980s, the Fund adheres to the view that there should be a concessional element in the cost of using the Fund's resources, reflecting the cooperative character of the organization. The basic rate of charge applied to the use of the Fund's resources is set at the beginning of each financial year as a proportion of the weekly **Special Drawing Right (SDR)** rate of interest, so as to achieve a predetermined net income target. The mechanism is designed to ensure that the Fund's operational income closely reflects its operational costs, which depend largely on the SDR interest rate since the rate of **remuneration** (i.e., the interest rate paid on members' credit balances) is linked to the SDR rate.

To strengthen its financial position against consequences of **overdue obligations**, the Fund has adopted "**burden sharing**" measures to accumulate additional precautionary balances and to distribute the financial burden of overdue obligations between debtor and creditor members. As part of this mechanism, adjustments are made to the rate of charge and the rate of remuneration. The resources so generated are intended to protect the Fund against risk associated with arrears and to provide additional **liquidity**.

At the most recent review of the Fund's income position in July 2008, the **Executive Board** agreed to set the rate of charge at 100 basis points above the SDR interest rate for FY 2009 (108 basis points in FY 2008). This decision was taken in light of the Fund's new income model and was consistent with the key principles to set a rate of charge that would cover the Fund's intermediation costs and the build-up of reserves, rather than the full range of Fund activities, and that would be broadly in line with long-term credit market conditions.

The projections for FY 2009, which did not assume any income from an expanded investment authority, indicate a net operational income shortfall of about SDR 150 million (roughly $242 million). At that time, the Executive Board also adopted a number of other decisions that have a bearing on the IMF's finances, including with respect to the use of FY 2008 investment income to meet the cost of conducting the business of the Fund during FY 2008, and the continuation of special charges on certain overdue obligations.

CHINA—HONG KONG SAR. *See* HONG KONG SAR.

CLASSIFICATION OF COUNTRIES. The Fund operates on the principle of **uniformity of treatment** for all members, and it was not until the second amendment to the **Articles of Agreement** (1978) that mention was made of **developing countries**. For analytical purposes, however, the Fund has established a comprehensive classification, grouping countries according to their key economic and financial characteristics. The classification must necessarily change to reflect world economic developments, and beginning in May 1997, the group of countries traditionally known as industrial countries was expanded to include the newly industrialized economies in Asia (**Hong Kong SAR**, **Korea**, Taiwan Province of China, Singapore, and Israel), and the category was renamed *advanced economies* in recognition of the declining share of employment in manufacturing common to all the countries in the group. All other countries were classified as *developing countries*, with subgroups of *economies in transition* (i.e., countries in central and eastern Europe and members of the former Soviet Union) and other subgroups as needed for analytical purposes. These groupings, which have no relevance for the operations of the Fund, are primarily used by the Fund in its surveys and analysis of world economic developments, published twice a year in the ***World Economic Outlook***. *See* TRANSITIONAL ECONOMIES.

COCHRAN, MERLE H. (1892–1973). A U.S. national, Merle Cochran was **Deputy Managing Director** of the Fund in 1953–1962. Before joining the Fund, he had been serving in the U.S. Foreign Service and resigned as Ambassador to Indonesia to take up his post in the Fund.

CODE OF CONDUCT FOR MEMBERS OF THE EXECUTIVE BOARD OF THE INTERNATIONAL MONETARY FUND. On 14 July 2002, the **Executive Board** adopted an official code of conduct for **Executive Directors** to reflect their status as entrusted representatives of member countries charged with helping to ensure that the Fund carries out the mandate set forth in its **Articles of Agreement**. The code of conduct provides guidance aimed at ensuring the highest of professional and ethical standards in individual Executive Director's personal and professional behavior in particular as it relates to their conduct within the Fund, the protection of confidential information, making public statements, avoiding conflicts of interest, conducting their personal financial affairs, accepting gifts and entertainment, and arrangements for post-

Fund employment. The standards set forth in the code of conduct also apply to Alternate Executive Directors, and Advisors to Executive Directors.

In adopting the code, the Executive Board also established an Ethics Committee to consider matters related to the Code and to provide guidance on ethical aspects of conduct, including the conduct of Alternates, Advisors, and assistants.

CODE OF GOOD PRACTICES ON FISCAL TRANSPARENCY. The Code of Good Practices on Fiscal Transparency was developed in 1998 as part of the **Standards and Codes Initiative**, a set of guidelines on governance designed to support improvements to the architecture of the international financial system. It puts forth a set of principles and practices to help ensure that governments are providing a clear picture of the structure and finances of government. While implementation and adherence to the Code is voluntary, it provides assurance to the public that the soundness of fiscal policy can be reliably assessed.

The Code is based on four general principles:

- **Clarity of roles and responsibilities:** There should be a clear distinction between government and commercial activities, and there should be a clear legal and institutional framework governing fiscal administration and relations with the private sector. Policy and management roles within the public sector should be clear and publicly disclosed.
- **Open budget processes:** Budget information should be presented in a way that facilitates policy analysis and promotes accountability. Budget documentation should specify fiscal policy objectives, the macroeconomic assumptions used in formulating the budget, and identifiable major fiscal risks. Procedures for collecting revenue and for monitoring approved expenditures should be clearly specified.
- **Public availability of information:** The public should be provided with complete information on the past, current, and projected fiscal activity of government. This should be readily accessible. Countries should commit to the timely publication of fiscal information.
- **Assurances of integrity:** Fiscal data and practices should meet accepted quality standards and should be subjected to independent scrutiny.

The Code was updated in 2007, based on assessments to date of country observance of fiscal transparency, relative to the good practices identified in it. In drafting the revised Code, views were sought from the general public, country authorities, development agencies, academics, and nongovernmental agencies working in the area of budget transparency.

COLLECTIVE ACTION CLAUSE (CAC). Under English law, CACs have traditionally been included in sovereign bond contracts as a way to (1) foster early dialogue, coordination, and communication among creditors and sovereign states experiencing debt problems; (2) provide effective means for creditors and debtors to agree to restructuring, without a minority of debt-holders obstructing the process; and (3) hinder disruptive legal actions by individual creditors that could impede a workout.

In 2002, the Fund bolstered its efforts to promote the more widespread use of CAC provisions in international sovereign bond contracts through its multilateral and bilateral **surveillance** activities. In particular, the Fund's country reports were adapted to incorporate important information for creditors to make decisions about the economic situation of sovereign issuers. While the Fund does not support or endorse any set of model clauses, which are the subject of negotiation among relevant parties, it encourages emerging market bond-issuers to improve data collection and dissemination, including through participation in the **Special Data Dissemination Standard (SDDS)**, and to implement effective programs to improve investor relations and transparency.

COLLECTIVE RESERVE UNIT (CRU). Early in the 1960s, the adequacy of the level of **international liquidity**, and the role that the U.S. **balance of payments** deficit played in the creation of international liquidity, began to be recognized as a growing problem. Several proposals, centered around the creation of a collective or composite **reserve asset**, were formulated with the aim of being able to control the growth of **international reserves**. The proposals had several basic features in common: the assets would be backed by gold or **currencies** in defined amounts; they would be exchangeable for currencies among the participants; they would not be available for direct intervention in **exchange markets**; they would be deliberately created by agreement among a defined group of countries; their creation, allocation, and withdrawal would be determined by the overall need for international liquidity and not based on the situation of any one country; the countries participating in and controlling the scheme would be limited to advanced industrial and trading countries; and reserve units would not be issued to **developing countries** or be used for development finance.

Many of these features were later included in the scheme for creating **Special Drawing Rights (SDR)** authorized by the first amendment to the **Articles of Agreement**, which became effective on 28 July 1969. The value of the SDR was first fixed in terms of gold and then later in terms of a basket of currencies; it was an asset for use only by national **monetary authorities** and other prescribed official holders; and it was to be created, and withdrawn, with reference to the world's need for international liquidity. The SDR, however, was conceived as a universal asset and not confined to an exclusive group of countries. It was established as a supplement to existing reserve assets and designed to have a hybrid appearance of part credit and part reserve unit. Although its value was at first fixed in terms of gold, it had no tangible backing, and it was an asset created by international law, which established the rules for its transfer and acceptance.

COMMITTEE OF TWENTY. Formally, the Committee of the Board of Governors on Reform of the International Monetary System and Related Issues, this committee was established in 1972 to negotiate the draft of a reformed **international monetary system** after the United States had announced in August 1971 that the convertibility of the dollar into **gold** was suspended, thus bringing the **Bretton Woods system** to an end. The Committee consisted of 20 members of the **Board of Governors** of the Fund, modeled on the representation of the same countries and constituencies forming the **Executive Board**. The inaugural meeting of the Committee was held in September 1972 and elected Ali Wardhana, the Governor for Indonesia, as its Chairman, and established a Committee of Deputies under the chairmanship of Sir C. Jeremy Morse, Alternate Governor for the United Kingdom and, at that time, a Director of the Bank of England. The Committee met at the ministerial level 6 times and the Deputies met 12 times during the next two years. During the course of its work, the Committee established seven technical groups to examine certain aspects of reform of the international monetary system in greater detail.

The Committee began its work on the presumption that some form of the **par value system** would eventually be restored. The confusion and stress of the 1970s, however, was not a background that lent itself to calm and orderly planning for the future. After two years of effort, the Committee was not able to reach agreement on a fully reformed international monetary system, admitted defeat, and in June 1974 submitted its final report to the Board of Governors, to which was attached an *Outline of Reform.* The report explained that the Committee had not been able to reach agreement on a full-fledged reform because of the uncertainties affecting the world economic outlook caused by gathering inflation, the repercussions of the sharp increase in international oil prices, and other unsettled conditions. It urged that immediate steps be taken to begin an evolutionary process of reform. In Part I of the *Outline of Reform*, the Committee indicated the general direction in which the international monetary system could evolve in the future. Part II of the *Outline* set forth the immediate steps that could be taken before final agreement could be reached on a comprehensive reformed system.

Part I of the *Outline of Reform* was based on the idea of retaining as much of the Bretton Woods system as possible, although the Committee foresaw the need for some additional flexibility in applying the reformed system. In discussing the future **exchange rate** mechanism, the Committee envisioned that exchange rates would continue to be a matter of international concern, **competitive exchange depreciation** and undervaluation of currencies would be avoided, the exchange rate system would continue to be based on stable but adjustable **par values**, and changes in them would still be subject to approval by the Fund. Countries could, however, adopt **floating exchange rates** in particular situations, subject to authorization, **surveillance**, and review by the Fund. On other aspects of the reformed system, the Committee was able to point to weaknesses in the Bretton Woods system, and to discuss possible remedies without reaching agreement on them. Thus, it recognized the need, among others, for improvements in the adjustment process, the management of **international liquidity** and **reserve currency**, and the need for special provisions for **developing countries** in the new system. A series of 10 annexes examined in detail possible approaches to a number of important aspects of the international monetary system. Prepared by the Chairman and Vice Chairman of the Committee of Deputies, the annexes were not endorsed by the full committee.

Part II of the *Outline* recognized that there would be an interim period before full reform came into existence. During this period, the Committee proposed that the Fund tighten its surveillance and consultative procedures, experiment with some aspects of reform, and begin drafting reformed **Articles of Agreement**. Many, but not all, of the ideas in the *Outline* eventually found their way into the second amendment to the Articles of Agreement, which became effective in April 1978.

COMMODITIES. During the postwar era, the instability of export earnings from primary products had had a severe impact on **developing countries**, a number of which were, and still are, heavily dependent on the export of just a few commodities for their receipts of foreign **currency**. The consequences were injurious "stop and go" policies as economies underwent boom and bust cycles, leading to inflation at home, a lack of confidence in the **exchange rate** abroad, and the disruption of long-term development plans. National **monetary authorities** and international organizations have attempted to ameliorate these adverse developments by adopting three complementary approaches—export diversification, stabilization of commodity prices through international action, and compensatory financing. Export diversification is a long-term approach, addressed in the Fund's annual consultations with members and taken into account in Fund-supported **adjustment programs**.

Stabilization of commodity prices through international agreements is, technically speaking, outside the Fund's jurisdiction, but, nevertheless, it is an endeavor that the Fund has been able to support by making finance available to members under the **buffer stock financing facility** established in 1969. As regards compensatory financing, the Fund's facility to offset shortfalls in export earnings was established as early as 1963 and has been liberalized several times since. Over the years it has been used extensively by developing countries.

COMPENSATORY AND CONTINGENCY FINANCING FACILITY (CCFF). As originally conceived, the Fund's financial **resources** were to be available to finance general **balance of payments** needs and, apart from **drawings** in the **reserve tranche** (previously **gold tranche**), countries using the resources would need to adopt corrective adjustment policies in order to be able to repay the Fund. No attempt was made to distinguish various elements in the balance of payments, and no allowance was made that some of these elements might be self-adjusting. In the 1950s, however, experience suggested that some balance of payments difficulties were caused by factors largely beyond the control of the country in question, such as a crop failure, a temporary decline in international **commodity** prices, or a natural disaster, and that these difficulties would be largely self-correcting over time without the need to adopt an **adjustment program**. Therefore, **special facilities** were established to meet such adverse developments, allowing a member to use the Fund's financial resources as a floating facility (i.e., over and above the use of other facilities) free of **conditionality**, subject to the proviso that the member was willing to cooperate with the Fund.

The first of the special facilities to be introduced was the compensatory financing facility, which was established in 1963 and covered export shortfalls. In 1979 the facility was widened to include receipts from tourism and workers' remittances, and in 1981 to cover excess cereal import costs. In 1988, a contingency financing element was added and all the elements were amalgamated into a single facility, the contingency and compensatory financing facility. The elements of this amalgamated facility are explained later. The special facility for **buffer stock financing** and the provisions for **emergency assistance** were dealt with in separate entries. The compensatory financing facility was established to provide additional assistance to member countries experiencing balance of payments difficulties arising from export shortfalls, provided the shortfalls were temporary and largely attributable to circumstances beyond the member's control. In theory, it is a contra-cyclical facility, enabling the member to borrow from the Fund when its export earnings and financial reserves are low and to repay the Fund when they are high.

In this way, fluctuations in a country's export earnings could be neutralized over the longer-term, enabling it to maintain its import capacity, and thus reduce potential disruption of its domestic economy.

Established in 1963, the facility was little used in its first 13 years. In 1975, however, when commodity prices were at their trough, the rules governing the use of the facility were substantially liberalized, and financing made available under it increased sharply. Part of that liberalization was achieved by modifying the method used to calculate the shortfall, which was calculated as the amount by which export earnings in the shortfall year were below the geometric average of export earnings for the five-year period centered on the shortfall year (i.e., the latest 12-month period for which data were available). Exports for the two post-shortfall years were based on projections worked out between the staff and the authorities in the member country.

In 1981, the facility was further widened to include coverage for balance of payments difficulties caused by excessive costs in cereal imports. An excess in cereal import costs was calculated as the amount by which the cost of cereal imports in a given year exceeded the arithmetic average of the cost of cereal imports for the five years centered on that year.

The distinguishing feature of the compensatory financing facility is that **drawings** under the facility were to compensate for a shortfall in export earnings or the rise in cereal import costs caused by temporary factors largely beyond the member's control, and thus the situation was self-regulating and might not require corrective adjustment policies. However, although drawings under the facility were not necessarily linked to corrective policies to restore balance of payments equilibrium, a fall in export receipts or a rise in cereal import costs could be associated with wider domestic economic problems that needed to be, or already were being, addressed under a Fund-supported program.

Compensatory financing was available to all member countries, but its beneficiaries tended to be exporters of primary products, particularly **developing countries** that were reliant on just one or two export products. Primary product exports are especially prone to temporary cyclical fluctuations in price and earnings that arise from changes in demand in industrial countries, as well as from changes in output owing to weather and other natural causes. The compensatory financing facility became a major source of financial assistance to members, amounting to about 15 to 20 percent of total outstanding credit from the Fund in the early 1990s, but has since fallen to much lower levels, amounting to only 3 percent of outstanding Fund credit in 1997.

Contingency financing was added to the facility in 1988. The aim was to provide additional financing to a member country following a Fund-supported adjustment program that has been blown off course by external developments. Contingency features attached to such programs were aimed at providing part of the additional financing required to keep the program on track in the face of adverse external developments. The external variables covered depended on the economic circumstance of the country in question, but included export earnings, import prices, and interest rates, as well as other factors, such as workers' remittances and tourist receipts, if they were important elements in a country's current balance of payments account.

Maximum **access limits** under the compensatory and contingency financing facility—export shortfalls, excess cereal costs, and contingency financing—were set after the ninth general review of **quotas** came into effect in November 1992 at 95 percent of a member's quota, with sublimits of 30 percent for compensatory financing, 30 percent for contingency financing, 15 percent for cereal import financing, and an optional tranche of 20 percent of quota to supplement any one of the three elements. Drawings beyond those levels would be subject to conditionality—a willingness to cooperate with the Fund and adherence to an adjustment program—but amounts up to 30 percent of quota could be available immediately, pending the implementation of appropriate adjustment policies.

Purchases under the contingency and compensatory financing facility, as well as those under the buffer stock financing facility, were made in addition to purchases under **credit tranche** policies. A member, therefore, could use the Fund's resources beyond the limit set for cumulative access under credit tranche policies and under the **enlarged access policy**. Repurchases under the facility were made in equal quarterly installments, beginning three years, and ending five years, after purchase.

As part of the ongoing review of the of the architecture of the global financial system and the effort to streamline the Fund's financing operations, in February 2000, the Executive Board agreed to eliminate the buffer stock financing facility and to replace the compensatory and contingency financing facility with the **compensatory financing facility (CFF)**. However, the CFF has been little used.

COMPENSATORY FINANCING FACILITY (CFF). *See* COMPENSATORY AND CONTINGENCY FINANCING FACILITY.

COMPETITIVE EXCHANGE DEPRECIATION. Identified as one of the destructive elements of the world's trade and payments system of the 1930s, competitive depreciation was a practice that the establishment of the Fund was designed to prevent. Manipulation of exchange rates for national advantage was to be prevented by the authority conferred on the Fund to accept or reject initial **par values** proposed by member countries, and by the requirement that the Fund approve any subsequent changes to initial par values. In fact, the term *competitive depreciation*, like its associated term ***fundamental disequilibrium***, was never defined by the Fund, although a number of **exchange rate changes** proposed by members aroused some concern and resistance on the part of the **Executive Board**.

By March 1973, the **par value system** had collapsed and all the major **currencies** were floating against each other. Nevertheless, the code of conduct established in the preceding 20 years survived largely intact. The main concern was that those countries that had adopted **floating exchange rate** systems should practice "clean" floating (as distinct from "dirty" floating) and that they should not resort to manipulating the system. Until the reform of the **Articles of Agreement** in 1978, very little international control could be exercised over exchange rates, since the provisions governing par values and **currency convertibility** had been abandoned. The Fund stressed, however, that members were still under their obligations regarding exchange stability set out in Article IV, Section 4, which stipulated that "each member undertakes to collaborate with the Fund to promote exchange stability, to maintain orderly exchange arrangements with other members, and to avoid competitive exchange alterations." It was a moral authority, and perhaps the only authority, that the Fund was able to use in the interim period between the breakdown of the **Bretton Woods system** and the second amendment to the Articles in 1978.

In the reformed **international monetary system** ushered in by the second amendment, stress was again laid on the need to avoid competitive alterations of exchange rates. Thus, in Article IV of the amended Articles, members are enjoined "to seek to promote stability by fostering orderly underlying economic and financial conditions" and "to avoid manipulating exchange rates or the international monetary system in order to prevent effective balance of payments adjustment or to gain an unfair competitive advantage over other members." Whereas the original Articles establishing the par value system could be said to have given the Fund direct power to control exchange rates, insofar as it had to approve changes in a member's par value, the reformed Articles of 1978 ceded to the Fund a broader, but a more indirect, power, that of "firm **surveillance**" over the exchange rate policies of its members. This implied that the economic and financial policies of members would also be of international concern, but experience has shown that, in practice, it has not been easy to exercise these broader powers effectively, particularly over powerful industrial countries that in recent years have not needed to use the Fund's **resources**. Nevertheless, the increasingly volatile nature of international financial markets in the 1990s has concentrated attention on the urgent need to improve the surveillance functions exercised by the Fund.

CONDITIONALITY. The term *conditionality* is the body of policies and procedures governing a member's use of the Fund's **resources** in support of **adjustment** policies that will enable the member to overcome its **balance of payments** problem in a manner that is not unnecessarily destructive of national or international prosperity and also enable the member to repay the Fund over the medium term. The rationale of the approach is that in the absence of unlimited outside resources, a country's external payments imbalance will not be able to endure forever, and that sooner or later adjustment will take place, either precipitately with widespread disruption or deliberately with corrective policy actions supported by financing, to bring about a smooth adjustment over time. Fund conditionality in earlier years concentrated primarily on macroeconomic policies involving monetary, fiscal, exchange rate, and pricing policies, and only to a lesser extent on more deep-seated, longer-term structural measures. With the growth in **membership** of **developing countries** and countries in transition after the collapse of the communist command economies, attention to the economic infrastructure, privatization, and institution-building has been an important and growing complement to the Fund's macroeconomic adjustment programs. Furthermore, the need for such programs was demonstrated anew in 1997, with the unexpected emergence of the **Asian financial crisis**. *See also* THE INTRODUCTION AND USE OF FUND RESOURCES.

CONSULTATIONS BY THE FUND. Regular consultations between the Fund and each member are required under Article IV of the Fund Agreement and are central to the Fund's mandate under its **Articles of Agreement** to "exercise firm surveillance over the exchange rate policies of members." These consultations comprehend those required under **Article XIV**—members that are maintaining exchange restrictions under the **transitional arrangements** set out in the Articles—and place on a formal basis the consultations that prior to the second amendment of the Articles (1978) were held on a voluntary basis with members that had accepted the obligations of **Article VIII**. The consultations under Article IV provide the data the Fund needs to exercise surveillance over the economic policies of member countries. They allow the Fund to analyze economic developments and policies in member countries; to examine members' fiscal, monetary, and **balance of payments** accounts; and to assess how policies influence their exchange rates and external accounts.

Article IV consultations may be held annually, or at intervals of up to 24 months, depending on the member country. The focus of Article IV consultation depends on the characteristics of the member country. In recent years, given the large payments imbalances among industrial countries and debt-servicing problems of many **developing countries**, the Fund has devoted greater attention to the medium-term objectives of sustaining economic growth and a viable balance of payments, restoring external creditworthiness, and improving structural policies. During the consultations, the Fund's staff analyze economic developments and policies; examine fiscal, exchange rate, and monetary policies; review balance of payments and external debt developments; and assess the impact of policies—including trade and **exchange restrictions**—on a member's external accounts. The basic procedure for these consultations is as follows: first, the staff carries out at headquarters a preliminary assessment of the country's economic and financial situation, assembling and making a preliminary analysis of all the economic data available on the economy; second, a mission visits the country in question and carries out discussions with the relevant authorities in the country; third, the staff prepares a detailed background report on the country's economic and financial situation, together with an assessment by the staff; fourth, the **Executive Board** discusses the staff report; fifth, the comments of the Executive Board are transmitted to the country in question; and sixth, subject to the approval of the country, the comments by the Executive Directors are published on the Fund's website. In 1994, the Fund made available to the public the staff's background economic reports prepared under Article IV consultations.

In addition to Article IV consultations, some members are on a periodic schedule of consultations for other reasons, such as having **stand-by** and other arrangements with the Fund. Special consultative procedures have also been introduced for selected countries in connection with the preparation of the Fund's report on world economic developments, published twice a year under the title ***World Economic Outlook***.

CONTINGENT CREDIT LINES (CCL). As part of its response to the rapid spread of turmoil through global financial markets during the **Asian financial crisis** of 1997–1998, the Fund introduced the CCL in the spring of 1999. The CCL was intended to provide a precautionary line of support for members with sound policies, who were vulnerable to contagion effects from capital account crises in other countries. Under the facility, a member that met the eligibility criteria could draw on a large prespecified amount of resources if hit by a financial crisis due to factors beyond its control. The CCL remained unused as of March 2003, and it was allowed to expire on 30 November 2003.

CONVERTIBILITY OF CURRENCIES. Convertibility is basic to the functioning of a freely operating multilateral payments system, as envisaged at the **Bretton Woods Conference**. The **Articles of Agreement**, in **Article**

VIII, Sections 2, 3, and 4, spelled out the obligations of members to avoid restrictions on current payments and discriminatory currency practices, and to maintain convertibility of their **currencies**.

The original Articles defined a convertible currency in Article XIX *(d)* as a currency of a member not availing itself of the **transitional arrangements** set out in **Article XIV** and the acceptance by the member of the obligations of Article VIII. By 1961, in fact, all the major trading countries had formally accepted the convertibility obligations prescribed in the Articles. The obligation of members to avoid restrictions on, and to maintain the convertibility of, their currency for current transfers and payments has been continued in the first, second, and third amendments to the Articles. By 2008, only 20 member countries—all developing countries or **economies in transition**—were still availing themselves of the transitional arrangements. Thus, the **international monetary system** by and large was operating in a manner envisaged by the Fund's founders, largely free of restrictions on current payments and transfers.

One aspect of convertibility, that of official convertibility of currency holdings into **gold**, was eliminated from the Articles by the second amendment in 1978. Only the United States had agreed to such conversions on demand, but it was the linchpin of the **Bretton Woods system**. When the United States announced in 1971 that it would no longer convert officially held U.S. dollar balances into gold, the Bretton Woods system collapsed.

COUNCIL OF THE BOARD OF GOVERNORS. Originally this Council was to have succeeded the **Interim Committee**, set up in 1974. Establishment of the Council requires an 85-percent majority vote of the **Board of Governors** and in the 25 years that the Interim Committee had been in existence, little interest has been shown in implementing the original intention, mainly because of political opposition by developing countries. In 1998, however, in the aftermath of the **Asian financial crisis**, and as one of a number of proposals to strengthen the architecture of the international monetary system, the replacement of the Interim Committee by the Council was mooted.

CRAWLING PEGS. Sliding **par values**, or crawling pegs, gained some favor, particularly in academic circles, late into the **Bretton Woods system**, and especially after that system collapsed in the 1970s. Its advocates sought to remove what they perceived had become rigidities in the **par value system**. Countries had found it difficult, for political or other reasons, to devalue their currencies. The crawling peg system seemed to offer the advantages of stability and of small, periodic adjustment, without the traumatic disruption caused by an announced **devaluation**. The proposal was thought of as an adjunct to the par value system, to be adopted optionally by individual members, with the aim of improving the working of the par value system.

In the event, the **Committee of Twenty** and national **monetary authorities** could not agree on a continuation of the par value system in any form, and the crawling peg, as a codified system, became irrelevant in the situation of generalized **floating** that came into effect after 1973. Nevertheless, some countries have adopted a variation of the crawling peg system and allow their **currencies** to appreciate or depreciate under controlled circumstances, in accordance with the implementation of their economic and financial policies.

CREDIT CONTROLS. Credit controls play a major role in the monetary approach to the **balance of payments**, an approach initiated and developed by the Fund through research and pragmatic experience. The approach recognizes that there is a defined relationship between domestic **monetary policy** and a country's external balance and that the curtailment of domestic absorption (i.e., cutting back on consumption, investment, and imports) will bring about an improvement on external account. The relationship among all the economic variables, however, may not be stable over time or uniform for all countries. Credit controls have proved to be the most direct, immediate, and effective instrument for applying monetary policy.

The Fund has nearly 50 years' experience in applying credit controls, and their implementation has become both more selective and precise. In addition to overall limits on the expansion of bank credit and the money supply, ceilings are applied to selected activities of the economy, such as central bank credit to the government and ease of access to it by the commercial banks, and commercial bank lending to the private sector. These ceilings, which are arrived at in detailed discussions with the **monetary authority** in question and from the Fund's own macromodeling, also serve as performance criteria to measure the progress of an **adjustment program**. **Stand-by arrangements** regularly include quarterly credit ceilings on selected sectors of the economy. Disbursements under stand-by arrangements may be phased and made subject to the member meeting performance criteria. Credit limits will normally be an important element in those criteria.

CREDIT TRANCHES. Credit tranche policies determine the level of **conditionality** attached to the use of the Fund's **resources**. A member can make use of the general resources of the Fund in four credit tranches, each equivalent to 25 percent of a member's **quota**. Use of Fund resources up to the limit of the first credit tranche (i.e., 25 percent of a member's quota) can be made on liberal conditions, provided that the member is making reasonable efforts to solve its **balance of payments** problems. Use of resources beyond the first credit tranche requires a convincing presentation on the part of the member that its balance of payments difficulties will be resolved within a reasonable period. Use of the Fund's resources in these upper credit tranches is usually made under a **stand-by arrangement** or an extended arrangement. Phasing of purchases, performance criteria, and reviews of progress made under the program apply to the use of the Fund's resources in the upper credit tranches. A member may use its **reserve tranche** without challenge.

CURRENCIES. A currency is issued by a single issuer—a central bank, government, or currency board—and may circulate as legal tender (1) only in the country of issuance; (2) independently, in other countries as well as the country of issuance (e.g., the U.S. dollar is legal tender in Panama, and the Panamanian balboa, which is pegged to the U.S. dollar, is limited to small denominations); and (3) in several countries belonging to a currency union, with a central currency board responsible for the issuance of the currency (i.e., the seven countries belonging to the West African Monetary Union or the six member countries of the Central African Monetary Union, each of which has a common currency area with a fixed exchange rate pegged to the euro). The important provision from the Fund's point of view is that each member country should be able to control effectively its own monetary conditions.

Internationally, a currency can (1) be used as an intervention currency in the world's **exchange markets** (i.e., a central bank or a central **monetary authority** may buy or sell a currency [such as the U.S. dollar] to influence the value of its own currency in the market); (2) be a vehicle currency, or one that is extensively used in world trade and payments; and (3) be a **reserve currency**, or one that countries use in which to hold their **international reserves**. The U.S. dollar is the principal currency that fulfills all these roles, but other currencies, such as the pound sterling, the **euro**, and the Japanese yen, also have significant international functions. All of these currencies make up the **Special Drawing Rights valuation basket**.

The Fund also employs a concept of "freely usable" currency in its operations. When a member uses the Fund's resources, it buys with its own currency other members' currencies that are being held by the Fund. If these other currencies are not recognized as being freely usable (and up to now, the Fund has recognized only the U.S. dollar, the pound sterling, the euro, and the Japanese yen as being freely usable in the principal foreign exchange markets), then the member whose currency is being purchased must itself convert its currency into one of the freely convertible currencies, as requested by the purchasing member, at the official exchange rate notified to the Fund. Similar conversion procedures apply in respect to repayments (**repurchases**) to the Fund.

As distinct from "freely usable," not all currencies held by the Fund are usable, because they are currencies of members that have weak **balance of payments** positions or are using the credit facilities of the Fund. In projecting future operations, therefore, the Fund draws up each quarter an **operational budget**, setting out currencies to be used in **drawings** (**purchases**) and repayments (repurchases).

CURRENCY CONVERTIBLE IN FACT. A concept employed under the first amendment of the **Articles of Agreement** to ensure that members wishing to transfer their **Special Drawing Rights** in return for a desired **currency** could do so at a rate that was not at variance with its market value. The concept, designed solely for transactions in SDRs, ensured that those members using SDRs would receive "equal value" (i.e., equal to its market value). Under the second amendment, the concept of a currency convertible in fact was eliminated, and members using SDRs were assured of equal value by the creation of a new concept, that of a "freely usable" currency.

CURRENCY STABILIZATION FUND. Several member countries of the Fund have established currency board arrangements, including **Argentina**, Djibouti, Estonia, and Lithuania. A currency board is a monetary arrangement that commits the authorities to issue domestic **currency** only in exchange for a specified foreign currency at a fixed rate, thus sharply limiting or eliminating the authorities' discretion to create money by extending credits. The chief advantages of a currency board is the simplicity of operation, the strengthened capability it provides in the conduct of monetary and fiscal policy, and the usefulness of this rule-based arrangement in enhancing transparency and encouraging financial discipline.

In 1995, the Fund's **Executive Board** discussed the conditions and modalities of possible Fund support for currency stabilization funds. In the light of experience, it recognized that, in certain circumstances, a nominal exchange rate anchor can be a powerful instrument when used in the context of strong macroeconomic stabilization policies, in bringing about a rapid decline in inflation. In the framework of an upper **credit tranche** stand-by or extended arrangement, Fund financial support for the specific purpose of establishing a currency stabilization fund could provide, for a transitional period, additional confidence in support of an exchange-rate-based strategy. Access could be up to 100 percent of **quota**, but would be subject to the limits applicable to stand-by and extended arrangements.

The most appropriate arrangement to be supported by a currency stabilization fund would be an exchange rate peg with relatively narrow margins, or a preannounced crawl. The policy condition required would include fiscal adjustment and credit creation consistent with targeted inflation, appropriate measures to deal with backward-looking automatic wage and other indexation schemes, establishment of current account convertibility and an open trade regime, contingency plans to deal with large capital account inflows or outflows, integrated management of foreign exchange reserves and intervention policy, and other structural and institutional elements designed to reduce inflation sharply. A staff study in 1996 found that currency board arrangements were especially attractive to three groups of countries: small open economies with limited central bank expertise and incipient financial markets, countries that wished to belong to a broader trade or currency area, and countries that wished to enhance the credibility of exchange-rate-based disinflation policies.

On the other hand, the study warned that currency board arrangements were not appropriate for every country. The inflexible commitment to a fixed exchange rate parity, for example, might deprive a government of a major tool in addressing real exchange rate misalignments. Similarly, the restrictions that such arrangements bring with them could seriously limit the freedom of the **monetary authorities** to take action in a financial crisis or in addressing the effect of destabilizing capital flows. The forgoing of important central bank functions in this way could have severe costs and frequently require a level of fiscal consolidation that would be difficult to attain or sustain.

The study also warned that doubt about the soundness of the banking sector is among the greatest threats to the credibility of a currency board arrangement. Countries experiencing banking sector problems require additional measures before initiating a currency board, including a restructuring or closing of banks that do not comply with established prudential standards. *See* CRAWLING PEGS.

CURRENCY SWAP ARRANGEMENT. Bilateral swap arrangements among central banks of the industrial countries have been used extensively over recent decades. Their use to influence movements in exchange markets has become increasingly problematic as the world has become a global economy. Even in the 1960s, when a network of reciprocal lines of credit was established among the main central banks to relieve pressure on the U.S. dollar in the **exchange markets** and ensure the smooth functioning of the **international monetary system**, the mechanism was ultimately not successful in easing the strains on the international monetary system and saving it from collapse. The growing swap arrangements, however, were symbolic of the "one-world" character of the international monetary system and the responsible attitude assumed by nations to sustain it. Since the breakdown of the **Bretton Woods system**, the network of swap arrangements has from time to time continued to be activated in selected conditions to facilitate coordinated central bank intervention in international exchange markets.

D

DALE, WILLIAM B. (1924–). William Dale, a U.S. national, was the fourth Deputy **Managing Director** from 1974 until 1984. Prior to becoming Deputy Managing Director, he was **Executive Director** appointed by the United States from 1962 to 1974. Before that, he had served with the U.S. Government in the Department of Commerce and in the Department of the Treasury.

DATA DISSEMINATION INITIATIVE. *See* DATA DISSEMINATION STANDARDS; DISSEMINATION STANDARDS BULLETIN BOARD (DSBB); GENERAL DATA DISSEMINATION SYSTEM (GDDS); SPECIAL DATA DISSEMINATION STANDARD (SDDS).

DATA DISSEMINATION STANDARDS. The financial market crises of the 1990s heightened awareness concerning the importance of data transparency in the smooth functioning of financial markets and reducing the likelihood of crises. In 1996 and 1997, the Fund established data dissemination standards to guide members in the publication (or "dissemination") of their economic and financial data. These standards consist of two tiers: a voluntary general standard, the **General Data Dissemination System (GDDS)**, which applies to all member countries and focuses on improving statistical systems; and a more demanding standard, the **Special Data Dissemination Standard (SDDS)**, which applies to members having or seeking access to international capital markets. The GDDS and the SDDS provide guidance on four dimensions of data production and dissemination, including coverage, periodicity, and timeliness of data; access by the public; integrity of the disseminated data; and quality of the disseminated data. For each of these four dimensions, the GDDS and the SDDS describe two to four good practices that countries should follow.

Participation in the GDDS and the SDDS is voluntary, and both the GDDS and the SDDS are reviewed periodically to make needed adjustments. As of the end of 2005, about one-third of Fund member countries had subscribed to the SDDS. About 45 percent participated in the GDDS system, while close to

20 percent of the member countries do not yet participate in either the GDDS or the SDDS.

As a cornerstone of the implementation of the GDDS and the SDDS, the Fund maintains an electronic **Dissemination Standards Bulletin Board (DSBB)** on the Internet at www.imf.org. The DSBB identifies member countries subscribing to the GDDS and the SDDS, and provides easy access to data that describe individual countries' statistical practices with respect to data production and dissemination. *See also* STANDARDS AND CODES INITIATIVE.

DATA QUALITY ASSESSMENT FRAMEWORK (DQAF). The DQAF was adopted in July 2001 as part of the Fund's overall data quality assessment program. Rooted in the **United Nations** *Fundamental Principles of Official Statistics*, the DQAF was developed through consultation with national and international statistical authorities and data users inside and outside the Fund. It focuses on the quality-related features of governance of statistical systems, core statistical processes, and statistical products. Under the DQAF, assessments have a six-part structure starting with a review of the legal and institutional environment. The DQAF has been applied to help enhance the effectiveness of Fund **technical assistance** programs. In particular, the set of 18 DQAF-based qualitative indicators and 16 quantitative indicators are used to provide a snapshot view of countries' statistical systems.

DATA QUALITY REFERENCE. This portion of the Fund's website (www.imf.org) assembles material related to the topic of quality of macroeconomic data. *See also* DISSEMINATION STANDARDS BULLETIN BOARD (DSBB); DATA DISSEMINATION STANDARD; SPECIAL DATA DISSEMINATION STANDARD.

DEBT REDUCTION MECHANISMS. Since the latter part of the 1980s, Fund-supported **adjustment programs** have included, where appropriate, specified amounts of financing earmarked for debt reduction purposes, particularly if the country in question is making a strong effort under an adjustment program. Some of these programs have been accompanied by the adoption of a number of devices to reduce the indebtedness of individual **developing countries**. One such device is the buyback mechanism, whereby countries are permitted to repurchase their debt at a discount for cash. Either the country's **international reserves** or **foreign exchange** donated or borrowed from official or private sources may be used for such operations. Another such device is the use of **swaps**, whereby foreign banks may swap their loans for an equity investment, while foreign nonbanks may purchase loan claims at a discount in the secondary market to finance direct investment or purchase domestic financial assets. Importers have also used swaps in this manner, buying bank debt in the secondary market and redeeming it at the central bank for local currency in order to pay the exporter. A third mechanism for debt reduction involves debt exchange, whereby old debt is exchanged for new debt, usually at a discount on the face value or at a lower rate of interest. Fourth, exit bonds have been introduced in a number of restructuring agreements, whereby a commercial bank that does not wish to remain part of a concerted restructuring package takes up an exit bond. Such a bond usually bears a rate of interest that is lower than the current market rate, and this discount is viewed as the cost of withdrawing from the concerted lending operation.

The Fund's strategy to the debt problem was based on a case-by-case approach with three basic elements: the pursuit of growth-oriented adjustment and structural reform in debtor countries; the provision of adequate financial support by official, multilateral, and private sources; and the maintenance of a favorable global economic environment. In May 1989, the **Executive Board** agreed that a certain portion of Fund **resources** committed under an extended or **stand-by arrangement** could be set aside to reduce the stock of debt through buybacks or exchanges. The Board stressed that this percentage would be determined on a case-by-case basis, but that it would normally be around 25 percent. The Board also agreed to consider additional access—up to 30 percent of a member's **quota**—to the Fund's resources for debt-service reduction in certain cases, providing that such support would be decisive in promoting further cost-effective operations and in catalyzing other financial resources.

Since the May 1989 guidelines were established, the Fund has approved stand-by and extended arrangements for several members (such as **Argentina**, Costa Rica, Ecuador, Mexico, **Philippines**, Uruguay, Venezuela) that have set aside 25 percent of the total financing provided under the arrangement for debt reduction, with the possibility of additional amounts for debt-service reduction. In November 1992, when new quota increases became effective, the Fund announced that the limit on the augmentation of arrangements to reduce the stock of debt and the service on debt would be 30 percent of quota, where such support would facilitate further cost-effective operations and catalyze other resources.

In September 1996, the **Interim Committee** authorized the Fund, in coordination with the **World Bank**, to introduce a new initiative for **heavily indebted poor countries**, aimed at assisting them, both through adjustment programming and financing, to meet their debt problems. *See also* PARIS CLUB.

DEBT SUSTAINABILITY ANALYSIS (DSA). *See* DEBT SUSTAINABILITY FRAMEWORK (DSF).

DEBT SUSTAINABILITY ASSESSMENT (DSA). The framework for DSA for low-income countries was developed in 2005. The primary purpose of DSAs is to form judgments about appropriate future borrowing policies taking into account country-specific circumstances. They form the basis for designing country-specific borrowing strategies that are compatible with countries' prospective repayment capacities. While DSAs form part of the Fund's policy analysis in **surveillance** and program contexts, a distinction is made between countries with significant capital market access and low-income countries. DSAs for low-income countries are modified to take into account special characteristics, such as reliance on official financing, the nature of the potential shocks, and constraints on the resources necessary to repay their debts. DSAs for countries with significant market access are undertaken mainly for emerging market countries, but also for industrialized countries.

The DSA has three core elements: a baseline projection of medium- and long-term debt sustainability indicators, scenario analysis to determine the impact of varying the assumptions about the future trend of key variables, and inferences about the vulnerability of the country to a crisis. The analysis is done separately for public debt (external and domestic) and external debt (public and private), and the results are used to derive an understanding of overall debt sustainability.

DSAs are prepared jointly by the Fund and **World Bank** staffs, and annual DSAs are required for all countries eligible to use the **poverty reduction and growth facility** and actual or potential beneficiaries of the **heavily indebted poor countries** initiative.

The DSA framework constitutes an important addition to the Fund's toolkit to assess the appropriate balance between adjustment, lending, grants, and debt restructuring or relief in low-income countries. It also enables other international financial institutions and donors to establish a coordinated approach to concessional lending.

DEBT SUSTAINABILITY FRAMEWORK (DSF). In April 2005, the **Executive Boards** of the Fund and the **World Bank** endorsed a joint framework for **debt sustainability analyses (DSAs)** in low-income countries to help guide borrowing decisions to match their need for funds with their current and prospective ability to service debt. Given the central role of official creditors and donors in providing new development resources to low-income countries, DSAs also provide guidance for lending and grant-allocation decisions. DSAs form the basis of the DSF aimed at ensuring that resources are provided to low-income countries on terms that are consistent with their long-term debt sustainability and progress toward achieving their medium-term growth objectives. The forward-looking nature of the DSF allows it to serve as an "early warning system" of the potential risks of debt distress so that preventive action can be taken.

DSAs consist of a standardized forward-looking analysis of the debt and debt service dynamics under a baseline scenario and in the face of plausible shocks; an assessment of debt sustainability given country-specific debt burden thresholds set on the basis of the quality of policies and institutions; and an advisable borrowing (and lending) strategy that limits the risks of debt distress.

The assessment of external debt-burden indicators in relation to policy-dependent thresholds reflects the key empirical finding that a low-income country with better policies and institutions can sustain a higher level of external debt. The DSF, therefore, classifies countries into one of three policy performance categories: strong, medium, and poor. On this basis, it establishes debt-burden thresholds for each group of policy performers, and provides a four-category assessment of the risk of debt distress: low risk, moderate risk, high risk, and in debt distress.

DE LAROSIÈRE, JACQUES (1929–). Jacques de Larosière, of France, became the sixth **Managing Director** and Chairman of the **Executive Board** in June 1978. He came to the Fund after a distinguished career in the French civil service: Director of the French Treasury, and for a time Personal Assistant and Director of the Cabinet Office of Valéry Giscard d'Estaing when he was Minister of Economy and Finance. He was well known among financial officials and had participated in meetings of the **Committee of Twenty**, the **Interim Committee**, and the **Development Committee**, and had served on the Economic Policy Committee and the Development Assistance Committee of the Organization for Economic Cooperation and Development. At the time he became Managing Director, Mr. Larosière was serving as Chairman of the Deputies of the **Group of Ten**. He was the Fund's Managing Director for eight-and-a-half years and was succeeded by **Michel Camdessus**, also of France, in 1987.

DE RATO, RODRIGO (1949–). Rodrigo de Rato, a Spanish national, assumed office as the ninth **Managing Director** of the Fund on 7 June 2004.

Prior to taking up his position at the Fund, Mr. de Rato was Vice President for Economic Affairs and Minister of Economy for the Government of Spain. He was also Governor for Spain on the **Boards of Governors** of the IMF, the **World Bank**, the Inter-American Development Bank, the European

Investment Bank, and the European Bank for Reconstruction and Development. He was a member of Spain's parliament from 1982 to 2004.

Mr. de Rato earned a law degree in 1971 from the Universidad Complutense in Madrid and a Master of Business Administration from the University of California at Berkeley in 1974. In 2003, he earned a PhD in Economics from the Universidad Complutense. On 28 June 2007, Mr. de Rato announced his intention to resign for personal reasons following the 2007 annual meetings, and he stepped down on 31 October 2007.

DEPUTY MANAGING DIRECTOR. The appointment of Deputy Managing Directors is approved by the **Executive Board** and is customarily for a term of five years. By convention, the position of First Deputy Managing Director has always been filled by a U.S. national, while the **Managing Director**, also by convention, has always been a European.

On 6 June 1994, the Fund announced that it would increase the number of Deputy Managing Directors from one to three, and it named **Stanley Fischer** (United States), **Alassane D. Ouattara** (Côte d'Ivoire), and **Prabhakar R. Narvekar** (India) to the positions. The three Deputies succeeded **Richard D. Erb**, the fifth Deputy Managing Director, who had been appointed in 1984 and had served two five-year terms in the position. To preserve the convention that the Deputy Managing Director should be a U.S. national, Stanley Fischer was designated as First Deputy Managing Director. When Prabhakar Narvekar retired in 1997, he was succeeded by **Shigemitsu Sugisaki** (Japan).

Working under the direction of the Managing Director, each Deputy Managing Director has the authority to chair Executive Board meetings and to maintain contacts with officials of member governments, Executive Directors, and other institutions.

The role of a Deputy Managing Director has never been defined. It is not a position that is enumerated in the **Articles of Agreement** or dealt with in any substance in the **by-laws** and **Rules and Regulations of the Fund**. In the absence of the Managing Director, a Deputy Managing Director serves as Acting Chairman and assumes in that role the power of the Managing Director. Like the Managing Director, a Deputy cannot vote, except in the event of an equal vote by Executive Directors, when the Acting Chairman may cast a deciding vote.

Deputy Managing Directors also assist in the administration of the staff. They are active in shaping the Fund's **administrative budget**, in the assignment of staff to missions to member countries, and in overseeing the day-to-day working of the Fund. They are integral members of the policymaking group, attend the Managing Director's meetings with staff and Executive Directors, and are the central links among various departments, divisions, and sectors of the Fund's staff. The precise role and the extent of a Deputy Managing Director's influence on the affairs of the Fund depend very much on the personal characteristics of the occupant.

Prior to Richard Erb, the position of Deputy Managing Director had been held by **Andrew Overby** (1949–1952), **Merle Cochran** (1953–1962), **Frank Southard** (1962–1974), and **William Dale** (1974–1984). *See also* FUND MANAGEMENT STRUCTURE CHANGE.

DEVALUATION. Under the **Bretton Woods system** the value of a **currency** was defined in terms of **gold**, and changes in a **par value** required the approval of the Fund. One of the perceived causes of the failure of the Bretton Woods system was that countries, particularly industrial and major trading countries, were reluctant to devalue their currencies for fear of political repercussions. Maintenance of the value of a country's currency in **exchange markets** became a prestige factor in domestic politics, and any lowering of that value tended to be associated with a failure of policy. After the collapse of the Bretton Woods system early in the 1970s, the Fund ceased to exercise direct authority over **exchange rate changes**, although it continued to have responsibility for the orderly and smooth functioning of the **international monetary system**.

Since the second amendment of the Fund's **Articles of Agreement** in 1978, member countries have opted for a variety of exchange arrangements—**pegging** to a single currency or to a trade-weighted group of currencies or to the **Special Drawing Rights**, maintaining a fixed rate under the **European Monetary System**, or allowing a freely **floating** rate. The new freedom to adopt exchange arrangements of choice has made it easier to adjust exchange rates or to let them find their market levels. Under these new arrangements, in fact, volatility, not rigidity, has been of concern as exchange rates of the major currencies have sometimes tended to gyrate against each other, with little or no change in the underlying economic and financial conditions.

DEVELOPING COUNTRIES. The term *developing countries* was not mentioned in the original **Articles**, even though there was some pressure on the part of developing countries at the **Bretton Woods Conference** to include a reference to the special position of developing countries. The term was included in the second amendment to the Articles, but only in connection with setting up a **Council**, which has never come into existence, and with the sale of the Fund's **gold** holdings and the distribution of their proceeds. An implicit principle embedded in the Articles is that all members should receive uniform treatment.

The term *developing countries* has itself evolved from what was considered pejorative terminology, first from backward countries and then from underdeveloped countries. Like most labels, it is understood as a term of art, rather than a depiction of reality, since all countries are developing, in one sense or another. In the Fund's classification, countries that are not classified as "advanced economies," a group which is composed of the **Group of Seven** and 15 other advanced economies, are classified broadly as "developing countries," although this large group of about 160 countries is broken down into subgroups for analytical purposes.

Over the years, the Fund has established a number of facilities, such as the **compensatory financing facility**, the **buffer stock financing facility**, and the **structural adjustment facility**, which are particularly beneficial to developing countries. The Trust Fund, which was funded largely by proceeds from the sales of the Fund's **gold** holdings, was specifically established for the benefit of the least developed or low-income countries. However, although some of its facilities are particularly beneficial to developing countries, and, indeed, have been designed to be so, its financial resources are open to all members on the same terms and on an even-handed basis.

DEVELOPMENT COMMITTEE. The Joint Ministerial Committee of the **Boards of Governors** of the Bank and the Fund on the Transfer of Real Resources to Developing Countries (known as the *Development Committee*) was established on 2 October 1974 under a parallel composite resolution adopted by the Boards of Governors of the World Bank and the Fund. It was one of two successor committees (the **Interim Committee** was the other) to the **Committee of Twenty**.

Members of the Committee are **Governors** of the **World Bank**, Governors of the Fund, ministers, or others of comparable rank, appointed for successive terms of two years by members of the World Bank or members of the Fund. There can be up to seven associates. The President of the World Bank and the **Managing Director** of the Fund participate in the meetings of the Committee, which are held at the time of the **a**nnual meetings and, in addition, at any other times deemed appropriate. In practice, the Committee usually meets twice a year at the same time and location as the International Monetary and Finance Committee (IMFC). Like the IMFC, the Development Committee issues a public communiqué at the conclusion of its meetings.

The Committee was founded mainly at the urging of the developing countries, which were disappointed that they had not been able to achieve a "link" between SDR allocations and development finance. It was established at a time when a sharp increase in the world price of crude oil, together with a slowdown in the growth of the world economy, was causing severe **balance of payments** difficulties for many developing countries. The Committee's terms of reference are:

> to maintain an overview of the development process and . . . advise and report to the Boards of Governors of the Bank and the Fund on all aspects of the broad question of the transfer of real resources to developing countries, and . . . make suggestions for consideration by those concerned regarding the implementation of its conclusions. The Committee shall review, on a continuing basis, the progress made in fulfillment of its suggestions. [The Committee shall] establish a detailed program of work, taking account of the topics listed in Annex 10 of the Outline of Reform. The Committee in carrying out its work shall bear in mind the need for coordination with other international bodies. [The Committee shall] give urgent attention to the problems of (i) the least developed countries and (ii) those developing countries most seriously affected by balance of payments difficulties in the current situation.

DEVELOPMENT FINANCE. The Fund does not provide development finance, which is the function of its sister institution—the **World Bank**. Development finance is long-term financing, often in grant form or on concessional terms, directed to a specific project or sector of the economy. The Fund provides short-term to medium-term **balance of payments** financing in support of macroeconomic and **structural adjustment programs**. All its financing, however, is in support of adjustment programs that are designed to bring about conditions for sustained economic growth.

DISCRIMINATION. Both the Fund and its members are obligated to deal with all of its members on the principle of uniformity. All members are able to use the Fund's **resources** on the same terms and all members must receive symmetrical treatment from the Fund. Similarly, no member can discriminate against any other member in the context of its **exchange rate arrangements**.

DISSEMINATION STANDARDS BULLETIN BOARD (DSBB). The DSBB is a tool for market analysts and others who track economic growth, inflation, and other economic and financial developments in countries around the world. It describes the statistical practices—such as methodologies and data release calendars—of countries subscribing to the **Special Data Dissemination Standard (SDDS)** in key areas: the real, fiscal, financial, and external sectors. It also describes steps subscribers have taken to improve practices to move toward full observance of the SDDS.

The DSBB was established as part of the **Data Dissemination Initiative**, which came about in the wake of the **Asian financial crisis** of 1997 and growing international recognition of the importance of accurate statistics as an essential prerequisite for the formulation of appropriate economic and financial policies and of the importance of transparency for the efficient functioning of markets. The Data Dissemination Initiative resulted in the creation of the SDDS in 1996 and the **General Data Dissemination System (GDDS)** in 1997.

Beginning in April 1997, electronic links (hyperlinks) between the bulletin board and actual data on national data sites were established, enabling users to move directly from the bulletin board to current economic and financial data on an Internet site maintained by the member country. (The presence of the links does not in itself indicate Fund endorsement of the data.) The bulletin board can be accessed on the Internet at http://dsbb.imf.org.

As of November 2007, participation in the SDDS and GDDS was substantial, with 64 and 89 IMF member countries participating, respectively. Taken together, this total accounts for 83 percent of the IMF's 185 members. *See also* DATA DISSEMINATION STANDARDS.

DOCUMENTS AND INFORMATION. For almost the first four decades of its operations, the discussions and negotiations that the Fund held with member countries, its staff reports on countries, and the **adjustment programs** supported by the Fund were all held to be confidential. The Fund attached great importance to preserving its confidentiality on these matters, since it believed that only under conditions of absolute trust and confidentiality would it be possible to have full and frank discussions with member governments on sensitive national issues. Thus, a vast amount of documentation on country-specific matters was never made public, even though the Fund was, and still is, charged under its **Articles** to "act as a center for the collection and exchange of information on monetary and financial problems." It was judged that publication of the Fund's economic journal, *Staff Papers*, and its statistical data base, *International Financial Statistics*, as well as one or two official reports, met this charge. Moreover, unlike many of its member governments and other international organizations, the Fund set no time period for breaking this confidentiality, and only in January 1996 was it decided to open material in the Fund's **archives** when it was 30 years old.

In the 1980s, however, the Fund went through a gradual transformation in its attitude to public relations and information services. Once content to be the "scapegoat" for public officials in member countries that were adopting unpopular adjustment policies, the Fund came to see that that such criticisms, particularly when they were indulged in by high authorities who were themselves responsible for steering the country into desperate situations, were counterproductive and seriously impeded its work. As a result, the Fund took a new approach to information services and over the following decade or so fundamentally changed the way the Fund operated in the public arena. It established an External Relations Department to replace an office that had been staffed by only two or three press officers, and became much more aggressive in its press and information activities. It expanded its publications programs and produced a video on the Fund's form, functions, and policies; organized seminars at headquarters and abroad on macroeconomic policies and financial reforms for government officials and local academics; made public its surveys and scenarios on the world economy; strengthened and expanded its training programs at the IMF Institute; and in general began a program to reach out to and service the academic communities, government officials, and the general public.

In the 1990s, galvanized by the suddenness of the **Mexican financial crisis** and the lack of information and transparency that contributed to the crisis, the Fund went further to bring about as much transparency as possible in its own activities. It encouraged members of its staff missions abroad to consult with important segments of opinion makers, to appear on television and radio to explain the programs that were being implemented; published its staff economic reports on member countries; made public **Executive Board** comments from its Article IV consultations with members and the reviews of member-country programs (**Public Information Notices**); and made public on its website (subject to the consent of the country authority involved) letters of intent from members undertaking Fund-supported adjustment programs. The bibliography includes a list of the Fund's publications.

DOLLARIZED ECONOMIES. Dollarization, or the holding by a country's residents of a large share of assets in instruments denominated in foreign currencies, is common among developing countries and economies in transition. Historically, dollarization has been associated with reactions to economic instability and high levels of inflation. However, in a globalized economy, characterized by increasingly free capital movements and deregulated financial markets, most countries experience some degree of dollarization. This may take the form of currency substitution, asset substitution, or a combination of the two.

The effects of dollarization present both benefits and risks. In some circumstances, deposits of foreign currencies can bolster the growth of the domestic financial sector and enable domestic banks to compete with cross-border accounts. In cases of extreme price instability or capital flight, dollarization can also help to remonetize an economy. However, in weak financial systems, dollarization can increase risks, especially if there is deterioration in the quality of the foreign currency loan portfolio or a sharp devaluation of the domestic currency. Most important, the likely higher volatility of money demand in economies with high levels of currency substitution can increase **exchange rate** instability and limit the effectiveness of **monetary policy**.

DRAWINGS. The term *drawing* is used synonymously with the term ***purchase*** in the Fund's lexicon. Technically, all operations with the Fund's **General Department** (i.e., its ordinary resources) are termed *purchases* and ***repurchases***. These terms reflect the fact that the Fund's **resources** consist of a pool of **currencies** (the Fund's holdings of **gold** are no longer used in any transaction) that has been subscribed by members. A member using the Fund's resources will purchase from the Fund a currency it needs by exchanging an equal amount of its own currency. When that member repays the Fund, it will repurchase its own currency by exchanging an equal amount of another member's currency, as designated by the Fund. *Purchases* and *repurchases* are not terms used in ordinary banking business and are often substituted by the more generally understood terms *drawings* and *repayments*.

E

EASTERN CARIBBEAN CENTRAL BANK (ECCB). The ECCB was established in 1983 to replace the British Caribbean Currency Board. It is the Monetary Authority for eight island economies—Anguilla, Antigua and Barbuda, Commonwealth of Dominica, Grenada, Montserrat, St. Kitts and Nevis, St. Lucia, and St. Vincent and the Grenadines. The purposes of the ECCB include regulating the availability of money and credit, maintaining monetary stability, and promoting credit and exchange conditions and a sound financial structure. The ECCB maintains a regional currency board arrangement with a fixed peg of the EC dollar to the U.S. dollar. The Fund conducts regular Article IV consultations with the ECCB under its program of regional surveillance.

EASTERN CARIBBEAN CURRENCY UNION (ECCU). The Eastern Caribbean Currency Union is a development of the Organization of Eastern Caribbean States. The member countries use a common currency, the East Caribbean dollar, which is pegged at EC$2.7169 to US$1. *See also* EASTERN CARIBBEAN CENTRAL BANK (ECCB).

ECONOMIC COUNSELOR. A position created on the staff of the Fund in May 1966, when **Jacques J. Polak**, who was Director of the Research Department, was also appointed to the position of Economic Counselor. At that time, the **Group of Ten** and its Deputies began to meet regularly to discuss the problem of **international liquidity** and the need for a contingency mechanism for reserve creation. Jacques Polak was one of the two representatives of the Fund to attend the meetings of the Deputies and report back to the **Executive Board**. After its creation, the position became permanent, and has been automatically conferred on the Director of the Research Department. Since Jacques Polak's retirement from the staff of the Fund, the Director of the Research Department has been recruited from outside the Fund and has generally been an esteemed member of the academic community.

ECONOMIC DEVELOPMENT. Unlike the **World Bank**, the Fund is not an organization with a primary or direct purpose of promoting economic development. The Fund is directly concerned with a member country's **balance of payments** position and the domestic monetary and fiscal policies that produce an imbalance in that position. But this concern has broader implications, because experience demonstrates that the domestic economic and financial policies of a country, its external economic position, and its rate of sustainable growth are all inextricably linked. Although not directly involved in economic development, the Fund's actions and policies have a crucial impact on economic development itself. The secondary, and indirect, purpose of the Fund's work, therefore, is to be supportive of the development efforts of its members and to help national governments raise the standard of living everywhere.

Fund policy is based on the belief that a stable economy, free from inflation and operating without artificial restrictions, affords the most promising grounds for sustainable economic development. It is a belief supported by many research and case studies conducted inside and outside the Fund. The key factors in a Fund-supported **adjustment program** also lead to the prerequisite conditions for growth and development. These include an appropriate balance between government revenue and expenditure, prudent monetary policies to avoid inflation, realistic exchange rates to promote a balance between a country's receipts from abroad and its external expenditures, the elimination of foreign **exchange restrictions** that hamper the growth of world trade, an open trading system to foster outward-orientated productive activities, and prudent policies on external borrowing. In addition, an extensive range of structural adjustments could include specific taxation policies; economic pricing of government services; free-market pricing wherever possible elsewhere in the economy; reduction of subsidies; privatization of loss-making state enterprises; and the development of institutions, such as securities exchanges, central banks, and investment banking, that would improve the economic management of the economy.

Moreover, a country adopting a **stabilization program** supported by the Fund sends a signal to the international financial community that it is putting its house in order and, therefore, is likely to attract finance, both official and private, for its economic development. Indeed, for many countries experiencing economic and financial difficulties, the Fund's seal of approval is critical in their efforts to attract external financing. During the 1980s, when international indebtedness was at its peak and many **developing countries** were having difficulty in debt servicing, the Fund was the only international organization in a position to initiate and coordinate efforts to round up external financing, including long-term finance, from other international organizations, national governments, and commercial banks in support of stabilization programs supported by Fund **stand-by arrangements**.

ECONOMIES IN TRANSITION. *See* TRANSITIONAL ECONOMIES.

EGYPT. In the early 1990s, Egypt faced severe financial imbalance evidenced by high inflation, large external deficits, and accumulated external arrears. With support from the Fund by means of two successive financial arrangements, in 1991 and 1993, the country made important progress toward reducing these imbalances. Real GDP growth accelerated to over 4 percent in 1995–1996, from virtual stagnation in 1991–1992, while the rate of inflation declined to 7 percent, from over 21 percent. The overall **balance of payments** remained in surplus, leading to a substantial accumulation of **international reserves**, equivalent to about 17 months of imports. With limited external borrowing and further debt relief from the **Paris Club**, the ratio of external debt to GDP fell to 47 percent in mid-1996 from about 75 percent in 1991–1992. Nevertheless, despite these promising developments, economic performance remained below potential, particularly in regard to structural reforms.

Against this background, Egypt adopted an ambitious reform program, in support of which the Fund approved a two-year **stand-by arrangement** in October 1996. In light of Egypt's strong external **reserve position**, the authorities viewed the arrangement as precautionary and had no intention to draw on it. The program focused on consolidating the gains on macroeconomic stabilization, while broadening and intensifying the structural reform agenda through privatization, deregulation, trade liberalization, and a revamping of the financial sector.

During the two-year period under the program, the aim was to achieve a further increase in real GDP to 6 percent and to maintain a viable external position, although the external current account position was expected to weaken slightly, reflecting the strong growth of imports driven by the recovery and higher investments. Structural reforms were aimed at expanding the private sector, in order to promote investment, growth, and employment. The central goal was to bring about a fundamental change in the ownership structure of the Egyptian economy, in which public enterprises accounted for as much as one-third of Egypt's manufacturing sector, half of investment expenditure, and about 15 percent of total employment. To this end, the program was based on a continued divestiture of nonfinancial sector enterprises.

Other key structural reforms included further liberalization of Egypt's international trade system; fiscal reforms, including the transformation of the general sales tax into a value-added tax; the rationalization of the income tax to make it simpler, broader-based, and more transparent and equitable; a medium-term program for improving the civil service; and an acceleration of financial sector reform, including the privatization of banks and insurance companies, and a further strengthening of banking supervision. At the same time, the authorities are committed to improving the country's health and education systems, to a further strengthening of the social safety net, and to providing increased assistance to displaced workers through compensation pay, retraining, and redeployment.

EMERGENCY ASSISTANCE. Since 1962, the IMF has provided emergency assistance in the form of outright purchases in the first and second **credit tranches** to countries facing payments problems arising from unforeseeable exogenous shocks. This can include natural disasters, such as floods, earthquakes, hurricanes, or droughts, as well as sharp declines in **foreign exchange** earnings arising from shortfalls in export earnings or increased imports. In 1995, the IMF's policy on emergency assistance was expanded to cover countries in postconflict situations.

These purchases are generally designed to be rapidly disbursing and do not involve adherence to formal performance criteria or the phasing of disbursements. However, they are limited to circumstances where a member facing an urgent **balance of payments** need has a limited capacity to develop and implement a economic program, owing to the affects of the exogenous shock. The member is required to describe the general economic policies that it proposes to follow and its intention to develop a more detailed policy program under one of the Fund's regular lending facilities. In such cases, Fund support is accompanied by policy advice and **technical assistance** aimed at rebuilding the capacity to implement macroeconomic policy. This includes rebuilding statistical capacity and establishing and reorganizing fiscal, monetary, and exchange institutions.

Emergency assistance can take a variety of forms, including for countries in postconflict situations using **emergency post-conflict assistance**, for countries afflicted by natural disasters using **emergency natural disaster assistance**, and for low-income countries under the **exogenous shocks facility**. Assistance is also provided under the **compensatory financing facility**, which assists countries experiencing either a sudden shortfall in export earnings or an increase in the cost of cereal imports caused by fluctuating world commodity prices.

EMERGENCY FINANCING MECHANISM (EFM). After the 1944 **Mexican financial crisis**, the Fund took a number of measures to strengthen its ability to respond promptly in support of its members. These included an agreement to formalize the procedures to be used in activating an emergency financing mechanism. The essence of the mechanism is that it would allow the **Executive Board** to give rapid approval for Fund financial support, while ensuring that appropriate **conditionality** would apply. In certain circumstances, it was also agreed that there might be a need for large and front-loaded access to Fund **resources**. The procedures were used extensively in 1997 to provide emergency financing for the Fund-supported adjustment programs for **Korea**, **Indonesia**, and **Thailand**.

In agreeing on the elements for such a procedure, the Board expressed caution on how it should be activated; it was to be used only in circumstances representing or threatening to give rise to a crisis in a member's external accounts that required an immediate response from the Fund. One consideration, but not necessarily an exclusively determining factor, would be whether there would be a spillover or contagion effects. The Board considered that the procedures should be used only in rare cases. Conditions for its activation would include the readiness of the member to engage immediately in accelerated negotiations with the Fund, with the prospect of an early agreement on and implementation of measures sufficiently strong to address the problem. A member's past cooperation with the Fund would be a factor in the speed at which the Fund could assess the situation and agree on necessary corrective measures; and until the emergency was resolved, there would be frequent assessments of the effectiveness of the member's policies. The Board also made it clear that there would be no automatic link between use of the emergency financing procedures and the **General Arrangements to Borrow** or other supplementary borrowing arrangements. Furthermore, the availability of the mechanism would not represent a guarantee against sovereign default. It was to be understood that if the financial crisis was resolved quickly, the member would make early repayments of resources drawn under the emergency procedures.

On another aspect relating to use of the emergency procedures, the Board also agreed that the Fund should be ready to give technical and financial assistance to postconflict countries. Such cases would include situations in which the country's institutional and administrative capacity had been disrupted as a result of conflict. In these circumstances, a member might not be able to develop and implement a comprehensive economic program that could be supported by a Fund arrangement. Nevertheless, Fund support could be part of a concerted international effort to catalyze support from other official sources when there was an urgent **balance of payments** need to rebuild **reserves** and meet essential external commitments and the country had sufficient capacity and commitment to plan and implement policy. It was foreseen, however, that the Fund would most probably not be the lead institution in such an internationally coordinated effort.

Directors agreed that access to Fund **resources** in these cases should as a rule be limited to one **credit tranche** (25 percent of a member's **quota**) and that access policy under the existing emergency financing mechanism would provide sufficient flexibility to handle exceptional needs. The proposed financing would be available only if the member intended to move within a relatively short time to an upper credit tranche or **enhanced structural adjustment facility** arrangement. The financing would be supplemented by a comprehensive **technical assistance** program, including the building and rebuilding of institutions.

EMERGENCY NATURAL DISASTER ASSISTANCE (ENDA). Since 1962, the Fund has provided emergency assistance to countries facing urgent **balance of payments** needs in the wake of natural disasters such as floods, earthquakes, hurricanes, or droughts. ENDA is designed to be disbursed rapidly. However, it is limited to cases in which the authorities are unable to develop and implement comprehensive economic programs because their capacity to do so has been adversely affected temporarily by the disaster. In these situations, although Fund support is accompanied by policy advice and, in many cases, **technical assistance**, it does not include adherence to performance criteria. Generally, the country is expected to indicate its intention to develop a more detailed follow-on policy program under one of the Fund's regular lending facilities.

In 1995, the Fund policies related to ENDA were expanded to cover postconflict situations. Assistance is usually limited to 25 percent of the member's **quota**, although amounts up to 50 percent of quota have been provided in certain circumstances. As of October 2009, 24 members affected by natural disasters had received emergency assistance on 27 occasions.

In May 2001, for countries eligible for the IMF's **poverty reduction and growth facility (PRGF)**, the interest rate on loans has been subsidized down to 0.5 percent per year, with the interest subsidies financed by grant contributions from bilateral donors. In January 2005, the **Executive Board** agreed to provide a similar subsidy for countries using ENDA for natural disasters. For example, countries affected by the December 2004 tsunami in South Asia benefited from this initiative. In March 2004, the Executive Board agreed to extend emergency postconflict assistance for a period of up to three years, with access to as much as 50 percent of quota, although no more than 25 percent of quota can be disbursed per year. On 29 July 2009, the Executive Board approved a new package of measures to help low-income countries. This package included the creation of a rapid credit facility, which would replace subsidized use of emergency assistance for PRGF-eligible countries.

EMERGENCY POST CONFLICT ASSISTANCE (EPCA). In 1995, the Fund policy on **emergency assistance** was expanded to provide finance to countries in postconflict situations. This assistance is limited to circumstances in which a member with an urgent **balance of payments** need is unable to develop and implement a comprehensive economic program that could be supported under the Fund's regular facilities, because its capacity has been damaged by a conflict. In such cases, the support from the Fund must form part of a comprehensive international effort to address the aftermath of the conflict.

ENHANCED STRUCTURAL ADJUSTMENT FACILITY (ESAF). The ESAF was part of the Fund's efforts to help its low-income members bring about reforms and structural adjustments to their economic and financial systems. The facility became operational in April 1988 and was extended and enlarged in December 1993. It followed the **structural adjustment facility (SAF)**, which was established in March 1986 and had been virtually phased out by 1995. In September 1996, the **Executive Board** decided to make the ESAF a permanent rather than a temporary facility, as the centerpiece of the Fund's strategy to help low-income countries. Subsequently, the ESAF was supplemented by the initiative to assist the **heavily indebted poor countries**. In December 1996, the Board approved an extension of the commitment period to 31 December 2000, with a corresponding extension through December 2003 of the drawdown periods in the agreements with lenders.

In establishing the SAF in March 1986, it had been recognized that the resources available under the facility might be insufficient to support the strong and comprehensive **adjustment programs** that the poorest countries needed to undertake to restore and maintain **balance of payments** viability while achieving high and sustainable rates of economic growth. The ESAF was thus established to continue the work of the SAF, and the conditions on its use by members were basically similar to those pertaining to the SAF. The facility was financed mainly by loans and grants from member countries to the ESAF Trust and, following the facility's extension in 1986, by the participation of a broad cross section of the Fund's membership.

As had been the case with the SAF, the Trust conducted its operations through three separate accounts—a Loan Account, which received loans from contributors for on-lending to members under ESAF arrangements; a Subsidy Account, which received contributions, including grants from members and earnings from the ESAF Administered Accounts, to subsidize the rate of interest charged on borrowings from the Trust; and a Reserve Account, which was set up to provide added security to lenders' claims on the Trust Fund and was financed mainly by resources provided by repayments of SAF and ESAF loans.

Borrowings by members from the ESAF Trust covered a three-year period under three annual arrangements (as under the SAF). Disbursements take place semiannually, the first disbursement coinciding with the approval of the arrangement, followed by a second disbursement after completion of a midyear performance review. Interest on ESAF loans has been kept at half of one percent. Access under the ESAF arrangements depends on a member's balance of payments need, the strength of its adjustment efforts, the amount of the member's outstanding credit with the Fund, and the record of its past performance. Total access is subject to a maximum of 190 percent of **quota**, with a provision that this limit may be exceeded in exceptional cases.

At the end of April 1998, 33 ESAF arrangements were in effect, and cumulative commitments under the ESAF and SAF arrangements had risen to SDR 10.3 billion, with over 60 **developing countries** benefiting from the Fund's concessional assistance.

The Fund's staff has conducted two internal reviews of the experience of countries under the ESAF and its precursor, the SAF. In regard to the first study, covering 19 countries and completed in March 1993, the Executive Board found that the experience under SAF/ESAF-supported programs had been generally favorable. The second study, completed in July 1997, covered 36 countries that had availed themselves of SAF and ESAF financing in support of 68 multiyear reform programs approved prior to 31 December 1994. This review was also positive, suggesting that countries undertaking reform and adjustment programs supported by the SAF/ESAF had brought their economies a long way from the doldrums of the early 1980s. By 1995, average real per capita output growth among ESAF users (excluding **transitional economies**) had caught up with that in other developing countries. The social indicators in most countries improved. Roughly three-quarters of ESAF-using countries moved closer to a viable external position. Budget deficits were trimmed and instances of very high inflation virtually eliminated.

The review made four recommendations for future programs:

1. Stronger fiscal adjustment based on durable budget economies, particularly from civil service reform and reduced support for public enterprises, while protecting growth-enhancing expenditures on health and education
2. More resolve in reducing inflation to single-digit levels by using monetary and exchange rate anchors, where appropriate
3. A more concerted effort to adopt "second-generation" structural reforms, especially trade liberalization, public enterprise reform, bank restructuring, and strengthened property rights

4. Steps to reduce policy slippage and encourage more sustained policy implementation by more intensive program monitoring, greater use of contingency planning in program design, and more proactive **technical assistance** to build institutional capacity

This internal review was complemented by an external evaluating panel, which presented its report for discussion by the Executive Board in March 1998. The panel, established in October 1996, comprised Dr. Kwesi Botchwey, Harvard Institute for International Development; Professor Paul Collier, Oxford University; Professor Jan Willem Gunning, Free University, Amsterdam; and Professor Koichi Hamada, Yale University. In accordance with its terms of reference, the panel concentrated on three specific areas: social policies and the composition of government spending, developments in countries' external position, and the determinants and influences of national ownership on ESAF-supported programs.

In its report the panel recommended the following:

1. At a sufficiently high management level, the Fund should engage in intensive and informal policy dialogue with the country's political leadership to understand a country's political constraints and possibilities.
2. The timing and duration of Fund staff missions should be arranged to allow adequate time for country preparation in advance of negotiation and consensus-building during the negotiation.
3. Steps should be taken to relieve concerns about the Fund's perceived inflexibility in negotiations through the introduction of an element of choice in the negotiation of the design of programs.
4. The Fund should develop a more systematic mechanism for providing ex-post support for country-initiated programs, enabling the Fund to play an important role in countries with balance of payments need but where agreement is impossible or delayed, although the areas of convergence between the Fund and government are substantial, or where a government feels unable to accede to formal agreement with the Fund for mainly political reasons.
5. Ways should be found to both humanize and demystify the Fund's image, so as to assuage the political hazard that countries perceive to be associated with dealing with the Fund.
6. The Fund/**World Bank** relations should be better coordinated.
7. Resident missions should be strengthened or established in all ESAF countries to reinforce strategies, foster country ownership, and assess the social impact of reform programs.

The ESAF was replaced by the **poverty reduction and growth facility (PRGF)** in November 1999. *See also* HEAVILY INDEBTED POOR COUNTRIES (HIPC).

ENHANCED STRUCTURAL ADJUSTMENT FACILITY SUBSIDY ACCOUNT. To enable enhanced structural adjustment financing to be provided at low concessional interest rates, subsidy contributions are received by the Trust Subsidy Account. Contributions to the Account take a variety of forms, including direct grants and deposits. At the end of the financial year on 30 April 1998, resources available in the Account totaled SDR 1.4 million; cumulative contributions by 22 countries amounted to SDR 1.6 million. The **enhanced structural adjustment facility** was replaced by the **poverty reduction and growth facility** in November 1999.

ENLARGED ACCESS POLICY (EAP). Introduced as a temporary measure in 1981, the enlarged access policy was terminated in November 1992, when the increase in members' **quotas** under the ninth general review of quotas became effective. The policy had served its purpose by allowing members to use the Fund's financial **resources** over and above the normal limits established by the Fund in a period when many countries, particularly **developing countries**, were suffering severe imbalance in their payments. The policy had been financed by Fund **borrowing**, in lieu of an adequate increase in its ordinary resources through a quota increase. When the quota increases under the ninth general review of quotas became effective in November 1992 (which took over five years from the start of the exercise to its completion), the Fund was able to meet members' needs for financing from its ordinary resources. Expressed in terms of the new quotas, the new **access limits** under **stand-by** and extended arrangements in support of members' economic programs were set at 68 percent of quota per annum and 300 percent of quota cumulatively, net of repayments falling due to the Fund during the period of the arrangement.

The EAP succeeded the **supplementary financing facility**, which was introduced in 1979, and came into effect when all available resources in that facility had been committed. Access limits under the enlarged access policy were determined by guidelines adopted periodically by the Fund.

ENVIRONMENT AND THE FUND. Early in 1991, the **Executive Board** informally considered the extent to which the Fund should address environmental issues. It was agreed that the staff should recognize linkages among economic policies, economic development, and the environment. This would help the Fund to avoid policies that could have undesirable environmental consequences, while ensuring that the thrust of its actions promoted **balance of payments** viability and sustainable growth. The Fund consults with other organizations with expertise in environmental matters, including the **World Bank**, the Organization for Economic Cooperation and Development, the United Nations Environmental Programme, and the United Nations Development Programme.

EQUAL VALUE PRINCIPLE. The equal value principle is designed to ensure that a member country transferring **Special Drawing Rights (SDRs)** in exchange for **currency** would receive equal value for the SDRs it was transferring, regardless of which currency was being provided in return for the SDRs received. Under the first amendment of the **Articles**, this requirement was met by the stipulation that a member receiving SDRs in exchange for currency had to supply currency **convertible** in fact. Under the second amendment to the Articles, this provision was changed, and a recipient of SDRs in exchange for currency had to supply "freely usable" currency (designated by the Fund as the euro, the Japanese yen, the pound sterling, and U.S. dollar).

ERB, RICHARD D. (1941–). Richard Erb (United States) was appointed **Deputy Managing Director** in 1984 and served for two five-year terms. Before his appointment as Deputy Managing Director, he had served the U.S. government in the Treasury Department. Upon the termination of his tenure in 1994, three Deputy Managing Directors were appointed, the first major change in the **Fund management structure** since the institution's founding.

ETHICS COMMITTEE. *See* CODE OF CONDUCT FOR MEMBERS OF THE EXECUTIVE BOARD OF THE INTERNATIONAL MONETARY FUND.

EURO. The euro was established as the third and final stage of **European Economic and Monetary Union (EMU)** on 1 January 1999, when 11 participating countries locked their bilateral **exchange** rates and adopted it as their common currency. While all 27 member states of the European Union are expected to participate in the EMU, as of August 2009, 16 member states had adopted it as their currency. Most notably, Denmark, Sweden, and the United Kingdom have not yet accepted the third stage and still use their own currencies.

The move toward European EMU officially began in May 1998, when the Council of the European Union, meeting at the level of the heads of state or government, announced that the 11 countries that had indicated their intent to be among the initial members—Austria, Belgium, Finland, France, Germany, Ireland, Italy, Luxembourg, the Netherlands, Portugal, and Spain—had qualified for full participation. As inputs to this decision, the Council of the European Union had the March 1998 reports published by the European Commission and the European Monetary Institute (EMI) assessing how countries had complied with the convergence criteria established by the Maastricht Treaty in the areas of price stability, public finances, interest rates, and exchange rates.

With a view to guiding markets in the run-up to EMU, it was agreed that exchange rate mechanism (ERM) central rates would be used as the basis for locking exchange rates on 1 January 1999, and Central Banks committed to ensure that these rates prevailed in the market on 31 December 1998. On 1 June 1998, the EMI ceased to operate and the European Central Bank (ECB) began operations, taking over responsibility for monetary policy in the euro area on 1 January 1999. From the start of EMU, participants' national currencies continued to circulate, but as subunits of the euro rather than as independent currencies. Euro notes and coins were introduced on 1 January 2002, and the national notes and coins of participating states were withdrawn by 30 June of that year.

The move toward EMU has largely been driven by the expectation of a number of economic benefits, including lower transaction costs, reduced exchange risk, greater competition, and a broadening and deepening of European financial markets. During the nearly 20-year existence of the ERM, cooperation among central banks steadily strengthened. The achievement of low inflation rates, in particular, provided a propitious starting point.

The countries participating in the EMU remain individual members of the Fund. Since the Fund's **Articles of Agreement** confine membership to countries, the euro area as such is not able to appoint a **Governor** or elect an **Executive Director**. In December 1998, the ECB was granted observer status at selected **Executive Board** meetings. The Fund continues to hold regular Article IV consultations with EMU countries. However, an Article IV consultation with a member cannot be completed without the Fund having had an opportunity to assess monetary policy. Therefore, discussions with representatives of the relevant EU institutions are needed as part of the Article IV consultations with individual euro-area countries. These discussions, and consideration by the Fund's Executive Board of the monetary and exchange rate policies of the euro area are, as a practical matter, held separately from those with individual euro-area countries, but are considered an integral part of the Article IV consultation process for each member. Executive Board discussions at the EU level also cover fiscal and structural policies from a regional perspective to provide a setting for the discussions on monetary and exchange rate policies.

Prior to EMU, the SDR basket included the currencies of the five members with the largest exports of goods and services. This included the U.S. dollar, the deutsche mark, the Japanese yen, the French franc, and the pound sterling. Since the launch of EMU, the euro has replaced the deutsche mark and the French franc in the SDR valuation basket.

EURO INTERBANK OFFERED RATE (EURIBOR). The rate at which **euro** interbank term deposits are offered by one prime bank to another within the **European Monetary Union**. At the regular five-year review of **Special Drawing Rights (SDR) valuation** concluded in October 2000, the Fund changed the method of valuation of the SDR and the determination of the SDR interest rate to take into account the introduction of the euro as the common currency within the European Union. In particular, the criteria used to select the currencies of member countries to be used in the SDR basket was extended to include exports by monetary unions that include IMF members. In addition, the method used to calculate the SDR rate adopted the three-month Euribor as the representative rate for the euro. The first SDR interest rate based on the new basked was announced on 5 January 2001.

EUROPEAN CENTRAL BANK (ECB). *See* EURO; EUROPEAN ECONOMIC MONETARY UNION (EMU) AND THE FUND.

EUROPEAN CURRENCY UNIT (ECU). ECUs were issued by the European Monetary Cooperation Fund to the central banks of participating countries in exchange for contributions of 20 percent of their **gold** holdings and 20 percent of their gross dollar holdings. These contributions were made under revolving swaps, of three months' duration, and could be unwound at the initiative of the participant at short notice. Furthermore, each participating central bank could, under contract, invest and manage the assets it had contributed. The exact amount of ECU holdings depended on the price of gold, the **exchange rate** for the U.S. dollar, and the amount of each asset held by the participating central banks. ECUs were used for partial settlements between participants on a monthly basis. At the end of 1996, ECUs accounted for about 5.9 percent of identified **reserve currency** holdings by all countries.

EUROPEAN ECONOMIC AND MONETARY UNION (EMU) AND THE FUND. 1 January 1999 marked the planned start of the European EMU, when a new single **currency**, the **euro**, would be used by 11 members of the European Union for trade throughout the world. Unlike other monetary reforms, the euro would replace the national currencies of participating members, a number of whose currencies were already widely used for international transactions.

A single currency had been seen as a necessary element to complete the European Union's single market. The signing of the Single European Act in 1986 led to the adoption, in April 1989, of the Maastricht Treaty, which set the path by which the European Union would proceed to EMU. The Treaty, which amended and supplemented the Treaty of Rome, proved to be highly controversial in a number of states and was signed by the heads of governments of the member states only after Denmark and the United Kingdom had negotiated their right to "opt out." The Treaty came into force on 1 November 1993 and imposed an obligation on the 13 states that had not negotiated to opt out to merge their currencies into a single currency if they met four macroeconomic criteria, relating to inflation, exchange rate stability, long-term interest rates, and government debt.

In May 1998, 11 member states were judged to have met the criteria, and a **European Central Bank (ECB)** was established. With the launch of the euro on 1 January 1999, the conversion rates of the national currencies for the euro were established and locked in; the euro became the currency of the participating states, and national currency units became denominations of the euro. The ECB took over control of monetary policy for the euro zone, and all new issues of government debt were to be issued in euro. In 2001, euro banknotes and coins would be introduced and all obligations denominated in national currency units would be redenominated in euro. On 30 June 2002, national banknotes and coins were to cease being legal tender.

The establishment of the EMU raised a number of issues for the Fund. These included how **surveillance** would be carried out, whether and how Fund **resources** should be made available to EMU members, how Fund **quotas** might be affected, whether the **SDR** would need to be redefined, and how the euro would be used in Fund operations. On 30 September 1998, the Fund announced that after the launch of the EMU on 1 January 1999, the euro would replace the currency amounts of the deutsche mark and the French franc in the SDR valuation basket.

With the advent of the EMU, the memberships of individual states in the Fund were not affected. The main reason for retaining individual membership, as opposed to all the states of the EMU being treated as a single member with a single quota share derived from the fact that membership in the EMU implied only a limited transfer of decision making at the supranational level. The transfer of competence would mainly concern the Union's monetary policy, which would be the exclusive responsibility of the ECB, and its exchange rate policy, which would be in the hands of the Council of Economic and Finance Ministers and the ECB. EMU member states would retain ultimate responsibility for other economic policies.

EUROPEAN MONETARY SYSTEM (EMS). The EMS began operating in March 1979 with the aim of establishing a zone of monetary stability among members of the European Community. Members of the Community electing to participate in the system were required to establish a central rate in terms of the **European Currency Unit (ECU)**. The ECU consisted of a basket of **currencies** containing agreed to amounts of currency of each Community member. Adjustments in **central rates** were subject to agreement by other members and the European Commission. Participants had to observe limits of 2.25 percent above and below the cross rate arising from their central rates established in terms of the ECU. They were given the option of observing a 6 percent margin upon entering the system, but this wider margin was to be gradually reduced to 2.25 percent. The establishment of this regional monetary system was seen as a step toward full economic and political integration of the European Community. It has been superseded by the establishment of the common European Union currency, the **euro**.

EUROPEAN RECOVERY PLAN. On 5 June 1947, the U.S. Secretary of State, General George Marshall, in a commencement address at Harvard University, announced a far-reaching plan (known forever after as the *Marshall Plan*) to aid the recovery of a dollar-scarce Europe in the postwar period. The plan, formally called the *European Recovery Program*, in addition to providing substantial amounts of financing, called for a number of macroeconomic reforms in the recipient countries—reforms that would have otherwise fallen under the aegis of the Fund. Much discussion ensued in the Fund's **Executive Board** as to what should be the reaction of the Fund to the Marshall Plan. The U.S. view was that in making substantial amounts of dollars available under the aid program, it would not be necessary for the countries receiving Marshall Plan aid to use resources from the Fund. In the event, the **Executive Directors** accepted this view and reached a decision that it would be in the best interest of members if the Fund's dollar resources were not used prematurely. A later clarification indicated that even drawings of **currencies** other than U.S. dollars by Marshall Plan recipients would be exceptional.

These decisions had important repercussions on the Fund's activities. Most of the previous drawings on the Fund had been by European members, and use of the Fund's **resources** by Western European members subsequently dropped precipitously. The decisions aroused widespread criticism of the U.S. authorities and the Fund, especially from the academic community, who felt that in shifting away from the **Bretton Woods** institutions, which they had helped to create, the Executive Board had moved the Fund to the sidelines for several years. Just when a new economic internationalism was about to be born, the Fund and Bank were shorn of much of their power and still awaited the dawn of the Bretton Woods age.

EXCHANGE CONTROLS. Exchange controls or **exchange restrictions**, imposed or maintained by member countries on current transactions, require the prior approval of the Fund. This was a major authority given to the Fund under the **Bretton Woods system**, and it has been perpetuated in subsequent amendments to the **Articles**, even though the second amendment (1978) no longer required member countries to obtain the Fund's prior approval for **exchange rate changes**. Restrictions on trade are closely linked to exchange restrictions, and although they are technically outside the Fund's jurisdiction, the Fund maintained a special and close relationship with the **General Agreement on Tariffs and Trade** and this has continued with its successor organization, the **World Trade Organization**.

EXCHANGE CROSS RATES. Broken cross rates, that is to say, rates between two **currencies** in a third market that differ from the bilateral relationship of the two currencies derived from their **par values** or **central rates**, were a problem in the early years of the **Bretton Woods system**. As the **convertibility** of currencies spread, restrictions were lifted, and **exchange markets** became more integrated, broken cross rates ceased to be a factor. Under the current **Articles of Agreement**, broken cross rates, if they exist, would be of concern to the Fund if they contributed to disorderly exchange rates or were judged to be a factor in the manipulation of the **international monetary system**.

EXCHANGE MARKETS. Made up of **monetary authorities**, commercial banks, brokers, and assorted finance houses, exchange markets exist in every country, although at different levels of sophistication, for the purpose of converting one **currency** into another. Only a few markets are broad enough to support reliable forward exchange market operations. Markets can be tightly controlled by monetary authorities or can operate freely. Dual exchange markets, auction markets, and other forms of regulated markets, once fairly widespread, are tending to be phased out in the developing world in favor of freely operating markets, enabling capital and financial flows to move around the world on a scale and at a speed never previously experienced. Under the Fund's **Articles of Agreement**, all member countries are obliged to collaborate with the Fund and other members to ensure orderly **exchange rate arrangements** and to promote a stable system of exchange rates.

EXCHANGE RATE ARRANGEMENTS. A term synonymous with exchange rate regime and exchange rate system. It refers to all the optional elements that can characterize a system: floating, crawling and sliding **pegs**, **flexible** and **fixed rates**, including **central rates** and **par values**, as well as dual exchange markets, exchange auctions, and multiple exchange rates.

EXCHANGE RATE CHANGES. Changes in exchange rates have not been subject to prior approval by the Fund, in practice since the collapse of the **par value system** in 1973, and legally since the second amendment (1978) of the **Articles of Agreement**. Under the current system, members are required to notify the Fund promptly of any change in their **exchange arrangements**, but this may be after the event. Under the Articles of Agreement, each member undertakes to collaborate with the Fund and other members to ensure orderly exchange arrangements and to promote a stable system of exchange rates. In addition, members must avoid manipulating exchange rates or the **international monetary system** in order to prevent effective **balance of payments** adjustment or to gain an unfair competitive advantage over other members.

EXCHANGE RATE MARGINS. Fixed or **pegged exchange rates** imply that a margin exists beyond which a movement of the exchange rate will not be allowed. Under the **par value system**, exchange rates had to be maintained within 1 percent either side of parity, allowing a maximum fluctuation between two currencies of 2 percent. Under the **Smithsonian Agreement** (1971), which was followed by an implementing decision by the **Executive Board** of the Fund, the margins were widened to 2.25 percent either side of parity or **central rates**, allowing a maximum fluctuation between two **currencies** of 4.5 percent. This was followed by the European narrow margins arrangement (known as the "snake") among a number of European countries whereby it was agreed that among their own currencies the maximum fluctuation should be reduced to 2.25 percent, and within this group of countries the Benelux countries (Belgium, Luxembourg, and the Netherlands) maintained an arrangement (called the "snake within a tunnel"), which terminated in 1976, that reduced the margins to 1.5 percent either side of parity.

The **European Monetary System** was established in 1979, under which members of the European Community agreed, in effect, to establish a regional par value system, based on the **European Currency Unit (ECU)**. In spot exchange transactions between currencies, participants had to observe limits of 2.25 percent above and below the bilateral relationship derived from the central rates established for their currencies in terms of ECUs. In May 1998, 11 members of the European Union agreed to participate in the **European Economic and Monetary Union** and convert their national currencies into a single currency, the **euro**.

EXCHANGE RESTRICTIONS. The Fund began operations in 1947 in a world that, apart from the U.S. dollar, was inundated with inconvertible **currency** and heavily enmeshed in trade and exchange trade controls, bilateral trade and payments arrangements, and restrictions on international trade of all kinds. The history of the first 25 years of the Fund's influence was the gradual disentanglement of its member countries from restrictions, first by the major trading countries and then later, more slowly and hesitantly, by **developing countries**. Indeed, it was only in the late 1980s and early 1990s that many major developing countries in Latin America and Asia finally took steps to sweep away their restrictive exchange and trade practices.

The record of this progress to a freer world economy was neither steady nor without setbacks. The early attempt in 1947 to make the pound sterling convertible for current transactions failed and it was not until toward the end of the 1950s that the industrialized countries of Europe were able to eliminate restrictions and to establish external **convertibility** for their currencies. Full currency convertibility was not established with the Fund until 1961. The Fund's **Articles of Agreement** had envisaged a period of **transitional arrangements** and after five years had called for annual reports on restrictions. The first of these annual reports, the *Annual Report on Exchange Restrictions*, appeared in 1952, and such reports—renamed in the 1970s the ***Annual Report on Exchange Arrangements and Exchange Restrictions***—have been published each year since then.

Although progress toward a free trade and payments system had been slower than originally envisaged, in some respects the removal of some restrictions—those on **capital movements**—has gone beyond what was thought possible, or desirable, by the founders of the Fund. Indeed, the freedom with which capital, particularly short-term capital, was allowed to flow through the world's **exchange markets** was perceived to be one cause of instability in the **international monetary system** during the 1960s and led to renewed attempts by some countries (notably the United States and the United Kingdom) to restrain such flows. The growth of international capital flows, and the accompanying economic and financial crises of the 1990s, led the Fund to seek new and expanded authority over international capital movements.

The progress toward a free trade and payments system was accompanied by international reductions in tariffs under a series of negotiations held by the

General Agreement on Tariffs and Trade, beginning with the initial round at Geneva (1947) and continuing in growing importance at Annecy (1949), Torquay (1950–1951), Geneva (1956, 1960–1961, 1964–1967), Tokyo (19731979), Geneva (1982), and finally the Uruguay Round (1986–1993). The result was a sharp increase in international trade, open **exchange markets**, the growth of multinational and transnational corporations, and the integration of the world's financial markets. Simultaneously, as the multinational transactions of private corporations, banks, and other interests have overrun national borders, national **monetary authorities** have attempted to close their ranks through summit, regional, and international meetings in an effort to harmonize policies, promote cooperation, and retain official influence over what has become an interdependent world.

EXCHANGE SURCHARGES. The practice of adding a surcharge to the buying rate of an exchange rate was adopted by a number of countries in the late 1940s and early 1950s. Usually, it was introduced as a temporary expedient in order to stem imports and correct an imbalance in the country's external accounts. Such a surcharge could also be used to raise revenue, as an alternative to raising tariffs. Surcharges can be applied to different categories of exchange purchases, such as financial remittances or nonessential imports. They are considered **multiple currency practices** and require approval by the Fund.

EXECUTIVE BOARD. Consisting of 24 **Executive Directors**, the Executive Board is responsible for conducting the day-to-day business of the Fund. It exercises for this purpose the powers assigned to it under the **Articles of Agreement** and those delegated to it by the **Board of Governors**. The Board is chaired by the **Managing Director**. Of the 24 Executive Directors making up the Board in August 2010, five were appointed by member countries with the largest quotas (the United States, Germany, Japan, the United Kingdom, and France); China, **Russia**, and Saudi Arabia each had sufficiently large quotas and thus sufficient votes to elect their own Executive Directors; and 16 others were elected by groups of member countries forming constituencies.

The number of countries in a constituency varies, ranging up to 24. Each Executive Director appoints an **Alternate Executive Director**, who, in the absence of the Executive Director, is authorized to act on his or her behalf. An appointed Executive Director holds office until a successor is appointed. Elections for elected Executive Directors are held every two years—in practice, at the time of the **annual meetings** in even-numbered years—or when needed. In recent years, as the number of countries in the electoral constituencies has grown to accommodate the enlarged Fund, Executive Directors have been authorized to appoint Advisors and Technical Assistants.

The Board functions in continuous session and is required to meet as often as the Fund business dictates. A quorum for the meeting exists when a majority of the Executive Directors having not less than one-half of the total voting power is present. Board meetings are held on a specific agenda, circulated in advance. Usually, the staff prepares the recommendations on which the policies and decisions taken by the Executive Board are based. Decisions on the more routine issues may be reached on a lapse-of-time basis, but the vast majority of decisions on matters of substance are reached by the Chairman ascertaining the "sense of the meeting."

Although Directors have the right to call for a formal vote, it has become a policy to try to avoid them, and formal votes are rare. If a vote is called for, an appointed Executive Director casts the number of eligible votes held by the member appointing him or her, and an elected Executive Director casts the total of eligible votes held by the members of his constituency. In the case of elected Executive Directors, they must cast their votes as one unit and cannot record individual country votes within their constituencies. Most voting decisions of the Board are made by a majority of the votes cast. *See also* Voting Provisions in the Fund.

EXECUTIVE BOARD COMMITTEES. **Executive Directors** are aided by a number of Board Committees, such as the Committee on Administrative Procedures, and, when needed, by several ad hoc committees, such as on the terms of **membership** for applicant countries or on regulations for the conduct of the biennial election of Executive Directors. Although such committees are established with a smaller, specified membership than the full Executive Board, all Executive Directors are entitled to attend them and to speak to the business at hand. There is no voting in committee.

EXECUTIVE BOARD PROCEDURES. The responsibilities of the **Executive Board** are comprehensive in relation to the day-to-day business of the Fund, covering the formulation of new policies and the establishment of new facilities, the approval of **stand-by arrangements** and other financial operations, country **consultations**, and staffing policies, as well as a range of housekeeping matters. Usually, the **Managing Director** and staff take the initiative in proposing the agenda and preparing the necessary papers for discussion and decision, but the influence of the Board and the need to obtain its final approval for any business of significance permeates all the work of the Fund. The management and staff may propose, but it is the Board that disposes.

Normally, the Board meets at fixed times in the mornings of Mondays, Wednesdays, and Fridays, allowing those **Executive Directors** who are also

Executive Directors of the **World Bank** to meet with the Bank's Board on Tuesdays and Thursdays. The pressure of work on the Executive Board, though varying with the extent of international and country business, has tended to escalate over the years, as the Fund's **membership** grew and its operational work expanded sharply.

Routinely, the Executive Directors meet as a Board, and it is in that format that Directors must approve decisions. Occasionally, in discussing particularly sensitive subjects, the Board meets in executive session, when attendance is restricted to management, members of the Board, and, if deemed appropriate, selected staff members. Executive Directors may also meet as a Committee of the Whole on important issues on which discussion is likely to be prolonged, affecting a large number of members, and requiring frequent referrals by Executive Directors to their **monetary authorities**. One such issue has traditionally been the general review of **quotas**, which in the past has required many Board papers and meetings of the Committee of the Whole over a period of many months before a proposal could be agreed to by the Executive Board for submission to and approval by the **Board of Governors**.

Also, Executive Directors may meet in informal session, sometimes when a major, sensitive topic or a new policy is to be discussed, when the management and staff, as well as Executive Directors, welcome the opportunity of sounding out views without taking firm positions. A similar format is used for discussion of the Fund's ***World Economic Outlook***, a twice-yearly review of the world economic situation and outlook prepared by the management and staff. Before the report is issued to the public, the staff takes into account factual comments made by Executive Directors, but the report remains a management and staff document.

The degrees of official status in these various formats of the Executive Directors' sessions are reflected in the character of the minutes of the meetings. Regular Board meetings are reported on in extensive (near verbatim) minutes and carefully checked by all those involved in the discussions. A summing up of the discussion prepared by the Managing Director is read to the meeting and later disseminated to the offices of Executive Directors and selected staff members. Since the beginning of 1998, the summings up by the Managing Director have been made available to the public in the form of **Public Information Notices**. Minutes of the other meetings are brief and deal only in outline with the substance of the discussion. Minutes become part of the official archives of the Fund and are tightly held, even among the staff.

EXECUTIVE DIRECTORS. Executive Directors are officers of the Fund, appointed or elected by members and remunerated by the Fund. Unlike the **Managing Director** and staff, however, Executive Directors do not owe their duty entirely to the Fund in the discharge of their official functions. Because they are appointed or elected by member countries, they have to balance their duties to the Fund with the interests of the countries that they represent.

The role and status of Executive Directors was much discussed at the **Bretton Woods Conference**, where it was the view of some that Executive Directors should be high officials of national governments, that they would attend **Executive Board** meetings, which would be called for only periodically, and that much of the day-to-day business of the Fund would be left in the hands of the management and staff. This was not how the **Articles of Agreement** finally emerged, however, and the requirement that the Board be in continuous session meant that Executive Directors would necessarily have to be full-time Fund officials, rather than practicing, hands-on members of their own governments. In fact, however, many Board members have been senior officials in their home governments, particularly in the earlier years of the Fund. With the revolution in the speed of communication since the 1960s, the tendency has been for governments to put forward less senior members of their administration, although a position on the Board is regarded as a prestigious experience. The closeness of the control exercised over Executive Directors by their home authorities differs for each incumbent, depending on personal factors and on national characteristics.

EXOGENOUS SHOCKS FACILITY (ESF). In January 2006, the ESF was established within the **poverty reduction and growth facility (PRGF)** and the **exogenous shocks facility (PRGF-ESF) trust**. It is intended to complement existing Fund arrangements in order to provide timely support to low-income countries that do not have existing PRGF arrangements that are faced with sudden exogenous shocks, such as natural disasters. In particular, the ESF facilitates quick access to more concessional financing than that available under the Fund's **emergency assistance** and the **compensatory financing facility**. It also serves as a safety net for countries wishing to graduate from continuous PRGF arrangements, including Policy Support Initiative users.

For the purposes of the ESF, an exogenous shock is considered to be any event that has a significant negative impact on the economy and that is beyond the control of the government. This could include sudden commodity price changes, natural disasters, and conflicts and crises in neighboring countries that disrupt trade.

Recent modifications to the ESF, in September 2008 and April 2009, have made it faster and easier to access and more flexible as well as capable of providing more finance, of up to 150 percent of quota. *See also* EMERGENCY ASSISTANCE.

EXPENDITURES OF THE FUND. *See also* INCOME AND EXPENDITURE OF THE FUND.

EXTENDED FUND FACILITY (EFF). Extended arrangements were introduced in 1974, on a recommendation of the **Committee of Twenty**. They come into effect when the Fund supports medium-term programs that usually run for three years (or up to four years in exceptional circumstances) and are aimed at overcoming **balance of payments** difficulties arising from structural as well as macroeconomic problems. The program sets out the general objectives and policies for the three-year period and the policies and measures for the first year; policies for subsequent years are established in annual reviews. The Fund's continued support and financing over the period of the arrangement is dependent on the country achieving performance criteria established for the program. Repayments begin after four years and must be completed within 10 years after making the **drawing** from the Fund. After the **quota** increases under the ninth general review of quotas came into effect in November 1992, members' **access limits** to the extended facility was established at 100 percent of quota per annum, with a cumulative limit of 300 percent of quota.

EXTERNAL AUDIT COMMITTEE. The **Articles of Agreement** provide for the Fund's financial accounts to be audited annually and for the auditor's report to be published in the Fund's ***Annual Report of the Executive Board***. The audit is conducted by an External Audit Committee consisting of either three or five persons, each of whom is nominated by a different member of the Fund and confirmed by the **Executive Board**. At least one person serving on each audit committee is nominated by one of the six members of the Fund having the largest quotas, and at least one person is nominated by a member that is a participant in the **Special Drawing Rights Department**. The procedures for conducting the audit are outlined in the **by-laws**.

EXTERNAL DEBT. External debt is the total amount of money a state's public and private sectors owe to nonresidents that is repayable in foreign currency, goods, or services. External indebtedness assumed crisis proportions for many **developing countries** in 1982. The disruptions caused by the sharp increases in oil prices in the 1970s, together with the easy availability of private financing and imprudent lending by some commercial banks as they recycled "oil dollars," led to the emergence of acute external debt-servicing problems in the 1980s, a problem that persisted in the 1990s.

The causes of the problems were varied and manifold: the inefficient use and control over borrowed funds by the recipient countries; inadequate investment returns to cover the cost of servicing the debt; the use of short-term debt for long-term projects; excessive debt levels in general; and adverse and unexpected international developments beyond the control of any individual country, such as rising interest rates, unfavorable terms of trade, restrictive and weak markets abroad, and a general decline in the growth of world trade and economic activity. The situation was compounded by a sharp reversal in the flow of external finance from the industrial countries to developing countries, principally caused by the commercial banks' need to cut back on new lending to the developing world in order to cope with their own portfolio and balance sheet problems.

Thus, some $130 billion of new private funds was lent to developing countries in 1981–1982, whereas only $30 billion (most of which was part of a package connected with Fund **adjustment programs**) was made available in 1982–1983. Thereafter, although existing debt was restructured, virtually no new money was made available through the second half of the 1980s. Subsequently, however, as confidence returned and international financial markets became more closely integrated, **capital movements** began to flow in increasing volume, a significant amount of which was of a short-term character.

During the 1980s, the Fund played an increasingly important role in facilitating discussions between its member countries and their creditors. It assisted countries in preparing statistical documentation, acted in many cases as "go-between" in bringing the debtor countries and private creditors together, and played a major role in supplying information and advice in the multilateral debt renegotiations held under the aegis of the **Paris Club**, which is the main forum for dealing with debt owed to or guaranteed by governments and official agencies of the participating creditor countries.

In some instances, the Fund went further and played a more positive role in debt renegotiations. It helped to devise programs that, on the one hand, required discipline and domestic restraint to meet a specified financing "gap" and, on the other, required external creditors to assemble a financial package of official grants, concessional financing, trade credits, and commercial loans to cover the country's internal financing gap. While preserving the confidentiality of Fund-membership relations, creditors were kept informed about the country's policies and the progress of their implementation. The link between debt restructuring and Fund-supported adjustment programs was, on the one hand, on an arms-length basis and, on the other, based on trust.

The 1994 **Mexican financial crisis** and the 1997 **Asian financial crisis** were compounded by large capital flows, in the form of both capital flight and the reversal of short-term capital movements. The Fund played an active role in helping countries cope with the crisis, by assisting in their domestic debt management programs, by expanding the access of these countries to Fund financing under the **enlarged access policy**, by taking the lead in coordinating the supply of external resources (from both official and private sources), and by helping countries to formulate and support adjustment programs that would bring effective domestic demand into balance with the available internal and external **resources**.

External debt became a systemic concern again as a result of the **global financial crisis**. In the period 2008–2010, the Fund provided over $200 billion in support of programs for countries affected by the crisis. In March 2009, the Fund introduced a major overhaul of its lending framework, including modernizing conditionality, introducing a new flexible credit line, enhancing the flexibility of the Fund's regular stand-by lending arrangement, doubling access limits on loans, adapting its cost structures for high-access and precautionary lending, and streamlining instruments in order to better assist advanced and emerging market economies, particularly in Europe.

In late 2008 and 2009, European economies experienced significant increases in fiscal deficits as a result of both federal stimulus measures and declining revenues associated with the recession. As of June 2010, the Fund staff projected that gross general government debt in the advanced economies would rise from an average of about 75 percent of GDP at the end of 2007 to about 110 percent of GDP at the end of 2014. Already in 2010, the average debt-to-GDP ratio in advanced economies was reminiscent of the level prevailing in 1950, in the aftermath of World War II. Moreover, this surge in government debt was expected to occur at a time when pressure from rising health and pension spending was building up.

At a meeting held in Toronto, Canada, in June 2010, heads of the **Group of Twenty** stated that the highest priority would be to safeguard and strengthen the recovery from the global recession and to bring general government debt ratios to the precrisis average of 60 percent by 2030. This effort would entail not only unwinding the discretionary stimulus measures used during the crisis, but also significant additional reform measures related to pension and health entitlements, containment of other spending, and increased tax revenues. *See also* GLOBAL FINANCIAL CRISIS.

EXTERNAL VULNERABILITY ASSESSMENTS. In response to the currency crises that afflicted several emerging market economies in the 1990s, the Fund launched a major effort to improve its ability to analyze whether, and to what extent, countries are vulnerable to such crises. Beginning in May 2001, the Fund incorporated vulnerability assessments in its normal surveillance work, and the use of vulnerability scenarios and indicators—such as external debt and reserve adequacy indicators—was made a part of staff reports for Article IV consultations with emerging market economies. Much of this effort relates to the assessment of countries' vulnerability to changes in external circumstances and, in particular, to capital market conditions. A prime objective is to forestall crises by recommending policies that reduce vulnerabilities and strengthen the economies' resilience to shocks. The external vulnerability assessments entail semiannual interdepartmental exercises to identify underlying vulnerabilities drawing on quantitative vulnerability indicators, qualitative staff assessments, market information, and analyses of different scenarios for the global economic and financial market environment. Countries identified as vulnerable are kept under continuous surveillance. Reports on the results of these exercises are sent to members of **Fund Management** and department heads. The **Executive Board** is kept informed through informal sessions on country matters, routine bilateral and multilateral surveillance reports, and ad hoc reports in times of particular turbulence.

F

FINANCIAL ACTION TASK FORCE (FATF). The FATF, a 35-member intergovernmental body, was established at the 1989 **Group of Seven** Summit to develop international standards in the area of **anti-money laundering (AML)**. In the wake of the terrorist attacks of 11 September 2001, the FATF's mandate was expanded to address efforts to **combat terrorist financing (CTF)**. The FATF works in close collaboration with other key international organizations, such as the IMF, the **World Bank**, and the **United Nations**, to promote AML/CTF policies and monitor members' progress in implementing necessary measures covering the criminal justice system, the financial sector, certain nonfinancial businesses and professions, and mechanisms of international cooperation. It also reviews money laundering and terrorist financing techniques and countermeasures. The FATF does not have an unlimited life span, and it reviews its mission every five years. In 2004, Ministry representatives of FATF members agreed to extend the mandate of the Task Force until 2012.

FINANCIAL PACKAGES. Financial packages consist of the Fund's financial **resources** and additional financing from international and national aid agencies, as well as the private sector of other Fund members. The assembly of financial packages became a regular practice in the late 1970s and 1980s and was aimed at assisting **developing countries** to cope with serious **balance of payments** problems through a coordinated approach of aggregating all available external resources in support of a country's **adjustment program** that tailored domestic absorption to available resources.

From its early days, a Fund **stand-by arrangement** with a member country has been accepted by the international financial community as a signal that the country was undertaking corrective programs to put its house in order. The adoption of a Fund-supported program has often been a catalyst to spur foreign aid and investment and, eventually, to enable the country to borrow in the world's financial markets. Thus, the relatively modest initial amount of financing received from the Fund often led to the inflow of funds several times the size of the Fund's commitment. The expectation that additional external financing would be forthcoming in connection with a successful Fund stand-by arrangement was one manifestation of growing international financial cooperation. Conversely, member countries came to understand that failure to reach agreement on a Fund-supported stand-by arrangement threatened isolation from regular sources of outside finance. The connection between a Fund-supported program and additional outside financing became stronger after the experiences of the 1970s, particularly as a result of the debt crises in 1982, the 1990s, and the great recession.

FINANCIAL PROGRAMMING. Financial programming is a set of coordinated policy measures—mainly in the monetary, fiscal, and **balance of payments** fields—intended to achieve certain economic targets in a relatively short period. In preparing such a program, the assumption is that a relatively stable relationship exists between financial variables (such as money and domestic credit) and nonfinancial variables (such as real national income and prices) and that in controlling the financial variables the **monetary authorities** can also control the real side of the economy.

In targeting a balance between real income and real absorption (consumption plus investment), a determination has to be made as to what changes are to take place in prices, **international reserves**, and the exchange rate, and what, if any, will be the resources flowing in from abroad. Short-term financial programs usually concentrate on establishing reasonable price stability and a given target for reserves by restraining domestic demand and by eliminating the most evident impediments to production, without attempting to tackle the more deep-seated problems. Longer term programs also address the more fundamental problems, such as measures to stimulate investment, implement appropriate exchange rate and pricing policies, promote financial markets, and initiate tax reforms.

A number of techniques can be used to draw up a financial program, including the construction of an econometric model. Experience in **developing countries** suggests that linkages between the relevant variables are not always stable, that the data used is not wholly reliable, and that accurate specification of the model can be extremely difficult. In the last analysis, therefore, judgmental considerations often dominate final decisions on the shape of the program. *See also* BALANCE OF PAYMENTS ADJUSTMENT; STABILIZATION PROGRAMS.

FINANCIAL SECTOR ASSESSMENT PROGRAM (FSAP). Following the financial markets crises of the late 1990s, the Fund and the **World Bank** launched a joint initiative, known as the *Financial Sector Assessment Program*, in May 1999 to strengthen **surveillance** of member countries, help countries identify and resolve financial sector vulnerabilities and thereby contribute to crisis prevention, and foster financial sector development and efficiency and thereby contribute to economic growth. For the purposes of these assessments, financial systems are seen to include the whole range of financial institutions, such as banks, mutual funds, and insurance companies, as well as the financial markets themselves (e.g., securities, foreign exchange, and money markets). They also include the payments system and the regulatory, supervisory, and legal framework that underlies the operations of the financial institutions and markets.

The FSAP draws heavily on the Fund's and the Bank's routine financial sector work. Traditionally, the Fund has focused on financial sector soundness and macroeconomic performance. It has support policies to improve oversight of financial institutions and markets to reduce excessive risk, improve these institutions' risk management, and promote sound intermediation of financial flows. At the same time, the World Bank has traditionally been concerned with the importance of the financial sector in economic development and poverty reduction. In this context, it has supported the development and strengthening of countries' financial sectors.

The FSAP seeks to alert countries to likely financial sector vulnerabilities and to assist the Bank and the Fund—and the international community more broadly—in designing appropriate assistance. In preparing individual assessments, the Bank and Fund staff draw not only on their own experience, but also on that of experts from a range of cooperating central banks, national supervisory agencies, international standard-setting bodies (e.g., the Basel Committee on Banking Supervision, the International Association of Insurance Supervisors, and the International Organization of Securities Commissions) and other institutions.

At the conclusion of joint Bank-Fund FSAP missions, the staffs report their findings and recommendations to country authorities in the form of an aide mémoire (previously referred to as the *FSAP main report*). Drawing on these findings, the Fund staff also prepares a **Financial System Stability Assessment (FSSA)**, which summarizes the FSAP findings on issues of relevance to Fund surveillance. The FSSA is provided to the **Executive Board**, usually as part of the Article IV **consultation**.

In light of the lessons learned during the global financial crisis, the FSAP was revamped in September 2009 to provide for more candid and transparent assessments, improved methodologies to identify linkages between the financial sector and the broader economy, to better tailor FSSAs to individual country circumstances and to better target the regulation and supervision of banks, securities markets, and insurance.

Although individual country participation in the FSAP is voluntary, more than three-quarters of Fund members had undergone FSSAs, *and a*ssessments for China, **Indonesia**, and the United States were underway as of October 2009.

FINANCIAL SOUNDNESS INDICATOR (FSI). As part of the overall initiative to strengthen financial systems launched in 1999, the Fund began an effort to develop financial soundness indicators that could be used to assess the strengths and weaknesses of the financial system. In June 2001, the Fund's **Executive Board** endorsed a list of core and encouraged indicators and supported the preparation of the *Financial Soundness Indicators: Compilation Guide* to assist countries in the compilation and dissemination of FSI data. The *Guide* was posted on the IMF website in 2004 and published in 2006.

In June 2003, the Executive Board of the IMF endorsed a coordinated compilation exercise (CCE) for FSIs to take place following completion of the *Guide.* Accordingly, in March 2004, the Fund embarked on the CCE with a view to (1) develop the capacity of the member countries to compile FSI data; (2) promote cross-country comparability of FSIs; (3) coordinate efforts by national authorities to compile FSIs; and (4) disseminate FSI data compiled in the CCE, along with metadata, to increase transparency and strengthen market discipline. To advance the implementation of the CCE, a meeting of 62 participating countries was held in November 2004 at the Fund's headquarters. Following that meeting, the CCE work program, its terms of reference, and the report forms for FSI data and metadata developed by the IMF Statistics Department were finalized.

The countries participating in the CCE were required to compile at least the 12 core FSIs as of the reference date, which was set at end-2005, in accordance with the *Guide*, and to provide the Fund with data for the core FSIs and the underlying data series, along with detailed metadata. Countries were also encouraged to compile and submit data and metadata for the 28 encouraged FSIs. The IMF disseminated this data for 57 countries via its website in January 2007.

On 31 July 2009, the first batch of member countries initiated regular reporting and dissemination of FSI data and metadata through the IMF website. The Fund will continue to promote the use of FSI data with a view to increasing the list of reporting countries in the period ahead.

FINANCIAL SYSTEM STABILITY ASSESSMENT (FSSA). *See* FINANCIAL SECTOR ASSESSMENT PROGRAM (FSAP).

FISCHER, STANLEY (1943–). Stanley Fischer, a U.S. national born in Zambia, served as the First **Deputy Managing Director** of the Fund from 1 September 1994 until the end of August 2001. He received his BSc (Econ.) and MSc (Econ.) from the London School of Economics and obtained his PhD in economics at the Massachusetts Institute of Technology (MIT) in 1969. He was Assistant Professor of Economics at the University of Chicago until 1973, when he returned to MIT as Associate Professor in the Department of Economics. Fischer became Professor of Economics at Massachusetts Institute of Technology in 1977, and held visiting positions at the Hebrew University, Jerusalem, and the Hoover Institution at Stanford. From January 1988 to August 1990, he served as Vice President of Development Economics and Chief Economist at the **World Bank**. He has also held consulting appointments and has published extensively.

After leaving the Fund, Mr. Fischer served as Vice Chairman of Citigroup, President of Citigroup International, and Head of the Public Sector Client Group. He became an Israeli citizen and Governor of the Bank of Israel on 1 May 2005.

FIXED EXCHANGE RATES. The Bretton Woods **par value system** was a fixed **exchange rate** system, based on **gold**. Changes could be made in the value of a currency only with the concurrence of the Fund. Otherwise, exchange rate movements were to be confined to a margin of 1 percent either side of the declared parity.

The **European Monetary System**, established in 1979, is an example of a regional par value or fixed-rate system, in which a participant fixes a **central rate** for its **currency** in terms of the **European Currency Unit (ECU)**. Under this system, the value of a currency could be changed by the mutual consent of the other participants, but otherwise participants had to observe, in "spot" transactions, a margin of 2.25 percent above and below each bilateral relationship with any other currency in the system. The system used a "divergence indicator" to give a signal that the exchange rate of a currency was moving out of line with the average exchange rate of all other currencies. If a currency crossed its "threshold of divergence," there was an intimation that the participant would take action to correct the situation.

The second amendment to the **Articles of Agreement** provided for a return to a par value system, if a majority of 85 percent of the **Board of Governors** voted for such a system. The Articles specifically preclude par values from being based on gold or a unit of currency. The evident intent of the drafters was that any new par value system operated by the Fund would be based on the **Special Drawing Right**. Under the system proposed in the Articles, the margin between pairs of currencies would be 4.5 percent, but the margin could be changed by an 85-percent-majority vote of the Board of Governors. Since the amendment to the Articles of the Fund, there has never been a serious proposal to return to the par value system.

FLEXIBLE CREDIT LINE (FCL). In the wake of the global financial crisis, the Fund introduced a new facility, the FCL, in March 2009, to replace the short-term liquidity facility (SLF). Access to the FLC is determined on a case-by-case basis for countries with very strong fundamentals, policies, and track records of policy implementation. Unlike the Fund's traditional **stand-by** and **extended arrangements**, disbursements under the FCL are not phased or subject to policy **conditionality**. The design features of the FCL—including its capped access and short repayment period, as well as the inability to use it on a precautionary basis—limit its value for most potential borrowers, but it is well suited for crisis prevention or resolution. In particular, the FCL provides assurance that qualified countries will have available large and upfront access to Fund **resources** under a renewable credit line that carried a repayment period of up to five years. Unlike the SLF, which had an access limit of 500 percent of **quota**, the FCL has no strict access limit and allows the member flexibility to draw at any time on the credit line or to treat it as a precautionary instrument (which was not allowed under the SLF).

FLOATING EXCHANGE RATES. The **Bretton Woods system** ushered in a system of fixed but adjustable exchange rates under which the countries themselves declared and notified the Fund of the **par value** of their **currencies**. The system did allow countries to float their currencies, but such practices were regarded as temporary expedients in order to arrive at a realistic par value, and floating was tolerated for only a few countries and in exceptional circumstances. Basically, the system was one of **fixed exchange rates**, and the only major trading country that maintained a **floating exchange rate** for any length of time was Canada.

The breakdown of the Bretton Woods par value system in 1971 led to the generalized floating of currencies in 1973, signaling the abandonment, in the short term at least, of the fixed-rate system—both the par value system, which had prevailed up to 1971, and the **central rate system**, which had been hastily put together at the end of that year. But the approach to floating was not a uniform one, and a fundamental disagreement rapidly emerged among the leading industrial nations as to whether currencies should be allowed to float freely in the **exchange markets** (the U.S. position) or whether movements in the exchange rate should be influenced by central bank intervention—mainly the European view. These two approaches came to be known as "clean" and "dirty" floating.

The new system, or "nonsystem" as some referred to it, evolved essentially into three currency blocs—the U.S. dollar, the Japanese yen, and the deutsche mark—each floating against the other. Within this floating system, the central bank of each country would, from time to time, try to influence the short-term movements of its currency in the market, and, more dramatically, sometimes the long-term movement of a particular currency (such as the U.S. dollar) in concert with other central banks. (A notable example of such a planned move was by the **Group of Seven** in the **Plaza Agreement**, New York, in September 1985, when it was announced that the participating national **monetary authorities** would cooperate to bring about a reduction in the value of the U.S. dollar. At the subsequent **Louvre** Palace agreement in Paris in February 1987, the Group announced that existing exchange rates were broadly consistent with the economic fundamentals and that they would "cooperate closely to foster stability around current levels"). A number of countries **pegged** their currencies to the U.S. dollar, some to the pound sterling, and others to the French franc, which itself was linked to the deutsche mark through the **European Monetary System**.

FLUCTUATING EXCHANGE RATES. The system of flexible or **floating exchange rates** that came into effect in 1973 proved to be more than just flexible. Indeed, since the floating rate system came into effect, rates have fluctuated quite sharply, often overshooting and undershooting without any clear relationship to the underlying fundamentals. At the outset, national **monetary authorities** that had chafed under what they had come to regard as the excessive rigidity of the **fixed-rate system** were disappointed to discover that the degree of freedom in setting their own national interest rate and monetary policies under the new fluctuating rate system was also severely constrained. Indeed, the European countries began to integrate their exchange rate policies into the **European Monetary System** as a move toward a fully fledged economic and political community. As a result of the marked fluctuations experienced in exchange rates, the main thrust of the Fund's **surveillance** role has been to place greater emphasis on the international coordination of **monetary** and exchange rate policies.

FOREIGN EXCHANGE. Foreign exchange is the market in which national **currencies** are bought and sold by persons, corporations, or entities that wish to convert a sum of money in one currency to that of another currency. Such transactions may be derived from exports and imports, corporate and business operations, or private remittances by individuals across national borders. The actual conversion of currency is carried out by brokers, banks, and other dealers, who charge a small commission for the operation.

With the growth of rapid means of communication in recent years, the dismantling of **exchange controls**, and the sharp expansion in international transactions, the **exchange markets** in individual countries have become almost instantaneously linked by an informal network of exchange dealers, where arbitrageurs buy and sell in the various markets to keep exchange rates, and their **exchange cross rates** with third currencies, in line throughout the world. Transactions in the exchange markets may be "spot," in which one currency is exchanged directly with another, or "forward," in which an exchange of currency is contracted for a future date.

According to the **Bank for International Settlements**, the average daily turnover in worldwide foreign exchange markets was equivalent to about $3.2 trillion in April 2007. This represents an unprecedented increase of 69 percent over the period since April 2004, and compares to unofficial estimates of an average daily turnover of roughly $1.6 billion in 1998. Over the period 2004–2008, the share of the four largest **currencies** fell, although the U.S. dollar and **euro** continued to be the most-traded pair of currencies. Notable increases in exchange activity had occurred, in particular for the Hong Kong dollar, which had benefited from rapid economic growth in China, and the New Zealand dollar, which attracted attention from investors as a high-yield currency. More broadly, the share of emerging market currencies in total turnover increased to almost 20 percent of all activity.

FORWARD COMMITMENT CAPACITY (FCC). The amount of **resources** the Fund has available for new (nonconcessional) lending. This amount includes its usable resources—the **quota**-funded holdings of currencies of financially strong economies used to finance lending and its own **Special Drawing Rights** holdings—plus projected loan repayments, less the resources already committed under existing lending arrangements and a prudential balance.

FRAMEWORK ADMINISTERED ACCOUNT FOR TECHNICAL ASSISTANCE ACTIVITIES (FAA). The FAA was established on 3 April 1995, to receive and administer resources contributed by individual members to finance **technical assistance** projects. The financing of technical assistance activities is implemented through the establishment and operation of subaccounts within the FAA. Resources are used in accordance with written understandings between the contributor and the **Managing Director**.

FUND MANAGEMENT STRUCTURE CHANGE. On 6 June 1994, the Fund announced that it would increase the number of **Deputy Managing Directors** from one to three, and named **Stanley Fischer** (United States), **Alassane D. Ouattara** (Côte d'Ivoire), and **Prabhakar R. Narvekar** (India) to the positions. The three Deputies succeeded **Richard Erb**, who had been appointed in 1984 and had served two five-year terms in the position.

This was the first major change in the structure of the Fund's senior management since 1949, when the position of Deputy Managing Director was established. The enlarged management structure was in response to the increased burden of responsibilities for a greatly expanded **membership** since the Fund's establishment in 1946. Traditionally, the Deputy Managing Director's position had always been filled by a U.S. national and to preserve the status of the United States in the management team, Stanley Fischer was designated First Deputy Managing Director. In this capacity, he was given broad responsibilities across the whole range of issues facing the institution and exercised comprehensive oversight.

Working under the direction of the **Managing Director**, each Deputy Managing Director has the authority to chair **Executive Board** meetings and to maintain contacts with officials of member governments, Executive Directors, and other institutions.

FUNDAMENTAL DISEQUILIBRIUM. The concept of a "fundamental disequilibrium" was essential to the working of the **Bretton Woods system**. Under the original **Articles** of the Fund, a member was not allowed to propose a change in the **par value** of its **currency** except to correct a fundamental disequilibrium. The drafters of the Articles had, it was thought, deliberately left the term undefined in order not to tie the hands of the Fund in its future operations. The Fund, itself, never defined the term *fundamental disequilibrium*, although numerous attempts were made, both inside and outside the Fund, to do so. In practice, the Fund assessed each proposed change in a member's par value on a case-by-case basis.

FUND–BANK RELATIONS. Both the International Monetary Fund and the International Bank for Reconstruction and Development, the formal name of the **World Bank**, were created at the **Bretton Woods Conference** of July 1944. Despite their common origin, however, they are separate, independent organizations, each with its own **Articles of Agreement**, its own governing body and staff, and its own defined terms of reference. The Fund is responsible for an international code of conduct governing exchange rates and international payments among countries, and has available to it a pool of

currencies that can be drawn upon, under suitable safeguards, by member governments that are in **balance of payments** difficulties. The World Bank, on the other hand, was conceived as an institution concerned with long-term **economic development** and has available to it resources from which it can make long-term loans to its member governments. After the reconstruction phase of the postwar world had been completed, when many warring nations, including Germany and Japan, had been helped in financing the rehabilitation of their war-torn economies, the World Bank concentrated entirely on the economic development of the Third World.

Both institutions were founded by farsighted but practical visionaries, who were dedicated to bringing about an essentially cooperative, open, free-market, postwar order. While the Fund was to oversee the international financial structure and the World Bank the world's economic development, a third institution, the International Trade Organization (ITO), was proposed to ensure fair and equitable arrangements for international trade. Aimed at the dismantling of tariffs, **quotas**, and other barriers to free trade between nations, the ITO never came into existence, although its ideals lived on, in a somewhat diluted form, in the **General Agreement on Tariffs and Trade (GATT)**. Nearly 50 years later, however, the ITO was resurrected when the new international organization, the **World Trade Organization**, replaced the GATT in 1995.

Facing each other across the street in Washington, D.C., cooperation between the World Bank and the Fund is close and practiced at all levels, both formally and informally. The World Bank's Articles of Agreement prescribe that a government must be a member of the Fund before it can become a member of the World Bank, and membership in the two institutions is virtually identical.

The Fund and the World Bank differ in their structure and size. The Fund has remained a single organization, with a relatively small staff, which had risen, after more than 40 years of operating, to only about 2,100. Most of its staff members work at its headquarters in Washington, D.C., although it has small offices in Geneva, Paris, Tokyo, and at the United Nations in New York, as well as seven regional training institutes. These include the IMF–Singapore Regional Training Institute, the Joint Africa Institute (in Tunisia), the Joint China–IMF Training Program (in Dalian, China), the Joint IMF–Arab Monetary Fund Regional Training Program (in the United Arab Emirates), the Joint India–IMF Training Program (in Pune, India), the Joint Regional Training Center for Latin America (in Brazil), and the Joint **Vienna Institute** (in Austria). The World Bank, on the other hand, has developed into the World Bank Group, comprising the World Bank, the International Development Association, the International Finance Corporation, the International

Center for Settlement of Investment Disputes, and the Multilateral Investment Guarantee Agency. The World Bank Group has a staff of over 7,000 and maintains about 40 offices throughout the world, although the main work of the Group is carried on at its headquarters in Washington, D.C. Whereas the Fund employs mainly professional economists specializing in macroeconomics, fiscal, and financial matters, the World Bank employs a vast range of professionals, such as economists, engineers, agronomists, urban planners, educationists, and experts in health care, water supply, sewage, transportation, rural development, communications, and other disciplines required to bring about the conditions of a modern state.

A member's use of the Fund's resources is determined by its need in terms of its balance of payments need in relation to its **quota** in the organization (the larger its economy, the larger the quota), whereas the World Bank Group invests its resources in member countries with creditworthy governments for viable development projects and sectoral and structural development programs. Both the Fund and the World Bank have funds available to them subscribed by their members, but most of the World Bank's resources for its lending is raised from private market operations, whereas the Fund relies heavily on the resources subscribed by members and borrows only exceptionally, and then only from official sources. The International Development Association, which provides concessional loans to poorer members, derives its resources from donations by wealthier members. Whereas the World Bank Group lends only to developing countries, the resources of the Fund are available to all countries, rich and poor, and over the years nearly all Fund members have used its resources.

The Fund's financing is available to its members at rates slightly below the market rate and is generally repayable in three to five years, and never more than 10 years. The World Bank loans have a maturity of 12 to 15 years and bear rates of interest slightly above the rate at which the World Bank pays for the funds from the market. Loans from the International Development Association, however, are interest free and have a maturity of 35 to 40 years.

During the first two decades of their operations, the Fund and the World Bank fulfilled clearly defined roles and conducted very different kinds of operations; the World Bank financed mainly specific long-term projects, such as dams, power stations, and transportation, and the Fund concentrated on an international code of conduct and providing medium-term financing to its members in support of corrective balance of payments programs. In the 1970s, however, following the world oil price increases, the resulting structural imbalances in the economies of many **developing countries**, and the subsequent debt crisis, both organizations were forced to broaden their respective roles. It became evident that the World Bank could no longer finance projects in isolation from general developments in the economy. Similarly, it became obvious that short-term **balance of payments adjustment** programs did not measure up to the severe structural problems persisting in many developing member countries.

The result was that the World Bank moved into structural and sector adjustment loans, while the Fund moved to longer term adjustment through **extended arrangements**, the **structural adjustment facility**, and the **enlarged access policy**. This broadening of the range of policies in both organizations brought them closer to each other operationally, with greater overlap and the necessity for even closer cooperation. Since the early 1980s, the two institutions have fielded a number of parallel and joint missions, cooperated in helping to prepare policy framework papers first for the structural adjustment and enhanced structural adjustment facilities and, now for the **poverty reduction and growth facility**. Throughout this period, the two institutions have intensified their cooperation at all levels. At the same time, they have maintained their regard for each other as independent institutions and upheld the confidential relationship that each has with its members. In particular, the two organizations have been careful to avoid "cross-conditionality," whereby the **conditionality** established by one organization for providing finance to a member is not a condition for receiving finance from the other. In the case of **overdue obligations** to either organization, the World Bank and the Fund cooperate closely with each other and the member, as well as with the regional development banks, such as the Inter-American Development Bank and the Asian Development Bank, to bring about normalization of the relations with the member. More recently, the Fund and Bank have agreed on a common approach under the **heavily indebted poor countries** initiative.

G

GENERAL ACCOUNT OF THE FUND. The General Account came into existence as a result of the first amendment to the **Articles of Agreement** in 1969, which created **Special Drawing Rights (SDR)**. The first amendment to the Articles designated the General Account as the operating account for the type of operations conducted by the Fund under the original, largely unchanged Articles, and established the SDR Account to handle the allocation and transfers of SDRs. The second amendment to the Articles (1978) changed the name from *General Account* to ***General Department***.

GENERAL AGREEMENT ON TARIFFS AND TRADE (GATT). The Fund had a special relationship with GATT, dating from 1950. In that year agreement was reached between the Fund and GATT under which the Fund would advise the Contracting Parties of the GATT as to whether a member's **balance of payments** position justified the imposition or maintenance of trade restrictions. In complying with this agreement, the Fund provided a report on the factual situation of the member in question and gave an evaluation of those facts in an advisory capacity. The Fund's office in Geneva maintained day-to-day contact with the GATT.

The GATT was signed in October 1947 and came into existence after negotiations for the establishment of the International Trade Organization failed to reach fruition. The Contracting Parties to the GATT, although not universal, accounted for the overwhelming value of world trade. The GATT was a form of multilateral trade agreement, in accordance with which signatories agreed, based on the principles of "reciprocity and mutual advantage," to negotiate a substantial reduction in customs tariffs and other impediments to trade and to eliminate discriminatory practices in international trade.

In addition to monitoring and negotiating bilateral trade agreements and helping to settle disputes between trading partners, GATT negotiated a series of worldwide tariff reductions at meetings, such as those held in Geneva (1947), Annecy (1949), Torquay (1950–1951), Geneva (1956, 1960–1961, and 1964–1967), Tokyo (1973–1979), and Geneva (1982). The latest of these, known as the **Uruguay Round**, began in 1986 and was expected to be completed in December 1990, but was delayed by protracted disagreements among the major trading countries on a number of sensitive issues, particularly agriculture. Finally completed at the end of 1993, the agreements not only brought about important tariff reductions, but also headed off a spate of protectionist measures waiting in the wings, and reached agreement on the establishment of a new international organization in place of GATT, the **World Trade Organization**, based on international law and with wider powers.

GENERAL ARRANGEMENTS TO BORROW (GAB). These arrangements came into existence in October 1962 when the Fund arranged to borrow, in certain circumstances, specified amounts of **currencies** from 11 industrial countries, consisting of 10 members of the Fund (Belgium, Canada, France, Germany, Italy, Japan, the Netherlands, Sweden, the United Kingdom, and the United States) and Switzerland, which was not a member at that time. The 10 member countries of the GAB originated the **Group of Ten**, which became prominent in international monetary affairs in later years.

The GAB were the first **borrowing** arrangements entered into by the Fund. They provided for the Fund to borrow up to a total of $6 billion in lenders' currencies to help to finance purchases by GAB participants when such financing would forestall or cope with an impairment of the **international monetary system**. The arrangements recognized that in the event of a financial crisis of any one of the participants, the Fund might not have sufficient **resources** of its own to cope with **drawings** of the magnitude required.

In 1982, faced with serious strains in the international financial system caused by the debt crisis, a thorough review of the arrangements was initiated, culminating in the completion of major reforms by the end of 1983. Under these new arrangements, the total of individual credit lines was increased to SDR 17 billion; the Swiss government became a participant in the arrangements, as distinct from an associate; provision was made for the Fund to enter, in association with the GAB, into borrowing arrangements with members that were not participants; and arrangements were agreed with Saudi Arabia to associate that country, on a bilateral basis, with the GAB. The revised arrangements also allowed the Fund, for the first time, to call on the participants to finance drawings by nonparticipants. Such drawings by nonparticipants are, however, subject to stricter **conditionality** than those made by participants. In addition, while the earlier GAB carried a rate of interest below market rates; this rate was raised, making it equal to the Special Drawing Rights interest rate. Since its establishment in 1962, the GAB has been renewed 10 times, most recently in November 2007 for a five-year period from December 2008.

The participants in the GAB and the amounts of their credit arrangements are:

Participant	Amount (In millions of SDRs)
United States	4,250.0
Deutsche Bundesbank	2,380.0
Japan	2,125.0
France	1,700.0
United Kingdom	1,700.0
Italy	1,105.0
Swiss National Bank	1,020.0
Canada	892.5
Netherlands	850.0
Belgium	595.0
Sveriges Riksbank	382.5
Total	17,000.0

See also BORROWING BY THE FUND; NEW ARRANGEMENTS TO BORROW (NAB).

GENERAL COUNSEL. This staff position was created in May 1966, when **Sir Joseph Gold**, who was the Director of the Legal Department, was also appointed as the General Counsel. He participated in the discussions of the Deputies of the **Group of Ten** as a representative of the **Managing Director** and was one of the main drafters of the amendment to the **Articles** establishing the creation of the **Special Drawing Rights** facility. The title is honorific and was also given to François P. Gianviti, of France, who became Director of the Legal Department in 1986 and General Counsel in 1987; and to Sean Hagan, who was named General Counsel and Director of the Legal Department in 2004.

GENERAL DATA DISSEMINATION SYSTEM (GDDS). The GDDS provides a framework for member countries to evaluate and prioritize their needs to improve the collection and dissemination of economic, financial, and sociodemographic data, and, where necessary, seek **technical assistance** in this area. Toward this end, the GDDS offers recommendations on good practice, based on the current practices of national statistical agencies, for producing and disseminating core and encouraged sets of data. The GDDS is designed to guide member countries in the dissemination of comprehensive, timely, accessible, and reliable statistics. *See also* DATA DISSEMINATION STANDARDS.

GENERAL DEPARTMENT. The General Department consists of the **General Resources Account**, the **Special Disbursement Account**, and the Investment Account, which was reactivated in May 2006. The **Borrowed Resources Suspense Account** was established in May 1981 within the General Department.

GENERAL RESERVE. The General Reserve is one of three precautionary balances maintained by the Fund to protect its assets from impairment and to demonstrate a sound financial management of the organization. The General Reserve is fed from the Fund's **income** after covering operational and administrative expenditures and any distributions to members that the Fund may decide upon. Apart from the first few years of its existence, the Fund has consistently had a surplus income over expenditure, yielding a net income that has been accrued in the General Reserve.

Periods of stringency have occurred, however, such as in 1970–1971 and during the 1980s, when some members were unable to meet their repayments and other obligations to the Fund. To meet this situation, the Fund established two **Special Contingency Accounts (SCAs)**, the first in 1987 and the second in 1990. The establishment of the first contingency account (SCA 1) was derived from the concept of **burden sharing**, when it was decided that both creditor members of the Fund and those paying **charges** on the use of the Fund's **resources** should contribute to the cost of covering the overdue repayments (**repurchases**) and charges. The second contingency account (SCA 2), an extension of the burden-sharing principle, was established to safeguard **purchases (drawings)** by a member that had been previously delinquent in its obligations to the Fund, but had accumulated sufficient "**rights**" to resume drawing on the Fund's resources.

GENERAL RESOURCES ACCOUNT (GRA). The General Resources Account is one of four accounts maintained in the **General Department**; the other three are the **Special Disbursement Account**, the Investment Account, and the **Borrowed Resources Suspense Account**. The bulk of transactions between member countries and the Fund take place through the GRA, including the receipt of **quota subscriptions**, **purchases** and **repurchases**, receipt and refunding of **charges** payment of remuneration on members' loan claims and on creditor positions in the Fund, and repayment of principal to the Fund's lenders. The assets in the account are held in the form of members' **currencies**, **Special Drawing Rights**, **gold**, and other assets. These holdings are derived principally from quota subscriptions plus any activated borrowings.

GHANA. When Ghana became independent in 1957, it enjoyed the highest per capita income in sub-Saharan Africa. It was the world's largest producer of cocoa, had a strong **balance of payments** position, and held external reserves equivalent to three years of imports. Over the 25 years, economic mismanagement led to an almost complete dissipation of these advantages. Government interventionist policies over all the critical areas of the economy, including **foreign exchange**, prices, credit, and imports; the absence of any discipline over public sector finances, leading to surging inflation and a negative balance of payments; and, finally, a severe drought and falling cocoa prices in 1982–1983, all brought the economy to the point of collapse.

Faced with a crisis situation, Ghana launched an ambitious economic recovery program, involving a progressive shift away from direct controls and government intervention toward greater reliance on market mechanisms. Over the next 15 years, with the support of several Fund-supported programs and its considerable financial backing, the government struggled to implement its program, but with only limited success. At the beginning of 1998, it was clear that the Ghanaian economy was still a work in progress.

The market-oriented program had initially achieved some positive results: inflation had been reduced to 10 percent by the end of 1991, the distorted exchange rate and trade system had been liberalized, and real GDP growth was averaging about 5 percent a year, resulting in appreciable increases in real per capita income. Nevertheless, inflation remained high and variable; private sector saving and investment continued to be inadequate; and the implementation of critical structural reforms in the financial, parastatal, and agricultural sectors was progressing, but only slowly. Export growth was disappointing and the country continued to depend on external assistance.

In 1992, a fiscal imbalance reemerged, with the primary domestic deficit jumping from 1.9 percent of GDP in 1991 to 4.9 percent in 1992, accompanied by a rapid growth in the money supply and the reemergence of inflationary pressures. For the next four years the government's record of economic management was marked by recurrent lapses in financial discipline. In 1995, the Fund approved a series of loans for Ghana over the next three years under the **enhanced structural adjustment facility (ESAF)** totaling SDR 164.4 million (about $258 million) in support of the government's 1995–1997 economic program. The implementation, however, of policies under the first year of the program was uneven, with the budgetary outturn falling well short of the target, resulting in the growth of arrears to private contractors and an annual rate of inflation of 71 percent. On the positive side, the privatization program remained on track, there was a bumper cocoa crop, an increase in foreign exchange reserves, and a GDP growth rate of 4.5 percent. In 1996, performance under the program was again mixed; most quantitative indicators and several structural benchmarks under the program were missed. Large fiscal slippages raised the budget deficit to 10.6 percent of GDP, 6 percent above the targeted amount. A bumper cocoa crop, however, helped to raise GDP growth to 5.2 percent, and inflation fell to 33 percent. The external deficit widened and gross **international reserves** declined. At the rate and pattern of economic growth that had been established over the previous years, it was estimated that it would take 30 years for the average poor in Ghana to cross the poverty line.

In 1997, the government launched a fiscal adjustment plan aimed at restoring budgetary discipline and thus generating the domestic primary surplus needed to reduce public borrowing and to lower inflation and interest rates. The plan succeeded in moderating the overall budget deficit, with a decline in tax receipts being more than offset by a decline in expenditures, brought about largely by a fall in capital outlays, where overruns had been concentrated in 1996. Owing mainly to a recovery in domestic foodstuff production and a slowdown in aggregate demand, inflation fell from 33 percent at the end of 1996 to 21 percent at the end of 1997. By the end of the year, a decade of reform had brought about some encouraging results, such as a drastic reduction in government regulations and interventionist policies; the enactment of significant legislation to provide the framework for private sector participation in the economy; and the divestitures of a total of 48 state-owned enterprises, from a predetermined list of 110 such enterprises.

In March 1998, in approving the second annual loan under the ESAF program, the Fund announced that the loan had been augmented by SDR 27 million (about $37 million) at the authorities' request, by rephasing the remaining amount available under the three-year program. The commitment period of the three-year ESAF arrangement had also been extended by one full year, to June 1999. In announcing its approval of the loan disbursement, the Fund said that the key macroeconomic targets of the 1998 program were (1) to achieve an annual rate of growth of real GDP of 5.6 percent; (2) to reduce annual inflation from 21 percent to 11 percent by the end of 1998, and to further halve it to 5.5 percent by the end of 1999; and (3) to contain the current account deficit at 7.3 percent of GDP, while maintaining gross official reserves at 2.7 months of imports. These objectives were to be achieved through an improvement in tax collection and the introduction of a value-added tax in December 1998, an intensification of tax reform, and tighter control over the money supply. Under the program of structural reform, the government would further deregulate the petroleum and cocoa sectors, and aggressively pursue its divestiture program, liberalize the financial sector, and reform the civil service and autonomous government agencies. Under the government's social programs, priority would be given to education, health, and roads.

On 23 March 1998, the Fund approved a second annual loan under the ESAF, in an amount equivalent to SDR 82.2 million. The loan was augmented by SDR 27.4 million (about $37 million) at the authorities' request, by rephasing the remaining amount available under the three-year loan program. The commitment period of the three-year ESAF arrangement was also by one full year to 29 June 1999.

The Fund approved an additional three-year load for Ghana under the ESAF, equivalent to SDR 155 million in May 1999. The loan was to be disbursed in seven installments over the period 1999–2001. This loan approval came in light of the significant progress Ghana had achieved in reducing macroeconomic imbalances and implementing structural reforms in 1997 and 1998. Thus, the main objectives of the 1999–2001 program were to consolidate further the progress made in macroeconomic stability and accelerate the pace of structural reform. The main objectives of the 1999 program were to obtain real GDP growth of 5.5 percent, end-of-period inflation of 9 percent, an external current account deficit, including grants, of about 2.5 percent of GDP, and gross official reserves equivalent to three months of imports. To achieve these objectives, domestic budget financing would be limited to about 2.8 percent of GDP and to bring the primary domestic balance to a surplus of about 3.5 percent of GDP. Monetary growth in 1999 would be geared toward supporting inflation and balance of payments objectives.

In November 1999, the ESAF was renamed the **poverty reduction and growth facility (PRGF)**. The Ghanaian government's agenda for poverty alleviation over the period 2002–2004 was set forth in the Ghana Poverty Reduction Strategy. On 28 June 2001, Fund and the World Bank's International Development Association agreed that Ghana had taken the necessary steps to reach its completion point under the enhanced **heavily indebted poor countries** initiative. Ghana thus became the fourteenth country to secure relief from its creditors, amounting to about $3.5 billion, under this initiative.

In reviewing Ghana's progress at that time, the **Executive Board** noted that the proportion of Ghana's population living in poverty had fallen steadily from 51 percent in 1992 to 39 percent in 2000, the country had achieved a fairly stable overall macroeconomic environment, and real GDP growth had accelerated from 3.7 percent in 2000 to 5.2 percent in 2003. Nevertheless, it was clear that the challenge of achieving long-term debt sustainability and sustained growth would require continued and fiscal vigilance and steadfast reforms.

On 27 October 2006, the Executive Board completed the sixth and final review of Ghana's economic performance under the PRGF arrangement.

However, it noted that further structural reforms efforts were needed to support efficiency and growth prospects. It also called for efforts to strengthen transparency and economic governance, which would contribute to the efficient use of resources—including those from debt relief—in line with the government's poverty reduction strategy.

On 16 July 2009, the Executive Board approved a new three-year arrangement under the PRGF for Ghana in an amount equivalent to SDR 387.45 million. In doing so, **Executive Directors** noted that Ghana's macroeconomic conditions had deteriorated substantially during 2008, reflecting global shocks to food and fuel prices and highly expansionary fiscal policies. Inflation had risen to about 20 percent and the current account deficit had widened appreciably, putting pressure on Ghana's **international reserves** and the **exchange rate**. Growth was projected to moderate in 2009, with potential additional downside risks stemming from the global recession.

In the period since 2000, growth had been supported by significant debt relief, which had provided the country with fiscal space to invest in infrastructure, and the social sectors. Thanks to the combination of higher growth, declining inflation and improved social spending, poverty levels had significantly declined, and Ghana was poised to achieve the **Millennium Development Goal** of halving extreme poverty by 2015. Nevertheless, fiscal performance had deteriorated sharply, partly due to a severe energy crisis in 2006–2007 and the global food and fuel crisis in 2008, but also importantly due to highly expansionary fiscal policies ahead of the end-2008 presidential elections. As a consequence, the fiscal deficit had jumped from 9.2 percent of GDP in 2007 to 14.5 percent in 2008.

In this context, the government's medium-term macroeconomic program was aimed at substantially reducing Ghana's large fiscal imbalances by 2011 and put in place strengthened institutions for public financial management. Toward this end, the macroeconomic framework for 2009–2011 was set to achieve: a real non-oil GDP growth of about 5.5 percent, a medium-term inflation rate of 7–9 percent per year, an overall budget deficit of 4.5 percent of GDP in 2011, and international reserves coverage equal to about three months of imports.

On 11 November 2009, the Fund announced that Ghana would be the site of a second **African Regional Technical Assistance Center** (**AFRITAC** West 2). AFRITAC West 2 will serve six countries (Cape Verde, The Gambia, Ghana, Nigeria, Liberia, and Sierra Leone). These countries despite their differences, face broadly similar macroeconomic policy challenges and capacity building needs. Commodities, minerals, and agriculture feature prominently in the aggregate output, and exports and fiscal revenues of most of them make sustainable management of resources a priority. At least a quarter of the population in these countries live below the poverty line and almost all of them rank in the lowest quartile of the UN Human Development Index. Technical assistance by AFRITAC West 2 will focus on tax and customs policy and administration, public financial management, financial sector regulation and supervision, public debt markets, and macroeconomic statistics.

GLOBAL FINANCIAL CRISIS. Also known as "the Great Recession," the global financial crisis that began in 2008 represents the most significant global downturn since the **Bretton Woods Conference** in 1944. Likened to "the perfect storm" by the Fund's **Managing Director**, **Domique Strauss-Kahn**, the crisis emerged in an environment characterized by a prolonged period of strong global growth, increased capital flows, low interest rates, and a breakdown of financial regulation and supervision. Fueled by the bubble in the U.S. housing market, financial institutions and other market participants lowered their lending standards in search of higher yields. At the same time, weak underwriting standards, unsound risk management practices, increasingly complex and opaque financial products, and consequent excessive leverage combined to create vulnerabilities in the system. The collapse of the global housing bubble, which had peaked in 2006, caused the values of securities tied to real estate to plummet.

The global crisis originated in the United States when the investment bank, Lehman Brothers, folded and the U.S. government intervened to rescue its financial sector. However, the problem quickly spread throughout the U.S. economy as difficulties related to bank solvency and credit availability eroded consumer confidence. Soon thereafter, global stock markets began to suffer unprecedented losses. As deleveraging cascaded across the global financial system, liquid assets were devalued, credit lines were slashed, and equity prices fell sharply. Even emerging markets and **developing countries** with only limited exposure to the U.S. subprime mortgage market were devastated as a result of falling commodity prices, weak export demand, dwindling flows of bank-related financing, and volatile exchange markets. Worldwide industrial production and merchandise trade plummeted in late 2008 and early 2009 as a result of a global credit crunch.

Despite the efforts of governments and central banks to respond rapidly with unprecedented fiscal stimulus packages, monetary policy expansion, and institutional bailouts, global GDP fell by 6.25 percent in the last quarter of 2008, and this trend continued through the first quarter of 2009. The fallout from the crisis had a profound effect on output and employment across the globe, but especially in countries with preexisting external vulnerabilities.

Among the emerging markets, the crisis took the form of a sudden stop in capital inflows, which added to the strains from the collapse in global activity and commodity prices. During the period September 2008 to July 2009, the Fund approved **stand-by arrangements** for 10 members in Europe and the CIS (Commonwealth of Independent States) region, including Armenia, Belarus, Bosnia and Herzegovina, Georgia, Hungary, Iceland, Latvia, Romania, Serbia, and Ukraine; two countries in Asia: Pakistan and Mongolia; as well as precautionary arrangements for Costa Rica, El Salvador, and Guatemala.

Compared with previous crisis scenarios, the financing packages arranged in the context of the 2008–2009 crisis were more timely and included more frontloading. Adherence to program **conditionality**, which was more focused than in previous cases, was also much stronger. The stance of fiscal policy was accommodative and adjusted to evolving conditions, in particular to ensure adequate spending on social safety nets and to avoid currency overshooting. Fiscal deficits were allowed to rise in response to falling revenues and, in cases in which domestic and external financing was lacking, this was facilitated by channeling Fund **resources** directly to the budget. In many instances, however, underlying concerns about debt sustainability and weak structural fiscal positions required limiting the full play of automatic stabilizers. Over time, the programs envisaged stronger structural reforms aimed at securing long-term fiscal sustainability.

In November 2008, the **Group of Twenty (G-20)** held its first leaders meeting in Washington, D.C., to formulate a response to the global economic crisis. The meeting was attended by heads of state and government of the members along with the Secretary-General of the **United Nations**, the President of the **World Bank**, the **Managing Director** of the Fund, and the Chair of the Financial Stability Forum (later reconstituted at the London Summit as the Financial Stability Board). This plan was reviewed and revised at two subsequent summit meetings held in London in April 2009 and Pittsburg in September 2009. In the context of these meetings, members of the G-20 agreed to coordinate policies aimed at strengthening transparency and accountability; enhancing sound regulation; promoting integrity in financial markets; reinforcing international cooperation; and reforming the international financial institutions. In this context, members of the G-20 endorsed a substantial increase in the financial resources available to the Fund, including a new increase in **quotas** and an expansion of the **New Arrangements to Borrow** by up to $600 billion, and a strengthening of its role in crisis prevention.

By the time the 2009 **annual meetings** took place, the world economy was showing early signs of recovery, led by strong performance of the Asian economies and a rebound in manufacturing. Global growth was projected to reach 3 percent in 2010 and average just above 4 percent over the period 2010–2014. Nevertheless, the pace of recovery was expected to be slow and uneven, as financial and corporate restructuring would continue to suppress economic activity and the need for both countries and households to rebuild savings would likely continue to dampen demand.

GLOBAL FINANCIAL STABILITY REPORT (GFSR). The GFSR replaced the International Capital Markets Report and the report on Emerging Market Financing in August 2001, as the main instrument of global financial market surveillance. The GFSR is prepared and published semiannually to provide timely and comprehensive coverage of both mature and emerging financial markets. Its main objectives are to identify potential vulnerabilities in the international financial system from a multilateral perspective and to analyze linkages between developments in mature financial centers and capital flows to emerging markets. Through the **Capital Markets Consultative Group**, the staff maintains a dialogue with representatives of private financial institutions on issues related to the operation of international capital markets, such as the development of investor relations programs and the promotion of standards and codes.

Like the ***World Economic Outlook***, GFSR reports are supplemented with regular informal **Executive Board** discussions on world economic and market developments and financial market updates. These sessions typically focus on recent developments, the near-term outlook, and policy implications.

GLOBAL MONITORING REPORT (GMR). The GMR is an annual report that assesses progress toward implementing the policies and actions needed to achieve the **Millennium Development Goals** and related outcomes. It is produced jointly by the **World Bank** and the Fund, in collaboration with other international partners.

GOLD. Referred to by central bankers and bullion brokers as "the metal," gold played a central role in the international monetary system established at **Bretton Woods**. It was the common denominator of the **par value system**, and the value of each **currency** had to be expressed in terms of the fixed, official price of gold or in terms of the U.S. dollar, which had a fixed valuation in terms of gold of the weight and fineness in effect on July 1, 1944. The United States maintained the gold value of the U.S. dollar by undertaking to buy and sell gold freely for officially held U.S. dollars. The **Special Drawing Right**, which had been introduced into the international monetary system under the first amendment to the **Articles** in 1968, was also initially defined in terms of gold. Gold was thus the primary **reserve asset** of the international monetary system, as it had been in the nineteenth century.

Originally, members had to pay one-fourth of their **subscriptions** to the Fund in gold (or, as an authorized exception, in U.S. dollars). This led to the concepts of the **gold tranche** and **credit tranches**, which set a basic framework for the use of the Fund's **resources**. The second amendment to the Articles of Agreement (1978) eliminated gold from the Fund's operations and transactions, provided for the sale of a portion of the Fund's gold holdings, and envisioned a gradual reduction in the role of gold in the international monetary system.

Nevertheless, gold remains an important asset in the reserve holdings of a number of countries, and the Fund is one of the largest official holders of gold in the world. Consistent with the new income model for the Fund agreed in April 2008, on 18 September 2009, the **Executive Board** approved **gold sales** strictly limited to 403.3 metric tons, representing one-eighth of the Fund's total holdings of gold. Resources accrued from these gold sales will also help boost the Fund's concessional lending capacity. *See also* GOLD AUCTIONS; GOLD POOL; REFORM OF THE INTERNATIONAL MONETARY SYSTEM.

GOLD, SIR JOSEPH (1912–2000). Sir Joseph Gold was a member of the Fund's Legal Department from October 1946 to July 1979. He was Director of the Legal Department from 1960 to 1979 and was also given the title of **General Counsel** in 1966. Sir Joseph represented the **Managing Director** at the meetings of the Deputies of the **Group of Ten** and accompanied the Managing Director to the ministerial meetings of the Group. He was responsible for advising the Managing Director on a wide range of topics and for making many innovative proposals. He played a major role in drafting the first amendment to the **Articles of Agreement** and was the principal drafter of the second amendment.

Upon his retirement, Sir Joseph was appointed to the position of Senior Consultant in the Fund. He was knighted by the Queen of England in 1980. Sir Joseph has published numerous books and articles on the Fund and international monetary law and has contributed greatly to the development of international law in the fields of money and finance. Sir Joseph was a major influence in molding the shape and influence of the Fund over its first 50 years.

GOLD AND FOREIGN EXCHANGE RESERVES. *See* INTERNATIONAL RESERVES.

GOLD AUCTIONS. The Fund held 45 **gold** auctions between 1976 and 1980, selling a total of 23.52 million ounces of gold at prices ranging from $108.76 an ounce in September 1976 to $718.01 an ounce in February 1980, for a total profit of $4.6 billion. The auctions were held in accordance with an agreement reached in the **Interim Committee** in August 1975, whereby it was agreed that one-sixth (25 million ounces) of the Fund's gold holdings should be sold for the benefit of the **developing countries** and another sixth should be "restituted" (distributed) to members.

Because under its **Articles of Agreement** then in effect, the Fund could sell its gold only to members with creditor positions in the Fund, only at the official price, and only to replenish its holdings of a member's **currency**, it was necessary to adopt a circuitous, but legal, method of auctioning the gold. Thus, the gold was sold at the official price to creditor members, who then resold the gold, also at the official price, to the **Trust Fund**. The Fund conducted the auctions on behalf of the Trust Fund, the proceeds of which were held by the Trust Fund and made available to a selected group of least developed countries under agreed upon **adjustment programs**. *See also* RESTITUTION.

GOLD MARKETS. *See* GOLD POOL.

GOLD POOL. The gold pool was formed in 1961 by the central banks of Belgium, France, Germany, Italy, the Netherlands, Switzerland, the United Kingdom, and the United States to intervene in the London gold market to keep the price of **gold** at its official level. The London market was the leading gold bullion market, and by keeping the price of gold at its official price in the London market, the authorities were able to keep the price in other markets, in Europe and elsewhere, in line.

In 1967 and in 1968, following the **devaluation** of the pound sterling and a continuing deficit in the U.S. **balance of payments**, a sharp loss of confidence in the U.S. dollar ensued and the demand for gold became so great that the market had to be closed. The gold pool arrangements were brought to an end in March 1968, when the eight central banks participating in the arrangements announced that they would continue official sales and purchases at the official rate, but that the price of gold in private transactions would henceforth be determined by supply and demand. The announcement ushered in a two-tier market for gold that lasted until the eight central banks that had formed the gold pool agreed that they would be free to sell gold from their official reserves in the private markets.

GOLD SALES BY THE FUND. The Fund had substantial holdings of gold, amounting to about 96.6 million ounces (3,005.3 metric tons) at the end of January 2010. As of 1 February 2010, its total gold holdings were valued at about $105.0 billion based on current market prices. The Fund acquired most of its gold holdings as a result of its original **Articles** requiring members to pay 25 percent of their **subscriptions** to the Fund in gold. It was from this provision that the concept of the **gold tranche** originated. In addition to these gold payment subscriptions, the Fund also accumulated gold as a result of the provision requiring members to pay **charges** in gold.

Until the second amendment to the **Articles of Agreement** (1978) came into effect, the Fund regularly sold gold to replenish its holdings of **currencies** that were in demand and in short supply. **Borrowings** from participants in the **General Arrangements to Borrow** were also often accompanied by sales of gold to participants that were lending resources to the Fund, seemingly to compensate them for lending the Fund their currencies. In 1976–1980, the Fund reduced its gold holdings by one-third (50 million ounces), half through a series of sales by **gold auctions** and half through **restitution** to members.

In December 1999, the **Executive Board** authorized off-market transactions in gold of up to 14 million ounces to help finance the Fund's participation in the **heavily indebted poor countries (HIPC)** initiative. Between December 1999 and April 2000, separate but closely linked transactions involving a total of 12.9 million ounces of gold were carried out with Brazil and Mexico. In the first step, the Fund sold gold to the member at the prevailing market price and the profits were placed in a special account invested for the benefit of the HIPC initiative. In the second step, the Fund immediately accepted back, at the same market price, the same amount of gold from the member in settlement of that member's financial obligations. In the end, these transactions left the balance of the Fund's holdings of physical gold unchanged.

As a key step in moving to the Fund's new income model, on 18 September 2009, the Executive Board approved the sale of 403.3 metric tons of gold (12.97 million ounces), which amounts to one-eighth of the Fund's total holdings of gold.

To avoid any disruption of the gold market, the Executive Board adopted specific modalities for gold sales by the Fund, as follows:

- Sales should be strictly limited to the amount of gold that the Fund has acquired since the second amendment of the **Articles of Agreement** (12,965,649 fine troy ounces or 403.3 metric tons, which represent one-eighth of the Fund's total holdings).
- The Fund's gold sales should not add to the announced volume of sales from official sources.
- The scope for sales of gold to one or more official holders should be explored. This would be advantageous because such transactions would redistribute official gold holdings without changing total official holdings. There would also be the practical advantage that the Fund could

receive sales proceeds earlier, thereby beginning to generate income from an endowment sooner.

- Absent sufficient interest from other official holders to purchase gold directly from the Fund, phased on-market sales would represent the most appropriate modality for potential gold sales. This would follow the approach adopted successfully over a number of years by current Central Bank Gold Agreement participants.
- A strong governance and control framework, together with a high degree of transparency, would be essential for gold sales conducted by the Fund. A clear, transparent communications strategy, including regular external reporting on sales, should be adopted, in order to assure markets that the gold sales are being conducted in a responsible manner.

GOLD TRANCHE. This term originated under the **Bretton Woods system** and was replaced after the second amendment to the **Articles of Agreement** by the **reserve tranche**. Under the original Articles, a member normally paid one-fourth of its **subscription** in **gold** and three-fourths in its own **currency**. In accordance with the Articles, the **Executive Board** took a number of decisions, dating from 1952, framing the tranche policies: (1) a member could purchase currencies that it desired (usually U.S. dollars) up to the point where the Fund's **holdings** of its currency reached 100 percent of its **quota**—that is, a member could purchase the equivalent of its gold tranche virtually without **conditionality**; and (2) a member may normally have total **purchases** outstanding from the Fund up to the point where the Fund's holding of that member's currency did not exceed 200 percent of quota. A member's gold tranche was the difference between the Fund's holding of a member's currency and its quota. If a member's currency is purchased (drawn) by other members, its gold tranche (reserve tranche) increases correspondingly. After the first amendment to the Articles the gold tranche became a floating facility, and after the second amendment it was renamed the *reserve tranche* and could be drawn upon without challenge.

GOOD GOVERNANCE. The declaration of *Partnership for Sustainable Global Growth*, which was adopted by the **Interim Committee** at its meeting in Washington on 29 September 1996, identified "promoting good governance in all its aspects, including ensuring the rule of law, improving efficiency and accountability of the public sector, and tackling corruption" as an essential element of a framework within which economies can prosper. The Fund's **Executive Board** then met a number of times to develop guidance on the issue and adopted in July 1997 a Guidance Note. The guidelines seek to promote greater attention by the Fund to governance issues, in particular through:

1. A more comprehensive treatment, in the context of both Article IV consultations and Fund-supported programs, of those governance issues within the mandate and expertise of the Fund
2. A more proactive approach in advocating policies and the development of institutions and administrative systems that eliminate the opportunity for bribery, corruption, and fraudulent activity in the management of public resources
3. An evenhanded treatment of governance issues in all member countries
4. Enhanced collaboration with other multilateral institutions, in particular the **World Bank**, to make better use of complementary areas of expertise

The guidelines seek to set boundaries for the Fund's involvement and specify that since the Fund is primarily concerned with macroeconomic stability, external viability, and orderly economic growth in member countries, the Fund's contribution to good governance arises principally in two spheres:

1. Improving the management of public resources through reforms covering public sector institutions (e.g., the treasury, central bank, public enterprises, civil service, and offices of official statistics), including administrative procedures (e.g., expenditure control, budget management, and revenue collection)
2. Supporting the development and maintenance of a transparent and stable economic and regulatory environment conducive to efficient private sector activities (e.g., price systems, exchange and trade regimes, and banking systems and their related regulations)

The guidelines stress that the Fund does not have a mandate to adopt an investigative role in member countries, but that the staff should address governance issues, including instances of corruption, on the basis of economic considerations within its mandate. This would involve an assessment of whether poor governance would have an impact on macroeconomic performance and the government's ability to pursue appropriate and agreed-upon economic policies, taking into account the need to safeguard the use of the Fund's **resources.** It is recognized, however, that there are practical limitations to the ability of the staff to identify deficiencies in governance, and it is proposed that the staff should urge governments to adopt greater transparency in their operations, so as to help build private sector confidence in government policies. In this regard, the Fund's **technical assistance** should contribute to improving transparency and the economic aspects of good governance. Finally, the staff was asked to keep abreast of activities in partner organizations and specific efforts in member countries to address governance issues.

To promote and ensure the integrity of its own organization, in June 1998, the Fund adopted a number of rules and regulations to ensure ethical conduct and prevent corruption among its staff, reflected in the Code of Conduct for Staff. These rules are bolstered by extensive financial certification and disclosure requirements, all subject to disciplinary sanctions in case of violations. On 14 July 2000, the Fund adopted a separate, but similar, **Code of Conduct for Members of the Executive Board** who, unlike the staff, are not subject to the authority of the **Managing Director**, as they are appointed or elected by member states.

GOVERNORS, BOARD OF. *See* BOARD OF GOVERNORS.

GREECE. Among the countries hardest hit by the **global financial crisis**, the Greek economy had suffered from lingering vulnerabilities dating back to its entry into the euro area. Throughout the period 2000–2008, Greece had taken advantage of access to low-cost credit to boost domestic demand and pursue procyclical fiscal policies, with tax cuts and increased spending on wages and entitlements. In 2009, output dropped by 2 percent and election-driven and partially unreported spending, amid weak overall expenditure control, worsened the fiscal deficit to 13.6 percent of GDP, straining Greece's ability to fund itself in the market. Greece's financial crisis was spurred when a significant revision to the 2008 and 2009 fiscal deficit data shocked markets. The revision entailed an increase in public debt from below 100 percent of GDP to 115 percent of GDP and revealed misreporting of official statistics. There was also evidence of significant domestic demand inflation and external competitiveness problems. When the new fiscal deficit and public debt data were revealed, markets reacted by increasing spreads on Greek bonds and lowering credit ratings. Concerns about fiscal sustainability quickly deepened, and market sentiment further eroded. Foreign funding dried up and spreads on government paper took off, threatening the banking system and the economy at large with a downward spiral of unfolding risks.

On 9 May 2010, the Fund approved a €30 billion three-year **Stand-by Arrangement** for Greece as part of a joint European Union–Fund €110 billion financing package to help the country ride out its debt crisis, revive growth, and modernize the economy. This package entailed exceptional access to Fund **resources**, amounting to more than 3,200 percent of quota, and was approved under the **Emergency Financing Mechanism** procedures. The underlying reform program focused sharply on fiscal consolidation measures, amounting to 11 percent of GDP over the three-year program period, including budget cuts, a freeze in wages and pensions, deep cuts in military expenditures, and tax increases. The program also included significant reforms designed to strengthen Greece's competitiveness and revive stalled economic growth.

GROUP OF EIGHT. The **Russian Federation** was invited to join the annual summit meetings of the **Group of Seven** in 1998 and fully participated in the meetings for the first time in May of that year, when the group met in Birmingham, England.

GROUP OF FIVE. This group consisted of France, Germany, Japan, the United Kingdom, and the United States, but subsequently evolved into the **Group of Seven** with the addition of Canada and Italy.

GROUP OF NINE. During the 1960s, especially in connection with the establishment of the **Special Drawing Rights** facility, the nine **Executive Directors** elected by the **developing countries** in the Fund used to meet informally to discuss their common problems and objectives. Subsequently, additional Executive Directors were appointed or elected to an enlarged Board—Saudi Arabia in the 1970s, China in the 1980s, and Russia and Switzerland in the 1990s.

GROUP OF SEVEN. Consists of seven industrial countries—Canada, France, Germany, Italy, Japan, the United Kingdom, the United States—and was an expansion of the **Group of Five**, with the addition of Canada and Italy. The leaders of these countries have had annual economic summit meetings since 1974. Their discussions and decisions are important for continued cooperation among the major **industrial nations** of the world, and often set the agenda for the **Group of Ten** meetings, the meetings of the **Interim Committee** (now the **International Monetary and Financial Committee**), and the Fund itself. Beginning in 1998, the **Russia Federation** was invited to attend the annual summit meetings of the group, making it a **Group of Eight**.

Meeting in Bonn on 20 February 1999, the group endorsed a proposal to establish a "financial stability forum." The forum would meet regularly and establish more formal coordination among finance ministers, central bankers, and other financial regulators to more effectively promote international financial stability, improve the functioning of markets, and reduce systemic risk. The forum will initially include only the Group of Seven countries, but over time it is envisaged additional national authorities would be included in the process.

GROUP OF SEVENTY-SEVEN. This group of countries emerged from the United Nations Conference on Trade and Development held in 1964, when the **developing countries** joined together to defend and promote their common interests. Subsequently, the number of developing countries in the group increased to over 100.

GROUP OF TEN. The group consists of the 10 member countries that agreed to participate in the **General Arrangements to Borrow** established in 1962. These countries are Belgium, Canada, France, Germany, Italy, Japan, the Netherlands, Sweden, the United Kingdom, and the United States. The group played a prominent role in shaping the **Special Drawing Rights** facility established by the first amendment to the Fund's **Articles of Agreement** and in the provisions of the second amendment, establishing the post–Bretton Woods **international monetary system**. The group, made up of the principal industrial countries, is a dominating influence in international monetary negotiations and has tended to spawn counter groups from developing countries. *See* GROUP OF SEVENTY-SEVEN; GROUP OF THIRTY-ONE; GROUP OF TWENTY-FOUR.

GROUP OF THIRTY-ONE. In 1966, **developing countries** briefly got together to put forward their views as to how the **international monetary system** should evolve, particularly in connection with the problem of the adequacy of **international liquidity**. The activity of the group was provoked by discussions in the **Group of Ten** proposing that a scheme to create **international reserves** should be confined to the leading industrial nations.

GROUP OF TWENTY (G-20). The G-20, made up of Finance Ministers and Central Bank Governors, was established in 1999 to bring together systemically important industrial and developing countries to discuss key issues in the global economy. The inaugural meeting of the G-20, hosted by the German and Canadian finance ministers, was held in Berlin, Germany, in December 1999. The G-20 currently serves as a major forum for discussions on matters related to international economic development and global economic stability. Its mandate is to support growth and development across the globe by contributing to a strengthening of the international financial architecture and providing opportunities for dialogue on national policies, international cooperation, and international financial institutions.

GROUP OF TWENTY-FOUR. An intergovernmental Group of Twenty-Four on International Monetary Affairs was set up in 1971, in part to have a counterbody to the **Group of Ten**. The group consists of 24 Finance Ministers or senior monetary or financial authorities, 8 appointed by the African, 8 by the Asian, and 8 by the Latin American members of the **Group of Seventy-Seven**. Although the group is formally limited to 24 members, in practice any member of the Group of Seventy-Seven can attend its meetings as an observer, and the People's Republic of China enjoys the status of "Special Invitee" and can address the plenary sessions of the Group. The group played an active role in discussions regarding the **reform of the international monetary system**, and in the final phase of those negotiations it held two joint, informal sessions with the **Executive Board** of the Fund. In addition to helping to shape the reformed system, the group is credited with having been responsible for promoting several innovations within the Fund and elsewhere. It remains an active body, and meets regularly, usually twice a year at the time that the Group of Ten meets.

GROUP OF TWENTY-TWO. This group consists of finance ministers and central bank governors of the **Group of Seven** plus those of 15 emerging **developing countries**—**Argentina**, Australia, Brazil, Canada, China, France, Germany, **Hong Kong SAR**, India, **Indonesia**, Italy, Japan, **Korea**, **Malaysia**, **Mexico**, Poland, **Russia**, Singapore, South Africa, **Thailand**, the United Kingdom, and the **United States**. The group met in April 1998 to examine issues related to strengthening the international financial architecture. The initiative was intended to complement ongoing efforts in the Fund, the **World Bank**, and other international institutions and fora and to help develop a broad international consensus on these important issues. At this meeting, three working groups were established on enhancing transparency and accountability, on strengthening financial systems, and on international financial crises. Each working group comprised representatives from finance ministries and central banks of countries in the Group of Seven, as well as those from developed and emerging market economies; international organizations were also invited to participate in the discussions; and contributions and views were sought from other international groups, countries not represented in the working groups, and the private sector.

Meeting for a second time, in October 1998, the group received the reports prepared by the working groups on the outcome of their discussions. The report of the working group on enhancing transparency and accountability attached particular importance to enhancing the relevance, reliability, comparability, and understandability of information disclosed by the private sector and recommended that priority be given to compliance with and enforcement of high-quality accounting standards. It agreed on the need to improve coverage, frequency, and timeliness with which data on **foreign exchange** reserves, external debt, and financial sector soundness were published. Furthermore, it recommended that consideration be given to compiling and publishing data on the international exposures of investment banks, hedge funds, and other institutional investors. Stressing the importance of transparency, the report recommended that international financial institutions adopt a presumption in favor of the release of information, except where release might compromise a well-defined need for confidentiality. It also emphasized the importance of being transparent about transparency and recommended that the Fund prepare a transparency report summarizing the extent to which an economy meets internationally recognized disclosure standards.

The report of the working group on strengthening financial systems identified several areas—corporate governance, risk management (including liquidity management), and safety net arrangements—where standards for sound practices needed to be enhanced and developed. It recognized that cooperation and coordination among national supervisors and regulators and international groups and organizations were crucial to the strengthening of domestic financial systems and set out several options for enhancing international cooperation, such as the establishment of a Financial Sector Policy Forum that would meet periodically to discuss financial sector issues.

The report of the working group on international financial crises stressed the need to encourage better management risk by the public and private sectors, and it recommended that governments limit the scope and clarify the design of guarantees that they offer. Effective insolvency and debtor–creditor regimes were identified as important means of limiting financial crises and facilitating rapid and orderly workouts from excessive indebtedness. The report urged countries to make the strongest possible efforts to meet the terms and conditions of all debt contracts in full and on time. Unilateral suspensions of debt payments were inherently disruptive and the report proposed a framework to promote the collective interest of debtors and creditors in cooperative and orderly debt workouts, with principles that could guide the resolution of future international financial crises. The working group added that its report should not be considered an agenda for addressing problems that were currently being experienced in many emerging markets.

The reports were forwarded to the Fund and other international financial organizations for further consideration and were published on the Fund's website. The initiative to bring together systemically important industrial and developing countries was institutionalized by the creation of the Group of Twenty in 1999. *See also* GROUP OF TWENTY.

GULF COOPERATION COUNCIL (GCC). Originally established on 25 May 1981 as a free-trade area comprising six member states—Bahrain, Kuwait, Oman, Qatar, Saudi Arabia, and the United Arab Emirates—the GCC was launched as a common market on 1 January 2008. At that time, its member states agreed to further advance economic integration and to put in place a Common Market and Economic and Monetary Union by 2010. Since 2003, the GCC member countries have pegged their currencies to the U.S. dollar, and they plan to maintain this parity at least until the GCC Monetary Union comes into effect.

GUTT, CAMILLE (1884–1971). Camille Gutt, of Belgium, was the Fund's first **Managing Director**, from 1946 to 1951. Before taking up his appointment with the Fund, he served in the Belgium government as Minister of State and Finance Minister.

H

HEAVILY INDEBTED POOR COUNTRIES (HIPCs). In September 1996, the **Managing Director** of the Fund and the President of the **World Bank** submitted to the **Interim Committee** and the **Development Committee** a joint report on a Program of Action to Resolve the debt problems of the HIPCs. The report included a proposed initiative to address the problems of HIPCs that followed sound policies, but for which traditional debt-relief mechanisms were inadequate to secure a **sustainable external debt** position over the medium term. The Committees endorsed the report and requested the implementation of the program.

The key features of the HIPC initiative were as follows: The initiative would be open to all members that were eligible to use the **enhanced structural adjustment facility (ESAF)** and the resources of the International Development Association (IDA), that is the poorest countries eligible to receive concessional loans from IDA.

Eligibility: The Boards of the Fund and the World Bank would decide on a country's eligibility typically after three years of strong performance under adjustment and reform programs supported by the World Bank and the Fund (the first stage). To qualify for exceptional assistance under the program, countries would have to face an unsustainable debt situation at the completion point after the full application of traditional debt-relief mechanisms and reform. This completion point would be reached after a successful second three-year period of adjustment and reform (the second stage). This six-year performance period would be implemented on a case-by-case basis, with countries receiving credit for programs that were already underway.

Debt Sustainability: The objective would be to bring a country's debt burden to sustainable levels, subject to satisfactory policy performance. This was defined as when the ratio of the net present value of a country's debt to exports was below the range of 200 to 250 percent and its debt service was below 20 to 25 percent of the value of its exports.

The First Stage: The program would build on the existing mechanisms for providing debt relief, including those of the **Paris Club**, which in December 1994, at a meeting in Naples, raised its rescheduling target to afford a 67 percent reduction in the net present value of eligible debt. During this first three-year period, countries would need to establish a track record of good performance.

Possible Country Situation: At the end of the first stage, the Fund and the World Bank would prepare an analysis of the country's situation to determine whether all the efforts made by the country itself, the Paris Club, other supporting institutions, and its creditors were sufficient to put the country into a sustainable debt position in the following three years. In the event that the efforts were sufficient (i.e., that the debt situation would be sustainable without further relief), the country would not be eligible for the program.

The Second Stage: For countries deemed eligible for support under the program, all creditors would commit at the decision point to provide the relief necessary to attain the targeted debt ratios in support of the country's continued reform efforts.

Action at the Completion Point: The Paris Club would provide a reduction in debt stock of up to 80 percent in present value terms on eligible debt, and comparable reductions would be sought from other bilateral official and commercial debtors, with the multilateral institutions also participating, but, at the same time, preserving their preferred creditor status.

Action by All Creditors: All creditors would be expected to participate in providing the exceptional assistance needed by the country to reach debt sustainability.

The Fund's Participation: The participation of the Fund in the program was to be through special ESAF operations and would take the form of a reduction in the present value of the Fund's claims on a country.

Use of Fund Reserves: It was agreed that if the need should arise, the Fund would have to be prepared to use its **reserves** to secure full financing under the program, and consideration would be given to the sale of up to five million ounces of the Fund's **gold** for this purpose. Not all Board members were in favor of such use of the Fund's gold reserves and it was further understood that only the proceeds from investments of the profits from such sales would be used to contribute to the financing of the debt reduction.

First Country Case: In April 1997, the Fund **Executive Board** approved **Uganda's** eligibility for assistance under the HIPC initiative, with an envisaged completion point one year later. The shortening of the second stage to one year was recognized as being exceptional, reflecting Uganda's success in implementing policies under previous Fund-supported programs.

In 1999, a comprehensive review of the Initiative allowed the Fund to provide faster, deeper, and broader debt relief and strengthened the links between debt relief, poverty reduction, and social policies.

In 2005, the HIPC Initiative was supplemented by the **Multilateral Debt Relief Initiative (MDRI)** to help further progress toward the achievement of the UN **Millennium Development Goals**. The MDRI allows for 100 percent relief on eligible debts by three multilateral institutions—the Fund, the World Bank, and the African Development Fund—when countries complete the HIPC process. In 2007, the Inter-American Development Bank decided to provide additional ("beyond HIPC") debt relief to the five eligible countries located in the Western Hemisphere.

As of 1 July 2009, 40 countries had qualified for, or were considered eligible or potentially eligible for assistance under the HIPC Initiative. These include:

	Post-Completion-Point Countries (26)	
Benin	Guyana	Niger
Bolivia	Haiti	Rwanda
Burkina Faso	Honduras	São Tomé & Príncipe
Burundi	Madagascar	Senegal
Cameroon	Malawi	Sierra Leone
Central African Republic	Mali	Tanzania
Ethiopia	Mauritania	Uganda
The Gambia	Mozambique	Zambia
Ghana	Nicaragua	
	Interim Countries (Between Decision and Completion Point) (9)	
Afghanistan	Democratic Republic of the Congo	Guinea Bissau
Chad	Côte d'Ivoire	Liberia
Republic of Congo	Guinea	Togo
	Pre-Decision-Point Countries (5)	
Comoros	Kyrgyz Republic	Sudan
Eritrea	Somalia	

HEDGE FUNDS. Hedge funds are collective investment vehicles, often organized as private partnerships and resident offshore for tax and regulatory purposes. Their legal status places few restrictions on their portfolios and transactions and allows their managers freedom to use short sales, derivative securities, and leverage to raise returns and cushion risk. The **Asian financial crisis** led to the collapse of one of the largest, most leveraged, and, up to then, one of the most successful hedge funds. Its collapse, and the need for a bail-out, was thought to have exacerbated the international financial crisis and led authorities, bankers, and other lenders to consider whether such funds should be subject to greater surveillance. Similar calls for greater regulation of hedge funds abounded during the **global financial crisis** that began in 2008.

HOLDINGS BY THE FUND. The Fund's holdings consist of **currencies**, **gold**, and, since 1972, **Special Drawing Rights (SDRs)**. These holdings are derived from **subscription** payments by members, reflecting their **quotas** when they joined the Fund and subsequent increases in those quotas. In addition, the Fund's holdings are increased by **charges** and service fees on the use of its **resources**, less the cost of remunerating members holding creditor positions in the Fund and interest payments on SDRs.

HONG KONG SAR. The return of Hong Kong to the People's Republic of China took place on 1 July 1997. The terms of the transfer, which are embodied in the Basic Law, included the establishment of the Hong Kong Special Administrative Region (SAR). The Basic Law also provides for Hong Kong to have a considerable degree of autonomy over economic and other policies and includes a commitment to continue the existing free-market system for 50 years.

The Basic Law's requirements in the area of fiscal policy include the avoidance of fiscal deficits and the principle of keeping the budget commensurate with the growth rate of the GDP. The Basic Law also requires Hong Kong's **currency** to be fully backed by **foreign reserves**, and the **exchange rate** linked to the U.S. dollar under a currency board-type arrangement. At the end of December 1997, foreign currency assets totaled $92.8 billion.

The **Asian financial crisis** contributed to substantial volatility in the Hong Kong markets during 1997. Stock and property prices rose strongly during the first half of the year; by the middle of the year, property prices were a third higher than their trough in the second quarter of 1994, and the Hang Seng price index reached a historic peak in early August, having risen by around 50 percent during the previous 12 months. Spillovers from the regional turmoil caused the Hong Kong dollar to come under speculative attack in the latter half of 1997.

These pressures were successfully resisted by means of intervention in the **foreign exchange** market and a corresponding tightening of domestic liquidity. Nonetheless, higher interest rates, which resulted from spillovers from the financial turmoil in the region and the resultant pressures on the exchange rate, contributed to a substantial correction in stock and property markets. By the end of January 1998, the Hang Seng index was roughly 45 percent below its 1997 peak, and property prices appeared to have fallen by 15 to 20 percent on average since mid-1997. Pressure on the financial markets continued throughout the first nine months of 1998 and the markets continued to react with volatility, but the downward slide slowed markedly. Pressure on the currency remained strong, but a devaluation was resisted, with foreign exchange reserves strengthening somewhat over the year.

Reviewing Hong Kong SAR's situation in February 1998, the Fund's **Executive Directors** observed that, notwithstanding the recent turmoil in the region, developments during the previous year had been satisfactory in many respects. The handover had been achieved smoothly, and confidence in a continuation of the existing economic and legal framework had been maintained under the "one country, two systems" framework. Hong Kong SAR's solid fundamentals and decisive policy actions had helped it withstand the regional financial crisis and the bouts of speculative attacks. In particular, the Directors welcomed the stance taken by the government in allowing a prompt tightening of domestic monetary conditions under the linked exchange rate system to counter the pressures in the foreign exchange market.

The Directors agreed that the linked exchange rate system had provided an important anchor for economic stability since 1983 and that it played a vital role in demonstrating the commitment to an independent monetary and exchange rate policy in Hong Kong SAR and in maintaining confidence in its status as an international financial center.

In the wake of the Asian financial crisis, Directors commended the authorities for the firm, prudential regulatory oversight of the financial sector and for improvements in disclosure requirements. They welcomed the willingness of the authorities to allow weaker financial institutions to fail, in line with an overall noninterventionist approach to policies.

Hong Kong SAR was again severely affected by the recent global financial crisis, experiencing a sharp economic contraction in early 2009. In response to the crisis, the authorities took swift, broad-based policy actions, in particular through a sizeable fiscal stimulus package, coupled with accommodative monetary conditions. This decisive action facilitated a rapid turnaround, with growth expected to strengthen steadily and unemployment to decline in 2010.

During the 2009 Article IV consultation on 2 December 2009, Executive Directors welcomed the action taken by the Hong Kong SAR authorities. Nevertheless, they noted that the more positive outlook for the period ahead was subject to downside risks, including a weaker-than-expected recovery in Hong Kong SAR's major trading partners.

Directors noted that strong capital inflows and the resultant large liquidity overhang in the financial system could potentially lead to rapid credit growth, fueling asset markets and creating macroeconomic volatility. They welcomed the authorities' contingency strategy to preempt asset price bubbles as well as ongoing efforts to increase the availability of land. Directors noted that strict enforcement of the existing regulatory regime would be essential, while countervailing prudential measures could play a role in mitigating the credit–asset price cycle.

Directors welcomed the robustness of the Hong Kong banking system, which was the result of the banks' careful risk management and the authorities' vigilant, prudent regulation and enforcement. Hong Kong SAR, in coordination with Singapore and Malaysia, was well advanced in planning an exit from the blanket deposit guarantee, which has been instrumental in restoring confidence.

I

IMF INSTITUTE AND REGIONAL INSTITUTIONS. The IMF Institute (called "the Institute") was established in 1964 to provide training in economic management to officials of member countries. The training is delivered in Washington, D.C., as well as through seven regional training centers, which have been established in collaboration with other regional training institutions and national governments, and through a distance learning program. In addition to courses and seminars, the IMF Institute offers lecturing assistance to other training institutions and administers a scholarship program for PhD candidates in economics at North American universities.

In 1992, the Fund, working in collaboration with others established the Joint **Vienna Institute (JVI)** in Austria. Supported by two primary members (the IMF and Austria), four contributing members—the European Bank for Reconstruction and Development, the **International Bank for Reconstruction and Development**, the Organization for Economic Cooperation and Development, and the **World Trade Organization**—and other bilateral donor organizations, the JVI organizes courses for officials from new European Union member countries and officials of former centrally planned economies in Europe and Asia that are in transition to market-based systems.

The IMF Institute has a long-standing cooperative relationship with the regional training institutions in Francophone Africa, namely, the training centers of the Central Bank of West African States (West African Training Center for Banking Studies) and the Bank of Central African States. The Institute offers a yearly regional course on Financial Programming and Policies or External Sector Policies, as well as periodic lecturing assistance to the centers. The regional courses benefit from cofinancing from the United Nations Development Programme and the European Union. To respond to the growing need for training in Africa, the Institute helped establish in 1997 the nine-member Macroeconomic and Financial Management Institute of Eastern and Southern Africa in Zimbabwe and the West African Institute for Financial and Economic Management in Nigeria.

Since the 1970s, the IMF Institute has been assisting the South-East Asian Central Banks Research and Training Center (SEACEN) in Kuala Lumpur in the formulation and implementation of its training program. The Institute and SEACEN have offered joint courses since the 1980s. On 4 May 1998, the IMF–Singapore Regional Training Institute was established to offer training on policy-related economics to selected government officials, mainly from developing countries in the Asia and the Pacific region. Courses and seminars focus on macroeconomic adjustment and reform policies, financial programming, the problems of transition economies, monetary and exchange operations, public finance, banking supervision, and macroeconomic statistics.

The Institute has maintained a close relationship with the training branch of the Arab Monetary Fund and the Economic Policy Institute since its inception in 1988, and it has been cooperating with the Islamic Development Bank on regional training courses since 1994. The Institute has also worked with the Center for Latin American Monetary Studies for several years. *See also* ORGANIZATION OF THE FUND; TECHNICAL ASSISTANCE AND TRAINING.

INCOME AND EXPENDITURE OF THE FUND. The Fund aims to be financially self-sufficient, covering its expenditure from income, and providing for a prudent financial reserve.

Income is derived from and determined by its financial operations with members, including the extent of the use of the Fund's **resources**, the rate of interest on **Special Drawing Rights (SDRs)**, the rate of **remuneration** paid by the Fund to members, and the rate of charge on the use of the Fund's **general resources**. About 90 percent of the Fund's income is derived from charges on the use of the Fund's resources, and the remainder is derived from interest on the Fund's holdings of SDRs and service charges on purchases of **currency** from the Fund.

The Fund's current expenditures are made up of two categories: operational expenditures and administrative expenditures. Operational expenditures include mainly remuneration on creditor positions in the Fund and interest payments on the Fund's **borrowings**. Administrative expenses are all those expenditures covered in the Fund's **administrative budget**, which includes personnel expenditures and travel expenses.

The Fund's net income, which is defined as operational income minus operational and administrative expenditures, is either distributed to members or placed in reserve. As part of the effort to strengthen its financial position in the face of a substantial volume of **overdue obligations**, the Fund established **Special Contingency Accounts (SCA)** in 1987 and 1990. Total precautionary balances (reserves, plus the two Special Contingency Accounts—SCA-1 and SCA-2) amounted on 30 April 1998 to SDR 4 billion, equivalent to 8 percent of credit outstanding to member countries in the **General Resources Account** at that date. Financing of SCA-2, planned to amount to SDR 1 billion and to cover the risks associated with the **rights accumulation** programs, was completed in 1996–1997. In April 1998, the Board considered the level of the Fund's precautionary balances against the background of heavy use of its resources and decided to accelerate the rate of accumulation of the precautionary balances by adding during the following 12 months the equivalent of 5 percent to general **reserves** and an equal amount to SCA-1. *See also* ADMINISTRATIVE AND CAPITAL BUDGETS OF THE FUND.

INDEPENDENT EVALUATION OFFICE (IEO). The IEO was established in 2001 to conduct independent and objective evaluations of Fund policies and activities. Under its Terms of References, it is fully independent from Fund Management and operates at arm's length from the Executive Board. The IEO's mission is to enhance the learning culture within the organization, strengthen external credibility, promote greater understanding of the work of the Fund, and support institutional governance and oversight.

INDONESIA. Indonesia used various Fund facilities in the 1960s and early 1970s, but its economic performance ranked among the best of developing countries, registering GDP growth of about 7 percent annually during the 1980s and 1990s. Nevertheless, the shift in market sentiment that swept through the Asian region during 1997 exposed deep structural weaknesses in the Indonesian economy, in particularly owing to the large amount of short-term foreign debt held by its private corporate sector. Even though the country introduced measures to combat the crisis early and called in the Fund while its exchange reserves were strong, the measures taken were insufficient to restore confidence.

On 5 November 1997, the Fund approved a **stand-by arrangement** for Indonesia, authorizing drawings of up to SDR 7.3 billion (about $10.1 billion) over a three-year period. In addition to the Fund financing, the reform program was supported by financing from the **World Bank** and the Asian Development Bank, which, together with Indonesia's substantial reserves, provided a first line defense of $23 billion.

Key elements of the initial stand-by arrangement made available under the Fund's **emergency financing mechanism** included financial sector restructuring, stabilization of the rupiah through tight monetary policy and flexible **exchange rate** policy, fiscal tightening equivalent to about 1 percent of GDP, and structural reforms to enhance economic efficiency, including through liberalization of foreign trade and investment, dismantling domestic monopolies, and expanding the country's privatization program.

Almost immediately following approval of the arrangement, substantial resistance surfaced in Indonesia to a number of aspects of the program. The poorer sections of the population revolted against the prospect of higher prices on a number of consumer staples, as well as gasoline, because of a reduction or elimination of subsidies. Some members and friends of the President's family resisted the proposed closing of nonviable banks and the dismantling of several government monopolies, with which they were closely identified. Resulting delays in the program's implementation, and the likelihood that the second installment of Fund financing would not be approved led to further declines in confidence.

The Fund's Managing Director, **Michel Camdessus**, and the First Deputy Managing Director, **Stanley Fischer**, together with a staff mission, visited Jakarta to discuss with President Suharto and his officials a strengthening of the program in the face of a deteriorating situation. This unusual participation of the Fund's management in direct negotiations with the Indonesian authorities demonstrated the concern with which the Fund viewed the situation.

On 15 January 1998, the Fund's Managing Director was able to announce in Jakarta that agreement had been reached on the financial and structural reform program. He said that President Suharto had indicated that he would take personal responsibility for the program and would, himself, sign the Letter of Intent. Further, in order to ensure that the program would be fully implemented and its objectives realized, President Suharto would appoint a high council of ministers that would report directly to him to oversee the implementation of the program.

In announcing the renegotiated agreement in January, the Fund's Managing Director summarized the program as follows:

1. The program was designed to avoid a decline in output, while containing inflation to 20 percent in 1998, with the aim of bringing it back to single digits the following year.
2. The 1998–1999 budget would be revised to accord with the newly agreed macroeconomic framework, while still adhering to Indonesia's long-standing balanced-budget principle. This would imply a small deficit of about 1 percent of GDP.
3. To promote further transparency, the accounts of the Restoration and Investment Funds would be brought into the budget.
4. Under current conditions, public spending would be limited only to those items of vital importance to the country. Twelve infrastructure projects would be canceled and a number of other government commitments would be discontinued.

5. The Bank of Indonesia would be given full autonomy to conduct monetary policy and begin immediately to decide interest rates unilaterally.
6. It was vitally important for the bank and corporate sectors to be restructured and specific plans formulated.
7. On structural reforms, virtually all of the restrictions that were currently in place would be swept away, including the monopoly on the import and distribution of sugar, as well as the monopoly over the distribution of wheat flour. Domestic trade in all agricultural products would be fully deregulated; the Clove Marketing Board would be eliminated; all restrictive marketing arrangements would be abolished and the cement, paper, and plywood cartels would be dissolved; all formal and informal barriers to investment in palm oil plantation would be removed; and all restrictions on investment in wholesale and retail trades would be lifted.
8. Measures would be taken to alleviate the suffering caused by the drought.

Finally, the Fund announced the appointment of **Prabhakar Narvekar**, a former **Deputy Managing Director** of the Fund, as resident special advisor to the President of Indonesia.

Despite the attempts to soften the impact of the austerity program on the more vulnerable sections of the population, its implementation was met with widespread riots and political turmoil. In the face of growing civil unrest and demands for his resignation, President Suharto announced, on 20 May 1998, his resignation from the presidency, and his Vice President, B. R. Habibie, was sworn in as president.

On 24 June 1998, the government issued a Second Supplementary Memorandum of Economic and Financial Policy, noting that the economic situation had worsened and the program had been driven off track by social disturbances and political change. The Fund and the Indonesian authorities announced agreement on a new program and financial package. The economic situation and outlook had worsened considerably, and the economy was facing a very serious crisis. The distribution network had been badly damaged; economic activity, including exports, had been generally disrupted; and business confidence had been severely shaken. As a result, the exchange rate had weakened substantially, rather than appreciating as originally envisaged, and inflation was higher than had been projected.

Under the revised macroeconomic scenario, in 1998, GDP was expected to decline by 10 percent, the exchange rate to stabilize at around 10,000 rupiahs to the dollar, and inflation to be about 80 percent, but an improvement in the situation was seen for 1999. A central feature of the program continued to be limiting the budget deficit to a level that could be offset by additional foreign financing. The pressure on the budget, however, had intensified in the deepening crisis, and, in view of its particular impact on the poor, there was an urgent need to strengthen the social safety net to cushion the impact of higher unemployment and the greater incidence of poverty. Although some savings were envisaged in greater efficiency in the management of state-run operations, most of the savings were to come from cuts in infrastructure projects, amounting to about 2.5 percent of GDP. It remained the objective to phase out subsidies on staple foods and fuels, but these measures would have to await the recovery of household income. Taken together, the budgetary actions were aimed at reducing the budget deficit to 8.5 percent of GDP in 1998–1999—a level that would be unsustainable over the long run and would require further measures to raise revenues and cut subsidies in the following years.

Fiscal policy was to be supported by a tight monetary policy and a switch from setting interest rates administratively on central bank paper to a system of auctions. The further weakening that had occurred in the banking system meant that the implementation of comprehensive reforms were to be given the highest priority. The revised strategy involved measures to strengthen relatively sound banks partly through infusion of new capital and to recapitalize weak banks or close them. Decisions regarding individual banks would be based on uniform and transparent criteria, drawing on the results of portfolio reviews by international accounting firms. In the area of financial restructuring of the corporate sector, it was envisaged that domestic as well as foreign creditors would participate in debt workouts for individual companies, with all creditors sharing in the burden of providing the necessary relief. In support of the negotiation of such restructuring, the government had issued a regulation, in lieu of legislation, that had modernized the bankruptcy system. A critical aspect of the program would be the government's efforts to improve food security by placing considerable emphasis on ensuring that there were adequate supplies of essential commodities, especially rice, and that these would be available through the distribution system at affordable prices.

Finally, the government remained committed to implementing all of the structural reforms agreed to earlier, in collaboration with the World Bank. The privatization program was proceeding on schedule and the projected receipts from privatization, at $1.5 billion, would be achieved. The Monetary Monitoring Committee, comprising representatives of Indonesia, the Fund, the U.S. Treasury, and the Bundesbank, which had been meeting since April 1998, would continue to meet regularly. Regarding external financing needs, despite the considerable support that was being provided by bilateral and multilateral sources, additional **balance of payments** support amounting to about $4–6 billion would be required in 1998–1999 to close the financing gap. At this critical juncture, the government would be seeking further support from the international community to bring about success in the program.

The Fund completed its first review of the program in July 1998 and announced an increase of about $1.3 billion in the financing available to Indonesia, bringing the total under the three-year arrangement to about $11.3 billion. Following completion of the review, about $1 billion was made available immediately, bringing total disbursement under the arrangement to $4.9 billion. The Fund also announced that additional financing was to be made available from Australia, China, the Asian Development Bank, and the World Bank amounting to nearly $5 billion, all to be made available before the end of March 1999.

By the end of 1998, there were signs that the worst of the crisis was over. Interest rates were declining, the currency was appreciating, and usable external reserves had risen sharply. A modest recovery was expected to begin in 1999, with a marked fall in the rate of inflation by the end of the year. *See also* ASIAN FINANCIAL CRISIS.

INELIGIBILITY TO USE FUND RESOURCES. If a member fails to fulfill any of its obligations under the **Articles of Agreement**, the Fund has the right to declare that member ineligible to use the Fund's **General Resources Account (GRA)**. Nonpayment of **charges** or failure to fulfill repayment (**repurchase**) obligations would, in the absence of an explanation satisfactory to the Fund, be reason to declare a member ineligible. The Fund has used this right sparingly and as a last resort. Typically, when a member has shown good faith, the Fund has made an effort to reschedule repayments or enter into new programs that would restore the member's position of "good standing."

A declaration of ineligibility by the Fund carries harsh repercussions for the member concerned, as it signals to the international financial community that the member in question is not honoring its commitments, and it generally leads to cutting off funds from private and other official sources.

An early test of the Fund's authority occurred in connection with the decision to demonstrate its authority in the sphere of exchange rates, and particularly in its authority to approve a multiple exchange rate system established by a member. The test of this nascent policy came early in January 1948 over the Fund's objections that a French proposal for a free market for some transactions would destroy the country's whole system of fixed and stable **par values**. The French went ahead, anyway, and devalued the franc, and, at the same time, established a free exchange market alongside the official rate. In response, the Fund declared France to be ineligible to use the Fund resources—a disbarment that lasted for six years.

In the 1980s, with the outbreak of an acute debt crisis among many developing countries, the amount of **overdue obligations** reached substantial proportions, rising from about $1.2 billion in 1987 to $3.5 billion in 1992. The number of members with overdue obligations to the Fund reached a peak in 1993 at 12, and the number of countries that had been declared ineligible to use the Fund's resources rose to 10 in 1990. In that year, the Fund adopted a strengthened cooperative approach designed to prevent cases of overdue obligations arising in the first place, tightening the deterrent measures against delinquent members and organizing a collaborative approach on the part of members of the international financial community—designated as the "rights" approach—aimed at helping delinquent members to restore their good standing. Thereafter, with the implementation of these strategies, by 30 April 1998, the number of members with overdue obligations had fallen to seven and the number of ineligible members to four. As of the end of October 2009, the number of members with overdue obligations had been reduced to three—Somalia, Sudan, and Zimbabwe. Although Zimbabwe settled its remaining overdue obligations to the GRA on 15 February 2006, it still had substantial arrears to the **poverty reduction and growth facility** and the **exogenous shocks facility**, and thus remained ineligible to use the Fund's resources.

INFORMATION AND PUBLICATIONS. *See* DOCUMENTS AND INFORMATION.

INTERIM COMMITTEE. The Interim Committee of the Board of Governors on the International Monetary System (called the "Interim Committee") was one of two committees (the **Development Committee** is the other) that succeeded the **Committee of Twenty** in 1974. The Interim Committee was replaced by the **International Monetary and Financial Committee (IMFC)** in 1999.

The terms of reference of the Interim Committee were to advise and report to the Board of Governors on supervising the management and adaptation of the international monetary system, including the operation of the adjustment process; considering proposals by the **Executive Board** to amend the **Articles of Agreement**); and dealing with sudden disturbances that pose a threat to the international monetary system.

The original aim in establishing the Interim Committee was to bring into existence a group of officials who held high office in their own countries and who, meeting from time to time, would bring informed authority into the affairs of the Fund. Accordingly, the committee was composed of Governors of the Fund, ministers, or other persons of comparable rank. As in the case with respect to the IMFC, each Fund member that appoints an **Executive Director** and each group of Fund members that elect an Executive Director was entitled to participate in the Interim Committee's meetings. Executive Directors, or in their absence, their **Alternates**, were also entitled to attend the meetings. Meetings of the Interim Committee were generally held twice a year and were usually attended by more than 200 officials, as were the meetings of the earlier Committee of Twenty.

The Committee was named an interim body because it was the intention of the drafters of the second amendment to the Articles of Agreement that the Committee would eventually be replaced by a Council. The Council, which requires an 85 percent majority vote of the Board of Governors to come into effect, would have terms of reference, composition, and functions comparable to the Interim Committee. The principal difference is that the Interim Committee is not created as an organ of the Fund and, therefore, could not exercise the powers of the Fund, such as taking decisions that bind members. It could make only recommendations, and although those recommendations carried great weight, the Board of Governors and the Executive Directors had the legal right to disregard them. The high majority of votes required under the Articles of Agreement to bring the Council into existence makes it unlikely that it will be established in the near future.

INTERIM POVERTY REDUCTION STRATEGY PAPER (I-PRSP). I-PRSPs summarize current knowledge and analysis of a country's poverty situation, describe the existing poverty reduction strategy, and lay out the process for producing a fully developed **poverty reduction strategy paper** in a participatory fashion. The country documents, along with the accompanying Fund–**World Bank** joint staff assessments, are made available to the public on the World Bank and IMF websites in agreement with the member country. *See also* POVERTY REDUCTION AND GROWTH FACILITY (PRGF).

INTERNATIONAL BANK FOR RECONSTRUCTION AND DEVELOPMENT (IBRD). *See* WORLD BANK.

INTERNATIONAL CAPITAL MOVEMENTS. *See* CAPITAL MOVEMENTS.

INTERNATIONAL LIQUIDITY. The adequacy of international liquidity was of central concern under the **Bretton Woods system** using **fixed exchange rates**. The relatively fixed supply of **gold**, together with an obvious limit to the role that could be played by the U.S. dollar as a **reserve currency** when those dollars could be converted, on demand, into gold at a fixed rate, raised questions of how an expansion of the world economy could be sustained on a relatively fixed reserve base. The issues, discussed with growing intensity both inside and outside the Fund in the 1960s, posed a number of questions: whether there was a need for more effective **adjustment programs** on the part of countries in **balance of payments** disequilibria or an increase in global **reserves**; whether the undersupply or oversupply of reserves would be deflationary or inflationary; and whether any increase in international liquidity should be in the form of conditional liquidity, through an increase of members' **quotas** in the Fund, or in the form of unconditional liquidity (i.e., owned reserves in the form of gold, the creation of **Special Drawing Rights (SDR)** as an unconditional form of international liquidity, in accordance with the first amendment to the Fund's **Articles of Agreement** in 1969. The amendment called upon members and the Fund to make "the special drawing right the principal reserve asset in the international monetary system."

Two years after creating the SDR facility, the **convertibility** of the U.S. dollar into gold was suspended, and 18 months later the adjustable peg system established at the **Bretton Woods Conference** had completely collapsed. Although discussions on the adequacy of international liquidity and a possible mechanism for controlling its growth were part of the negotiations on reform of the **international monetary system**, the legalization of the freely **floating exchange rate** system authorized by the second amendment (1978) effectively brought the debate to a close. Since the beginning of the 1980s, the issue of international liquidity has not been of concern, in part because the need for international liquidity had been substantially reduced in a freely floating exchange rate system, and in part because of the abundant supply of international credit that became available in the 1970s as a result of the recycling of "petrodollars" and subsequently through the integration of capital markets.

SDRs have continued to play a very minor role in the international monetary system and have not become the principal **reserve asset** envisaged under the 1978 amendment. Instead, there has been an explosion in foreign exchange holdings, which now are by far the largest component of **international reserves**. With the integration of the world's financial markets, liquidity for creditworthy governments has not been a critical problem. For many **developing countries**, a shortage of reserves has been chronic, but the attention of the international community has been focused more on their need for adequate development finance and for the maintenance of stable domestic economic conditions, rather than their liquidity needs.

INTERNATIONAL MONETARY AND FINANCIAL COMMITTEE (IMFC). The IMFC was established in September 1999 to replace the **In-**

terim Committee of the Board of Governors on the International Monetary System (the Interim Committee) established in 1974. The **Board of Governors** Resolution initiating this change signified a strengthening of the role of the Committee as the primary advisory committee of the Board of Governors. It also included an explicit provision calling for preparatory meetings of representatives (Deputies) of Committee members prior to the official meetings of the Governors.

The IMFC advises and reports to the Board of Governors on matters pertaining to:

- The management and adaptation of the international monetary and financial system, including the continuing operation of the adjustment process, and developments in global liquidity and the transfer of real resources to developing countries
- Proposals by the **Executive Board** to amend the **Articles of Agreement**
- Sudden disturbances that might threaten the international monetary and financial system
- Ad hoc requests by the Board of Governors

IMFC members are Governors of the Fund, Ministers, or others of comparable rank. Each member of the IMF that appoints an **Executive Director** and each member or group of members that elects an Executive Director is entitled to appoint one member of the IMFC. Thus, the Committee membership reflects the composition of the Executive Board.

The IMFC selects a Chair from among its members, who serves for such period as the IMFC determines. Members of the IMFC, their associates, and Executive Directors or their alternates are entitled to attend the meetings of the IMFC unless the IMFC decides to hold a more restricted session. In addition, the **Managing Director** participates in all IMFC meetings. The Secretary of the IMF serves as the Secretary of the IMFC. In addition, a number of international institutions, including the **World Bank**, participate as observers in the IMFC's meetings.

The IMFC meets twice a year, in September or October before the joint World Bank–IMF **annual meetings** and in March or April at the time of the spring meetings.

The IMFC issues a communiqué after each meeting summarizing the outcome of its discussions and giving strategic direction to the IMF's policy work for the near to medium term. On the basis of the communiqué, the Managing Director draws up a work program for the Fund for the coming 6 to 12 months. After discussion in the Executive Board, the agreed work program forms the basis for the Board's work. Thus, an interactive relationship exists between the IMFC and the Executive Board, in which the IMFC sets the strategic direction of the institutions based on a thorough review of the progress made by the Executive Board during the preceding period.

INTERNATIONAL MONETARY SYSTEM. There are many definitions of the *international monetary system*, but basically the system is concerned with a member's economic and financial policies as they affect other members. It is concerned with the process of how a member influences its **balance of payments** positions, since one member's surplus is the obverse of a deficit or deficits elsewhere in the system, and vice versa. A country's balance of payments position is influenced in some degree by almost anything that happens in or to the economy, especially in an interdependent world economy such as has developed over the past 20 years. Nevertheless, the main factors that impact on the international monetary system are (1) a country's **exchange rate**, (2) the openness and nondiscriminatory character of the payments system, (3) the free and prudential movements of capital across borders, and (4) the form in which **international reserves** are held.

In the area of exchange rates, the world has moved from the fixed and unalterable exchange rates under the **gold** standard at the beginning of the century, through the floating era and "beggar-thy-neighbor" policies of the 1930s, to the **Bretton Woods system** of fixed but adjustable exchange rates of the postwar world, and finally to the freely **floating** system of exchange rates functioning under Fund **surveillance**.

The mechanism for settling accounts between countries has also gone through parallel developments. Dating from the 19th century, the pound sterling was the principal transaction **currency**, and operation of the gold standard hinged on London as the world's financial center. The interwar years saw the breakdown of the gold standard (or, more accurately, the gold exchange standard) and the emergence of a chaotic system, in which the pound sterling and the U.S. dollar were the principal transaction currencies, but in which bilateral trade and payments agreements and discriminatory arrangements proliferated.

This interwar period was followed by the postwar Bretton Woods system, which recognized that setting exchange rates was a matter of international concern and that the international behavior of nations should be governed by a code of conduct and monitored by a central international institution, the International Monetary Fund. The Bretton Woods system saw the gradual elimination of bilateral and discriminatory arrangements; the emergence of the U.S. dollar, based on gold, as the main vehicle and reserve currency; an attempt to introduce **Special Drawing Rights (SDRs)** into the international monetary system to supplement international reserves; a gradual lowering of the barriers to trade; a reduction in government interventionist policies and greater reliance on free markets; the spread of **convertibility** among currencies; a transformation in global communications brought about by the computer and sophisticated international telecommunications systems; and a growing integration of the world's financial markets.

With the collapse of the Bretton Woods system in the early 1970s, the U.S. dollar still remained the dominant reserve currency and currency of payment, but other currencies, such as the deutsche mark and the Japanese yen, grew in importance. The link with gold was severed, and although the Fund and central banks continued to hold substantial quantities of gold in reserve (although some central banks decided to reduce their gold holdings in the 1990s), official convertibility of currencies into gold had been eliminated. International reserves increased sharply over the past 25 years, mainly in the form of U.S. dollars, but with a significant shift away from the dollar to other currencies, such as the euro, the Japanese yen, and the pound sterling. SDRs remain a neglected component of the international monetary system. *See also* PAR VALUE SYSTEM; REFORM OF THE INTERNATIONAL MONETARY SYSTEM.

INTERNATIONAL RESERVES. Reserves perform the same function for national economies as shock absorbers do for a car. They protect an economy from having to make sharp, and perhaps disruptive, policy adjustments to cope with adverse domestic or external developments affecting its **balance of payments** position. The aim of allowing countries sufficient time to make orderly **adjustment** was one reason for establishing the Fund with a pool of **currencies**. The Fund is a large supplier of conditional **liquidity** (i.e., the use of the Fund's **resources** on condition that a country will adopt an appropriate **adjustment program**), but for unconditional liquidity, a country has to look mainly to the **reserve assets** that it owns and can use without challenge.

Reserve assets consist of **gold**, foreign exchange reserves, reserve positions in the Fund, and **Special Drawing Rights (SDRs)**. The role of gold in international reserves is ambiguous. It is the traditional reserve asset of last resort and is still esteemed by central bankers, although there has been an incipient movement by some central banks to sell small amounts of gold on the markets and there has been a slight decline in total gold reserves. However, there is no official price for gold, and any substantial sales of gold on the free market by a national **monetary authority** runs the risk of endangering its market price.

Gold is held mainly by industrial countries, with the United States holding about 30 percent of the world total. For official valuation purposes, in both its own accounts and those relating to its members, the Fund continues to value gold at SDR 35 per fine troy ounce. As of 28 August 2009, the IMF's holdings amounted to $98.8 billion at current market prices. At that time, total international reserves amounted to about $6.8 trillion. U.S. dollar holdings accounted for about 64 percent, the euro about 27 percent, the Japanese yen 3 percent, and the pound sterling 4 percent. Foreign exchange is the fastest growing component of international reserves, growing fivefold in the decade of the 1970s, doubling in the 1980s, increasing by nearly 70 percent in the first seven year of the 1990s.

INVESTMENT ACCOUNT. The **Articles of Agreement** authorized the establishment of an Investment Account, which specifically would allow the Fund to invest its holdings of **gold** and **currencies** in interest-bearing assets to help meet the expenses of conducting the business of the institution. The amounts that may be transferred to the Investment Account may not exceed the total amount of the Fund's **general reserves** and special reserves. Eligible **investments** include the domestic government bonds of member countries, their central banks, and other official agencies; and marketable obligations of international financial organizations. During the period 1956–1972, the Fund invested a small amount of its resources to supplement its **operational budget**. The earnings from these investments served to offset a deficit that had accumulated as income fell short of expenditure in the early years of the IMF's operations. Investments were continued after the deficit had been cleared and were accumulated in a special reserve. However, a decision to establish the Investment Account and make it operational was taken only in May 2006.

On 5 May 2008, the **Board of Governors** approved an amendment of the **Articles of Agreement** to introduce a new income model that would expand its investment authority in order to reduce the institution's overreliance on income from lending operations to cover administrative expenses. The new income model included the establishment of an endowment to be funded by the profits from a limited sale of 403.3 metric tons of the Fund's gold holdings. The endowment would then be invested with the objective of generating income while preserving the long-term real value of its resources. The Fund's investment policies will reflect the public nature of the funds to be invested and include safeguards to ensure that the broadened investment authority does not lead to actual or perceived conflicts of interest.

In accordance with the new income model, the Board approved on 18 September 2009 the sale of up to 403.3 metric tons, or about one-eighth of the Fund's total gold holdings, to be phased over time, following an approach similar to the one used successfully by the central banks participating in the Central Bank Gold Agreement. *See also* INVESTMENT BY THE FUND.

INVESTMENT BY THE FUND. From the period 1956–1972, the Fund invested a small amount of its **resources** to supplement its **operational budget**. The second amendment to the **Articles of Agreement** authorized the establishment of an **Investment Account**, which specifically allowed the Fund to invest its holdings of **gold** and **currencies** in interest-bearing assets of member countries. As part of the new income model for the Fund, the **Board of Governors** approved on 5 May 2008 a Resolution to broaden the Fund's investment authority to allow the institution to generate revenues from a variety of sources, including limited gold sales. It also authorizes the Fund to create an endowment, based on gold sales, to be invested with a view to generating income while preserving the long-term real value of these resources.

The Proposed Amendments will enter into force for all members once three-fifths of the members (111), holding 85 percent of the total voting power, have accepted the Proposed Amendments. As of 19 November 2009, 44 members had accepted the Amendment on Voice and Participation, and 41 members had accepted the Amendment to Expand the Fund's Investment Authority. *See also* INVESTMENT ACCOUNT.

ISTANBUL DECISIONS. The 2009 joint **World Bank**–IMF **annual meetings** held in Istanbul were concluded in the wake of the first truly **global financial crisis**, or "Great Recession," that had taken place since the founding of the Bretton Woods institutions in 1944. The decisions taken, called the *Istanbul Decisions*, set the foundation for permanent changes in the international monetary and financial system and in particular the work of the Fund. These decisions address four key reform areas related to the Fund's mandate, its financing role, multilateral **surveillance**, and governance.

This reform will focus on a review of the Fund's **mandate** to encompass the whole range of macroeconomic and financial sector policies that affect global stability and a greater role in crisis prevention. It will also entail examination of ways to enhance the Fund's financing instruments and facilities, in particular the **Flexible Credit Line**, to provide further assurance to market participants and more credibility to the Fund as the lender of last resort. An assessment will also take place on whether the Fund's enhanced financing instruments can help reduce the need for countries to self-insure against crisis by building up large **foreign exchange** reserves. Finally, the Fund was asked to build on its multilateral surveillance to assist the **Group of Twenty's** mutual assessment of policies.

J

JACOBSSON, PER (1894–1963). Per Jacobsson, a Swedish national, was the third **Managing Director** of the Fund, serving in that position from 1956 until he died in office in 1963. He joined the **Bank for International Settlements (BIS)** in 1931 as economic advisor and became General Manager of the BIS in 1946.

JAMAICA AGREEMENT. The meeting of the **Interim Committee** in Jamaica in January 1976 put into place the last pieces of the second amendment to the **Articles of Agreement**. At this meeting, new provisions for the Articles of Agreement were concluded on exchange arrangements, the role of **gold** in the **international monetary system** and in the Fund, and a number of other technical problems that the **Executive Board** of the Fund had been unable to resolve. The Committee requested the Fund's **Executive Directors** to complete the work of amending the Articles and submit the amendments, along with a report, to the **Board of Governors** in a matter of weeks. The Jamaica meeting virtually brought to an end the negotiations on a reformed international monetary system. The initial proposals for a new system had been put forward by the Fund's staff in 1971, taken up by the **Committee of Twenty** in 1972, formulated in broad principles by an *Outline of Reform* in June 1974, discussed and completely changed by the Interim Committee and the Executive Board over the next two years, and finally came into effect in 1978. *See also* REFORM OF THE INTERNATIONAL MONETARY SYSTEM.

JOINT FUND–BANK LIBRARY. An early example of cooperation between the Fund and the **World Bank** was the establishment of the Joint Fund–Bank Library, to serve the staff of each institution. The library is administered by the Fund, under the aegis of a joint Fund–Bank staff advisory committee, and its cost is shared by both institutions. The library's collection concentrates on contemporary works, rather than on historical or rare treatises and manuscripts. It has more than 200,000 volumes, subscribes to more than 4,000 separate journals, receives newspapers from nearly every member country, and has files of the major newspapers dating back to 1946.

Over time, the library has expanded to include a network of eight libraries and resource centers, all located in Washington, D.C., that serve the Fund and the World Bank Group. Its mandate is to provide information products and services to support the two institutions. It offers research services, consulting, procurement of information products, content organization, and document delivery. The Library Network also monitors the latest information industry trends and business challenges and focuses on bringing external print and electronic information products and services to client groups in both institutions.

The library has an online cataloging system, subscribes to a nationwide commercial database, and is a member of a national network of library catalogs. It is not open to the general public. However, it is open to visitors by appointment each Thursday between the hours of 10:00 AM and 4:00 PM.

JOINT IMF–WORLD BANK IMPLEMENTATION COMMITTEE (JIC). The JIC was established on 1 May 2000 to coordinate work on the **heavily indebted poor countries (HIPC)** initiative and the **Poverty Reduction Strategy Papers (PRSP)** program. The JIC oversees implementation of the HIPC initiative and PRSP program to ensure the effective resolution of any differences in approach that may arise between the **World Bank** and the Fund. Toward this end, it monitors progress in implementing both programs and coordinates the production of regular reports and briefings to the **Executive Boards**. The JIC also works with the External Relations departments of both institutions to ensure consistent and effective external communications.

JOINT MINISTERIAL COMMITTEE OF THE BOARDS OF GOVERNORS OF THE BANK AND THE FUND ON THE TRANSFER OF REAL RESOURCES TO DEVELOPING COUNTRIES. *See* DEVELOPMENT COMMITTEE.

JOINT STAFF ADVISORY NOTES (JSANs). JSANs are documents prepared jointly by the staffs of the Fund and the **World Bank**, containing an analysis of the strengths and weaknesses of a member's poverty reduction strategy. The JSANs are submitted with a member country's **Poverty Reduction Strategy Paper (PRSP)** or **Interim PRSP (I-PRSP)**. The JSANs replaced Joint Staff Assessments in 2005.

K

KATO, TAKATOSHI (1941–). Takatoshi Kato, a national of Japan, assumed office as **Deputy Managing Director** of the Fund on 2 February 2004. Prior to his service at the Fund, Mr. Kato held a series of senior positions at the Ministry of Finance of Japan. These include Vice-Minister of Finance for International Affairs (1995–1997) and Director-General of the International Finance Bureau (1993–1995). From 1985–1987, Mr. Kato served as Executive Director for Japan at the Asian Development Bank (ADB). Previously, he held positions at the Ministry of Finance and the Organization for Economic Cooperation and Development Secretariat. Mr. Kato has served as a member of advisory panels, including the World Health Organization's Commission on Macroeconomics and Health (2001) and an ADB panel on poverty reduction in Asia and the Pacific (1999–2000). In 2002, he published a book on **exchange rate** policy. He was Advisor to the President of Tokyo-Mitsubishi Bank and a Visiting Professor at Waseda University as well as a Visiting Professor at Princeton University (1998–1999). Mr. Kato has a BA from Tokyo University (1964) and an MPA. from Princeton University (1968).

KEYNES, LORD JOHN MAYNARD (1883–1946). John Maynard Keynes, the British economist, journalist, and financier, was the most outstanding economist of the 20th century, best known for his *General Theory of Employment, Interest, and Money*, published in the mid-1930s, which changed the focus of economic theory and public policy throughout the noncommunist world. Working for the British Treasury during World War II, Keynes was one of the chief architects of the International Monetary Fund and played a dominant role in negotiating the drafts of the agreements establishing the Fund and the **World Bank** at the **Bretton Woods Conference** of July 1944. See *also* KEYNES PLAN.

KEYNES PLAN. First published in 1942, the Keynes Plan was titled *Proposals for an International Currency (or Clearing) Union* and was conceived as an international central bank for national central banks. The unit of account was to be **Bancor**, the value of which was to be fixed in terms of **gold**, but not unalterably so. Debit balances, when they arose, were to take the form of overdrafts and not of specific loans. Reflecting Keynes' view that adjustment of **balance of payments** disequilibria should be shared by countries in deficit and surplus, the Union was to charge a rate of interest on credit as well as debit balances. **Exchange rates** were to be fixed in terms of Bancor and were not to be altered without permission of the **Governing Board**, except when the member had a debit balance with the Union of more than one-fourth of its **quota**, when it would be entitled to reduce the value of its **currency** by 5 percent annually. Persistent and growing debtors to the Union were to take increasingly severe action to correct their external position. At the same time, creditor countries were to be subject to similar action in reverse. As put forward by Keynes, the plan dealt only with the Clearing Union, but it did envisage the establishment of a number of parallel organizations, including international bodies charged with postwar relief, rehabilitation, and reconstruction.

The Keynes Plan was being drafted at the same time as the **White Plan** was being put together in the United States. Subsequently, other plans were also issued, such as the French plan, the Canadian plan, and the U.S. Federal Reserve Board plan. Discussions on these plans intensified in 1943 and culminated in the **Bretton Woods Conference** of July 1944. All the plans went through mergings and major revisions, but it is generally agreed that the final **Articles of Agreement** owed more to the White Plan than to Keynes.

KÖHLER, HORST (1943–). Horst Köhler, a German national, served as the eighth **Managing Director** of the Fund. He directly succeeded **Michel Camdessus**, who retired from the IMF on 14 February 2000. Prior to taking up his position at the Fund, Mr. Köhler was the President of the European Bank for Reconstruction and Development, a post to which he was appointed in September 1998. He was President of the German Savings Bank Association from 1993 to 1998. From 1990 to 1993, he served as Germany's Deputy Minister of Finance. During this time, he led negotiations on behalf of the German government on the agreement that became the Maastricht Treaty on European Economic and Monetary Union, was closely involved in the process of German unification, and held the position of Deputy Governor for Germany at the **World Bank**. He was educated at the University of Tübingen, where he earned a doctorate in economics and political science.

Mr. Köhler resigned from the Fund on 4 March 2004, following his nomination to serve a five-year term as President of the Federal Republic of Germany. He was reelected to a second term on 23 May 2009.

KOREA. Over a period of 50 years, Korea, like other Asian economies, has passed through periods of poverty, stagnation, and miraculous growth.

Although it had used the Fund's **resources** under a variety of **stand-by arrangements**, by the end of 1987 Korea had repaid all its outstanding credits and loans to the Fund. For several decades per capita GDP growth had risen by 7 percent annually, and by the end of the 1980s a once-poor agrarian economy had been transformed into an advanced industrial economy. It was thus a great shock, both to those at home and abroad, when the deep economic and financial crisis broke in 1997.

During 1996, warning signs of financial stress began to emerge, but they were largely ignored by the authorities. Reflecting a weaker external demand, a collapse in computer chip prices, and loss of competitiveness as result of the depreciation of the Japanese yen, export growth slowed markedly. Productive capacity became increasingly underutilized, raising costs when sales were already weakening. Corporate profits deteriorated, leading to losses and debt servicing problems, and to an unusually high number of bankruptcies, including the large conglomerates (chaebols).

These ailing enterprises increased the pressures on the banking sector, which in turn adversely affected overseas creditors' confidence. By mid-November, confidence had fallen so low that foreign creditors began declining requests to roll over maturing debts. At the same time, a number of merchant banks faced serious liquidity problems and were virtually insolvent. Finally, the political uncertainty brought on by the presidential elections in December 1997 triggered a financial crisis, intensifying the pressures that the market had already been facing following the decline in the **Hong Kong SAR** stock market prices late in October. The exchange rate for the won declined precipitously in a chaotic market, as did stock market prices.

On 7 November 1997, the Korean authorities asked the Fund for support in implementing an economic stabilization and reform program. The Fund's **Executive Board** approved Korea's request for a three-year **stand-by credit** for $21 billion on 4 December 1997. The Board subsequently reviewed the situation three times—on 18 and 30 December 1997 and 8 January 1998, and disbursed substantial installments of the credit after each meeting.

In addition to the Fund's financing, the **World Bank** stood ready to provide up to $10 billion in support of specific structural reforms, and the Asian Development Bank indicated a willingness to provide a further $4 billion in support of policy and institutional reforms. At the same time, no less than a dozen industrial countries announced that they would be willing, in the event of unanticipated adverse circumstances, to provide a second line of defense, expected to be in excess of $20 billion.

The centerpiece of the government's program was a comprehensive restructuring and strengthening of the financial system to make it sound, transparent (i.e., open), and more efficient. This involved an exit strategy that would ensure the rapid resolution of troubled financial institutions in a way that would minimize systemic stress and avoid **moral hazard**. Nine insolvent merchant banks were suspended and other merchant banks that were not able to submit appropriate restructuring plans were warned that they would have their licenses revoked. All banks were to meet the **Basle Committee's** capitalization standards. The deposit guarantee system was set to be eliminated by the year 2000 and replaced by a deposit insurance system, financed solely by contributions from the financial sector.

To improve transparency in the financial sector and upgrade accounting and disclosure practices to international standards, large financial institutions would be required to have their financial statements audited by internationally recognized firms. Disclosure standards would require the publication of key data by financial institutions twice a year, including nonperforming loans, capital structure, ownership, and affiliations.

Supervision of the financial sector would be strengthened by setting up a central agency that would consolidate all the supervisory functions. Early legislation would be sought to make the Bank of Korea independent, with price stability as its overriding mandate. To promote competition and efficiency, the authorities would allow foreigners to establish bank subsidiaries and brokerage houses by mid-1998.

To further the substantial trade liberalization that had taken place since the early 1980s, the program called for a timetable to be set up in line with the **World Trade Organization (WTO)** commitment to eliminate trade-related subsidies, restrictive import licensing, and the import diversification program. The government also undertook to accelerate its ongoing capital account liberalization program, raising the ceiling on aggregate foreign ownership of listed shares to 55 percent by the end of 1998 and the ceiling on foreign ownership from 7 percent to 50 percent by the end of 1997. Finally, labor market flexibility was to be enhanced by easing the restrictions on dismissals under mergers and acquisitions and corporate restructuring. To ease the burden of layoffs and expedite reemployment, the employment insurance system was strengthened and private job placement agencies and temporary employment agencies were allowed to operate.

The impact of the crisis on the real economy was severe. After growth of 5.5 percent in 1997, real GDP contracted by 3.8 percent in the first quarter of 1998 and was not expected to recover until later in the year. The slowdown in recovery was hampered by the continued recession in the Japanese economy, for although exports to Europe and the United States expanded, this positive development was negated by a fall in exports to Japan. In its consultations with Korea at the end of May 1998, **Executive Directors** commended the authorities for their steadfast implementation of their wide-ranging stabilization and reform program. In the third quarter, the won stabilized at around 35 to 40 percent below its precrisis level and short-term interest rates were about 8 to 9 percent.

There was promise of resumed growth in 1999, when the GDP was expected to grow 2–3 percent. By the end of 1998, Korea's external reserves had grown to $47 billion, compared with only $4 billion a year earlier, and it was able to repay the Fund $2.8 billion of drawings made under the **supplemental reserve facility**. Interest rates continued to moderate and the stock market turned bullish. *See also* ASIAN FINANCIAL CRISIS.

KRUEGER, ANNE (1934–). Anne O. Krueger served as First **Deputy Managing Director** of the Fund from 1 September 2001 to 31 August 2006. She was also Acting Managing Director of the Fund on a temporary basis between the time that **Horst Köhler** resigned on 4 March 2004 and **Rodrigo de Rato** took up the post on 7 June 2004.

Before coming to the Fund, Ms. Krueger was the Herald L. and Caroline L. Ritch Professor in Humanities and Sciences in the Department of Economics at Stanford University. She was also the founding Director of Stanford's Center for Research on Economic Development and Policy Reform and a Senior Fellow of the Hoover Institution. From 1982 to 1986, she was the **World Bank's** Vice President for Economics and Research. Ms. Krueger received her undergraduate degree from Oberlin College and her PhD in economics from the University of Wisconsin. She is a Distinguished Fellow and past President of the American Economic Association, a member of the National Academy of Sciences, and a Research Associate of the National Bureau of Economic Research. A recipient of a number of economic prizes and awards, she has published extensively on policy reform in developing countries, the role of multilateral institutions in the international economy, and the political economy of trade policy.

After leaving the Fund in the spring of 2007, Ms. Krueger assumed the position of professor of international economics at the Johns Hopkins School of Advanced International Studies in Washington, D.C.

L

LANGUAGE OF THE FUND. The working language of the Fund is English, and all its transactions, papers, Board discussions, policy decisions, and documentation are conducted or prepared in English. Several key publications are, however, translated and issued in French and Spanish, and other selected documents and **publications** are translated from the English into Arabic, Chinese, French, German, Portuguese, Russian, and Spanish.

LATVIA. Latvia's economy grew extremely rapidly for a number of years prior to the **global financial crisis** of 2008. Capital inflows, including from foreign parent banks, and expansionary macroeconomic policies had bolstered growth rates, but also fueled unsustainable credit and housing bubbles, as well as a current account deficit above 20 percent of GDP. The combination of these bubbles deflating, the global financial crisis, and acute banking pressures in Latvia culminated in a severe financial crisis in late 2008, following a run on Parex Bank, the largest domestically owned financial institution. This led to one of the sharpest economic downturns in the world, with a decline in GDP of about 18 percent in 2009 and unemployment hovering above 22 percent.

Economic instability gave way to political unrest on 13 January 2009, when Latvia experienced the most severe riots since the collapse of the former Soviet Union (FSU). More than 10,000 people engaged in protests in Riga against the government's handling of the crisis, and on 20 February, the Latvian coalition government headed by Prime Minister Ivars Godmanis collapsed.

In December 2008, the **Executive Board** approved a 27-month **Stand-By Arrangement** in the amount of €1.7 billion for Latvia as part of a coordinated international effort that included contributions from the European Union (€3.1 billion); the Nordic countries (€1.8 billion); the **World Bank** (€400 million); the Czech Republic (€200 million); and the European Bank for Reconstruction and Development, Estonia, and Poland (€100 million each).

The main objectives of the underlying program were to address the immediate liquidity crisis and ensure long-term external stability, while maintaining the exchange rate peg. Toward that end, the program emphasized measures to stabilize the financial sector and restore depositor confidence. It also included substantial fiscal policy tightening to reduce financing needs and foster real exchange rate depreciation. Structural reforms and incomes policies were also included to improve competitiveness and facilitate external adjustment.

By the time of the Fund's Article IV consultation with Latvia in July 2010, **Executive Directors** noted that the recession appeared to be bottoming out, with positive annual growth expected to return in 2011. By early 2010, Latvia's foreign currency reserves had reached €4.8 billion, up from €3.4 billion at the height of the crisis in November 2008. Pressures on the exchange rate had abated, and overnight interest rates had fallen from a peak of 33 percent in June 2009. As a result, financial market confidence was improving.

LETTER OF INTENT (LOI). The document prepared by a member country to formally request an arrangement to use the Fund's financial **resources**. This document describes the member's commitments to strengthen its economic and financial policies. The letter of intent may be accompanied by a more detailed Memorandum of Economic and Financial Policies.

LIBRARIES. The Fund maintains separate fiscal and legal libraries, and, in conjunction with the **World Bank**, the main library, the **Joint Fund–Bank Library**, which serves both organizations.

LIPSKY, JOHN. John Lipsky assumed the position of First **Deputy Managing Director** of the Fund on 1 September 2006. Prior to taking up this position, he was Vice Chairman of the JP Morgan Investment Bank. In this position, he advised the firm's principal market risk takers, published independent research on the principal forces shaping global financial markets, was actively engaged with JP Morgan's key clients, and represented the firm around the world with senior public and financial sector decision makers.

Previously, Mr. Lipsky served as JP Morgan's Chief Economist, and as Chase Manhattan Bank's Chief Economist and Director of Research. He served as Chief Economist of Salomon Brothers, Inc., from 1992 until 1997. From 1989 to 1992, Mr. Lipsky was based in London, where he directed Salomon Brothers' European Economic and Market Analysis Group.

Before joining Salomon Brothers in 1984, Mr. Lipsky served for more than a decade as a member of the Fund staff, where he helped manage the Fund's procedure for **surveillance over exchange rates** and analyzed developments in international capital markets. He also participated in negotiations with several member countries and served as the Fund's Resident Representative in Chile during 1978–1980. In 2000, he chaired a Financial Sector Review Group, established by former Managing Director **Horst Köhler**, to provide the IMF with an independent perspective on the Fund's work on international financial markets.

A graduate of Wesleyan University, Mr. Lipsky earned a bachelors degree in economics. He later earned a PhD in economics from Stanford University.

LIQUIDITY, INTERNATIONAL. *See* INTERNATIONAL LIQUIDITY; INTERNATIONAL RESERVES.

LIQUIDITY OF THE FUND. The liquidity of the Fund determines its lending capacity, that is, the maximum amount of financing that the Fund can make available to its members. The liquid **resources** of the Fund consist of usable currencies and **Special Drawing Rights (SDRs)** held in the **General Resources Account**, supplemented as necessary by borrowed resources. Usable **currencies**, the largest component of liquid resources, are the currencies of members whose **balance of payments** and gross reserve positions are considered sufficiently strong to warrant inclusion of their currencies in the **operational budget** for use in financing Fund operations and **transactions**. At the end of 2009, the Fund's uncommitted usable resources totaled about SDR 213 billion, compared with 132.1 billion a year earlier. This includes funds available to the Fund under borrowing agreements with Japan (US$100 billion), Canada (US$10 billion), Norges Bank (SDR 3 billion), the United Kingdom (SDR 9.92 billion), Deutsche Bundesbank (EUR 15 billion), De Nederlandsche Bank NV (EUR 5.31 billion), Danmarks Nationalbank (EUR 1.95 billion), Banco de Portugal (EUR 1.06 billion), France (EUR 11.06 billion), National Bank of Belgium (EUR 4.74 billion), Central Bank of Malta (EUR 120 million), Slovak Republic (EUR 440 million), and Czech National Bank (EUR 1.03 billion); and note purchase agreements with People's Bank of China (SDR 32 billion), Brazil (US$10 billion), and Reserve Bank of India (US$10 billion).

LONDON INTERBANK OFFERED RATE (LIBOR). The LIBOR is a daily reference rate based on the interest rates bank offer to lend unsecured funds to other banks in the London wholesale (or "interbank") money market.

LOUVRE ACCORD. The Louvre Accord of February 1987 among the **Group of Seven** industrial countries meeting in the Louvre, Paris, was meant to stem an excessive depreciation of the U.S. dollar and to stabilize

currencies around the then-current levels, which were considered to be "broadly consistent with underlying economic fundamentals." These objectives were to be supported by central bank intervention and agreed macroeconomic policies. Since 1988, the Group of Seven has held discussions covering a broad range of macroeconomic policy issues. The group has made specific efforts, including coordinated intervention, to resist exchange rate movements regarded as unwarranted by economic fundamentals or contrary to policy objectives, but it has made no commitment to a more formal arrangement. *See also* PLAZA AGREEMENT.

M

MADRID DECLARATION. Meeting in Madrid in 1994, the **Interim Committee** issued a *Declaration on Cooperation to Strengthen Global Expansion.* Two years later, meeting in Washington, D.C., the Committee noted that the strategy set out in the *Declaration*, which emphasized sound domestic policies, international cooperation, and global integration, remained valid. It reiterated the objective of promoting full participation of all economies, including the low-income countries, in the global economy. Favorable developments in, and prospects for, many industrial, developing, and **transitional economies** owed much to the implementation of sound policies consistent with the common medium-term strategy.

The Committee saw a need to update and broaden the *Declaration* in light of the new challenges of a changing global environment, and to strengthen its implementation, in a renewed spirit of partnership. In the new *Declaration on Partnership for Sustainable Global Growth*, known informally as the "11 Commandments," the Committee attached particular importance to the following:

1. It stressed that sound monetary, fiscal, and structural policies were complementary and mutually reinforcing: steady application of consistent policies over the medium term was required to establish the conditions for sustained noninflationary growth and job creation, which were essential for social cohesion.
2. The implementation of sound macroeconomic policies and the avoidance of large imbalances were essential to promote financial and exchange rate stability and to avoid significant misalignments among currencies.
3. Creation of a favorable environment for private savings.
4. Consolidation of the success in bringing inflation down and building on the hard-won credibility of monetary policy.
5. Maintenance of the movement toward trade liberalization, resistance against protectionist measures, and the upholding of the multilateral trading system.

6. Encouragement of current account **convertibility** and careful progress toward increased freedom of **capital movements** through efforts to promote stability and financial soundness.
7. Achievement of budget balance and strengthened fiscal discipline in a multiyear framework. Continued fiscal imbalances and excessive public indebtedness, and the upward pressures they put on global real interest rates, were threats to financial stability and durable growth. It was essential to enhance the transparency of fiscal policy by persevering with efforts to reduce off-budget transactions and quasifiscal deficits.
8. Improvement of the quality and composition of fiscal adjustment by reducing unproductive spending while ensuring adequate basic investment in infrastructure. Because the sustainability of economic growth depended on the development of human resources, it was essential to improve education and training, reform public pension and health systems to ensure their long-term viability and enable them to provide effective health care, and alleviate poverty and provide well-targeted and affordable social safety nets.
9. Bold structural reform, including labor and product market reforms, with a view to increasing employment and reducing other distortions that impeded the efficient allocation of resources, so as to make members' economies more dynamic and resilient to adverse developments.
10. The promotion of **good governance** in all its aspects, including adherence to the rule of law, improvements in the efficiency and accountability of the public sector, and tackling corruption, as essential elements of a framework within which economies could prosper.
11. Strong prudential regulation and supervision of the banking system to ensure its soundness, improved coordination, better assessment of credit risk, stringent capital requirements, timely disclosure of banks' financial conditions, action to prevent money laundering, and improved management of banks.

MALAYSIA. Since the late 1980s, Malaysia's economy, sustained by high levels of investment (over 40 percent of GDP in recent years) and savings (well over 30 percent of GDP)—a federal government surplus and a favorable balance of trade—and generally strong macroeconomic fundamentals, had achieved considerable success, reflected in high growth and a very substantial reduction in poverty. In 1997, however, Malaysia was seriously affected by regional developments. From the second half of 1997, economic activity slowed and there was a large outflow of short-term capital; from the end of 1996 through April 1998, gross **international reserves** fell by $7 billion to

$20 billion. The ringgit depreciated by 44 percent, and the stock market fell by almost 50 percent between mid-1997 and January 1998. In the next three months, however, the ringgit strengthened by 20 percent and the stock market recovered by 9 percent.

In March 1998, the government announced a new package of measures, which built on earlier initiatives and was designed to broaden the overall policy response within the changed macroeconomic framework. The measures included action to strengthen the financial sector and address emerging problems in financial institutions. Fiscal policy was aimed at ensuring a small surplus, despite an increase in spending to strengthen the social safety net. There was to be a significant reduction in credit and monetary growth, and a more active use of interest rates to stabilize the **foreign exchange** market and restrain inflation. The government also renewed its commitment to improve transparency and steadily to implement structural measures aimed at improving corporate governance and competition.

Upon the conclusion of the **Executive Board's** Article IV consultation with Malaysia in April 1998, the **Executive Directors** welcomed the package of measures announced by the Malaysian authorities in March, noting that it constituted a more comprehensive approach to restructuring the Malaysian economy. Directors placed strong emphasis on the tightening of monetary policy, on improvements in corporate governance and fiscal transparency, and on the early implementation of commitments to deepen structural reform.

As the contagion spread, however, the Malaysian economy was subjected to continuing pressure, and in September 1998, the government introduced capital controls and pegged the exchange rate of the ringgit to the dollar in order to insulate domestic interest rates from continuing pressures and volatility in the foreign exchange market. These measures were followed by interest rate reductions as well as more direct measures aimed at stimulating credit growth, an expansionary government budget, and accelerated implementation of the financial and corporate sector restructuring program. In February 1999, the capital controls were modified with the replacement of the one-year holding period restriction on portfolio capital flows with a system of exit levies.

By 1999, there were increasing signs of a pickup in economic activity in Malaysia as well as in other countries in the region. Improved economic prospects were reflected in stabilizing property prices and a significant recovery in equity market prices. Inflation had also fallen to a little under 3 percent as the effects of the earlier depreciation of the ringgit wore off. *See also* ASIAN FINANCIAL CRISIS.

MANAGING DIRECTOR. The Managing Director of the Fund is selected by the **Executive Board** for an initial term of five years. He is Chairman of the Executive Board and participates in meetings of the **Board of Governors**, the **International Monetary and Financial Committee**, and the **Development Committee**. The Managing Director is also chief of the Fund's **staff** and, under the direction of the Executive Board, conducts the ordinary business of the Fund. Subject to the general overview of the Executive Board, he is also responsible for the organization, appointment, and dismissal of staff. The position has traditionally been filled by a national of one of the Fund's European members. The First **Deputy Managing Director** has traditionally been from the United States. *See also* CAMDESSUS, MICHEL; DE LAROSIÈRE, JACQUES; DE RATO, RODRIGO; GUTT, CAMILLE; JACOBSSON, PER; KÖHLER, HORST; ROOTH, IVAR; SCHWEITZER, PIERRE-PAUL; STRAUSS-KAHN, DOMINIQUE; WITTEVEEN, H. JOHANNES.

MANILA FRAMEWORK GROUP (MFG). The MFG was created in November 1997 in the midst of the Asian financial crisis by 14 Asia-Pacific countries (including Australia, Canada, New Zealand, and the United States) for the purpose of maintaining an in-depth dialog on regional economic issues and crisis management. Finance Ministers and central bankers from the member countries and senior representatives of the Fund, the **World Bank**, and the **Bank for International Settlements** met semiannually at the level of Deputy Finance Ministers. By the early 2000s, the Asian financial crisis had subsided and the significance of the MFG meetings had dwindled. The group was disbanded in 2004.

MEDIUM-TERM STRATEGY (MTS). In light of the economic transformation wrought by globalization, particularly throughout the 1990s, the Fund embarked on a review of its mandate and future direction. This effort culminated in the publication of the **Managing Director's** *Report on Implementing the Fund's Medium-Term Strategy* in April 2006.

The strategy concluded that the emergence of new economic powers, integrated financial markets, unprecedented capital flows, and new ideas to promote economic development required an updated interpretation of the Fund's mandate as the steward of international financial cooperation and stability. Without a renewed focus and carefully chosen priorities, the institution risked being pulled in too many directions simultaneously and losing its relevance to large parts of the membership.

The proposals put forward in the MTS covered **surveillance**; the Fund's role in emerging market countries; its engagement in low-income countries; and issues related to **good governance**, capacity building, and the institution's budget requirements.

The difficulties in tackling unprecedented global imbalances throughout the 1990s, and the challenges facing individual countries, called for stronger exercise of Fund surveillance. At the global level, the MTS called for efforts to identify—and promote effective responses to—risks to economic stability, including from payments imbalances, **currency** misalignments, and financial market disturbances. At the country level, it called for the Fund to focus on effectiveness rather than comprehensiveness, with deeper analysis of financial systems, a greater multilateral perspective, and more regional context and outreach

With respect to emerging market countries, the MTS called for efforts to augment candid and focused macroeconomic analysis with enhanced surveillance over financial and capital markets. At the same time, the MTS called for efforts to improve crisis prevention and response.

With respect to low-income countries, it called for efforts to marshal the expected rise in aid flows, including from debt relief, to achieve higher growth rates and the UN **Millennium Development Goals**. This would call for a deeper and more focused engagement in low-income developing countries, including through new understandings with the **World Bank** and other agencies on the division of labor.

The reform of governance within the Fund, including through a revision of **quota** shares was seen as central to the legitimacy and effectiveness of the institution. During the 2006 Singapore annual meetings, a two-year package was initiated with, as a first step, an ad hoc increase in quotas for four countries: **China**, **Korea**, Mexico, and Turkey. The MTS also called for efforts to address other aspects of governance, including transparent selection of Fund management and more clearly defining the role of the **Executive Board**.

The MTS called for targeted efforts to increase capacity building to help members implement reforms. This was also an important part of the strategy to address vulnerabilities identified in surveillance. The Fund's efforts to assist countries build macroeconomic institutions needed to be strengthened through better prioritization and country ownership. The MTS also called for action to streamline and control internal procedures and documentation, lest the work, messages, and governance of the institution to better enable Fund management and members of the Executive Board shift attention from routine and detail to broader, strategic issues.

Finally, the MTS called for these efforts to be reconciled within a medium-term budget that would effectively address the projected fall in the Fund's income. Moreover, the MTS noted that a new business model would be needed to finance the Fund's activity over the longer term, with less reliance on margins from lending and more on steady, long-term sources of income.

MEMBERSHIP OF THE FUND. Membership in the Fund is open to every country that controls its foreign relations and is able and prepared to fulfill the obligations of membership contained in the Fund's **Articles of Agreement**. At the end of April 2009, membership was virtually universal, amounting to 186 members, compared with only 30 original members in 1946. The collapse of communism and the breakup of the **Union of Soviet Socialist Republics** was followed by the memberships of the three Baltic states, the other 12 newly independent countries that formerly made up the Soviet Union, the rest of the former communist countries in eastern Europe that had not already joined the Fund, and Switzerland.

The **Board of Governors** is the only authority in the Fund to approve applications for membership, and it does so by a simple majority vote. In matters of procedure, a committee of **Executive Directors** is formed which, along with the **staff** of the Fund, helps the applicant gather the necessary economic data and agrees with the applicant on the terms of membership. The most critical aspects of the **Membership Resolution** are the size of the new member's **quota** and the form in which the **subscription** is to be paid.

In determining whether an applicant is a country, and thus eligible to become a member, the Fund makes its own finding, although it will take into account the recognition given to it by other members and by the **United Nations (UN)**. Membership in the UN, however, is not a sufficient condition for membership in the Fund. The sole determinants for membership are that the applicant is a country able to control its foreign relations and fulfill the obligations of its membership. Membership does not depend on the geographic or economic size of the country, or whether it has its own currency or central bank, or whether it is a centrally planned economy. The Fund has accepted into membership many small states, several countries not possessing their own currencies or central banks, and countries in various parts of the world having centrally planned economies.

MEMBERSHIP RESOLUTION. A country is admitted to membership in the Fund after the **Board of Governors** has voted on a Membership Resolution and the terms of the Resolution have been complied with by the member. The Resolution specifies the size of the member's **quota**, the method of paying the **subscription**, notification by the member of its **exchange arrangements**, the terms on which it can engage in **transactions** with the Fund, confirmation that it has taken all legal steps necessary under its own constitutional arrangements to become a member, and the period of time for accepting membership.

MEXICAN FINANCIAL CRISIS. Mexico has a long history of financial relations with the Fund and from the early years made frequent use of the

Fund's **resources** in moderate amounts. It was not until the late 1970s that Mexico's **drawings** on the Fund became substantial in a period when international payments were badly out of balance because of escalating oil prices. Mexico's difficulties partly resulted from inconsistent policies that encouraged domestic consumption spending, and from the practice that sprang up among the international banks of making unwise loans to **developing countries** through syndicated lending in their efforts to recycle the petrodollars deposited with them by the oil-producing countries

It was Mexico's 1982 debt crisis that led the Fund into new fields of international finance. As the weight of international debt grew dramatically, mounting concern about Mexico's financial viability spread through the international financial community. The international banks suddenly stopped lending to Mexico and, in order to avoid declaring a default on its loans, the country turned to the Fund for support. Up to this point, the Fund had always followed a passive role in cofinancing: it had established the amount of financing that it could itself provide under its institutional rules and then it ascertained what other creditors would be willing to contribute, framing the **adjustment program** to the total external resources available. In the situation that Mexico and many other developing countries found themselves in the early 1980s, the international banks were unwilling to make any further new loans or to roll over existing loans.

This led to what became known as *concerted lending*. The **Managing Director** of the Fund went before a meeting of creditor banks in New York and informed them that the Fund would lend Mexico $3.8 billion over three years under an **extended Fund facility** only if the Fund received a written assurance from the banks that, as a group, they would increase their own lending to Mexico by $5.8 billion. His perception was that the banks' long-term common interest in saving Mexico from default was greater than the dubious short-term advantage that they would achieve if, as individual institutions, they attempted to reduce their exposures unilaterally. Concerted lending became the wave of the future for the next three or four years, until debt-reduction strategies were put in place.

A remarkable economic transformation had been achieved by Mexico through prudent macroeconomic programs and structural reforms since the 1982 crisis. These programs emphasized three aspects:

1. Fiscal and budgetary reforms that brought about a broader tax base, an increase in revenues, lower tax rates, and the elimination of loopholes, which, combined with cuts in government expenditures, converted a deficit amounting to 7 percent of GDP in 1982 to a surplus of 8 percent of GDP in 1990.

2. Privatization, which first focused on making the private sector self-sufficient and weaning it away from subsidized inputs and interest rates, and then converted state-owned enterprises into private hands so that by 1991 the government owned only 257 firms, compared with 1,155 at the end of 1982.
3. Trade liberalization, which included unilateral initiatives, as well as reciprocal trade liberalization under the **General Agreement on Tariffs and Trade**, which Mexico joined in 1985, in time to participate in the Uruguay Round.

Despite the progress made since 1982, concerns about the sustainability of the current account deficit began to rise sharply in 1994. Dramatic political unrest, intense foreign competition for savings in other emerging markets, and generally higher interest rates abroad led to a sharp decline in capital inflows and even to significant outflows. To stem capital outflows, the Mexican authorities raised interest rates, allowed the **currency** to depreciate, and substituted short-term indebtedness denominated in foreign currency for local currency-denominated debt. The level of **reserves** was stabilized for about six months during 1994, but in October of that year a resurgence of investors' fears put further pressure on the **foreign exchange** and financial markets, forced the government to float the peso, and precipitated another crisis.

Mexico again turned to the Fund. At first the Fund intended to lend Mexico $7.8 billion under a **stand-by arrangement**, but when the U.S. Congress refused the U.S. Administration's request for $40 billion in loan guarantees late in the evening of 30 January, the Fund promptly raised its loan amount by $10 billion, to $17.8 billion, said at that time to be the largest amount ever lent to anyone (although not all the credit was subsequently drawn on). In making such a huge loan available to Mexico, the Fund's rationale was not only to restore confidence in Mexico, but also to head off the contagion (Tequila) effect that the loss of confidence was having on other countries in the region and the broader threat to the **international monetary system**. In addition to Fund **resources**, the U.S. Administration, despite the opposition by the U.S. Congress, agreed to provide $20 billion in credit from the Exchange Stabilization Fund, and the **Bank for International Settlements** raised its loan offer from $5 billion to $10 billion, thereby restoring the original amount of financing.

Tighter fiscal and monetary policy, along with greater privatization and other structural reforms, led to sharp economic and financial improvements. Interests rates, although remaining high, began to fall and the trade surplus increased dramatically. Overall, however, economic growth was slow to recover, although the country's external position improved markedly, with a strengthening of its **international reserves** and some recovery in its foreign exchange and financial markets. As a consequence, Mexico was able to resume borrowing from private markets abroad and to begin repaying its creditors ahead of schedule.

The 1994 Mexican crisis, as in the crisis 12 years earlier, was followed by a number of improvements in the international financial mechanism. Although there had been some earlier indications that the underlying economic conditions were not entirely satisfactory, the force and severity of the crisis when it did come took the international community by surprise and provoked a sharp overreaction by the international financial markets not justified by the economic fundamentals. In the succeeding years, steps were taken to significantly strengthen the Fund's financial resources by establishing the **New Arrangements to Borrow (NAB)**, the renewal of the **General Arrangements to Borrow (GAB)**, and a general 45 percent increase in quotas under the eleventh general review of **quotas**. Its mechanism for coping with unexpected demands for resources was expedited by the emergency financing mechanism and the **supplemental reserve facility**. Finally, the data and other information made public by the Fund were improved and expanded; the Fund's **surveillance** procedures over members' economies were intensified; the Executive Board's views on members' policies under Article IV consultations were made available to the public in the form of **public information notices**; **letters of intent**, spelling out the **adjustment programs** supported by the Fund, were made available on the Fund's website, subject to the consent of the member involved; **special data dissemination standards** for statistical data were established for improving the quality and transparency of the data supplied by member countries; and, in general, the range of the Fund's publications was expanded sharply to include staff reports on countries, working papers, and other analytical and explanatory material.

In the period following the 1994 financial crisis, Mexico significantly strengthened policy credibility and public and private sector balance sheets. It also achieved considerable progress in strengthening the regulatory framework and soundness of the banking sector. This progress, combined with strong economic performance, with growth averaging over 3.5 percent over the period 2003–2007, and the flexible exchange rate regime placed it in a strong position prior to the onset of the **global financial crisis**.

Nevertheless, Mexico's resilience was severely tested during the global crisis. The surge in risk aversion following the collapse of Lehman Brothers in September 2008 triggered a sharp retrenchment of financial flows from emerging markets, including Mexico, resulting in liquidity strains and marked currency depreciation. Meanwhile, reflecting close U.S. linkages, Mexico experienced a rapid decline in manufacturing exports in the first half of 2009. Unanticipated large losses on corporate foreign exchange derivate positions disclosed in late 2008 further weighed on confidence, while the H1N1 virus outbreak in mid-2009 put an additional drag on activity. Against this background, output contracted by 6.5 percent in 2009, while the peso fell 25 percent against the dollar in the nine months to mid-2009.

The Mexican authorities took prompt and effective policy measures in response to the crisis. Macroeconomic policies were eased significantly, providing a fiscal impulse of 2.5 percent of GDP in 2009. Targeted assistance was also extended to financial intermediaries to address funding shortages. At the same time, Mexico's Central Bank (Banxico) made substantial interventions (US$31.4 billion in total) to maintain orderly liquidity conditions in the foreign exchange market, and secured contingent financing through the Federal Reserve swap line ($30 billion) and the Fund **Flexible Credit Line** ($47 billion) to further support confidence.

Based on these strong policy measures, growth resumed starting in mid-2009, the peso exchange rate rebounded, and domestic financial stability had been maintained. *See also* GLOBAL FINANCIAL CRISIS.

MILITARY EXPENDITURES. The Fund estimated that military spending in the early 1990s amounted to about 5 percent of the world's GDP. In discussing military expenditure and the role of the Fund toward the end of 1992, the Directors indicated that such expenditure had an important bearing on a member's fiscal policy and external position. They recognized, however, that judgments about the appropriate level of military spending were the prerogative of national governments and were not part of the Fund's work. The **Executive Board** emphasized that aggregate data on all fiscal expenditures, including off-budget items, should continue to be reported to the Fund.

According to a Fund staff analysis of 132 countries, military expenditures declined to 2.3 percent of GDP in 1996 and 1997, from 3.5 percent in 1990—allowing some $357 billion of resources to be applied to more productive endeavors, assuming the maintenance of the 1990 level of expenditures throughout the period. The sharp drop and eventual leveling off of military expenditures during the 1990s were most notable in **stand-by** and extended Fund arrangements. This was mainly due to the significant number of **transitional economies** seeking Fund assistance under these arrangements and their high levels of military expenditures before they entered into the arrangements. Low-income countries, which typically enter into adjustment programs or enhanced structural adjustment arrangements, also managed to reduce their military expenditures significantly.

Military expenditures as a share of GDP in countries receiving Fund-supported programs have remained below the worldwide average, particularly in those countries with programs extending for two years or more. Military expenditures in countries with programs under the **structural adjustment facility** and the **enhanced structural adjustment facility** had fallen from 4.4 percent of GDP in 1990 to 2.8 percent in 1997, in countries with extended Fund facility programs from 4.8 percent to 1.7 percent, and in countries with stand-by arrangements from 3.8 percent to 1.9 percent.

MILLENNIUM DEVELOPMENT GOALS (MDGs). The MDGs are a set of eight measurable targets established at the United Nations Millennium Summit in September 2000. These targets aim to reduce poverty and improve the welfare of the world's poorest by 2015. The first seven goals focus on eradicating extreme poverty and hunger; achieving universal primary education; promoting gender equality and empowering women; reducing child mortality; improving maternal health; combating HIV and AIDS, malaria, and other diseases; and ensuring environmental sustainability. The eighth goal calls for the creation of a global partnership for development, with targets for aid, trade, and debt relief.

The Fund contributes to this effort through its advice, **technical assistance**, and lending to countries, as well as its role in mobilizing donor support. It also tries to ensure that developed countries' policies are supportive of low-income countries' development efforts, by promoting increased foreign aid, opening markets to developing countries' exports, and the need for a healthy and stable international economic climate. Together with the **World Bank**, the Fund assesses progress toward the MDGs through an annual **Global Monitoring Report (GMR)**, which examines policies and actions aimed at achieving the MDGs and related outcomes.

At a meeting held in Monterrey, Mexico, in March 2002, the international community adopted a two-pillar strategy toward the achievement of the MDGs based on rewarding the sustained pursuit of sound policies and **good governance** by providing larger and more effective international support.

The pressures to meet the MDGs by 2015 have further focused the Fund's efforts in individual country cases. Specifically, the Fund **staff** tries to help countries assess the macroeconomic consequences of scaling up both their own policy efforts and external financial support. In this context, it encourages countries to develop and analyze alternative frameworks for achieving the MDGs and to incorporate detailed policies in their poverty reduction strategies. Increasingly, it is recognized that macroeconomic stability and growth depend heavily on structural and institutional factors. Therefore, in contributing to the achievement of the MDGs, the Fund has increased its collaboration with the World Bank and other multilateral and bilateral providers of aid and financing.

According to the 2008 GMR, the international community was on course to achieve the first MDG of halving extreme poverty between 1990 and 2015. The number of people living on less than $1 a day had declined by 278 million between 1990 and 2004. The most significant declines in poverty had been achieved by the regions such as East Asia, which had experienced the strongest overall economic growth. However, based on 2008 trends, it was unlikely that most of the MDG would be met at the global level by 2015. In particular, countries in sub-Saharan Africa and South Asia were likely to fall short of the MDGs, particularly as they related to child and maternal mortality, access to basic sanitation, and reducing child malnutrition. While the HIV prevalence rate declined in Africa, it rose in some other regions, albeit from much smaller levels than in Africa.

MINISTATES. *See* SMALL STATES.

MONETARY APPROACH TO BALANCE OF PAYMENTS. In the 1950s, the Fund developed what came to be known as the *Polak model*, reflecting the work of **Jacques J. Polak**, Director of the Research Department from 1958 to 1979, a monetary model that was designed to allow the Fund to judge whether a country's policies would be sufficient to restore economic balance. The main feature of the model was its simplicity, confining inputs to the economic data (banking data and trade data) generally available in many member countries at that time, and the necessity to keep the model based on the key variable that governments could control (domestic credit creation). The model contained two behavioral equations—a demand-for-money function that was proportional to income and a correlated demand-for-import function. The set of four equations in the model constitutes the logical core of the Fund's programming exercise, known as ***financial programming***. Over the years, for practical purposes the model has remained simple, with a limited number of standard variables. It has, however, been subject to elaboration on an ad hoc basis.

MONETARY AUTHORITY. Monetary authorities are the treasury, central bank, stabilization fund, or any similar fiscal agency of a member country. Normally, a monetary authority is responsible for applying the rules governing the relationship between the country and the Fund insofar as the country's **balance of payments** and related matters are concerned.

MONETARY POLICY. Monetary policy is one of several short-term policy instruments used as part of a broader approach to structural and **balance of payments adjustment** that may include fiscal and exchange rate policies, as well as institutional and structural reforms. Regulation of the money supply is controlled through central banking instruments of policy—interest rates, special central bank deposits, open-market operations, and other techniques. **Adjustment programs** supported by the Fund usually include quarterly credit ceilings—on the public and private sectors, and on overall bank credit. Curtailment of the money supply reduces domestic absorption (consumption and investment), releases resources for export, cuts down on imports, and brings about an improvement in the **balance of payments**. Other factors, financial and nonfinancial, may need attention, and the relationship between the money supply and the balance of payments requires assumptions about the demand for money, which may differ from country to country, and over time. Nevertheless, the monetary approach to the balance of payments is a proven, pragmatic, practical approach, based on readily available and up-to-date statistics that are easy to monitor. *See also* FINANCIAL PROGRAMMING.

MONETARY RESERVES. Used in the original **Articles of Agreement**, the term has been eliminated from the current Articles. The term was never defined, but refers to **reserve assets**. *See* INTERNATIONAL RESERVES.

MORAL HAZARD. As the Fund moved into crisis management, first with the **Mexican financial crisis** in 1982 and subsequently with the critical crisis that arose again with Mexico in 1994 and the **Asian financial crisis** three years later, it came under strong criticism from many quarters for what were labeled its "bail-out" policies. It was contended by these critics that the marketplace was the appropriate place to bring about any needed adjustment, that the chips should fall where they may, and that the intervention of an international organization was not only unnecessary but damaging to the long-run health of the free enterprise system. It was charged that the Fund, by providing assistance to countries in crisis, encouraged more reckless behavior on the part of borrowers and lenders in the future. Further, it was contended that the very participation of the Fund in a country's economy, no matter what long-term benefit there would be, sent a strong signal that in the short term the country was in trouble, and thus caused an exacerbation of the situation.

Addressing this issue in a speech given in February 1998, the Fund's **Managing Director**, **Michel Camdessus**, said that the notion that the availability of Fund programs encouraged countries to behave recklessly was not plausible; no country would deliberately court such a crisis, even if it thought international assistance would be forthcoming. The economic, financial, social, and political price paid was simply too great. "Nor do countries," he added, "show any great desire to enter Fund programs unless they absolutely have to."

Further, the Managing Director noted, despite the constant talk of bailouts, most investors were taking heavy losses in the crisis. With stock markets and **exchange rates** plunging, foreign equity investors had lost nearly three-quarters of the value of their holdings in some Asian markets. Many firms and financial institutions in these countries would go bankrupt, and their foreign and domestic lenders would share in the losses. International banks were also sharing in the cost of the crisis.

The Managing Director concluded his defense of the Fund by saying there was a trade-off in how the international community chose to handle the Asian financial crisis. It could step back, allow the crisis to deepen, bring additional suffering to the people of the region, and in the process possibly teach a handful of international lenders a better lesson. Or it could step in and try to do what it could to mitigate the undesired side effects. "In my view," he said, "the global interest lies in containing and overcoming the crisis as quickly as possible. And working through the Fund offers the most expeditious and cost-effective way of doing this." The controversy parallels the arguments that sometimes reappear in some countries as to whether central banks or other government authorities should indulge in bailouts for domestic banks. In practice, however, no country, however sparse its regulations over the financial sector may be, can stand aside and watch its national banking system collapse. And so far, no country has done so. Similarly, the Fund and other international institutions would be failing in their responsibilities to allow a major international financial crisis to develop to a point where there is a danger of the international system suffering severe disruption or even collapsing, as happened in the 1930s, when the troubles of a relatively small Austrian bank were followed by a worldwide depression.

On the question of "bailing-in" the private sector, the **Interim Committee** and the **Executive Board** have given much consideration as to how private creditors can be encouraged to stay with a country in crisis, without pulling out their funds in unison, and as to how this can be done on a voluntary basis, without the creditors withdrawing their funds from other markets. The November 1998 agreement on the economic and financial program with **Brazil** was an experimental attempt along these lines.

MULTILATERAL DEBT RELIEF INITIATIVE (MDRI). The MDRI was established by the **Group of Eight (G-8)** major industrial countries in June 2005. It calls on the Fund, the International Development Association (IDA) of the **World Bank**, and the African Development Fund (AfDF) to provide for 100 percent relief on eligible debt for low-income countries that reach the completion point under the joint IMF–World Bank enhanced Initiative for **heavily indebted poor countries (HIPC)**. The initiative is intended to help these countries achieve the **Millennium Development Goals (MDGs)**, which are focused on halving poverty by 2015.

While the HIPC Initiative provides for coordinated action by multilateral organizations and governments to reduce to sustainable levels the external debt burdens of the most heavily indebted poor countries, the MDRI goes further by providing full debt relief so as to free up additional resources to help countries reach the MDGs. Unlike the HIPC Initiative, the MDRI does not propose any parallel debt relief on the part of official bilateral or private creditors, or of multilateral institutions beyond the IMF, IDA, and the AfDF. In early 2007, the **Inter-American Development Bank** announced that it would provide similar debt relief to the five HIPCs in the Western Hemisphere.

The Fund and the World Bank collaborate closely in the implementation and monitoring of the MDRI. The first progress report on the IMF's implementation of the MDRI was presented to the **Executive Board** in April 2006. Subsequent reports have been folded into the regular joint Bank–Fund HIPC Initiative status of implementation report.

MULTILATERAL EXCHANGE RATE MODEL (MERM). The MERM was an early worldwide econometric model devised by the Fund's **staff** that, in analyzing a country's overall competitiveness in terms of changes in its **exchange rate**, calculated effective exchange rates by taking into account the commodity composition of a country's trade, the relevant elasticities of supply and demand, and the relative importance of other countries as trading partners and as competitors in third markets. The MERM was phased out during the 1980s and has been replaced by a more generalized model.

MULTILATERAL SURVEILLANCE. Multilateral surveillance is a key function of the Fund. It monitors developments in individual countries, the global economy, and financial markets with a view to detecting and heightening awareness of systemic risks, highlighting the potential spillover effects of policy changes in systemically important countries.

The key instruments of multilateral surveillance are two semiannual publications, the ***World Economic Outlook*** **(WEO)** and the ***Global Financial Stability Report*** **(GFSR)**. The WEO provides detailed analysis of the state of the world economy, addressing issues of pressing interest, such as the current global financial turmoil and economic downturn. The GFSR provides an up-to-date assessment of global financial markets, highlighting imbalances and vulnerabilities that could pose risks to stability. The Fund also publishes Regional Economic Outlook reports, which provide more detailed analyses of developments within the five major regions. *See also* SURVEILLANCE OVER EXCHANGE RATES.

MULTIPLE CURRENCY PRACTICES. Members must obtain the approval of the Fund before engaging in multiple currency practices. Despite the fact that under the second amendment to the **Articles** members have freedom to choose their exchange arrangements, unitary **exchange rates** continue to be the principle to be upheld under the Articles. Multiple currency practices are objected to because they can be restrictive, discriminatory among members, and unfairly competitive. Under the original Articles, multiple rates were legally identifiable if some exchange transactions took place within the legal margins and others outside that margin. Under the current system of exchange arrangements, there are no legal margins, which are set by the market.

As a guideline, therefore, in defining a multiple currency practice, the Fund has adopted a decision reasoning that official action should not cause spreads between a buying and selling rate for a currency, or discrepancies between cross rates among currencies, that differ unreasonably from the rates that would emerge if they were affected only by normal commercial costs and risks of exchange transactions. For the purpose of applying this decision, the Fund has established a margin of 2 percent. If a spread exceeds 2 percent without official action, it will not be considered a multiple currency practice. But if this is caused by official action, such as, say, a tax on exchange transactions of more than 2 percent, then the Fund will judge that to be a multiple currency practice.

MULTIPLE RESERVE CURRENCY PROPOSALS. A number of plans were advanced late in the 1950s and in the 1960s, mainly by private economists, proposing a deliberate diversification of foreign **currency** holdings by central banks, in order to reduce reliance on the U.S. dollar. The proposals had many variations in their details, but they were never seriously considered by the **monetary authorities**. Instead, the **Special Drawing Rights** facility was established in the Fund under the first amendment of the **Articles** (1969). *See also* MUTUAL CURRENCY ACCOUNT PLAN.

MUTUAL CURRENCY ACCOUNT PLAN. A scheme to increase **international liquidity** and reduce the role of **gold** in the **international monetary system** was first put forward in 1962 by Robert V. Roosa, at that time Undersecretary for Monetary Affairs of the U.S. Treasury. He suggested that the industrial countries should be prepared to hold each other's **currencies** in their monetary **reserves**: a country in surplus in its **balance of payments** would receive and hold the currency of an industrial country in balance of payments deficit, thereby avoiding its conversion into gold, U.S. dollars, or sterling. At that time, the U.S. dollar and sterling were the principal **reserve**

currencies and the effect of the Roosa scheme would have been to increase the number of currencies held in reserves.

Later in the same year, Reginald Maudling, of the United Kingdom, built on the idea put forward by Roosa by suggesting that the Fund establish a mutual currency account into which the mutual holdings of currencies could be converted into a **reserve asset** defined in terms of gold. The plan was cast in terms of voluntary action, but its details were never fully formulated, since the United States, which was in balance of payments deficit, resisted the idea of establishing a two-tier dollar holding structure with a defined and guaranteed value in terms of gold established under the mutual currency account and the other consisting of U.S. dollars held by countries in their reserves outside the mutual currency plan.

Although these early schemes to counter the shortage of international liquidity and to reduce the role of the U.S. dollar as a reserve currency did not get far, they laid the groundwork for a number of other proposals. These included a mechanism to control international liquidity put forward by Professor Robert Triffin and others; a reserve asset scheme suggested by Edward M. Bernstein, who had played a prominent role in the negotiation of the original **Articles of Agreement**; and the establishment of the **Special Drawing Rights** facility in the Fund in 1969. Although the concept of a substitution account was seriously considered and even outlined in some detail by the **Committee of Twenty**, the differing proposals could not be reconciled. Subsequently, in 1980, the **Interim Committee** agreed to abandon further study of the proposal.

N

NARVEKAR, PRABHAKAR R. (1932–). Prabhakar Narvekar, a national of India, was appointed one of three **Deputy Managing Directors** in June 1994. He had been Special Advisor to the **Managing Director** of the Fund since August 1991. He joined the staff of the Fund in 1953 as a Research Assistant, and he held various positions in the Asian and European Departments before being appointed Director of the Asian Department in 1986. He holds degrees in economics from Bombay University and Columbia University and also studied at Oxford University. Mr. Narvekar retired from the Fund's staff in 1997 but was appointed by the Managing Director as Special Advisor to the President of **Indonesia** in 1998, following that country's economic crisis and the inauguration of a Fund-supported **adjustment program**. He later became a founding member and Vice-Chairman of the Centennial Group, a consulting group composed of internationally recognized figures from the public and private sectors that provides high-level policy and strategic advice to top business executives, senior public officials, and multilateral financial agencies.

NEED FOR FINANCING. *See* REQUIREMENT OF NEED.

NEW ARRANGEMENTS TO BORROW (NAB). Under the NAB, approved by the Fund's **Executive Board** on 27 January 1997, 25 participant countries and institutions stand ready to lend the Fund additional resources—up to SDR 34 billion (about $47 billion)—to supplement its regular **quota** resources when needed to forestall or cope with an impairment of the **international monetary system** or deal with an exceptional situation that threatens the stability of the system. The NABs do not replace the supplemental credit lines available to the Fund under the **General Arrangements to Borrow (GAB)**, which remain in force. Under the GAB, the **Group of Ten** industrial countries and Switzerland stand ready to lend up to SDR 17 billion (about $24 billion); in an associated agreement, Saudi Arabia is prepared to make available SDR 1.5 billion (about $2.1 billion). The NAB, however, will be the facility of first recourse.

It entered into force on 17 November 1998—for five years and subject to renewal—when it was approved by participants with credit arrangements totaling SDR 28.9 billion (about $40 billion), including the five participants with the largest credit arrangements. NAB credit lines may be drawn on for the benefit of all NAB participant countries, or for nonparticipant countries under circumstances similar to those under the GAB. Activation procedures for nonparticipants under the NAB credit lines may be drawn on for the benefit of all NAB participant countries, or for nonparticipant countries under circumstances similar to those under the GAB. Activation procedures for nonparticipants are, however, somewhat more flexible. A country or institution not currently a participant may become one when the NAB is renewed, if the Fund and participants representing 80 percent of credit arrangements agree.

The wider participation under the NAB reflects the changing character of the global economy and a broadened willingness to share responsibility for managing the international monetary system. The credit contributions (except for the Hong Kong Monetary Authority) are based initially on the strength and size of the economies of the participating members as reflected by their quotas in the Fund. In approving the new arrangements, the Board reiterated that they were in no way a substitute for the strengthening of quotas—which is the capital basis of the Fund.

The first activation of the NAB came in December 1998, when 21 countries lent a total of about $12.5 billion to the Fund to help finance the arrangement approved for Brazil.

In the wake of the global financial crises, on 2 April 2009, the **Group of Twenty** industrialized and emerging market economies agreed to further increase the Fund's ability to borrow resources by up to $500 billion. This increase will entail two steps. First, the Fund will be given immediate access to bilateral financing from member countries. Second, this financing will be incorporated into an expanded and more flexible NAB. As of December 2009, six countries had signed bilateral loan agreements with the Fund worth $169 billion.

NONMETROPOLITAN TERRITORIES OF MEMBERS. Dependencies or nonmetropolitan territories of members cannot be admitted to **membership** of the Fund, even though the dependency may have a separate **currency** and a separate **balance of payments**, full internal autonomy, and, in terms of economic size, may be far larger than many existing members of the Fund (e.g., as was **Hong Kong**). Members accepting the obligations of the **Articles of Agreement** do so for all the territory under their authority and are solely responsible for carrying out those obligations, which cannot be shared with a dependency.

O

OBLIGATIONS UNDER ARTICLE VIII. Members accepting the obligations of the **Articles of Agreement** undertake to refrain from imposing restrictions on the making of payments for current international transactions or engaging in discriminatory currency arrangements or **multiple currency practices** without Fund approval. Members that are not in a position to accept **Article VIII** can avail themselves of the **transitional arrangements** set out in **Article XIV**. At the beginning of December 2009, 167 members, including all the major trading countries, had accepted the obligations of Article VIII.

OFFICES OUTSIDE THE UNITED STATES. The Fund maintains four small liaison offices outside of the United States in Guatemala City, Paris, Tokyo, and Warsaw. The office in Paris serves mainly as a liaison office for the Fund with the European Union, the Organization for Economic Cooperation and Development, and the national **monetary authorities** in Europe. *See also* AFRICAN REGIONAL TECHNICAL ASSISTANCE CENTER (AFRITAC); CARIBBEAN REGIONAL TECHNICAL ASSISTANCE CENTER (CARTAC).

OIL FACILITIES. In 1974 and again in 1975, the Fund established a temporary facility to help members meet the increased costs of imports of petroleum and petroleum products as a result of the sharp rise in oil prices occurring at the end of 1973. These large increases in oil prices had given rise to **balance of payments** difficulties of unprecedented magnitude for most oil-importing countries. **Drawings** by these members under the Fund's normal **credit tranche** policies would have been inadequate to meet the serious imbalances caused by the oil price escalation, and would have virtually rendered the Fund a bystander at a time when a serious payments crisis was threatening to overwhelm the world economy.

The establishment of the oil facilities of 1974 and 1975 was based on the view that neither the oil-exporting countries nor the oil-importing countries could quickly adjust to their new payments situations. The capacity of the major oil-exporting countries to increase imports was limited in the short run, while measures to rectify the balance of payments of the oil-importing countries could only aggravate the general imbalance in payments through widespread deflationary policies or trade restrictions. Financing rather than adjustment was the principal objective to be achieved by establishing the oil facilities. The facilities were funded by borrowing from those members that were in balance of payments surplus, mainly the major oil-exporting countries, thereby recycling the so-called petrodollars.

In accordance with this policy, **conditionality** on the use of the two oil facilities was minimal, although the terms of the 1975 facility were tightened somewhat. Repayments of drawings under the facilities were to begin in the fourth year after purchase and be completed within seven years. All told, 55 members drew SDR 6.9 billion under the facilities, which were funded by borrowings from 17 lenders. *See also* OIL FACILITY SUBSIDY ACCOUNT.

OIL FACILITY SUBSIDY ACCOUNT. In August 1975, the Fund established a subsidy account to assist its most seriously affected members to meet the cost of using resources made available under the **oil facility**. Members eligible to receive assistance from the subsidy account were 18 Fund members on the list of countries prepared by the Secretary-General of the **United Nations** that had been most seriously affected by the increased price of petroleum and petroleum products. Contributions to the subsidy account were made by 24 members of the Fund and Switzerland, in the amount of SDR 160 million. The account enabled the effective cost of using the resources of the oil facility to be reduced by about 5 percent, to about 2.75 percent a year. The account was administered by the Fund as trustee, and in that guise the resources of the account were able to be directed to a specific list of 25 **developing countries** without violating the spirit of the **Articles of Agreement**, which imply that all members be treated equally.

The subsidy account was the forerunner of the **Trust Fund**, which was established the following year.

OPERATIONAL BUDGET. The Fund's **financial resources** consist essentially of a pool of **gold**, **Special Drawing Rights (SDRs)**, and national **currencies** subscribed by members. Not all the currencies held by the Fund are usable at all times. Only currencies of members in sufficiently strong **balance of payments** and reserve positions are sold by the Fund in its **transactions** and operations. A considerable portion of its currency holdings is not, therefore, available for use.

Currencies to be used in **drawings** (purchases), repayments (**repurchases**), and other Fund operations are selected by the **Executive Board** for successive quarterly periods by drawing up an operational budget. This budget specifies the amount of SDRs and currencies that the Fund is expected to use in the three-month period. In preparing the budget, the selection of currency is determined by the strength of the balance of payments and gross reserves of members and by developments in **exchange markets**. In addition, the Fund tries to promote, over time, balanced positions in the Fund, so that the amount of individual currencies transferred through the budget are consistent with the member's gross holding of gold and **foreign exchange** reserves and with the need for the Fund to maintain minimum working balances in all currencies.

The operational budget is a practical example of members cooperating within the institution. Members that are in strong balance of payments and reserve positions make resources available to members experiencing balance of payments difficulties. In preparing the budget, the Fund makes a projection of the overall use of its resources that will be required in the following quarter and assesses which currencies will be available to use in drawings by other members. The purpose of the exercise is to ensure that only the stronger currencies are used, temporarily, to help the weaker currencies. *See also* ADMINISTRATIVE AND CAPITAL BUDGETS OF THE FUND; INCOME AND EXPENDITURE OF THE FUND.

ORGANIZATION OF THE FUND. The organizational structure of the Fund is set out in its **Articles of Agreement**. They provide for a **Board of Governors**, an **Executive Board**, a **Managing Director**, and a **staff** of international civil servants. The highest authority in the Fund is the Board of Governors. Each Fund member country appoints one Governor and one Alternate Governor. The Governors are usually ministers of finance or heads of central banks. The second amendment to the Articles provided for the Board of Governors to establish a Council as a permanent body at the ministerial level to supervise the management and functioning of the **international monetary system** and to consider any proposals to amend the Articles of Agreement, but the Board has not done so. Instead, the **Interim Committee** and later the **International Monetary and Financial Committee** have served as high-level advisory bodies for the institution. In 1974, the Board of Governors also established the **Development Committee** to advise and report to the Fund and Bank Boards of Governors on developing issues.

The Board of Governors has delegated many of its powers to the Executive Board, which is the day-to-day decision-making authority. The Executive Board selects the Managing Director of the Fund, who serves as its Chairman and the head of the Fund's staff. The **Deputy Managing Directors** are selected by the Managing Director, subject to the approval of the Executive Board.

Beneath the Office of the Managing Director and reporting directly to it are five area departments; seven functional and special services departments; and five information, liaison, and support departments, including a Secretariat at headquarters and five offices located overseas.

The area departments advise management and the Board on the economies and economic policies of the countries in their areas, assist in the formulation of Fund policies toward these countries, and carry out these policies. Area departments also negotiate arrangements for the use of Fund financial **resources** and review performance under Fund-supported arrangements. Together with other departments, the area departments provide member countries with policy advice and **technical assistance** and maintain contact with regional organizations and multilateral institutions in their area. Much of the Fund's bilateral **surveillance** work is carried out by the area departments through their direct contacts with member countries, supplemented by staff in functional departments.

Functional and special services departments are individually responsible for a wide range of activities. The *Strategy, Policy, and Review Department* is responsible for designing, implementing and evaluating Fund policies related to **surveillance** and the use of its financial resources. *The Monetary and Capital Markets Department* monitors financial sectors and capital markets, and monetary and foreign exchange systems, arrangements, and operations. It also provides **technical assistance** to members in areas of its specialization and prepares the **Global Financial Stability Report (GFSR)**. The Fiscal Affairs Department is responsible for all activities involving the public finance of member countries. It participates in area department missions on fiscal matters, reviews the fiscal content of Fund policy advice and of Fund-supported **adjustment programs**, and provides technical assistance in public finance. It also conducts research and policy studies on fiscal issues, as well as on income distribution and poverty, social safety nets, public expenditure policy issues, and the environment.

The IMF Institute provides technical assistance through training officials of member countries, particularly **developing countries**, in such topics as **financial programming** and policy, external sector polities, **balance of payments** and government statistics, and public finance.

The Legal Department advises management, the Board, and the staff on the applicable rules of law. It prepares most of the decisions and other legal instruments necessary for Fund activities. It serves as counsel to the Fund in litigation and arbitration cases, provides technical assistance on legislative reform in member countries, and responds to inquiries from national authorities and international organizations on the law of the Fund.

The Research Department carries out policy analysis and research in areas relating to the Fund's work. The department also plays a prominent role in the development of Fund policy concerning the **international monetary system** and surveillance. It cooperates with other departments in formulating the Fund's policy advice to member countries. It also coordinates the semiannual ***World Economic Outlook*** exercise and the GFSR, as well as analysis for the **Group of Seven** policy coordination exercise and for the Board's seminars on World Economic and Market Developments. The department also develops the Fund's contacts with the academic community and with other research organizations.

The Statistics Department maintains a database of country, regional, and global economic and financial statistics and reviews country data in support of the Fund's surveillance role. It is also responsible for developing statistical concepts in balance of payments, government finance, and money and financial statistics; and for producing methodological manuals. The department provides technical assistance and training to help members to develop statistical systems and produces the Fund's statistical publications. In addition, it is responsible for the development and maintenance of standards for the dissemination of data by member countries.

The Secretary's Department assists in preparing and coordinating the work program of the Board and other official bodies, including scheduling and assisting in the conduct of Board meetings. The department also manages the **annual meetings** in cooperation with the **World Bank**, and is responsible for the Fund's **archives** and communications with member countries.

OSSOLA GROUP. The Ossola Group was established by the Deputies of the **Group of Ten** in June 1964 to study the various proposals for the creation of **reserve assets**, headed by Rinaldo Ossola, of the Bank of Italy. The Group's report, submitted in May 1965, was an important step in the subsequent formulation of the **Special Drawing Rights** facility.

OUATTARA, ALASSANE D. (1942–). Alassane Ouattara served as **Deputy Managing Director** of the Fund from July 1994 to July 1999. He studied at the Drexel Institute of Technology and the University of Pennsylvania, where he received his PhD in economics. He joined the **staff** of the Fund in 1968 as an economist in the African Department, leaving in 1973 to join the Central Bank for West African States (BCEAO), where he became Vice Governor in 1983. He joined the Fund staff again in November 1984 as Director of the African Department and was appointed Counselor in May 1987. Mr. Outtara returned to the BCEAO as Governor in November 1988, was appointed Chairman of the Economic Committee of the Government of Côte d'Ivoire in April 1990, and between November 1990 and December 1993 served as Prime Minister of Côte d'Ivoire.

OVERBY, ANDREW (1909–1984). Andrew Overby, who had been appointed to the **Executive Board** by the United States in July 1947, was appointed as **Deputy Managing Director** from February 1949 to January 1952. He was formerly Assistant Vice President of the Federal Reserve Bank of New York, and immediately before becoming Deputy Managing Director was Special Assistant to the Secretary of the Treasury in charge of international and monetary affairs.

OVERDUE OBLIGATIONS TO THE FUND. Members' overdue obligations to the Fund began to be a serious problem in the second half of the 1980s. In the financial year ending 30 April 1986, 11 members had obligations overdue by six months or more, amounting to a total of SDR 489 million. The amount overdue rose dramatically in the following years, reaching a peak of SDR 3.5 billion at the end of the 1991–1992 financial year, accounted for by 10 members. By 30 April 1998, total **arrears** had fallen to SDR 2.3 billion, and the number of delinquent members had fallen to seven, after rising to a peak of 12 five years earlier. On 30 April 1998, seven members—Liberia, Sierra Leone, Somalia, Sudan, Vietnam, Zaire, and Zambia—had been declared **ineligible to use Fund resources** and three of them, Liberia, Sudan, and Zaire, had been declared to be not cooperating with the Fund.

In 1990, the Fund introduced a strengthened cooperative strategy on overdue obligations, consisting of three key elements—prevention, deterrence, and intensified collaboration. Preventive measures seek to make certain that **adjustment** programs are drawn up so that members will be able to meet their obligations to the Fund when they fall due. Potential risks and dangers are highlighted, and every effort is made to address these risks in the design, implementation, and financing of the program. Deterrent and remedial measures include a tightening of the timetable for dealing with members with overdue obligations by shortening the period between the emergence of arrears and the declaration of ineligibility and by setting a specific date for a declaration of noncooperation and the initiation of the procedures for compulsory withdrawal.

The collaborative approach requires the "ineligible" member to embark on and adhere to an adjustment program that is monitored by the Fund. Although the member would not be eligible to receive Fund financing, successful completion of the program, together with clearance of its arrears to the Fund, would place it in a position to acquire "**rights**" to use the Fund's financing under a successor program. The member would be expected to obtain the financing and other assistance needed for a Fund-monitored program from a support group, whose assembly would be encouraged by the Fund. At a minimum, the financing generated for such a program would include funds to settle financial obligations falling due to the Fund and the **World Bank** during the program period. The rights approach allows a member following a comprehensive economic program to restore its good standing in the Fund and accumulate rights toward future drawings. Encashment of accumulated rights would take place only after clearance of arrears to the Fund and would be associated with a successor financial arrangement. The new program would involve some Fund financing beyond that provided for the encashment of rights.

By June 2005, the number of members with protracted overdue financial obligations to the Fund had fallen to four—Liberia, Somalia, Sudan, and Zimbabwe. The three members with arrears dating back to the mid-1980s—Liberia, Somalia, and Sudan—accounted for 90 percent of total arrears to the Fund, with Sudan alone accounting for 53 percent. Liberia cleared its arrears to the Fund in 2008. Zimbabwe, which became a protracted arrears case on 14 August 2001, settled its remaining overdue obligations to the **General Resources Account** on 15 February 2006, but it still had substantial arrears to the **poverty-reduction growth facility** and the **exogenous shocks facility**. As of December 2009, total overdue obligations amounted to SDR 1.3 billion.

P

PAR VALUE SYSTEM. The par value system established at the **Bretton Woods Conference** was a major departure from the experience in the period between World War I and World War II, when countries held the view, and acted accordingly, that the setting of an exchange rate was a sovereign decision and beyond the purview of other countries. In addition to bringing exchange rates under international supervision, a second objective of the **Bretton Woods system** was to avoid the rigidity of the **gold** standard and establish a stable system of exchange rates, but at the same time allow them to be adjusted, with the approval of the Fund, if a country was faced with a fundamental disequilibrium in its **balance of payments**.

The rules for operating the par value system were both broad and specific. Competitive **exchange rate** alterations were forbidden. The value of each member's **currency** was fixed in terms of **gold** or in terms of the U.S. dollar of the weight and fineness in effect on 1 July 1944. The **fixed rate** of exchange of one currency against another was determined by the ratio between the two currencies based on their par values, and transactions had to be kept within a specified margin of 1 percent either side of parity. **Floating exchange rates** were not allowed, although temporary floating in order to reach a viable par value for a currency was tolerated in a few cases by the Fund. Exchange systems were to be unitary; **multiple currency practices**, discriminatory exchange rates, and **exchange restrictions** were to be outlawed.

The Bretton Woods par value system was fatally disrupted on 15 August 1971, when the United States suspended the conversion of official dollar balances into gold, and it finally expired in March 1973 when all the major trading countries had resorted to letting their currencies float on the world's **exchange markets**. The second amendment to the **Articles of Agreement** legalized the freely floating exchange rate system that had emerged, but included provisions for a return to a par value system (one that would not be based on gold) if 85 percent of the total voting power of the **Board of Governors** voted in favor of its restoration. *See also* INTERNATIONAL MONETARY SYSTEM; REFORM OF THE INTERNATIONAL MONETARY SYSTEM.

PAR VALUES. Par values were the central feature of the **Bretton Woods system**. The **Articles of Agreement** gave the Fund authority to bring exchange rates under international supervision. **Exchange rates** were to be unitary, fair, and no longer regarded as the sole preserve of national authorities. Under the Bretton Woods system, a member had to notify the Fund of the initial par value of its **currency** expressed in terms of **gold** as a common denominator or in terms of the U.S. dollar of the weight and fineness in effect on 1 July 1944. Agreement of the Fund was necessary when an initial par value was communicated to the Fund, and the concurrence of the Fund was required when a change in par value was proposed going beyond a cumulative 10 percent from the initial par value. A member was entitled to change the par value of its currency after consulting with and obtaining the concurrence of the Fund, but only to correct a fundamental disequilibrium in its **balance of payments**. Temporary balance of payments disequilibria were not grounds for a change in a par value. The member was expected to finance short-term disequilibria, with the assistance of the Fund's **financial resources**, if necessary. Exchange transactions taking place in the territory of a member were not permitted to differ from parity by more than 1 percent for spot transactions.

PARIS CLUB. The Paris Club is an informal group of creditor governments mainly from industrial countries that has met regularly in Paris since 1956, with the French Treasury providing the Secretariat. The Club assumed importance after many **developing countries** in the 1970s incurred a sharp increase in **external debt** that led to debt-servicing difficulties and to **payment arrears**. Meetings of the Club are usually called on the initiative of the debtor country in order to bring all its creditors together at one meeting to discuss possibilities of a multilateral debt relief, instead of bilateral negotiations with each creditor. In addition to the debtor and creditor countries, meetings are attended by the Fund, the **World Bank**, the Organization for Economic Cooperation and Development, and the United Nations Conference on Trade and Development. The international organizations do not attend in official capacities, but provide **technical assistance** and information. The Fund's role is primarily to act as a "go-between," to help the debtor country prepare its submission to the meeting and, if requested, to make presentations analyzing the impact that various levels of debt restructuring would have on the debtor's **financial programming** and its **balance of payments** situation over the medium term. Over the years, the meetings of the Paris Club became more formal, and debt relief became linked to an understanding that a debtor country would enter into a **stand-by arrangement** with the Fund to implement a **stabilization program**.

In the 1980s, the Paris Club became extremely active, and the Fund also took the initiative in embarking on a more innovative and broader role in multilateral debt negotiations. At first, in its early attempts to provide relief in the new indebted situation, the Club creditors provided reschedulings for low-income countries on nonconcessional standard terms, with relatively short grace (5 years) and maturity periods (10 years), and on market-related interest rates. Many countries, however, continued to have difficulties in adhering to their new payments schedules and it became obvious that such repeated reschedulings over a prolonged period would not solve their debt problems. In the late 1980s, therefore, the Paris Club creditors, meeting in Toronto, agreed to provide concessional rescheduling on what came to be known as the **Toronto menu**—a menu of options for debt and debt-service reduction to reduce the net present value of rescheduled amounts by up to one-third. These new terms provided substantial relief, but within a few years it again became obvious that more far-reaching measures would be required. Thus, meeting in London in December 1991, creditors introduced what came to be known as the *London terms*, which increased the level of debt relief up to 50 percent. Subsequently, meeting in Naples at the end of 1994, the level of concessionality was increased to 67 percent—the Naples terms.

Under the Naples terms, eligibility is determined on a case-by-case basis, based primarily on a country's income level. Most countries receive a reduction in eligible nonofficial development assistance debt of 67 percent of net present value terms, with somewhat less easy terms for countries with a per capita income of $500 or more and a ratio of debt to exports in present value terms of less than 350 percent. The coverage of the debt to be included in the rescheduling is also decided on a case-by-case basis, but previously rescheduled debts are not excluded from the Naples terms. Creditors have a choice of two concessional options: a debt reduction option, with repayment over 23 years with a six-year grace period, or, a debt-service reduction option, under which the net present value reduction is achieved by concessional interest rates, with repayments over 33 years. There is a third option that allows creditors to enter into a commercial or long-term maturities option, providing for no net present value reduction, with repayment of 40 years with 20 years' grace. Finally, a stock-of-debt operation is available under which the entire stock of eligible debt is rescheduled concessionally. This option is reserved for countries with a satisfactory track record for a minimum of three years with respect to both payments under rescheduling agreements and performance under Fund arrangements. Creditors must be confident that the country will be able to respect the debt agreement as an exit rescheduling (with no further rescheduling required), and there must be a consensus among creditors to choose concessional options.

To ensure concerted support by the international community, Paris Club rescheduling agreements include a comparability clause under which the rescheduling country commits itself to seek at least comparable debt relief from commercial and non–Paris Club bilateral creditors.

As of August 2010, the Paris Club, and related ad hoc groups, had reached over 416 agreements covering 87 debtor countries.

PAYMENTS ARREARS. *See* ARREARS IN PAYMENTS.

PEGGING OF EXCHANGE RATES. After the collapse of the **fixed exchange rate** system in 1973, each country was faced with the choice of letting its currency float freely in the **exchange market** (and thus have its value determined by supply and demand) or of pegging to another currency or composite unit. While the national **monetary authorities** of the major **currencies**, such as the U.S. dollar, the Japanese yen, and the deutsche mark, chose to allow their currencies to float (the deutsche mark in the context of the **European Monetary System**), many smaller economies chose to peg their currencies to one of the major currencies, to a composite unit made up of a basket of currencies of their main trading partners, or to the **Special Drawing Right**. *See also* CRAWLING PEGS; FLOATING EXCHANGE RATES.

PER JACOBSSON FOUNDATION. Established in 1964, the Per Jacobsson Foundation was founded as a permanent memorial to **Per Jacobsson**, the third **Managing Director** of the Fund, who died in office in May 1963. The Foundation was sponsored by the Fund, the **Bank for International Settlements**, and a group of 45 former finance ministers, heads of central banks, and other friends of Per Jacobsson.

The Foundation sponsors a lecture series, to be given by an authority in the field of international economics and finance. The lectures are usually held annually at the same time and place as the **annual meetings** of the Fund and **World Bank** and are thus convened for two consecutive years in Washington, D.C., followed by a meeting every third year outside the United States.

PERU. The government that took office in 1990 immediately began to address the crisis facing the Peruvian economy by carrying out a program of macroeconomic adjustment and structural reform aimed at sharply reducing inflation, and creating the conditions for sustained economic growth and a progressive return to external viability. At that time, Peru had heavy external indebtedness and had **overdue obligations** to the Fund. The program was initially supported by a Fund-monitored Rights Accumulation Program through the end of 1992. Following through on the improvement of economic performance under that program, the government developed a three-year program that was supported by an extended Fund facility in an amount equivalent to SDR 1,018 million (about $1,467 million), which expired in March 1996. After an initial disbursement of SDR 642.7 million (about $926 million), Peru opted not to make any further **drawings** under the arrangement. All quantitative performance criteria through December 1995 were met with margins to spare, reflecting an impressive real performance; during 1993–1995, output grew at an average of 8.5 percent a year, inflation was reduced to 10 percent during 1995, and the net **international reserve** position of the Central Reserve Bank improved significantly. These results were the fruits of prudent fiscal and **monetary policies**, a comprehensive program of structural reform, and continued support from the international financial community, including **Paris Club** rescheduling of debt.

In July 1996, the Fund approved a second three-year extended arrangement in the amount equivalent to SDR 248.3 million (about $358 million) in support of the government's medium-term economic and reform program during the period 1996–1998. Building on the progress that had been made under the previous program, performance under the new program was again strong. In 1997, output grew by 7.4 percent, inflation dropped to 6.5 percent, from 11.8 percent in 1996, and the external current account narrowed somewhat. About two-thirds of the external current account was covered by long-term capital flows, and the net international reserves of the Central Reserve Bank rose by $1.6 billion in 1997, with gross reserves reaching the equivalent of nearly 12 months of goods and services by the end of the year. This performance took place in the context of a flexible exchange rate regime, with open trade and capital account. As in the previous years, all performance criteria under the program were observed.

During 1997, the Fund supported a disbursement of SDR 160.5 million (about $223 million) to support Peru's debt and debt-service reduction operation with its external commercial creditors. After the completion of this operation, the ratio of Peru's debt-service obligations to commercial banks was reduced to 3.1 percent of exports of goods and nonfactor services in 1997, from 7.4 percent in 1995. A debt rescheduling, granted in July 1996 by the Paris Club creditors, provided additional debt relief over the medium term, substantially improving the prospects of Peru's external viability by the end of 1998.

In a May 1998 Letter of Intent to the Fund from the Minister of Economy and the President of the Central Reserve Bank, it was noted that, as in previous years, all performance criteria had been observed in 1997; real GDP rose by 7.4 percent, the external current account deficit narrowed to 5.2 percent, and net international reserves rose by $1.6 billion. In 1998, as a result of the adverse affects on the economy by El Niño, real GDP was expected to grow 4–5 percent, with inflation in the range of 7–9 percent. The efforts to reduce tax evasion would be intensified, government expenditure kept under strict control, and the flexible exchange rate policy maintained. The government would continue to implement its policy on privatization, reform the pension system, continue in its efforts to improve education and health, and maintain open trade, capital, and exchange regimes. Finally, it would be the main priority of the government's program to reduce poverty, it being noted that the share of the population living in extreme poverty had been reduced from 24 percent in 1991 to 18 percent in 1996 and that access to basic services, such as drinking water and electricity, had increased significantly over the past five years.

Over the period since 1999, Peru's economic performance has been impressive by domestic and international standards. Under a series of precautionary stand-by arrangements with the Fund, the Peruvian authorities have maintained strong economic fundamentals, a sound institutional policy framework, and a solid track-record for prudent macroeconomic policies. This helped the country reduce vulnerabilities, accelerate economic growth, and achieve meaningful progress in poverty reduction. Peru was granted investment grade by Fitch and Standard & Poor's in 2008 and by Moody's at the end of 2009, consolidating its standing among major emerging market economies. Despite the continuing risks to the global economy, Fund staff projections in 2010 indicated that Peru's medium-term prospects remained bright, in particular given its sustained commitment to an ambitious structural reform agenda.

PHILIPPINES. At the time that the economic and financial crisis spread through Southeast Asia, the Philippines was in the third year of a Fund-assisted program under its **extended Fund facility (EFF)** that was due to expire on 23 July 1997. While the macroeconomic program remained broadly on track in the first quarter of 1997, the economy began to face a number of stresses in the second quarter, including increasing turbulence in the **foreign exchange market**, slippages in fiscal performance, and delay in the passage of proposed tax reforms. Following the float of the Thai baht on 2 July 1997, the foreign exchange market in the Philippines came under increased pressure, causing a significant depletion in the Philippines' **international reserves**.

The authorities responded decisively to the pressures on the peso by floating the currency on 11 July and supporting this action by strong fiscal and monetary policies. They requested an extension and augmentation of the EFF program until the end of 1997 to allow passage of tax reforms and completion of the final review of the EFF credit, and also to support their action to float the peso to discourage speculative capital flows. The amount under the EFF credit, originally set at $650 million, was augmented by an additional $435 million, bringing the total immediately available to the Philippines to about $700 million.

Under the extended program, the government sought passage of a comprehensive tax reform package to strengthen the financial sector by the adoption of measures to tighten the limits of exposure of banks to the real estate market, to discourage the growth of foreign currency liabilities through new liquidity requirements, and by removing tax disincentives to peso deposits.

At the end of March 1998, the Fund approved financial assistance amounting to $1.4 billion under a two-year **stand-by arrangement**. The arrangement was regarded as a precautionary measure and the authorities had expressed their intention to draw on it only if necessary. The program under the stand-by addressed the dual goals of managing the current crisis while creating the conditions for sustained growth over the medium term, providing for an orderly adjustment to lower capital inflows in the wake of the crisis. The main macroeconomic objectives for 1998 and 1999 were to contain the slowdown of real GDP growth to 3 percent in 1998 and to 5 percent in 1999; limit inflation to 8 percent in 1998 and to 6 percent in 1999; and reduce the current account deficit to 3.1 percent of GNP in 1998 and 2.7 percent in 1999, compared with a 5.7 percent deficit in 1997. The program also included banking sector reforms, such as increasing capital requirements, tightening regulatory oversight, and dealing with problem banks.

The program also addressed the need to reduce poverty, on which progress had lagged behind other countries in the region. This involved a strengthening of agriculture and improvements in education and health services, with a focus on primary education in the rural areas.

On 30 October 1998, the Fund's **Deputy Managing Director**, **Shigemitsu Sugisaki**, announced that the **Executive Board** had completed first and second reviews under the stand-by credit and had approved the release of the first credit tranche, amounting to $280 million, for the Philippines. The Philippine authorities had decided to draw on the credit, which up to that point they had treated as precautionary. The statement also said that the program had been modified to take into account the continued difficult economic environment and to incorporate the policy agenda of the new government, which had taken office in July 1998. The revised program for 1998–1999 aimed at deepening the stabilization gained, cushioning the impact of the financial crisis on vulnerable sections of the population, and setting the stage for an early, strong, and sustainable recovery. Sugisaki emphasized the need for the government to proceed quickly and forcefully with the structural reform agenda, with emphasis on banking, tax, and public reform issues.

At the 2010 Article IV consultation with Peru, Executive Directors commended the authorities for their implementation of sound economic policies over the period since the Asian financial crisis. They noted that the authorities' pursuit of supportive macroeconomic policies, together with resilient remittances, had provided a cushion against the global economic crisis. Although the Philippines had experienced recession in line with global developments, recovery was expected in 2010. They noted that, like other countries, a timely return to a sustainable fiscal path while avoiding a premature exit from a supportive monetary policy would be important for the Philippines. *See also* ASIAN FINANCIAL CRISIS; THAILAND.

PLAZA AGREEMENT. Meeting at the Plaza Hotel, New York, in September 1985, the **Group of Five** reached an understanding on a specific coordinated action to intervene in the **exchange markets** to reduce the value of the U.S. dollar. In the succeeding months, the **monetary authorities** of the five countries sold U.S. dollars in their markets and brought about a substantial reduction in the value of the dollar. Meeting at the Louvre Palace, Paris, in February 1987, the **Group of Seven** announced that existing exchange rates were broadly consistent with the economic fundamentals and they would "cooperate closely to foster stability around current levels." The lessons of that episode were variously interpreted: some commentators saw it as an example of what coordinated policy action could achieve; others felt that the value of the dollar was due to decline in any event, and that central bank intervention had only assisted in the movement of the market. *See also* LOUVRE ACCORD.

POLAK, JACQUES J. (1914–2010). Jacques J. Polak, of the Netherlands, joined the **staff** of the Fund in 1947, became Director of the Research Department in June 1958, and later, while he continued to hold that position, was appointed **Economic Counselor**. After his retirement from the staff of the Fund in 1979, Polak served briefly as advisor to the **Managing Director** and then, in January 1981, he was elected as **Executive Director** for the constituency of Cyprus, Israel, the Netherlands, Romania, and Yugoslavia. Polak contributed greatly to the work of the Fund by furthering its research work (he was a leading exponent of the monetary approach to the **balance of payments**) and by the development of the Fund's operational policies. He also made a particular contribution in the 1960s with his analytical work on **international liquidity** and was a leading authority and proponent on the establishment of **Special Drawing Rights**, the world's first international **reserve asset** to be created by international treaty. *See also* MONETARY APPROACH TO BALANCE OF PAYMENTS.

POLAND. Poland was an original member of the Fund, but withdrew voluntarily from membership in 1950 on the grounds that the Fund was no more than a mouthpiece for the U.S. government. It rejoined the Fund in 1986 and since then has been one of the most successful economies of the east European countries. Poland adopted an ambitious economic program supported by a **stand-by arrangement** in 1990 with the aim of reducing hyperinflation and shifting the economy to market mechanisms, involving measures to liberalize prices and the **foreign exchange** and trade systems, as well as introducing a wide range of market economy institutions. Poland continued its program of converting to a free-market economy with the support of a series of arrangements with the Fund through 1996, making only partial **drawings** on the finances available to it, and for the most part reducing its debtor position in the Fund.

In concluding the Article IV consultations with Poland in March 1998, the **Executive Board** noted that Poland had been able to combine strong economic growth—the fastest in eastern and central Europe over the previous four years—with substantial declines in inflation. Close to two-thirds of all jobs in the economy were in the private sector, illustrating that the country's transition was firmly on track. Strong investment spending and the fastest real retail sales since the transition began resulted in a real GDP growth of 6.9 percent during 1997 (compared with increases of 6.1 percent in 1996 and 7 percent in 1995) with a marked decline in unemployment. The strong domestic demand, however, had led to a deterioration in the current account of the **balance of payments**, from a surplus of more than 3 percent of GDP in 1995 to a 3.2 percent deficit in 1997.

The **monetary authorities** tightened policy several times in 1997, both by raising reserve requirements and raising interest rates. In the foreign exchange market, the zloty, which was being managed via a **currency** basket arrangement with a plus or minus 7 percent band and a **crawling** central rate that was allowed to depreciate by 1 percent each month, weakened in the second half of 1997 under the impact of the Asian currency gyrations, but strengthened markedly in the first three months of 1998.

The Fund's **Executive Directors** praised the Polish authorities for the progress that had been made in advancing structural reforms and saw Poland as a leader among the **transitional economies**.

PORTUGAL, MURILO (1948–). Murilo Portugal, a Brazilian national, assumed the position of **Deputy Managing Director** of the Fund on 1 December 2006. Prior to joining the Fund, Mr. Portugal was the Deputy Minister of Finance of Brazil. From 1998 until 2005, he served as the **Executive Director** of the Fund for Brazil, Colombia, Dominican Republic, Ecuador,

Guyana, Haiti, Panama, Suriname, and Trinidad and Tobago. From 1996 to 2000, he was an Executive Director at the **World Bank** Group. Prior to that, Mr. Portugal serviced in several senior positions in the government of Brazil, including as the Secretary of the National Treasury, in the Office of the President, and at the Ministry of Finance and the Ministry of Planning.

Mr. Portugal, who holds degrees in law and economics, was educated at Universidade Federal Fluminense, Rio de Janeiro, Brazil, and at the Universities of Cambridge and Manchester in the United Kingdom.

POVERTY AND FUND-SUPPORTED ADJUSTMENT PROGRAMS. As governments of **developing countries** increasingly took steps in the 1970s and early 1980s to respond to adverse shocks and to correct for earlier excess borrowing and spending, the burden of these adjustments often fell on the most vulnerable groups in society. Social disturbances occurred in several countries, resulting from the severe strains caused by **adjustment programs**. The Fund came under increasing criticism from nongovernmental organizations, academics, and other organizations for paying insufficient attention to the social consequences of its adjustment programs. In March 1989, in a letter published in major newspapers, the Fund's **Managing Director**, **Michel Camdessus**, responded to this criticism by pointing out that it was the prerogative of member states to decide for themselves what measures were required for recovery, however unpleasant those measures might be.

The Fund's **staff**, however, carried out much research on the effect of adjustment programs and on how their adverse effects could be mitigated. In a number of cases, it could demonstrate to the relevant government authorities what effects a program would have on income distribution, and provide them with alternative scenarios. Nevertheless, the staff has not been able to come up with a watertight theory defining the relationship of income distribution to economic growth and, thus, is unable to recommend to governments the "right" type of income distribution that should result from structural adjustments. As a result of this work, however, the Fund is able to focus on programs that benefit the poor, to help in setting up social safety nets for the disadvantaged, to target subsidy programs to those who really need them, and, in general, to streamline and make more efficient, at less cost, existing social programs. Many countries implementing Fund-supported adjustment programs, particularly those of the Former Soviet Union and Africa, have benefited from the Fund's advice and **technical assistance** in improving their **social policies**, including the establishment and reform of safety nets.

POVERTY REDUCTION AND GROWTH FACILITY (PRGF). The Fund first put in place a concessional lending facility through the establishment of the **Trust Fund** in 1976. In 1986, the **structural adjustment facility (SAF)** was created to provide concessional assistance to low-income countries by recycling resources lent under the Trust Fund. This was followed in 1987 by the establishment of the **enhanced structural adjustment facility (ESAF)** to foster stronger adjustment and reform measures than those under the SAF and to augment the Fund's resources for concessional lending. In 1999, the ESAF was renamed the PRGF, and the facility's objective was amended to include an explicit focus on poverty reduction in the context of a comprehensive growth-oriented strategy.

The PRGF is currently financed through bilateral loans and grants. However, in the near future the PRGF is due to become self-sustaining through the revolving use of resources accumulating in the Reserve Account of the PRGF–ESAF Trust, possibly supplemented by additional loan resources.

Eligibility for access to the PRGF is based primarily on a country's per capita income, drawing on the cutoff point for eligibility to **World Bank** concessional lending. PRGF loans are provided under three-year PRGF arrangements (which can be extended for a fourth year). Disbursements are normally on a semiannual basis, and are subject to phasing and the observance of performance criteria. In cases in which closer monitoring is needed, the arrangement may provide for quarterly phasing, performance criteria, and reviews.

An eligible country may borrow up to 140 percent of its quota under a three-year arrangement, and up to 185 percent of quota in exceptional circumstances. Unlike access to the Fund's **General Resources** facilities, there are no annual or cumulative access limits under the PRGF. However, there is a general presumption that access will decline under successive PRGF arrangements. In March 2004, the **Executive Board** approved the following norms for access under successive PRGF arrangements: 90 and 65 percent of quota for first and second arrangements, and 55, 45, 35, and 25 percent of quota for third, fourth, fifth, and subsequent arrangements, respectively. These norms should not be seen as either maxima or entitlements. In addition, the Executive Board agreed that even lower access (such as 10 percent or less of quota) would be appropriate for countries that have limited **balance of payments** need for concessional resources.

POVERTY REDUCTION STRATEGY PAPER (PRSP). Poverty Reduction Strategy Papers are prepared by member countries through a participatory process involving domestic stakeholders and external development partners, including the **World Bank** and the Fund. These papers are updated every three years with annual progress reports. PRSPs describe the country's macroeconomic, structural, and social policies, and programs to promote broad-based growth and reduce poverty. They also cover associated external financing needs and major sources of financing. These documents, along with the accompanying Fund–World Bank Joint Staff Assessments, are made available on the World Bank and IMF websites in agreement with the member country. *See also* POVERTY REDUCTION AND GROWTH FACILITY (PRGF).

PRESS INFORMATION NOTICES. *See* PUBLIC INFORMATION NOTICES (PINS).

PRICE CONTROLS. The Fund is a strong advocate of eliminating price controls, which hide underlying inflationary pressures, distort demand and production, and bring about bureaucratic rigidities in the economy. The freeing of prices, or setting them at realistic levels, is often a central feature of Fund-supported **adjustment programs**, whether it be for agriculture, consumer goods, public services, interest rates, or **foreign exchange** rates.

PUBLIC INFORMATION NOTICES (PINS). On 25 April 1997, the **Executive Board** agreed to the issuance of Press Information Notices (PINs), subsequently called *Public Information Notices*, following the conclusion of Article IV consultation discussions, for those members seeking to make known to the public the Fund's views about their economies.

The action, taken after the experience of growing, and sometimes volatile, capital flows was intended to strengthen the Fund's **surveillance** over the economic policies of member countries by increasing the transparency of the Fund's assessment of these policies, while preserving the integrity and confidentiality of the Article IV consultation process.

PINs are issued at the request of the member country shortly after the Executive Board discussion. They consist of a background section with factual information on the member country's economy and the Fund's assessment of the member country's economic policies and prospects, as reflected in the Executive Board's discussion of the Article IV review of the member country.

The first PIN was issued on 27 May 1997, and by the end of May 1998, 74 PINs had been issued. The full texts of PINs are available on the Fund's website (http://www.imf.org), and beginning in 1998, PINs were also reproduced in a Fund publication entitled *IMF Economic Reviews*, which appears three times a year containing all the PINs that have been issued in the preceding four-month period. The publication carries the summary material on Article VI consultations previously included in the ***Annual Report of the Executive Board.***

PUBLICATIONS OF THE FUND. *See* DOCUMENTS AND INFORMATION AND THE BIBLIOGRAPHY.

PURCHASES OF CURRENCY FROM THE FUND. When a member uses the Fund's **resources**, it purchases needed usable **currencies** by exchanging its own currency. Thus, for example, a member's initial position in the Fund may be a **subscription** held by the Fund consisting of 25 percent in **Special Drawing Rights** and 75 percent in the member's domestic currency. When the country makes a **drawing** on the Fund, it purchases usable currency with its own currency. As a result, the Fund's holdings of the currency of the member making the drawing will rise and its holdings of usable currencies (such as U.S. dollars, **euros**, yen, and others) will fall. Similarly, repayments to the Fund will be effected by a reverse procedure, with the member repurchasing its own currency by providing a designated usable currency to the Fund.

The cycle of purchase and repurchase operations, effected over the short- to medium-term, illustrates the cooperative concept on which the Fund was founded. A member, by purchasing usable currency with its own currency, and then subsequently repurchasing its own currency with a usable currency designated by the Fund, returns to its initial accounting position of being neither a debtor nor a creditor to the Fund. In this manner also, the Fund maintains its resources in the form of a revolving pool of currencies that can be drawn upon by members, always on the understanding that **repurchases** will be executed over the medium term. Technically speaking, therefore, Fund operations consist of purchases and repurchases, and are not loans and repayments.

In practice, only relatively few currencies held by the Fund are usable in international payments. The Fund draws up quarterly **operational budgets** based on estimates of the likely use of the Fund's resources and establishes the amounts for those currencies whose countries' economic positions and **international reserves** are sufficiently strong to be used in Fund operations and international payments.

Q

QUOTA REVIEWS. The Fund is required by its **Articles of Agreement** to conduct, at intervals of not more than five years, a general review of quotas and propose any adjustments that it deems appropriate. It may also, if it thinks fit, consider at any other time the adjustment of any particular **quota** at the request of the member concerned.

The Fund has completed twelve general reviews of quotas since it was founded. The first general increase in quotas took place in 1959, when **membership** in the Fund had risen to 69, an increase of 40 members since 1945. A general increase of 50 percent in quotas, as well as special increases for four countries, raised total quotas to SDR 14.6 billion. No increase in quotas was proposed in the third quinquennial review, but the fourth general review (1965) and the fifth general review (1970) each approved general increases of 25 percent, raising total quotas to SDR 28.8 billion, with a membership of 116 countries. The sixth general review (1976) resulted in a substantial increase in total quotas, with increases distributed among members in a way that would provide more balance among the different groups of countries. The seventh general review (1978) raised total quotas by 50 percent; the eighth (1983) by 19 percent, along with substantial increases for individual countries; and the ninth (1990) by 50 percent, bringing total quotas to about SDR 145 billion.

By the end of the fiscal year, 30 April 1995, payments of quota increases under the ninth general review had been completed by all members that had consented to their increases. Including the quotas of new members, this brought the total amount of Fund quotas to SDR 145 billion. At the end of April 1995, six members had **overdue obligations** to the Fund's **General Resources Account** and, as provided for in the **Board of Governors** Resolution on the ninth general review of quotas, they could not consent to their quota increase until their **arrears** were cleared.

The ninth general review of quotas was completed seven years after the previous review, and this delay in its completion meant that the tenth general review, which was to have been completed by 31 March 1993, in accordance with the five-year timetable specified in the Articles of Agreement, had to be extended. In December 1994, the **Executive Board** concluded that the ninth general review, which was then still being implemented, would provide the Fund with substantial additional usable resources and that the tenth general review should be concluded without an increase in quota.

The eleventh general review of quotas was completed early in January 1997, when the Board of Governors adopted a Resolution proposing an increase of 45 percent in the total Fund quotas, to approximately SDR 212 billion (about $288 billion) from SDR 146 billion. With the resurgence of a U.S. Congress dominated by the Republican Party after the 1996 congressional elections, resistance to U.S. participation in the quota increase stiffened, reflecting a variety of reasons ranging from a general distrust of international organizations, to a belief that adjustments to national economies were best left to free-market forces and that the policies and structure of the Fund, in any case, required radical reform. Thus, the increase in quotas did not come into effect until January 1998, and no increase in quotas was approved under the eleventh or twelfth general review.

However, in the wake of the **global financial crisis**, the Board of Governors approved on 28 April 2008 a large-scale quota and voice reform aimed at not only strengthening the Fund's resources, but also making quotas more responsive to economic realities by increasing the representation of fast-growing economies and giving low-income countries more say in the Fund's decision making. The reform includes a tripling of the number of **basic votes** as well as measures to protect the share of basic votes in total voting power in the future. This reform will become effective when the reform package is accepted by 111 member countries representing at least 85 percent of the total voting power. As of 23 October 2009, 42 members representing about 64 percent of total voting power had accepted.

In April 2009, the **International Monetary and Financial Committee** called for a prompt start to the fourteenth general review of quotas and for its early completion by January 2011—some two years ahead of the original schedule. *See also* VOTING PROVISIONS.

QUOTAS. A member's quota in the Fund establishes its fundamental relationship with the organization. It determines how much the member will subscribe to the Fund, its maximum **access** to financing, its **voting** strength, and its share in **Special Drawing Right (SDR)** allocations.

The amount of a member's quota is expressed in terms of SDRs and is equal to the **subscription** the member must pay, in full, to the Fund. Up to 25 percent of the subscription is paid in **reserve assets** specified by the Fund (SDRs or usable currencies) and the remainder in the member's own currency. The maximum access of a member to Fund **resources**, no matter to what facilities or under what policies, is determined in proportion to its quota. Similarly, **SDR allocations** are made to all participants as a percentage of quotas. Each member has 250 basic votes plus an additional vote for each SDR 100,000 of quota. On 28 April 2008, the **Board of Governors** approved a large-scale quota and voice reform that includes a tripling of the number of basic votes as well as measures to protect the share of basic votes in total voting power in the future. This reform will become effective when the reform package is accepted by 111 member countries representing at least 85 percent of the total voting power. As of 24 October 2009, 42 members representing about 64 percent of total voting power had accepted.

The size of members' quotas in the Fund is determined mainly by economic factors, but a judgmental approach is used to make the final determination. The original quotas in the Fund were determined in large part by the so-called **Bretton Woods** formula, which took into account such basic economic variables as the values of annual average import and export flows, **gold** holdings and U.S. dollar balances, and national income. In the 1960s, this formula was revised and has since undergone various permutations, changing the components of the formula and the weights attached to them, and using as many as 10 formulas in a single **quota review** for comparative purposes. The central purpose is to measure, in as comprehensive a way as possible, members' relative economic positions in the world economy.

R

REFORM OF THE FUND. Reform of the Fund refers to the first amendment of the **Articles of Agreement**, which became effective in 1969, as distinct from **reform of the international monetary system**, brought about by the second amendment to the Articles of Agreement, which became effective in 1978. The principal objective of the first amendment was to establish a facility in the Fund based on **Special Drawing Rights (SDRs)**. The establishment of the SDR facility necessitated the addition of 12 new Articles and a number of related changes in the rest of the text. At the same time, however, the opportunity was taken to make minor amendments to a number of other Articles affecting the technical operations of the Fund. The most important of these was the amendment to clarify that a member's **gold tranche** (now the **reserve tranche**) could be drawn upon without challenge from the Fund, and thus could be counted as part of a member's unconditional liquidity. Among other changes were a simplification of the complicated and technical provisions governing **repurchase** requirements, a provision to allow members to use their gold tranche to meet capital transfers, and a clarification in the definition of a member's monetary **reserves**.

REFORM OF THE INTERNATIONAL MONETARY SYSTEM. Reform of the **international monetary system** did not start out as an attempt to replace the **Bretton Woods system** in its entirety. After the **par value system** broke down, the immediate reaction of the **Group of Ten** was to try to patch up the system, pending agreement on a more thoroughgoing reform. Meeting at the Smithsonian Institution in Washington, D.C., in December 1971, the Group of Ten countries (plus Switzerland) introduced the option of **central rates**—fixed but alterable—with wider margins. This interim system, known as the **Smithsonian Agreement**, lasted for about 15 months, during which time all the major countries, one by one, gradually abandoned the **fixed exchange rate** for their currency. By March 1973, all the major countries had abandoned their par values or central rates and had let their **currencies** float against each other.

Within the Fund, **staff** studies on a reformed system had begun almost immediately after the U.S. action of August 1971, and when the **Board of Governors** approved a Resolution just six weeks later at the 1971 Annual Meeting requesting **Executive Directors** to prepare a report on the reformed system, the staff was able to produce a sketch of a new system early in 1972 for consideration by the **Executive Board**. The drafting of the report by the Executive Board revealed deep differences of viewpoints among member countries. Although there was a general desire to return to a par value system, with modifications to the Bretton Woods system, there was no agreement on other proposed improvements, such as asset convertibility and the role of the U.S. dollar. When the report was published in August 1972 under the title of *Report on Reform of the International Monetary System*, it contained a number of new ideas and proposals but its tone was tentative, suggesting that a great deal more work was required on a number of fundamental issues.

Meanwhile, as a result of initiatives taken within the Fund, a committee of Governors, known as the **Committee of Twenty**, or more formally the Committee of the Board of Governors on Reform of the International Monetary System and Related Issues, was established in July 1972. The committee replicated the structure of the Executive Board at the ministerial or central bank governor level, but included seven associate members and observers—about 200 officials in all. At its first meeting, the Committee established a Committee of Deputies, which, in turn, established seven technical groups. The Committee met six times over a period of two years, the Deputies met 12 times, and the technical groups held innumerable formal and informal sessions. The Committee's progress was slow and uncertain, and when the Organization of Oil Exporting Countries quadrupled international oil prices in December 1973, placing unprecedented strain on the world payments system, the Committee concluded that a fully reformed system was out of reach.

The Committee's report was published in June 1974, together with an incomplete *Outline of Reform*. Part I of the *Outline* indicated the general direction in which the Committee believed that the system could evolve. However, recognizing that a new system could not come into being for some time, the Committee recommended in Part II of the *Outline* that a number of immediate steps be taken in the interim to begin an evolutionary process of reform. Among the recommendations included in Part II was a proposal to establish an Interim Committee of the Board of Governors on the International Monetary System that would examine draft amendments to the **Articles of Agreement** "for possible recommendation at an appropriate time for the Board of Governors." The Committee of Twenty was dissolved and the **Interim Committee** came into existence.

The Interim Committee was structured on the same lines as was the Committee of Twenty, replicating the representation on the Fund's Executive Board and, like the Committee of Twenty, provided for each committee member to appoint seven associates to attend meetings, along with the **Managing Director**, his Deputy, Executive Directors, and a limited number of observers. In its new incarnation, however, there was no Committee of Deputies or outside working groups; these roles were performed by the Executive Board and the Fund's staff.

The staff provided the Executive Board with drafts, redrafts, and explanatory memoranda for nearly two years. The Executive Directors, on their part, debated and negotiated the amendments for 280 hours over 146 sessions, and were in constant communication with their national authorities, reporting on each stage of the discussions and receiving directions from them. Sensitive and divisive issues were referred to the Interim Committee, but the Committee itself had difficulty in reaching a decision on a number of key issues, and did so on several occasions only after government-to-government agreements had been negotiated. In April 1976, the prolonged negotiations were ended and the proposed second amendment was submitted to members for acceptance.

The key areas of disagreement related to the exchange rate system, the growth of **international liquidity**, and the role of **gold** in the system. In the end, the idea of returning to a par value system was abandoned, at least for the foreseeable future, but the new system did not go much further than legitimizing existing practices. It allows members to choose their own **exchange rate arrangements**, including **floating**. It upheld the authority of the Fund by requiring members to collaborate with the Fund in an endeavor to promote stability and order through economic and financial policies, and to avoid manipulating exchange rates to gain an unfair advantage over other members. The Fund, on its part, is required to oversee the compliance of each member with its obligations and exercise firm **surveillance** over the exchange rate policies of its members. The official price of gold was abolished and the role of gold in the system was to be gradually reduced; the denomination of any exchange rate arrangement in terms of gold was prohibited and the obligation of the Fund and members to receive gold under the Articles was eliminated. At the same time, the Fund was required to dispose of a portion of its gold holdings. In place of gold, the amendment sets out a clear objective of making the **Special Drawing Right** the principal **reserve asset** of the international monetary system.

More than two decades after the reform of the 1970s, the onset of a worldwide economic and financial crisis generated another wave of concern and proposals for reforming the international monetary system. The central problem was seen to be the volatility of free capital flows, particularly short-term **capital movements**. Several initiatives were floated, including greater international control over the liberalization of capital markets, the setting up of some kind of insurance institution to cover the risks associated with capital movements, a new facility within the Fund to protect countries in a sound position from being overthrown by unjustified adverse capital movements, as well as a variety of measures to make the existing facilities and instruments more effective. Clearly, the more adventurous of these proposals raised critical practical problems.

The recent **global financial crisis** has brought the question of a reform of the international monetary and financial system to the fore again. The recent **Istanbul Decisions** together with the reform of quotas and voice represent a turning point in the ongoing reform of the international monetary system that will likely be a focal point for Fund activities for the foreseeable future. *See also* ASIAN FINANCIAL CRISIS.

REGIONAL OFFICE FOR ASIA AND THE PACIFIC. The Fund officially opened the Regional Office for Asia and the Pacific in Tokyo on Thursday, 4 December 1997. In the wake of the **Asian financial crisis**, the establishment of the new regional office reflects the importance of the Asia–Pacific region in the global economy and for the operational work of the institution. As part of the Asia and Pacific Department, the main functions of the Office include monitoring regional economic and financial developments, participating in regional fora on monetary and finance cooperation, and helping to promote dialogue within the region on current issues and challenges in the international financial system as well as on the Fund and its policies. The office also undertakes a wide range of external relations activities, and facilitates the delivery of technical assistance and training in the region. *See also* ORGANIZATION OF THE FUND.

REGIONAL SURVEILLANCE. In addition to bilateral and multilateral **surveillance**, the Fund undertakes surveillance over developments in individual regions and policies pursued by supranational authorities. This level of surveillance is aimed at complementing bilateral Article IV consultations by providing a regional dimension to policy issues. Regional surveillance is particularly relevant for members of **currency** unions, such as the European Union (EU), the West African Economic and Monetary Union (WAEMU), **Central African Economic and Monetary Community (CEMAC)**, and the East Caribbean Currency Union (ECCU). Discussions with regional authorities are coordinated with the Article IV discussions that take place with individual country officials.

Given the systemic importance of the **euro**, formal procedures exist for conducting surveillance over the monetary and exchange rate policies of the EU. These involve twice-yearly discussions with the EU institutions responsible for common policies. While these discussions are held separately from the Article IV consultations with individual countries, they are considered an integral part of bilateral surveillance. There is an annual staff report and **Executive Board** discussion on the euro area. A summing up of the Board discussion is produced, which is cross referenced in the summings up for bilateral Article IV consultations with individual euro-area countries and, if relevant, in the bilateral consultations with EU member countries that are not part of the euro area.

Formal discussions at the regional level are also held with the three other currency unions—the WAEMU, the CEMAC, and the ECCU—in addition to the bilateral consultations with the member countries of these groups. Annual regional reports are prepared by the staff and discussed by the Executive Board, and a summing up of the Board discussion is produced.

Regional surveillance outside the main currency unions encompasses the preparation of regular regional outlook documents, the maintenance of a dialogue with various regional fora, and research on regional issues. However, most of these activities are conducted informally. The results feed into bilateral surveillance through information sharing, strengthened policy analysis, and enhanced policy outreach.

With respect to Asia, the Fund maintains a regional office in Tokyo, and it serves as the technical secretariat of the **Manila Framework Group** that was established specifically to undertake macroeconomic surveillance.

REMUNERATION OF MEMBERS. The Fund remunerates (pays interest) on that portion of a member's **currency** holdings that the Fund uses to meet the outstanding **drawings** of other members, referred to as the remunerated **reserve tranche** position. A remunerated reserve tranche position exists whenever the Fund's holdings of a member's currency falls below the norm. A member's norm is the total of 75 percent of its **quota** prior to the second amendment of the Articles of Agreement on 1 April 1978, plus the amounts of any subsequent increases. For countries that became members of the Fund after 1 April 1978, the norm is the weighted average of the norms applicable to all other members on the date the member joined the Fund plus any increase in its quota after that date. As quotas are increased, the norm will gradually rise over time.

REPURCHASES. The Fund's **resources** consist of a pool of **currencies** subscribed by members, and whenever a member draws from that pool by exchanging its own currency for that of another member's currency in the pool (i.e., by making a **purchase**), it is under an obligation to reverse that process when its **balance of payments** and international **reserves** allow it to do so (i.e., it must repurchase its own currency by using **Special Drawing Rights** or a currency selected by the Fund). The **Articles of Agreement** prescribe that normally repurchases should be made over a term of three to five years from the date of purchase. The objective is to maintain the revolving character of the Fund's financial resources.

The Fund's repurchase policies, however, are flexible, and longer terms may be allowed in exceptional cases of hardship. In addition, the **Executive Board** can vote to establish policies under individual facilities that reflect the changing needs and circumstances of members. The **extended Fund facility**, which addresses structural adjustment, has repurchase schedules up to 10 years, and facilities financed by borrowed funds have repurchase terms of up to seven years.

The overriding principle is that a member is obligated to make repurchases when its balance of payments and **international reserves** strengthen, even if such repurchases would be in advance of its repurchase schedule. Such early repurchases can, if desired by the member, be effected by the Fund selling its currency to another member in a purchase operation when that member is making a **drawing** on the Fund. A member that wishes to effect repurchases by having the Fund's holdings of its currency reduced in this manner must notify the Fund in advance, so that the transaction can be accommodated in the **operational budget**.

REQUIREMENT OF NEED. Any use of the Fund's **resources** is subject to the representation of a **balance of payments** need by the member. All such representations are subject to challenge by the Fund, except for **reserve tranche** purchases. The balance of payments need of a member is assessed both as to the magnitude of the financing required and the **adjustment program** to be followed by the member to correct the underlying balance of payments disequilibrium. The Fund's assessment is determined by three elements—a member's balance of payments position, its **international reserve** position, and developments in its reserve position. The assessment may be made on the basis of any single one of these elements, or by a combination of all three.

A similar requirement of need also pertains to transactions in **Special Drawing Rights (SDRs)** under the Fund's designation procedure. Under this procedure, the Fund may designate a participant to provide **currencies** in exchange for SDRs on the basis of the strength of its balance of payments. A participant's obligation to provide currency, however, does not extend beyond the point at which its SDR holdings amount to three times its cumulative **Special Drawing Rights allocations**. Participants can also exchange SDRs against currency by agreement. These transactions can be effected without balance of payments need, and in recent years all transactions of SDRs for currency have taken place by agreement between members, without the Fund's designation.

RESERVE ASSETS. The attributes of a reserve asset are that it must maintain its value over time, be known and widely accepted internationally, and be in adequate but not excessive supply. Currently, reserve assets are reserve **currencies**, **Special Drawing Rights**, **gold**, and reserve positions in the Fund. During the 1950s and 1960s, the U.S. dollar was the principal currency held in countries' reserves and accounted for the major part of total reserves. Since the mid-1970s, the growth of reserve currency holdings has continued, but the earlier movement away from the U.S. dollar has not continued in the 1990s. At the end of 2008, total currency reserves of all countries amounted to $6.8 trillion, of which about 64 percent was accounted for by the U.S. dollar, 27 percent by the **euro**, 3 by the Japanese yen, 4 percent by the pound sterling, and the remaining 2 percent in other currencies. Foreign currency is the largest and fastest growing reserve asset. *See also* INTERNATIONAL RESERVES; RESERVES, RESERVE CREATION PLANS; RESERVE CURRENCY; RESERVE POSITION IN THE FUND; RESERVE TRANCHE.

RESERVE CREATION PLANS. The problem of an expanding world economy and a relatively fixed level of **international reserves** attracted the intense attention of international economists in the 1950s and 1960s. In addition, there was a somewhat visionary view, held by a number of economists, that the world ought to have a central institution—and the International Monetary Fund was the only existing organization that could possibly fulfill the role—that would, eventually, be able to regulate the supply of international reserves in accordance with need. The establishment of a mechanism that would allow a deliberate incremental increase or decrease in world reserves would be a first step toward creating an international central bank.

Proposals for deliberately creating international reserves began to come forward in the latter part of the 1950s and continued through the 1960s. Early suggestions centered around so-called **multiple-currency** accounts, by which means central banks would hold controlled amounts of each other's currency and have reciprocal claims on such an account. A proposal of this kind was studied at some length in the Fund in 1963–1964, calling for the establishment of members' special accounts in the Fund. These special accounts would enlarge members' potential drawing rights, but in such a way that members with a zero net position in the Fund would be able to draw on the account without **conditionality**, while **drawings** of members with a net debtor position would be subject to conditionality.

A second set of schemes revolved around the creation of collective or composite reserve units (CRUs). All these composite unit schemes differed in detail, but basically they envisioned the creation of a reserve unit that would be transferable among central bank or national **monetary authorities** and not for trading in private markets. The units would be established, in a trustee organization, in exchange for liabilities from each participating country, in the form of either claims on **gold** or promissory notes. CRU schemes were usually conceived as being confined to a select group of countries, such as the industrial countries.

The end result of the many ideas propagated was the establishment of the **Special Drawing Right (SDR)** facility in the Fund, created by the first amendment to the **Articles of Agreement** in 1969. The new asset was a breakthrough in international money; neither a monetary unit nor credit, and dubbed by the press "funny money," the new mechanism did have several unique characteristics. First, the facility was a universal one, although participation in it was voluntary. Second, the SDR itself was an unconditional drawing right backed by an international agreement (the Fund's Articles of Agreement) and not a unit backed by financial claims or liabilities. Third, SDRs were to be allocated to members in proportion to their **quotas** in the Fund. And fourth, the **Special Drawing Rights allocations** were to be made as a result of deliberate decisions, based on an informed assessment of need, concurred in by participants, and approved by 85 percent of the Fund's total voting power. With the growing integration of international financial markets in the 1980s and 1990s, fears of a scarcity of international liquidity faded. Indeed, the survival of the SDR and the SDR system is becoming questionable, as more and more academics and officials see the SDR as an anachronism of the past.

International **liquidity** had been an underlying concern of the founders of the **Bretton Woods system** and a growing concern for a quarter of a century throughout the postwar era. The establishment of the SDR facility was welcomed as a significant follow-through in an ongoing attempt to instill stability and order into the **international monetary system**.

RESERVE CURRENCY. During the 19th century and in the early part of the 20th century, the United Kingdom was the leading industrial and trading country, and the pound sterling, its value based on **gold**, was the primary reserve **currency**. During the interwar years, the United Kingdom's trading position weakened, the gold exchange standard was abandoned, and the pound sterling lost its preeminent position as a reserve currency to the U.S. dollar. Under the **Bretton Woods system** established after World War II, the United States became the principal industrial and trading country, and the U.S. dollar, which was the only currency convertible into gold, became the principal reserve currency. After the U.S. authorities abrogated the gold **convertibility** obligation for the dollar in 1971, the dollar remained the preeminent reserve currency, but other currencies, notably the deutsche mark and the Japanese yen, began to be widely held by national **monetary authorities** as reserve currencies. *See also* INTERNATIONAL RESERVES.

RESERVE POSITION IN THE FUND. A member's reserve position in the Fund comprises the **reserve tranche** position and its creditor position under various borrowing arrangements. A member's reserve position is equivalent to a **reserve asset** owned by a member and can be drawn upon without challenge.

RESERVE TRANCHE. A member's reserve tranche (before the second amendment to the **Articles** it was known as the ***gold tranche***) is equal to the amount by which a member's **quota** exceeds the Fund's **holdings** of its **currency** after excluding those holdings that reflect the member's use of Fund credit. Excluding holdings that reflect the use of a member's Fund credit means that the member can preserve its reserve tranche, even though it makes a **drawing** in the **credit tranches**. Reserve tranche positions are liquid claims of members on the Fund arising from that part of **quota** subscriptions that are paid in **reserve assets**, plus any outstanding sales by the Fund of the member's currency to other members that are drawing on the Fund.

RESERVES. *See* INTERNATIONAL RESERVES; RESERVE ASSETS.

RESOURCES OF THE FUND. The resources of the Fund consist of ordinary resources and borrowed resources. Ordinary resources arise from members' **subscriptions** to the Fund in accordance with their **quotas** and from undistributed net income derived from the use of those resources. The value of these resources is established and maintained in terms of **Special Drawing Rights (SDRs)**, the Fund's unit of account. An amount not exceeding 25 percent of a member's quota is paid in **reserve assets** specified by the Fund (SDRs or usable currency) and the remainder in the form of promissory notes in the member's own currency.

Although quota subscriptions are the basic source of Fund financing, the Fund is authorized to borrow from its members and does so if it believes that a particular size, duration, or distribution of payments imbalances warrants a large temporary expansion of Fund credit. In this way, **borrowing** can provide a prompt and temporary supplement to usable quota resources and thus avoid the delay of a Fund-wide quota increase. There is nothing in the Fund's **Articles of Agreement** to preclude it from borrowing in private markets, but so far the Fund has borrowed only from official sources, such as from member governments, central banks, and the **Bank for International Settlements**.

The liquid resources of the Fund consist of usable **currencies** and SDRs held in the **General Resources Account**, supplemented as necessary by borrowed resources. In the fiscal year ended 30 April 1998, the Fund's usable resources declined to SDR 47.3 billion, compared with SDR 62.7 billion a year earlier, reflecting a historically high level of outstanding **drawings** at the end of the year. The stock of uncommitted usable resources, that is, usable resources less the amount of resources committed under current arrangements and considered likely to be drawn, also declined sharply during the period, to SDR 32 billion at the end of April 1998, from SDR 55.7 billion a year earlier. The Fund's liquidity ratio had thus declined precipitously to 44.5 percent, compared with a ratio of 120.5 percent a year earlier. The pressure on the Fund's resources continued throughout the rest of 1998, and in July the **General Arrangements to Borrow** had to be activated for the first time in 20 years. These developments lent great urgency to the need for the eleventh quota increase, which would raise total quotas by 45 percent to SDR 212 billion, to be fully subscribed and become effective as soon as possible. *See also* CHARGES ON THE USE OF THE FUND'S RESOURCES; USE OF FUND RESOURCES.

RESIDENT REPRESENTATIVES. These posts, typically filled by a single staff member, are intended to enhance the provisions of the Fund's policies and Fund-supported arrangements in the country concerned. In August 2010, the Fund had roughly 77 resident representatives in 73 countries.

RESTITUTION. The term *restitution* relates to the distribution of the Fund's **gold** in four annual installments beginning in January 1977. The decision, reached by the **Interim Committee** in August 1975, was to sell one-third of the Fund's gold holdings, or 50 million ounces. One-half of this amount, 25 million ounces, would be sold at **gold auctions**, and the remaining 25 million would be distributed, or "restituted" to members at the official price for gold (SDR 35 per fine ounce). This was the first and only occasion on which the Fund had made an across-the-board distribution of gold to its members, although it had on many occasions previously sold gold to individual members in connection with specific operations of the Fund, mostly to replenish its depleted holdings of members' **currencies**. The term *restitution* was, itself, an attempt to mask a difference of view on the ownership of the gold. Gold subscribed by members belongs solely to the Fund, but some members felt that in the case of a general disposition of gold held by the Fund, the gold ought to be returned to those members that had subscribed it.

The agreement reached in the Interim Committee to dispose of a portion of the Fund's gold was an attempt to remove gold from the central position in which it had been placed under the **par value system** established at the **Bretton Woods Conference** and reflected the treatment given to gold in the 1978 amendments to the **Articles of Agreement**. One-sixth (25 million ounces) of the Fund's gold was to be sold at auction in order to maximize the sale proceeds so as to yield a surplus or profit over the official price that would be available to the Fund to lend to low-income countries. The **Trust Fund** was established to receive these surplus proceeds and to lend them to 55 low-income countries.

RIGHTS ACCUMULATION. Aimed at resolving a member's **overdue obligations** to the Fund, the rights accumulation program allows a member to earn "rights" toward future financing through the implementation of a comprehensive economic program that the Fund would monitor but not assist in financing. Upon successful completion of such a program, and once the payments **arrears** to the Fund and the **World Bank** had been cleared, the member would be eligible to use the Fund's resources under a Fund-supported successor program. At the review of the program in August 2009, the Board extended the deadline for entry into the rights program until August 2010. Of the 11 countries eligible to take advantage of the rights program when it was first introduced in 1990, five had cleared their arrears without recourse to the rights approach, three other members had adopted the rights accumulation program and had successfully cleared their arrears with the Fund, and two others remained eligible and continued to have overdue obligations.

ROOTH, IVAR (1888–1972). Ivar Rooth, of Sweden, was the Fund's second **Managing Director**, serving from 1951 until 1956. He had been Governor of the Riksbank from 1929 to 1948, and for three years preceding his Fund appointment had been chairman of the Economic Research Institute of Sweden.

RULES AND REGULATIONS OF THE FUND. The Rules and Regulations supplement the **Articles of Agreement** and the **by-Laws** and are subordinate to both. The Rules and Regulations deal with the day-to-day business of the Fund and are periodically reviewed, amended, and published.

RUSSIAN FEDERATION. The **systemic transformation facility (STF)**, established in April 1993, was designed to help the Fund assist countries of the former Soviet Union (FSU) to transform themselves from command economies to market economies. In accordance with this objective, the Fund mounted a vast assistance program for the 15 former countries of the Soviet Union, among which the Russian Federation was the largest former member and absorbed the greatest amount of the Fund's resources, both in terms of manpower and finances.

Russia signed its first program with the Fund in June 1993, and received disbursements of $1.5 billion that year and a further $1.5 billion in 1994. The programs were aimed at eventually sweeping away the framework of the preceding communist command economy and substituting freely working private markets. Because, perhaps, of the very size of Russia, combined with the established decentralization of controls operated by autonomous institutions under the former communist regime, the progress in transforming Russia to a free enterprise system was slower than in many other FSU countries.

In the two years under the 1993 STF program, an important start had been made on the transformation of the economy, but the extent of the progress had been disappointing. In 1995, the Fund approved a request by the Russian Federation for a 12-month **stand-by arrangement**, authorizing **drawings** up to $6.8 billion, an amount that was at the time exceeded only by the **Mexican** arrangement signed three months earlier. The stand-by credit was aimed at bringing about decisive progress in stabilization and structural reform in 1995 and setting the stage for a sustained recovery in output and living standards. The key objectives were to bring inflation down to an average of 1 percent a month in the second half of the year and to accelerate the move to a market economy through wide-ranging structural reforms. In 1993, real GDP fell by 12 percent; in 1994, by 15 percent; and in 1995, by 4 percent. Inflation remained high, although falling from an annual rate of nearly 900 percent in 1993, to 300 percent in 1994, and to 190 percent in 1995. At the end of 1995, the monthly increase had fallen to a single digit—an improvement, however, that was not maintained in the following year.

In 1996, the Fund approved an arrangement under the **extended Fund facility (EFF)** for the Russian Federation, authorizing drawings amounting to about $10.1 billion over a period of three years. Progress under this program finally became markedly more positive, and in 1997, for the first time since 1992, the economy grew, albeit barely. At the end of 1997, the situation seemed to be positive. The current account of the **balance of payments** was in surplus; the Central Bank of Russia had proved its professionalism by overseeing a further decline in inflation, successfully fighting off contagion from the **Asian financial crisis**, and maintaining the currency band, which had been established in 1995. In 1998, however, the internal political situation weakened considerably, legislative progress on fiscal and structural reforms slowed sharply, and contagion from the Asian financial crisis all combined to halt the reform effort and throw the economy into a deep crisis.

Going into the third year of the EFF, a major problem still to be overcome was a deficit in the federal budget, amounting to about 7.5 percent of GDP, reflecting a complex and inadequate tax system that, together with a weak tax collection system, discouraged domestic and foreign investment, encouraged tax evasion, and fostered the expansion of underground activities. On the expenditure side, needed improvements included the strengthening of management and control over expenditures; reform of the civil service and the shedding of redundant workers; downsizing the workforce in public health and education; improved targeting of social benefits and strengthening the social safety net; and reform of public pension schemes.

Urgent structural reforms included faster, more transparent privatization and improved management of state-owned enterprises; the restructuring and pricing of natural monopolies (gas, electric power, district heating, and railways); urban land and real estate reform; further development of the capital market; development of a sound and efficient banking system; setting up a legal and institutional framework to make it easier to exercise and transfer property rights and to enforce contracts; liberalization of the housing market; the promotion of agricultural efficiency and productivity; a continued open economy to foreign trade and investment; and elimination of arbitrary and corrupt practices by public officials.

The situation deteriorated progressively, however, as 1998 wore on. The Russian economy was impacted by the Asian financial crisis; the recession in Japan; unfavorable developments in Russia's external markets, notably oil; and the failure on the part of the Russian parliament, the Duma, to pass critical reform legislation. On 19 February 1998, the Fund's **Managing Director**, **Michel Camdessus**, and the Prime Minister of Russia, Victor Chernomyrdin, announced that, following a review of the medium-term strategy supported by the EFF, they had reached agreement on an extension of one year to the three-year agreement signed in April 1996 and on an augmentation of the financial support for the program. In a communiqué issued after the meeting, they said that they "shared a common assessment of the situation, of the strategy, and of the policies needed to bring the program to full success." The communiqué went on to say that, notwithstanding substantial achievements in the areas of macroeconomic stabilization and the establishment of market mechanisms and institutions, a number of remaining challenges required decisive action without delay. These included, as noted in the communiqué, structural reform to promote the principles of good corporate governance and reduction in the fiscal imbalance. The draft 1998 budget as amended by the government, the communiqué said, was fully consistent with the EFF program, which also envisaged a strengthening of structural reforms in areas such as private sector development, fiscal institutions, banking, and natural monopolies.

The pronouncement of these measures, however, did nothing to halt the deteriorating situation, and in mid-1998 the Russian economy was in the midst of serious economic, financial, and political crisis, facing the specter of having to devalue the ruble and/or default on its **external debt**. In July 1998, bearing in mind the risks associated with a collapse of the Russian economy, the Fund again reached agreement with the authorities on a new financing plan, along with an undertaking by the government that it would, either by legislative action or under presidential authority, implement the reforms that had been previously agreed to, particularly in regard to the budget for 1999 and voluntary debt restructuring scheme. Under the terms of this latest agreement, the budget for 1999 was expected to produce a deficit of 2.8 percent of GDP, which would be about one-half of the deficit of 5.6 percent expected in 1998. In addition, authorities had agreed to convert, on a voluntary basis, treasury bills (known as *GKOs*), maturing through June 1999, into longer term dollar-denominated liabilities of 7 and 20 years maturity. This scheme was expected to help in avoiding the problem of rolling over GKOs and save a substantial amount in interest payments.

The **financial package** negotiated with the Russian authorities included an additional $11.2 billion from the Fund for 1998. In addition, there would be two tranches, each of $670 million under the previous arrangement, that would be disbursed when conditions were met on schedule in 1998. Thus, in 1998, if the economy stayed on track, Russia would be eligible for another $12.5 billion in financing from the Fund. In addition, the Russian Federation requested that the EFF arrangement be replaced by a new EFF, starting at the beginning of 1999, that would last for three years. Under that arrangement, the Fund's Managing Director said that he would recommend to the **Executive Board** disbursements on roughly the same scale as the current EFF, that is to say, $2.6 billion a year. By the end of 1999, therefore, if the Russians carried out the program, the Fund would have disbursed about $15.1 billion.

Under separate arrangements, the **World Bank** would be disbursing $1.25 billion in the second half of 1998 and a further $3 billion in 1999. With further money in the pipeline, it was expected that during the second half of 1998 through the end of 1999 total assistance from the World Bank would be $6 billion. Furthermore, the Japanese government had agreed to provide $1.5 billion in balance of payments support in cofinancing with the World Bank. All told, the total financing available to Russia would thus amount to $22.6 billion—a figure that had been announced in the Russian press and slightly in excess of the amount that the Russian government was reported to have been requesting. In order to secure the financing, the Fund announced that it would be activating the **General Arrangements to Borrow**.

On 20 July 1998, the Executive Board announced that the package represented a strong and appropriate response to overcome Russia's current difficulties. It noted, however, that parliamentary backing had not been forthcoming for needed action relating to personal income tax, nor had there been permanent measures to strengthen the pension fund. The Board welcomed the government's intention to seek parliamentary approval of measures in these areas in a special parliamentary session scheduled for August.

Subsequently, the Duma rejected the tax measures, the voluntary debt restructuring scheme became a nonstarter, and the government was unable to deliver on its policy commitments. Faced with the choice of **devaluation**, debt restructuring, and default, the government chose all three. The ruble was let float, theoretically in a band from 6 to 9 to the U.S. dollar, but promptly fell to 16; the restructuring was imposed unilaterally; and a temporary moratorium was imposed on private debts payments.

The new government, which contained for the first time since the overthrow of communism, several members in important positions who were known to be lukewarm or even opposed to the market orientation policy, announced that it was proceeding to put together an economic plan, but at the same time indicated that it would be resorting to controls and money printing. In October 1998, the international community awaited Russia's return to stability and the reform movement, to determine whether it might be able to financially reengage with Russia.

Following lengthy program negotiations, the Fund's Executive Board approved a 17-month stand-by arrangement equivalent to SDR 3.3 billion ($4.5 billion) on 28 July 1999.

In the light of allegations that emerged in the world press that the Russian central bank had diverted funds allocated by the Fund to an offshore subsidiary, FIMACO, to hide its reserves from external creditors, arrangements were made to ensure that all funds disbursed to Russia under the stand-by arrangement would be held at the Fund and repayments to the Fund from earlier loans to Russia would be made from that account.

During 1999, Russia made important progress in the implementation of its economic reform program, exceeding previous expectations with respect to economic growth, the containment of inflation, the fiscal balance, and international reserves. It completed an early repayment of its entire outstanding obligations to the Fund on 31 January 2005.

Throughout the early to mid-2000s, Russia experienced an economic boom, characterized by large capital inflows and steadily rising oil prices. By

August 2008, international reserves had increased to almost US$600 billion, the third highest in the world. This apparent stellar performance made Russia an attractive destination for foreign capital inflows, which came largely in the form of loans to corporations and commercial banks, with a much smaller portion in the form of portfolio and direct investment. Buoyed by ever increasing oil prices, gross private capital inflows increased from about $70 billion in 2005 to $100 billion in 2006 to over $200 billion in 2007. Domestic demand growth reached 13.5 percent in 2007, driven by booming consumption and investment. With the economy at full capacity, real wages rose by close to 20 percent that year.

However, the combination of pro-cyclical macroeconomic policies and structural weaknesses contributed to excessive capital inflows and overheating, and left Russia extremely vulnerable in the midst of the **global financial crisis**. In 2009, the economy contracted by 7.9 percent. Domestic demand fell sharply, following plunging oil prices and an abrupt reversal of capital flows that brought a multiyear credit boom to an end. Private consumption and fixed investment declined strongly, with the effects on growth compounded by a large rundown of inventories. The contribution of net exports, meanwhile, turned positive as imports contracted.

Given large bank and corporate exposures in foreign currency, the authorities allowed a controlled depreciation of the ruble, while providing significant ruble liquidity. However, this strategy entailed the loss of one-third—$200 billion—of the central bank's reserves, and the economy sank into a deep recession.

Fortunately, the oil stabilization fund mechanism provided sufficient scope for a vigorous policy response. The authorities put in place measures to effect a turnaround in the fiscal position from a large surplus to a large deficit—amounting to about 10 percent of GDP—while pursuing an accommodating monetary policy stance. The federal government also provided massive support to the banking system and to private entities that had large, unhedged foreign exchange exposures.

By August 2010, the rate of inflation had fallen, the current and capital accounts had both rebounded from sharp deteriorations, and the ruble has strengthened. Although the banking system was under strain and financial markets remained vulnerable, the Fund staff projected an overall resumption of growth of more than 4 percent. *See also* ASIAN FINANCIAL CRISIS; GLOBAL FINANCIAL CRISIS; USSR AND THE FUND.

S

SCARCE CURRENCY CLAUSE. Article VII, Section 2, of the **Articles of Agreement** states that "if the Fund finds a general scarcity of a particular **currency** is developing, the Fund may so inform members and may issue a report setting forth the causes of the scarcity and containing recommendations designed to bring it to an end." Section 3 goes further and authorizes the Fund to declare a currency scarce if demand for it seriously threatens the Fund's ability to supply that currency and it allows members to impose restrictions on operations in that currency. The provisions survived the first, second, and third amendments to the Articles, but neither Section 2 nor Section 3 has ever been invoked.

Article VII was a compromise, one of many, reached by the drafters of the original Articles. **Lord John Maynard Keynes** and others felt that the responsibility for adjusting **balance of payments** imbalances should not necessarily fall only on countries in deficit and that countries in surplus had a responsibility to pursue policies that were compatible with their surplus positions. The United States negotiators, however, understanding that there would be a global dollar shortage after World War II and that application of the scarce currency clause would negate any progress that could be made toward a free and open trading and financial system, held out for only the milder sanction—of a report by the Fund—as provided for in Section 2. Acceptance by the United States of Section 3, which would have authorized other members to use a potentially powerful weapon of **discrimination** against the United States, was regarded as a generous and good-faith concession on the part of that country, demonstrating the spirit of cooperation that was to prevail in the postwar world.

SCHWEITZER, PIERRE-PAUL (1912–1994). A French national, Pierre-Paul Schweitzer became the fourth **Managing Director** of the Fund in September 1963. He had been Deputy Governor of the Bank of France since 1960 and before that Director of the French Treasury. In 1947–1948, he had been **Alternate Executive Director** of the Fund for France. Schweitzer completed two terms as Managing Director, serving until August 1973. During the crisis of 1971, he had appeared on television seemingly endorsing a proposal to devalue the U.S. dollar in terms of **gold**. The U.S. authorities were shocked, even outraged, and a third term for him as Managing Director was thereby placed out of reach.

SINGAPORE REGIONAL TRAINING INSTITUTE. The Fund and the government of Singapore inaugurated the Singapore Training Institute on 4 May 1998. The establishment of the Institute will allow the Fund to expand its training in Asia. The Fund also participates with other international organizations in a training institute in Vienna. *See also* AFRICAN REGIONAL TECHNICAL ASSISTANCE CENTER (AFRITAC); CARIBBEAN REGIONAL TECHNICAL ASSISTANCE CENTER (CARTAC); TECHNICAL ASSISTANCE; VIENNA INSTITUTE.

SMALL STATES. In the early years of the Fund, it was thought that potential members should have economies large enough to justify at least the "minimum quota" of SDR 250,000 that would correspond with the basic votes. However, in practice, geographic size, population, the existence of a national **currency**, possession of its own central bank, or the strength of its economy no longer have any bearing on whether a country is eligible to become a member of the Fund. There are only three criteria: the applicant must be a country, it must be in formal control of its external relations, and it must be able and willing to perform the obligations of **membership** contained in the **Articles of Agreement**.

The Fund's weighted **voting provisions** for its members have avoided most of the problems that membership of small states has posed in other international organizations. In 1998, for instance, after the 45 percent increase in **quotas** under the eleventh general review of quotas became effective, the United States was the largest member of the Fund with a voting power with 17.521 percent of total votes, whereas the Republic of Palau, the smallest member, will have a tiny voting power of 0.003 percent of the total power. The weighted voting system has facilitated the policy of not denying membership to small countries and of judging all applications on the criterion of whether the applicant has the ability to perform the obligations of membership, as set out in the Articles of Agreement. Denial of membership in the Fund would automatically deny the applicant membership in the **World Bank**, and thus cut off **development finance** to the country in question.

The sharp increase in membership of small states has, however, created a number of problems for the Fund. The sheer increase in the number of members has sharply expanded the constituencies of some **Executive Directors** and complicated their responsibilities in representing a diversity of interests. It has added to the workload and size of the **staff**, with more overseas missions, greater demands for **technical assistance**, and the need for policy prescriptions on problems that can be almost as intractable as in more sophisticated economies. Decision making in the Fund has also become more difficult, especially at the level of the **Board of Governors**, when majorities are specified in terms of a proportion of the number of Governors and total votes.

SMITHSONIAN AGREEMENT. The Finance Ministers and central bank governors of the **Group of Ten** (Belgium, Canada, France, Germany, Italy, Japan, the Netherlands, Sweden, the United Kingdom, and the United States), Switzerland, and the **Managing Director** of the Fund met in Washington, D.C., in the Old Red Castle of the Smithsonian Institution on 17 and 18 December 1971, to negotiate a new pattern of **exchange rate** relationships among **currencies**. The United States agreed to devalue the dollar by 7.89 percent against **gold**, France and the United Kingdom were to maintain the **par values** for their currencies, and the Canadian dollar was to continue to float. The other six countries agreed to establish **central rates**, involving revaluations against the dollar of 16.88 percent for the yen, 13.58 percent for the deutsche mark, 11.57 percent each for the Belgian franc and the Netherlands guilder, 7.48 percent for the Italian lira, and 7.49 percent for the Swedish krona.

It was the first time that the major trading countries had sat around a table and reached agreement on a new pattern of exchange rates for their currencies. It was hailed as a milestone in international monetary cooperation, and was seen by many as a reconstitution of the fixed rate system. The new exchange rates were not to last, however, and 14 months later they had been overwhelmed by underlying economic developments and by speculative attacks in the **exchange markets**. By March 1973 the mixed par value and central rate system had been overthrown and all the major currencies were floating against each other.

SOCIAL POLICIES AND FUND PROGRAMS. The Fund's mandate is to promote international monetary cooperation, balanced growth of international trade, and a stable system of exchange rates, and it is the belief in the Fund that fulfilling this mandate is its primary contribution to sustainable economic and human development. In general terms, social development requires a strategy of high-quality economic growth, macroeconomic stability to generate low inflation, and promotion of the agriculture sector, where many of the poor work.

During the 1950s and 1960s, when the Fund provided financial assistance mainly to industrial countries, its policy advice concentrated primarily on macroeconomic policies. With the shift to lending to **developing countries** since the 1970s and **transitional economies** since the late 1980s, much greater attention has been given to structural reform, and the interrelationship between macroeconomic policies and social issues. Experience has shown the need to protect vulnerable groups during the adjustment period by constructing well-targeted social safety nets and by safeguarding their access to basic public services, such as primary health and education. Such measures make structural reforms (which tend to bring benefits in the longer term) more acceptable to the vulnerable and to be politically sustainable.

The major components of social safety nets (SSNs) are typically as follows: (1) targeted commodity subsidies and cash compensation schemes aimed at protecting the consumption of basic food items by the poor in the face of rising prices, while reducing budgetary expenditure; (2) adaptation of permanent social security arrangements, such as pension and disability insurances, and child allowances, which can be improved and bolstered through restructuring, targeting, and improved incentives; and (3) the enhancement of unemployment benefits, severance pay, and public works schemes to cope with a temporary increase in unemployment brought about by structural reforms.

The aim of targeting is to reduce fiscal costs by limiting social benefits to those most in need. Where sophisticated means testing is not possible, resort to category targeting can be a useful substitute, whereby the benefits are limited to children or pensioners, or to households in certain regions. Commodity subsidies can be limited to goods consumed disproportionately by the poor or by limiting the quantity that each household can consume, for example, via coupons. The construction of incentives to encourage beneficiaries to move out of SSNs is a question of tailoring social programs to the tax structure. SSNs must be crafted taking into account the specific circumstances of each country, including its administrative capacity, the strength of its informal and formal social support systems, and the characteristics of the poor.

Examples of the advice and **technical assistance** provided by the Fund in recent years cover a wide range of countries and a variety of social measures. For example, in Italy, where the expenditure on public health care services was similar to other Organization for Economic Cooperation and Development countries, but the quality of the care was seen to be declining as costs rose, the Fund counseled in its Article IV consultations with Italy in 1992 that health care spending should avoid untargeted across-the-board cuts and should aim for long-lasting savings. It recommended a strategy of increasing local responsibility for expenditure decisions, reinforcing the managerial authority and financial accountability of local health administrators, and giving patients a greater degree of choice.

In Jordan, a generalized system of food subsidies was replaced in 1990 by subsidies targeted through a coupon scheme. The scheme allowed coupon recipients to purchase fixed quantities of subsidized sugar, rice, and powdered milk equal to quantities consumed, on average, by the poorest 10 percent of the population. As a result, the budgetary costs of the subsidy declined from 3.4 percent of GDP in 1990 to 1 percent of GDP in 1994, while the real consumption of the poor was shielded. In another variation of a subsidy scheme, general subsidies in the Kyrgyz Republic were replaced by a cash compensation scheme to pensioners and families with three or more children, together with the introduction of means testing.

In **Ghana**, where a comprehensive program of economic and structural reform was being supported by the Fund, the impact of a reduction of more than 32,000 positions in the civil service was cushioned by a comprehensive severance scheme that paid a lump sum to departing workers based on length of service and provided employment counseling and retraining, credit facilities, and food-for-work programs for those unable to find alternative employment.

In Sri Lanka, which in 1989–1994 implemented successive programs supported by the Fund and the **World Bank**, the main programs designed to alleviate poverty—the JanaSaviya, the Midday Meal, and the Food Stamp Program—were all poorly targeted and cost some 3 percent of GDP. After reform, when the benefits were confined to those in need, the cost declined substantially without a reduction in the benefits available to the vulnerable.

In **Uganda**, after almost a decade of war and civil strife, the infrastructure was devastated, agricultural lands widely abandoned, public services paralyzed, and its population largely impoverished. Real GDP fell by 8 percent between 1983 and 1986, external financing declined, and inflation rates were at extreme levels. A series of Fund-supported **adjustment programs**, starting in 1987, restored economic stability, reduced inflation to single-digit levels in 1993, and revived economic growth, which averaged 5 percent a year in the period 1987–1994. More than 40,000 ghost workers were eliminated from public payrolls, and the public sector was reorganized. The reorganization, combined with a system of mainly donor-financed severance payments, allowed the retrenchment of 66,000 temporary public employees and 14,000 civil servants. Moreover, more than 23,000 soldiers were reintegrated into civilian life through the provision of a support package that included a six-month subsistence allowance, the distribution of construction materials and agricultural inputs, as well as labor-intensive public works, and training programs. The peace dividend, in combination with the efficiency gains from the public sector reorganization, set free resources to effectively double the share of health expenditure and increase the share of education in government expenditures.

In **Peru**, as part of its efforts to stabilize and liberalize the economy in 1990, the authorities entered into a series of programs supported by the

Fund and the World Bank. The programs were successful in reducing annual inflation to 16 percent by the end of 1994, from an annual average of 3,800 percent during 1988–1990, and raised economic growth in 1994 to 11 percent. Hyperinflation had led to the virtual collapse of revenues, with the consequence that real wages of civil servants and critical government services had declined dramatically. As a result of fiscal reforms, current revenues rose from 7 percent of GDP in 1989 to 12 percent in 1994, allowing a gradual recovery in social and other expenditures. In 1991, the government stepped up its efforts to combat poverty by establishing a social investment fund to improve the access of the poor to social services and, in 1994, launched a basic social program to coordinate efforts in five priority areas—education, health services, nutrition, justice, and the creation of jobs. Through privatization of public enterprises, better targeting of social programs, enhanced budgetary expenditures, and improved management, the effectiveness of social spending was substantially improved.

SOUTHARD, FRANK A., JR. (1907–1989). A U.S. national, Frank Southard was the third **Deputy Managing Director** of the Fund, serving from October 1962 to March 1974. Before becoming Deputy Managing Director, he had been the **Executive Director** appointed by the United States since February 1949. Prior to that appointment, He had held senior posts in the U.S. Treasury and the Federal Reserve Board. Earlier he had taught economics at the University of California and at Cornell University, where he became Chairman of the Department of Economics in 1946. Frank Southard spent 25 years with the Fund in its most formative years and, more than any other individual, was a major influence on its evolution and development.

SPECIAL CONTINGENCY ACCOUNT (SCA). In view of protracted **overdue obligations** to the Fund on the part of members, beginning in 1987, the Fund decided to establish SCAs, in addition to the precautionary balance that it maintained in its general **reserve**. At the end of April 1998, these balances amounted to SDR 1.9 billion, held in two different accounts, designated as SCA-l and SCA-2. SCA-1 was established in 1987 with an initial balance of SDR 26.5 million and has been fed by amounts derived from higher **charges** and lower rates of **remuneration** under a **burden-sharing** mechanism.

A second contingency account, SCA-2, was established in 1990 to raise SDR 1 billion over a five-year period from a further increase in the rate of charge and a further adjustment in the rate of remuneration. The SCA-2 reached its target of US$1 billion in 1996 and further accumulation in the account has been terminated. The amounts in reserve are to safeguard **drawings** made on the Fund after a **rights accumulation** program has been successfully completed by members with protracted **arrears** to the Fund at the end of 1989, and they will also be used to finance such drawings.

When overdue obligations have been cleared, balances held in SCA-1 will be returned to those members that paid additional charges or received reduced remuneration. Similarly, balances held in SCA-2 will be refunded to contributors when the credits have been repaid, or earlier at the discretion of the Fund. At the end of the 1997–1998 financial year, the general reserves, together with the precautionary balances, amounted to SDR 4 billion, equivalent to 8.1 percent of total outstanding **General Resources Account** credit as of 30 April 1998.

SPECIAL DATA DISSEMINATION STANDARD (SDDS). As part of the **Data Dissemination Standard**, the SDDS applies to countries that either already have or are seeking access to international capital markets. Thus, it focuses on data dissemination by countries that, in general, already meet high data quality standards. Its purpose is to guide member countries in the provision to the public of comprehensive, timely, accessible, and reliable economic and financial statistics. In this respect, it is more prescriptive than the General Data Dissemination Standard in establishing specific standards that must be observed by subscribing countries. Participation in the SDDS carries a commitment to provide certain information about the member's practices with respect to the compilation and dissemination of economic and financial data. In particular, subscribers must agree to post information about their data dissemination practices on the **Dissemination Standards Bulletin Board (DSBB)** and to establish an Internet site containing the actual data, called a National Summary Data Page, which is accessible via hyperlinks on the DSBB. In 2006, the Fund began preparing annual observance reports for each SDDS subscriber. *See also* STANDARDS AND CODES INITIATIVE.

SPECIAL DISBURSEMENT ACCOUNT (SDA). The SDA, activated in 1981, received transfers from the **Trust Fund** derived from repayments of loans and interest payments to the Trust, which in 1992 was in the process of being wound up. Amounts received by the SDA were transferred to the supplementary financing facility **Subsidy Account**, which was established for the purpose of reducing the cost to eligible members that used the Fund's **resources** under the **Supplementary Financing Facility**. In 1985, the Fund determined that the resources in the Subsidy Account were sufficient to meet its estimated needs, and transfers to that account from the SDA were terminated. Thereafter, amounts received from the Trust Fund were held in the SDA pending their use in loan arrangements under the **structural**

adjustment facility and the **enhanced structural adjustment facility**. At the end of the 1997–1998 financial year, the balance held in the SDA was SDR 0.9 billion.

SPECIAL DRAWING RIGHT (SDR). The SDR was the first **international reserve asset** to be created by international law, coming into existence under the authority of the first amendment to the **Articles of Agreement** in 1969. SDRs are purely book entries maintained by the Fund, and they do not have any traditional reserve backing, such as gold or **reserve currencies**, or any other tangible property. They were created as a supplement to existing **reserves** and are neither reserve units nor credits, but combine features of both. They are for use among nations participating in the SDR facility—for settling accounts between national **monetary authorities**, but not for conducting private transactions or buying and selling in private markets, including **foreign exchange** markets. SDRs actually came into existence in 1970–1972, the first so-called basic period, when a total of SDR 9.3 billion was allocated. A second **Special Drawing Rights allocation** was made in the third basic period, 1978–1981, for a total of SDR 12.1 billion, bringing total allocations to SDR 21.4 billion.

The acceptability of the SDR in settlements, the use to which they can be put, and the value to be placed on them are mandated and circumscribed by international law, namely that of the Articles of Agreement. The unit value of the SDR was originally defined in the first amendment to the Articles as being 0.888671 gram of fine gold, equivalent to SDR 35 per one ounce of gold, but from 1974 until 1980, after the **Bretton Woods system** had collapsed, it was valued daily in terms of an SDR basket of 16 currencies, each currency in the basket carrying a weight determined by its share of world exports and services over a five-year period, with a special weight for the U.S. dollar. Subsequently, the valuation process was simplified to a weighted average of five major **currencies** (U.S. dollar, deutsche mark, Japanese yen, pound sterling, and French franc). The Fund publishes daily the **exchange rates** for nearly 50 currencies in terms of the SDR.

The amount of SDRs allocated to each participant is based on the size of its **quota** immediately preceding the allocation. Participants may exchange SDRs for usable currencies from other participants, either by agreement between the participants or by designation. Transfers by agreement with participants are now the predominant method for using SDRs. Under this procedure, there is no requirement of need and the Fund acts only as an intermediary in bringing the parties together. Transactions by agreement can be used for a wide range of purposes—to obtain usable currency, in **currency swap arrangements**, in forward operations, to make loans, to settle financial obligations, as security for financial obligations, and for donations. In the first few years of the life of the SDR facility, however, most transfers were conducted under the designation procedure, whereby the Fund can designate a participant to receive SDRs if its gross reserves and **balance of payments** position is considered sufficiently strong. A designated participant is obliged to provide usable currency in exchange for SDRs only up to three times its net allocations (i.e., allocations, minus cancellations). The designations procedure can be used only to meet a balance of payments need.

After the second amendment to the Articles came into effect, several measures were taken to enhance the attractiveness of SDRs. The requirement that participants must hold, over a five-year period, an average of 30 percent of their net allocations (called the **Special Drawing Rights reconstitution** provisions) was abrogated. The rate of interest on holdings of SDRs was raised to market levels and is calculated weekly, using the weighted average of interest rates of short-term instruments in the money markets of the five countries whose currencies compose the SDR valuation basket.

Although SDRs are allocated only to participants, the Fund is authorized to prescribe other official institutions as holders of SDRs. By the end of 1998, 15 such institutions had been prescribed by the Fund, including 3 central banks, 3 intergovernmental agencies, and 9 development banks. These designated entities can acquire and use SDRs in transactions by agreement and in operations with participants and other holders under the terms and conditions prescribed by the Fund for participants.

Cumulative allocations of SDRs amount to less than 2 percent of the world's total nongold reserves, an amount too small to make it the principal **reserve asset** of the **international monetary system**, the goal stipulated in the current Articles of Agreement. Nevertheless, the SDR is used as a unit of account in a number of international and regional organizations, as well as a limited number of private arrangements. SDRs can be held and traded only by official entities, and thus they have only a limited role as a medium of exchange. In 1980 and 1981, bonds and other financial instruments denominated in SDRs were placed in the private capital markets, but the demand for the private SDR has faded.

Since the allocation of SDRs in 1979–1981, no further SDRs have been allocated because 85 percent of the Fund's **voting** membership could not agree on whether there was a need for a further allocation. Several major countries believed that there was no need for an allocation, since the world's **liquidity** needs had been taken care of by the global movement of funds through private international capital markets and that, therefore, the SDR was something of an anachronism in the modern world.

On the other hand, a broad array of members, including many **developing countries**, felt strongly that there was a need for an allocation of SDRs, partly in terms of a distribution of real resources, partly in terms of equity, and partly to keep the SDR in play as an international reserve asset. They pointed out that 39 of the current members of the Fund had never received SDRs and that another 37 members had participated in some, but not all, allocations.

Within the **Executive Board**, there had been broad agreement that the Fund should make a special "equity" allocation of SDRs to correct for the fact that many members had either never received SDRs or had not participated in all the allocations made. The **Interim Committee**, at its meeting in September 1996, endorsed an Executive Board proposal for a special one-time allocation—through a fourth amendment to the Articles of Agreement—that would raise each member's ratio of cumulative allocations to **quota** to a common benchmark level. This would have enabled all members of the Fund to participate in the SDR system on an equitable basis. The Committee, at the time, emphasized that this would not affect in any way the Fund's existing power to allocate SDRs on the basis of a finding of a long-term, global need to supplement reserves when that need arose.

At its April 1997 meeting, the Interim Committee welcomed the progress in the Board toward a proposed amendment of the Articles of Agreement that would provide for a special one-time allocation of SDRs and requested it to continue its work. Later, at the 1997 annual meetings in **Hong Kong SAR**, the Board of Governors adopted a Resolution approving the special one-time allocation, amounting to SDR 21.4 billion, which would equalize all the ratio of SDRs to quotas for all members at 29.3 percent, allow the 38 members that have never received an allocation to participate in the SDR system, and double the total amount of SDRs in existence. The fourth amendment became effective for all members on 10 August 2009, when the United States joined 133 other members in supporting it. The special allocation of SDR 21.5 billion was implemented 30 days later on 9 September 2009. *See also* SPECIAL DRAWING RIGHTS ALLOCATIONS; SPECIAL DRAWING RIGHTS DEPARTMENT; SPECIAL DRAWING RIGHTS, RECONSTITUTION OF; SPECIAL DRAWING RIGHTS TRANSFERS; SPECIAL DRAWING RIGHTS VALUATION BASKET.

SPECIAL DRAWING RIGHTS ALLOCATIONS. Allocations of **Special Drawing Rights (SDRs)** are made by the Fund to those members that have agreed to become participants in the **Special Drawing Rights Department** and are made annually in proportion to participants' **quotas** in the Fund. In considering a decision to allocate SDRs, the Fund is obligated under its **Articles of Agreement** to "seek to meet the long-term global need, as and when it arises, to supplement existing **reserve assets** in such a manner as will promote the attainment of its purposes and will avoid economic stagnation and deflation as well as excess demand and inflation in the world." Because the decision to allocate SDRs gives the Fund a unique power to create unconditional **international liquidity**, the procedure to be followed is hedged around with precautionary features, designed to ensure that the Fund will exercise due care and caution in using its power.

First, the **Managing Director** is required to make a proposal for an SDR allocation, consistent with the criteria established in the Fund's Articles, at least six months before a basic period begins or within six months of a request for a proposal from the **Executive Board** or **Board of Governors**. In making such a proposal, the Managing Director must ascertain that it has widespread support among SDR participants. Second, the Executive Board must concur in the proposal. Third, the Board of Governors has the power to approve or modify the proposal by a majority of not less than 85 percent of its total voting power. If the Managing Director, after consulting with participants, concludes that broad support for an SDR allocation does not exist or that he cannot make a proposal that he considers to be consistent with the terms of the Articles, he is required to submit a report on his finding to the Executive Board and the Board of Governors.

Decisions on allocations of SDRs are made for successive basic periods of up to five years, although the Fund can alter the duration of the basic period. The first basic period was for three years (1970–1972), when a total of SDR 9.3 billion was allocated. In the following basic period (1973–1977), no allocations were made, but in the third basic period (1978–1981), SDR 12.1 billion was allocated. No allocations of SDRs were made during the period from 1981 until 2009.

At the 1997 meetings of the Board of Governors, the Governors adopted a Resolution approving a special one-time allocation of SDRs, amounting to SDR 21.4 billion, that would equalize the ratio of SDRs to quotas for all members at 29.3 percent and allow the 38 members that have never received SDRs to participate in the SDR system. This special allocation required an amendment to the Articles of Agreement, which was before the Board of Governors at the end of 1998. However, it did not become effective until 10 August 2009 when the Fund certified that at least three-fifths of the membership (112 members) with 85 percent of the total voting power had accepted it. On 5 August 2009, the United States joined 133 other members in supporting the Amendment. The special allocation of SDR 21.5 billion was implemented 30 days after the effective date, on 9 September 2009.

Meanwhile, on 7 August 2009, the Board of Governors approved by far the biggest allocation to date, equivalent to $250 billion, to provide liquidity to the global economic system in the wake of the global financial crisis.

This general allocation, which took place on 28 August 2009, was made in response to the call by the **Group of Twenty** Heads of State and the **International Monetary and Financial Committee** at their respective meetings in April 2009. The allocation aimed to provide significant unconditional financial resources to liquidity-constrained countries in order to smooth the need for adjustment and bolster expansionary policies, where needed in the face of deflation risks. The 2009 allocation was particularly important for emerging market and low-income countries that had been hit hard by the crisis. Over the longer term, the allocation could also reduce the tendency for countries to pursue destabilizing and costly reserve accumulation policies that could contribute to global imbalances. It was also expected to result in an increased volume of transactions initiated by members seeking to exchange SDRs for freely usable currencies.

SPECIAL DRAWING RIGHTS DEPARTMENT. An accounting entity rather than an organizational unit of the Fund's **staff**, this department records and administers transactions and operations in **Special Drawing Rights (SDRs)**. SDRs do not constitute claims by holders against the Fund to provide **currency**, except in connection with termination of participation or liquidation. Participation in the SDR Department is voluntary, but currently all Fund members are participants.

SPECIAL DRAWING RIGHTS (SDRs), RECONSTITUTION OF. Compulsory reconstitution of **Special Drawing Rights (SDRs)** was a feature of the SDR facility from its inception in 1969 to April 1981, when the requirement was abrogated. At the time of the facility's inception, participants were obligated to maintain over a five-year period average holdings of SDRs at 30 percent of their net cumulative **Special Drawing Rights allocations**. In the ensuing years, however, as changes were made to widen the uses of SDRs and to increase the interest rate on holdings of SDRs to near market levels, the compulsory holding requirement was no longer considered necessary. Participants, however, are still expected to maintain over time a balanced relationship between their holdings of SDRs and their other **reserves**.

Reconstitution was one of several difficult and divisive issues that preceded the establishment of the SDR facility. Many countries had basic doubts as to whether it was wise to put the power to create **international liquidity**, that is, create an international **reserve asset**, into the hands of officials of an international organization that was, in the last analysis, controlled by national political influences. During the course of the negotiations, the concept of a reserve unit, to be distributed to an exclusive group of countries, was changed to a universal drawing rights scheme designed only to supplement **interna-**

tional reserves. The decision, moreover, to allocate SDRs—normally over a basic period of five years—was hedged around with a complicated procedure and required approval of 85 percent of the participants' total voting power. As part of this cautious approach, the reconstitution provisions were made compulsory, partly to obligate national **monetary authorities** to accept and hold this new and unfamiliar supplement to reserves (dubbed in the press "funny money"), and partly because of the strongly held view by some members that reserves should not be a mechanism to effect the permanent transfer of real resources from industrial countries to **developing countries** in order to finance economic development.

SPECIAL DRAWING RIGHTS TRANSFERS. Total transfers of **Special Drawing Rights (SDRs)** during the financial year ended 30 April 1998 amounted to SDR 20.3 billion, compared with SDR 19.8 billion in 1996–1997, and annual average of SDR 18.7 billion over the past nine years. Transfers among participants and prescribed holders in 1997–1998 amounted to SDR 9.8 billion, compared with SDR 8.4 billion in the previous year, and an annual average of SDR 5.8 billion over the past nine years. Since September 1987, there have been no transactions with designation because potential exchanges of SDRs for **currency** have been accommodated through voluntary transactions.

SPECIAL DRAWING RIGHTS VALUATION BASKET. The current **Special Drawing Right (SDR)** valuation basket comprises the **currencies** of the four largest member countries in the Fund: the **euro**, the Japanese yen, the pound sterling, and the U.S. dollar. The basket composition is reviewed every five years by the Executive Board to ensure that it reflects the relative importance of currencies in the world's trading and financial systems. At the most recent review in November 2005, the weights of the currencies in the SDR basket were revised based on the value of the exports of goods and services and the amount of reserves denominated in the respective currencies that were held by other members of the IMF. These changes became effective on 1 January 2006. The next review will take place in late 2010.

SPECIAL FACILITIES. The Fund's special facilities consist of the **compensatory and contingency financing facility** and the **buffer stock financing facility**.

STABILIZATION PROGRAMS. The terms *stabilization program* and ***adjustment program*** are used synonymously, but a stabilization program has the connotation of policy measures aimed at correcting a financial imbalance, and is usually short-term, whereas an adjustment program may address structural maladjustments, as well as financial instability, and be planned for the longer term. A stabilization program is basically directed at restoring equilibrium to the economy in the near term through demand management policies, such as fiscal, monetary, and exchange rate policies.

Most of the early Fund-supported programs were of this character. In the mid-1970s, however, when many of the newly independent **developing countries** were experiencing the effects of unfavorable trends in their primary export markets, increased oil import prices, overambitious domestic development plans, and inflation, more fundamental and more enduring structural problems emerged. Demand management policies were by themselves no longer sufficient and needed to be underpinned by a broader economic strategy involving the mobilization of the country's resources, the integration of the various sectors of the economy, the removal of bottlenecks, the modernization of the taxation and banking systems, and policies to increase domestic savings and expand food production. These reforms could not be completed in the traditional 12 months of a stabilization program, and required implementation over the course of several years.

Stabilization measures are basic to all adjustment programs, for without financial stability, economic development and a viable **balance of payments** position cannot be sustained. In the postwar era, many earlier Fund stabilization programs included measures of structural adjustment that were introduced under 12-month **stand-by arrangements** and were only fully implemented after the duration of the arrangement.

All Fund programs are based on the understanding that deficits that are neither temporary nor self-reversing cannot be financed indefinitely and must be corrected through internal policy adjustments. Commitment on the part of a government to an appropriate Fund-supported adjustment program can bring in financing from other public, as well as private, sources, and thus provide breathing space for corrective policies to be implemented with less disruption than would otherwise be possible. *See also* FINANCIAL PROGRAMMING.

STAFF OF THE FUND. Unlike the **United Nations**, the Fund is not subject to nationality quotas in recruiting its staff. The **Articles of Agreement** specify that the staff owes its duty entirely to the Fund and to no other authority. In recruiting staff, the **Managing Director** is charged, subject to the paramount importance of securing the highest standards of efficiency and of technical competence, to pay due regard to the importance of recruiting personnel on as wide a geographical basis as possible. The Fund's professional staff is predominantly composed of economists, mostly with advanced qualifications or specialized knowledge in national accounts and macroeconomics.

The regular budgeted staff of the Fund at all levels has grown from 1,444 on 30 April 1980, to 2,181 on 30 April 1997, of which 46 percent were women and 54 percent men. Of this total, 693 were support staff (593 women and 100 men); 1,179 were professional staff (390 women and 789 men), of which 770 were economists (150 women and 620 men) and 409 other career streams (240 women and 169 men); and 309 were managerial staff (31 women and 278 men).

Distribution of professional staff by nationality and region was as follows: Africa, 5.2 percent; Asia, 15 percent, of which Japan accounted for 1.6 percent; Europe, 33.2 percent, of which France was 4.5 percent, Germany was 3.8 percent, Italy was 2.8 percent, the United Kingdom was 7 percent, and other European countries were 15.1 percent; Middle East, 6.1 percent; Western Hemisphere, 40.5 percent, of which Canada was 3.5 percent, the United States was 25.5 percent, and other countries in the Western Hemisphere were 11.5 percent.

On 30 April 1997, the Fund's regular staff numbered 2,181. In addition to its regular staff, the Fund had 480 authorized positions for outside experts and consultants. *See also* ORGANIZATION OF THE FUND.

STANDARDS AND CODES INITIATIVE. The standards and codes initiative (also called "the initiative") was launched in 1999 as a key part of the effort to strengthen the international financial architecture. The initiative was designed to promote greater financial stability, at both the domestic and international levels, through the development, dissemination, adoption, and implementation of international standards and codes. Its three main objectives include assisting countries in making progress in strengthening their economic institutions, informing the work of the Fund and the World Bank, and informing market participants.

The initiative covers 12 areas and associated standards, which were recognized by the **Boards of Governors** of the Fund and the **World Bank** as relevant for the operational work of the institutions. The standards relate to policy transparency, financial sector regulation and supervision, and market integrity. They include accounting, auditing, anti-money laundering and countering the financing of terrorism (AML/CFT), banking supervision, corporate governance, data dissemination, fiscal transparency, insolvency and creditor rights, insurance supervision, monetary and financial policy transparency, payments systems, and securities regulation.

The initiative includes sets of provisions that relate to the institutional environment—the "rules of the game"—within which economic policies are implemented. While the benefits of good institutions on economic performance has long been recognized, the initiative reflects a more explicit acknowledgment that financial stability is more likely to be achieved in institutional environments that meet certain standards. Over time, the initiative has evolved to recognize that, at the domestic level, implementation of standards can contribute to economic functioning and efficiency, not just to financial stability.

The initiative has required the development of appropriate standards and assessments of the extent to which these standards are implemented by various countries. Thus, together with member countries, key actors in the initiative are the "standard setters" and the "standard assessors." An assessment results in a Report on the Observance of Standards and Codes. For financial sector standards, longer documents (Detailed Assessments) are also produced.

As of the Executive Board review of the implementation of Standards and Codes in 2005, 723 assessments and updates had been completed in 122 countries, of which 592 were initial assessments. The pace of completing initial assessments has fallen in recent years. After peaking at 148 in 2003, it fell to 85 in 2005.

Participation in the initiative has been high for emerging market countries and advanced economies, and somewhat lower for developing countries. However, developing countries have been catching up since 2003, constituting the bulk of first-time participants. Regional participation rates remain uneven, with participation highest for Europe, including Eastern Europe, and lowest for East Asia and sub-Saharan Africa. There is evidence of "self-selection," with the best performers more willing to participate than poorer performers.

STAND-BY ARRANGEMENTS. A stand-by arrangement is a decision of the Fund by which a member is assured that, in accordance with the terms of the decision, the member will be able to purchase the **currency** of other members from the Fund during a specified period and up to a specified amount. Analogous to a confirmed line of credit, the stand-by arrangement was a novel instrument of international law and finance devised in the early years of the Fund. The stand-by arrangement has become the main instrument for making the **resources** of the Fund available to members.

The first stand-by arrangement with Belgium in 1952 was for a duration of 6 months, but shortly thereafter the standard period for a stand-by arrangement became 12 months until 1974, when the **extended Fund facility** was established, providing for three-year programs.

As noted previously, a stand-by arrangement provides an assurance to a member that a specified amount of financing will be made available to that member over the life of the arrangement, but this assurance is dependent on the member observing the terms and conditions set out in the arrangement.

Normally, the stand-by document will include economic performance criteria, such as budgetary and credit ceilings, **exchange rate** policies, interest rate policies, avoidance of restrictions on current payments and transfers, limits on indebtedness, and minimum levels of net **foreign exchange reserves**. In addition, the arrangement may provide for periodic reviews of the progress being made under the program and set out a schedule for the disbursement of finance at quarterly or half-yearly intervals. In the case of extended arrangements, members are expected to present a program outlining their objectives and policies for the whole period of the arrangement, as well as a detailed statement of policies and measures that will be followed during each 12-month period. Under these arrangements, the program will establish the macroeconomic criteria, as well as the structural maladjustments that are to be reformed.

STRAUSS-KAHN, DOMINIQUE (1949–). Dominique Strauss-Kahn, a French national, assumed office as the tenth **Managing Director** of the Fund on 1 November 2007.

Prior to taking up his position at the Fund, Mr. Strauss-Kahn was a member of the French National Assembly and Professor of Economics at the Institut d'Etudes Politiques de Paris. From 2001 to 2007, he was reelected three times to the National Assembly, and in 2006, he ran for the Socialist Party's nomination for the French presidential election. Earlier, Mr. Strauss-Kahn served as Minister of Economy, Finance and Industry of France. In this capacity, he managed the launch of the **euro**. He also represented France on the Board of Governors of a number of international financial institutions, including the Fund.

Mr. Strauss-Kahn holds a PhD in economics from the University of Paris. He also graduated in law, in business administration, in political studies, and in statistics. As an academic, his research fields include household saving behavior, public finance, and social policy.

STRUCTURAL ADJUSTMENT FACILITY (SAF). This facility, established in 1986, enables the Fund to provide financial resources on highly concessional terms to support medium-term macroeconomic and **adjustment programs** in low-income countries facing protracted **balance of payments** problems. The programs are explicitly directed toward the elimination of structural imbalances and rigidities in the economies of the poorer countries, for which the facility has been specifically established. Under its terms, the member develops and updates, with the assistance of the **staffs** of the Fund and the **World Bank**, the framework of a medium-term policy for a three-year period. Within this framework, detailed yearly policy programs are formulated and supported by financing from the Fund in the form of annual loan disbursements. The programs include quarterly benchmarks to assess performance. The overall **access limit** for the SAF was set in November 1992 at 50 percent of **quota** over a three-year period, with annual limits in the first, second, and third years of the program of 15 percent, 20 percent, and 15 percent, respectively. The rate of interest on SAF loans was set at 0.5 percent a year, and repayments were to be made in 5.5 to 10 years. The SAF was gradually phased out after an **Executive Board** decision was made in 1993 to extend and enlarge its successor, the **enhanced structural adjustment facility**.

SUBSCRIPTIONS TO THE FUND. A member's subscription is equal to its **quota** and must be paid in full before **membership** becomes effective. An amount not exceeding 25 percent of quota has to be paid in **reserve assets** specified by the Fund (currently in SDRs or usable currencies, but formerly in **gold** until the second amendment to the Articles in 1978) and the balance in the member's own currency. Normally, that part of the quota subscription paid in the member's own currency is provided in the form of promissory notes.

SUBSIDY ACCOUNTS. *See* ENHANCED STRUCTURAL ADJUSTMENT FACILITY SUBSIDY ACCOUNT; OIL FACILITY SUBSIDY ACCOUNT; SUPPLEMENTARY FINANCING FACILITY SUBSIDY ACCOUNT.

SUEZ CRISIS. The Suez crisis provided the opportunity for the Fund to become a major player on the international financial scene at a time of crisis after a period in which it had been sidelined in Europe by the introduction of the Marshall Plan and had played only a marginal role elsewhere. **Egypt** nationalized the Suez Canal in July 1956 and three months later Egypt was attacked by France, Israel, and the United Kingdom. The Suez Canal remained closed for many months and all four combatants approached the Fund for financial assistance. The first to do so was Egypt, which, making its first use of the Fund's **resources** since joining the Fund as a founding **member**, drew $15 million in its **gold tranche** and subsequently a further drawing of $15 million in its first **credit tranche**. Second was France, which obtained in September 1956 a one-year **stand-by arrangement** for its gold and first credit tranches, amounting to $262.5 million. In December, the British government also drew out its gold and first credit tranches, amounting to $561.5 million, and entered into a one-year stand-by arrangement for $738.5 million. Finally, early in 1957, Israel drew out its gold and credit tranches, amounting to $3.8 million.

Thus, 1956–1957 was a turning point for the Fund. The volume of **drawings** made on the Fund during the year, amounting to nearly $1.7 billion, was larger than the total **resources** made available by the Fund in the preceding nine years. In addition, new stand-by arrangements, amounting to $1.2 billion, were approved during the year, completely dwarfing the volume of stand-by arrangements that the Fund had previously approved. Of the total drawings, nearly $1 billion (or 59 percent) had been drawn by the four principals in the Suez affair.

SUGISAKI, SHIGEMITSU (1941–). Shigemitsu Sugisaki, a national of Japan, served as **Deputy Managing Director** from February 1997 to January 2004. Before his appointment as Deputy Managing Director, he had served as Special Advisor to the Managing Director since August 1994. A graduate of the University of Tokyo and Columbia University, Mr. Sugisaki joined Japan's Ministry of Finance in 1964 as a member of the Minister's Secretariat. He held various positions in the International Finance Bureau and the Tax Bureau, and was appointed Personal Assistant to the President or the Asian Development Bank. After rejoining the Ministry of Finance in 1979, he held a number of positions, including that of Deputy Director General of the International Finance Bureau in 1991–1992 and Commissioner of the Regional Taxation Bureau in 1992–1993. From mid-1993 until appointment to the Fund, he held the position of Secretary of Executive Bureau, the Securities and Exchange Surveillance Commission.

After leaving the Fund, Mr. Sugisaki served as Chairman of Sompo Japan Research Institute before becoming Vice Chairman of Goldman Sachs Japan Co., Ltd., on 29 December 2006.

SUPER GOLD TRANCHE. The super gold tranche, now an outdated term, referred to the amount that the Fund's **holdings** of a member's **currency** fell below 75 percent of its **quota** (assuming that the member had paid 25 percent in **gold**) because of net outstanding use of its currency by other members. **Gold** was eliminated from the Fund's operations by the second amendment to the **Articles** in 1978, and the terms ***gold tranche*** and *super gold tranche* no longer apply. Although the term *gold tranche* has been replaced by ***reserve tranche***, the use of the prefix *super* has been dropped.

SUPPLEMENTARY FINANCING FACILITY (SFF). Widening payments imbalances throughout the 1970s resulted in the need for financing **balance of payments** needs that were large in relation to members' **quotas** and, building on the experiences of the **borrowing** arrangements for the 1974 and 1975 oil facilities, the Fund entered into borrowing agreements with 13 members and the Swiss National Bank to borrow the equivalent of SDR 7.8 billion as supplementary financing to meet the rising demand for Fund **resources** that could not be met from ordinary resources. Available resources in the facility were fully committed by March 1981 and **repurchases**, which had a maximum repayment term of seven years, were completed by 1991. Use of the facility was subject to the standard requirement of balance of payments need and also to three other criteria: (1) that the period required for satisfactory adjustment of the balance of payments must normally be longer than one year; (2) that the financing required by the member must exceed the amount available in the **credit tranches** or under the **extended Fund facility**; and (3) that access must be in conjunction with an upper credit tranche **stand-by arrangement** or an extended arrangement with the Fund, and that **purchases** under the facility would be subject to the same **conditionality** as purchases under those arrangements.

Financing from the supplementary facility was mixed with financing from the ordinary resources of the Fund in varying proportions, depending on the type of arrangement that the facility supplemented and on the extent of the financing required. The Fund borrowed resources for the supplementary facility at market-determined interest rates, and its **charges** to members on outstanding balances under the facility were correspondingly higher than those on ordinary resources.

SUPPLEMENTARY FINANCING FACILITY SUBSIDY ACCOUNT. The supplementary financing facility subsidy account, which was administered by the Fund and separated from all other accounts, was established in 1980 to assist low-income **developing countries** to meet the cost of using resources made available through the Fund's **supplementary financing facility** and under the policy on exceptional use. Resources of the account were derived from contributions (SDR 57.4 million) and loans (SDR 4.6 million) from members and interest income earned on **investments** (SDR 61.4 million). The account also benefited by transfers of amounts received in interest and loan repayments from the **Trust Fund** through the **Special Disbursement Account**.

Subsidy payments to eligible members were made on a two-tier basis. Members with per capita incomes in 1979 equal to or below the per capita level used to determine eligibility for assistance from the International Development Association (the concessional lending facility of the **World Bank** Group) received the full rate of subsidy, with a maximum limit of 3 percent a year. Those with per capita income in 1979 above that level, but not more than that of the member with the highest per capita among the countries that were eligible to receive assistance from the Trust Fund, received subsidies at half the full rate (i.e., at 1.5 percent). The subsidy payment was calculated on the average daily balances of the Fund's **holdings** of a member's **currency** that resulted from **purchases** under the supplementary financing facility, but it was stipulated that the subsidy could not reduce the cost of using the facility below that of using the ordinary (unborrowed) resources of the Fund. After 1988, the rate of subsidy declined from the maximum of 3 percent and 1.5 percent, owing to the reduction in the **charge** on purchases under the supplementary financing facility in relation to the cost of the Fund's ordinary resources.

SUPPLEMENTAL RESERVE FACILITY (SRF). Following the experience of the **Mexican financial crisis** of 1996 and the more recent **Asian financial crisis**, which were marked by sharply adverse capital flows, the Fund introduced a new facility in December 1997 to provide financial assistance to a member experiencing exceptional **balance of payments** difficulties caused by a large short-term financing need resulting from a sudden and disruptive loss of market confidence, as reflected by movements in the member's capital account and reserves. Assistance under the facility will be available when there is a reasonable expectation that the implementation of strong adjustment policies and adequate financing will result, within a short period, in an early correction of the balance of payments difficulties.

Although resources of the Fund are available to all members, in setting up the SRF the Fund had in mind its use by members when the magnitude of an outflow created a risk of contagion that could potentially threaten the stability of the **international monetary system**. In approving a request by a member to use the SRF resources, the Fund takes into account the financing provided by other creditors. To minimize moral hazard, a member using the SRF resources is encouraged to maintain the participation of creditors—both official and private—until the pressure on the balance of payments ceases. The facility is part of the Fund's efforts to strengthen its **surveillance** procedures and encourage members to implement appropriate policies in order to prevent crises from occurring.

Financing under the new facility will be available in the form of additional **resources** under a **stand-by** or **extended** arrangement and be committed for up to one year, generally available in two or more tranches. The amount of financing available to a member under the facility will be determined by taking into account the financing needs of the member, its capacity to repay, the strength of its economic program, its outstanding use of Fund credit, and its record of cooperating with the Fund in the past. Countries will be expected to repay within 1 to 1.5 years after each tranche is drawn, although the Fund may extend this repayment period for up to a year. During the first year, borrowers pay a surcharge of 300 basis points above the rate of charge on Fund drawings. This rate increases by 50 basis points at the end of the first year and every six months thereafter until the surcharge reaches 500 basis points. *See also* ASIAN FINANCIAL CRISIS; BRAZIL.

SURVEILLANCE OVER EXCHANGE RATES. The Fund is charged under its **Articles of Agreement** "to exercise firm surveillance over the exchange rate policies of its members" to help ensure orderly exchange arrangements and promote a stable exchange rate system. The Fund has approved three principles to guide members in their conduct of exchange rates. The first of these reaffirms the obligation of members to refrain from manipulating exchange rates or the **international monetary system** in order to prevent **balance of payments** adjustment or to gain an unfair competitive advantage over other members. The second directs members to intervene in the **exchange markets** if necessary to counter disorderly conditions that may be characterized by, among other things, disruptive short-term movements in the exchange value of its **currency**. The third requires members to take into account in their intervention policies the interest of other members, including those of the countries in whose currencies they intervene.

In applying these principles, developments that might prompt the Fund to have discussions with a member are (1) a protracted, large-scale intervention in one direction in the exchange market; (2) an unsustainable level of official or quasiofficial borrowing, or excessive and prolonged short-term official or quasiofficial lending, for balance of payments purposes; (3) the introduction, substantial intensification, or prolonged maintenance, for balance of payments purposes, of restrictions on, or incentives for, current transactions or payments, or the introduction or substantial modification for balance of payments purposes of restrictions on, or incentives for, the inflow or outflow of capital; (4) the pursuit, for balance of payments purposes, of monetary and other domestic financial policies that provide abnormal encouragement or discouragement to capital flows; and (5) behavior of the exchange rate that appears to be unrelated to underlying economic and financial conditions, including factors affecting competitiveness and long-term **capital movements**.

The appraisal of a member's exchange rate policies is conducted within the framework of a comprehensive analysis of the general economic situation and the policy strategy of the members. First, the **Executive Board** regularly reviews each member's economic policies and performance and their interaction with economic developments in other countries. These reviews are based on staff reports prepared on the basis of regular Article IV consultation discussions with authorities of member countries, normally conducted on an annual basis. Second, broad developments in exchange rates are reviewed periodically by the Executive Board within the context of discussions on the world economic outlook, allowing members' policies to be reviewed and analyzed from a multilateral perspective. In this connection, the ***World Economic Outlook*** is prepared and published twice a year.

In addition, the Board holds, somewhat more frequently, discussions on exchange market developments in the major industrial countries. The **Managing Director** also participates in the meetings of finance ministers and central bank governors of the major industrial countries (the Group of Seven, increased to eight in 1998), to which he is able to provide a global view and analysis of national policies in terms of their international interactions.

Underlying the Fund's examination of members' exchange rate policies are the comprehensive data that the Fund routinely demands and receives on members' economic conditions, the close contact that the staff maintains with the officials in member countries responsible for formulating and implementing policy, and the comparative analysis that a multinational staff, in close contact with all member countries, can bring to the task of **multilateral surveillance**. Among the numerous indicators that are monitored and analyzed are economic growth rates, inflation, unemployment rates, fiscal and monetary trends, external debt developments, structural indicators, trade and current account balances, capital flows, investment, savings, exchange rates, and **reserves**. The staff prepares medium-term projections for these indicators as a means of monitoring and reviewing the policies and performances of the large industrial countries, and it draws up medium-term scenarios that illustrate the effects of alternative policies and identify potential conflicts. An important objective of the exercise is to examine the outlook for various categories of its members, such as advanced economies, **developing countries**, debtor countries, heavily indebted countries, and oil-exporting countries.

As a complement to other approaches, the Fund also uses macroeconomic models to identify possible exchange rate misalignments. These involve (1) a trade equation model to calculate the underlying current account position that would emerge at prevailing market exchange rates if all countries were producing at their potential output levels; (2) a separate model to estimate normal or equilibrium level of the saving-investment balance consistent with medium-run fundamentals, including the assumption that countries were operating at their potential levels; (3) a calculation of the amount by which the exchange rate would have to change, other things being equal, to equilibrate the underlying current account position with the medium-term saving-investment norm; and (4) an assessment whether the estimates of exchange rates consistent with the medium-term fundamentals suggest that any currencies are badly misaligned, taking into account the prevailing cyclical conditions and the degree to which macroeconomic policies are appropriate. *See also* REGIONAL SURVEILLANCE.

SWAPS. *See* CURRENCY SWAP ARRANGEMENT.

SYSTEMIC TRANSFORMATION FACILITY (STF). This new temporary facility, established in April 1993, was designed to help member countries facing **balance of payments** difficulties arising from a disruption of their traditional trade and payments arrangements caused by a shift from reliance on trading at nonmarket prices to multilateral, market-based trade. The countries that were expected to benefit from the facility were those that belonged to the former Council for Mutual Economic Assistance, the republics of the former Soviet Union, and other countries experiencing similar transformation. Access to the facility was limited to no more than 50 percent of **quota**, with financing being provided in two equal disbursements. Members using the facility were required to commit themselves to an interim program that could be succeeded by a full-fledged **adjustment program** with the Fund. Disbursements under the facility were made from the Fund's **general resources**, the rate of charge was the same as for other use of those **resources**, and the repayment period was set at from 4.5 to 10 years. *See also* ECONOMIES IN TRANSITION; RUSSIAN FEDERATION; TRANSITIONAL ECONOMIES.

T

TECHNICAL ASSISTANCE AND TRAINING. The provision of technical assistance and training has been an important part of the Fund's activities almost since its inception, but during the 1990s, particularly in the aftermath of the collapse of systems based on central planning, requests for technical assistance escalated sharply. In the year ended 30 April 1998, technical assistance accounted for an estimated 16.5 percent of the Fund's total expenditures. The assistance provided by the Fund covers a wide range of fields, including fiscal, monetary, and **balance of payments** policies; debt management; banking; exchange and trade systems; government finance; and statistics. Recipients are member countries, dependent territories of member countries, countries about to join the Fund, and some multinational institutions. Assistance is provided mainly through **staff** missions, field assignments by staff members or outside experts, and studies and recommendations prepared at headquarters.

The IMF Institute trains officials from member and prospective member countries through courses at Fund headquarters, at the IMF–Singapore Regional Training Institute, the Joint **Vienna Institute**, and in regional technical assistance centers. Courses in Washington, D.C., are offered in Arabic, English, French, and Spanish; courses in Vienna are offered in English, with Russian interpretation, and in French; and courses in other overseas locations are offered in Arabic, French, or Spanish, with interpretation into the local language, as needed.

The Fiscal Affairs Department provides technical assistance in fiscal matters to help country authorities with the building of tax administration and public expenditure management institutions.

The Legal Department provides technical assistance in the areas of central banking, commercial banking, foreign exchange, fiscal, collateral, and bank insolvency laws. The assistance includes drafting legislation, commenting on draft legislation prepared by the authorities of member countries, drafting implementing regulations, and providing other legal advice. The assistance is directed to a broad range of countries, but in the 1990s the larger share was to members with **transitional economies**.

Monetary and Capital Markets Department provides advice and assistance to members on the establishment and strengthening of central banks, currency boards, and other currency arrangements; the issuance of new currencies; central bank accounting and internal audit; and associated legislative, regulatory, and organizational reforms. It also provides advice on the design and implementation of monetary policy instruments and operations; money and exchange market intervention; and the institutional framework and instruments for public debt management. It also provides technical assistance in the areas of financial market development, banking supervision and regulation, including bank restructuring and banking safety nets, and the implementation of international standards.

The Strategy, Policy, and Review Department provides technical assistance in the creation of wide-coverage, high-frequency debt monitoring systems aimed at helping country authorities monitor the participation by banks or other creditors and prevent or resolve financial crises.

The Statistics Department, as other departments of the Fund, directs much of its technical assistance to countries in transition, centered on balance of payments, government finance, money and banking, national accounts, and price and international trade statistics. The Department has been active establishing the **Special Data Dissemination Standard (SDDS)** and guiding member countries that are seeking to participate in subscribing to the SDDS.

Other assistance provided by the Fund covers, from time to time, technical aspects of membership and operations, as well as help in the modernization of member countries' computer systems in central banks, ministries of finance, and statistical offices. *See also* AFRICAN REGIONAL TECHNICAL ASSISTANCE CENTER (AFRITAC); CARIBBEAN REGIONAL TECHNICAL ASSISTANCE CENTER (CARTAC); ORGANIZATION OF THE FUND.

THAILAND. Although Thailand had made extensive use of the Fund's resources in the period 1976–1989, by the early 1990s, it had cleared its outstanding use of Fund credit and had begun to build up its **reserve position in the Fund**. Indeed, it had enjoyed a decade of robust and strong economic growth prior to the outbreak of the **Asian financial crisis** in August 1997.

Thailand's economic crisis, like others in the region, was rooted in serious weaknesses in the domestic financial sector, which were exacerbated by a sharp slowdown in exports and GDP growth, growing difficulties in the property market, and a sharp fall in stock market prices. The introduction of a managed float of the baht in July 1997 was followed by a 20 percent depreciation in its value. Although the Thai authorities took some early measures to address the growing difficulties, their actions were inadequate to correct a deepening crisis, and the baht came under a series of increasingly serious speculative attacks as the markets lost confidence in the economy.

On 20 August 1997, the Fund's Executive Board approved a **stand-by arrangement** for Thailand, authorizing drawings of up to $3.9 billion, or up to 505 percent of Thailand's quota, over a 34-month period to support the government's economic program. An additional total of over $12 billion was pledged by the **World Bank**, the Asian Development Bank, and bilateral lenders in the region.

The main thrust of this short-term program was financial sector restructuring, initially focusing on the identification and closure of unviable financial institutions (including 56 finance companies), intervention in the weakest banks, and the recapitalization of the banking system; fiscal measures equivalent to about 3 percent of GDP to correct the public sector deficit to a surplus of 1 percent of GDP in 1997–1998, support the necessary improvement in the current account position, and provide for the costs of financial restructuring, including through an increase in the value-added tax rate from 7 percent to 10 percent. A new framework for monetary policy was also introduced to support the new managed float for the baht; and structural initiatives were put in place to increase efficiency, deepen the role of the private sector in the Thai economy, and reinforce its outward orientation. These initiatives included civil service reform, privatization, and initiatives to attract foreign capital.

As the recession deepened more sharply than initially expected, the program was modified five times, in November 1997, February 1998, May 1998, August 1998, and December 1998, to put in place additional measures to maintain the public sector surplus at 1 percent of GDP; provide a more comprehensive approach to bank and corporate restructuring, including strategies for the preemptive recapitalization and strengthening of the financial system; and to accelerate programs aimed at protecting the weakest sectors of society. Additional measures were also geared toward quickly stabilizing the exchange rate and bringing about an early recovery, including by providing a large fiscal stimulus to bolster domestic demand and restore confidence.

Despite bouts of international nervousness caused by the burgeoning crises in **Russia** and Latin America, progress continued in Thailand throughout 1998. Inflation stayed lower than expected, money market rates fell below their precrisis level, and the baht appreciated. A large swing in the external current account led to a substantial build-up in external reserves. At the beginning of 1999, prospects were for a modest 1 percent growth in GDP for the year.

TORONTO MENU. In June 1988, the leaders of the **Group of Seven** major industrial countries, participating in the fourteenth economic conference in Toronto, endorsed a debt-relief plan for the official bilateral debts of low-income countries undertaking macroeconomic and **structural adjustment** programs. The relief measures consisted of a reduction in debt service, a rescheduling at concessional interest rates, or a rescheduling at longer maturities. Subsequently, the menu was enlarged at the Group of Seven meeting in Trinidad in September 1990 to encompass debt reduction and was adopted by the **Paris Club** in December 1991.

TRAINING. *See* TECHNICAL ASSISTANCE AND TRAINING.

TRANCHE. *See* GOLD TRANCHE; RESERVE TRANCHE; SUPER GOLD TRANCHE.

TRANSACTIONS OF THE FUND. In the years since 1946, all industrial countries have purchased **currencies** from the Fund (although several, including the United States, have drawn only on their **reserve tranche**). **Drawings** on the Fund by industrial countries, however, dropped sharply in the 1970s, and no major industrial country has used the Fund's financial **resources** since 1976, when a total of SDR 2.6 billion was drawn by eight industrial countries. In 1976–1984, several of the smaller industrial countries made limited use of the Fund's resources, but since 1984 no industrial country has found it necessary to approach the Fund for financing.

Developing countries, on the other hand, have continued to make extensive use of the Fund's resources, with drawings reaching record levels through the 1980s and 1990s. The oil shocks of the 1970s, the debt crisis of the 1980s, and the economic and financial crises of the 1990s all posed serious problems for many developing countries, requiring a growing volume of resources from the Fund. In 1984, the Fund committed over SDR 28 billion under Fund-supported programs, and although the level declined thereafter in the 1980s, it began to rise again sharply in the 1990s, reaching a peak in 1997–1998, when total Fund credit outstanding rose to a record SDR 56 billion, an increase of SDR 16 billion during the year. By April 1998, the Fund had committed a total of over SDR 310 billion under about 1,170 Fund-supported programs. In financing these programs, the Fund has drawn on its ordinary resources as well as loans made to it for the oil facilities, the enlarged access policies, the supplementary financing, and the **Trust Fund**, amounting to over SDR 30 billion, not taking into account the activations of the **General Arrangements to Borrow** (GAB) over the years of its establishment. *See also* BORROWING BY THE FUND.

TRANSITIONAL ARRANGEMENTS. Article XIV, Section 2, of the **Articles of Agreement** allows a member to avail itself of transitional arrangements under which it may maintain and adapt to changing circumstances the restrictions on payments and transfers for current international transactions that were in effect on the date on which it became a member. Members are under an obligation to withdraw such restrictions as soon as conditions permit. Originally, members were given a transitional period targeted at five years, but the provision was replaced by more general language in the second amendment to the Articles. Under its Articles the Fund must report annually on restrictions in force in countries that are availing themselves of the transitional arrangements, and the Fund does so by publishing the ***Annual Report on Exchange Arrangements and Exchange Restrictions***. By 30 April 1998, 144 members, including all the main trading countries, had accepted the obligations of **Article VIII**, under which they had undertaken to refrain from imposing restrictions on the making of payments and transfers for current international transactions or engaging in discriminatory currency arrangements or **multiple currency practices**. At that time, about 40 members, all **developing countries**, **transitional economies**, or new members, were availing themselves of the transitional arrangements.

TRANSITIONAL ECONOMIES. A group of countries, mainly from the former Soviet Union (FSU), that had unusual problems in changing from a command economy to one based on free markets. With the end of central planning in many countries of eastern Europe and the breakup of the FSU, the Fund entered into a close relationship with the these 27 countries. Since 1990, it has provided a vast amount of financial and technical assistance to these economies, most of which have made good progress, with the resumption of economic growth, macroeconomic stabilization, and the inception of structural reforms. Progress has been mixed, however, with some countries forging ahead of others, depending to a large extent on the nature of their initial problems and the steadfastness with which they have pursued their goals.

Between 1 January 1990 and 31 December 1997, the Fund committed a total of SDR 30.7 billion (about $40.3 billion) to 27 economies in transition, including the Baltic countries, the **Russian Federation**, and other states of the FSU. These commitments were made through all the facilities of the Fund, such as under regular and extended **stand-by arrangements**; the concessional window, the **enhanced structural adjustment facility**; the special temporary facility created for these economies, the **systemic transformation facility**; and the **compensatory and contingency financing facility**. At the end of January 1998, outstanding credit amounted to SDR 15.6 billion (about $20.3 billion). The largest commitment was to the Russian Federation, amounting to SDR 14.1 billion (about $18.2 billion); followed by **Poland**, SDR 2.7 billion (about $3.5 billion); Ukraine, SDR 2.5 billion (about $3.2 billion); Hungary, SDR 2.1 billion (about $2.7 billion); Romania, SDR 1.8 billion (about $2.3 billion); and Bulgaria, SDR 1.7 billion (about $2.2 billion).

Technical assistance provided by the Fund to the economies covered four broad categories: design and implementation of fiscal and monetary policies; institution building (such as improving tax collection and through the strengthening of tax administration); collection and refinement of statistical data; and reviewing legislation and providing assistance, when asked, in its drafting. Technical assistance also included training officials at the IMF Institute at headquarters and at the Joint **Vienna Institute**. By the end of 1997, 8,300 participants from 33 countries had received training through courses and seminars at the Joint Vienna Institute.

By the end of the 1990s, the experience of the countries remained diverse. However, most of them had started on the growth process and had reduced inflation to moderate levels (e.g., Poland, the Baltic countries, Croatia, the Czech and Slovak Republics, Hungary, and Slovenia). In Russia, the long-awaited renewal of growth in output began very modestly only in 1997. Overall GDP in 1997 for all economies in transition grew by 1.7 percent, compared with negative results of 1.3 percent and 0.2 percent in 1995 and 1996, respectively. Inflation for the group fell from 119 percent in 1995 to 40 percent in 1996 and 31 percent in 1997.

The **global financial crisis**, which was triggered in 2007 by a liquidity shortfall in the United States banking system and resulted in the collapse of large financial institutions and downturns in stock markets around the world, sparked a series of crises in the transitional economies of Europe. Because of the tremendous diversity in the region, the affects of the crisis were mixed, ranging from Poland, which virtually escaped recession altogether, to Ukraine, the Baltic states, Romania, and Hungary, all of which suffered severe downturns. In particular, the states that had experienced relatively easy access to inexpensive foreign money in the early 2000s along with excess consumption, the formation of asset price bubbles, and unsustainable current account deficits, found themselves terribly exposed when foreign capital inflows came to an abrupt halt in 2008.

In the most vulnerable and hard-hit countries, coordinated assistance from the Fund, the European Union, and other multilateral institutions was provided to help ease the inevitable adjustment. During 2008–2009, the Fund provided more than $81 billion in financing for Belarus, Bosnia and Herzegovina, Hungary, Latvia, Poland, Romania, Serbia, and Ukraine. While the design of the underlying programs reflected individual country circumstances, they contained a number of key features. First, the financing was larger and more front-loaded than typically seen in the past. Second, program conditionality was streamlined to focus on measures aimed at addressing vulnerabilities that magnified the impact of the shock. For example, improvements in financial supervision, enhanced macroprudential regulation, and structural or entitlement reforms with a durable impact on public finances figured prominently in many programs. Third, the preservation or enhancement of social safety nets to protect the poor and vulnerable was emphasized.

By the middle of 2010, projections indicated a resumption of growth in 2010–2011. However, unemployment was expected to increase, and lingering difficulties in banking sectors were likely to restrain credit supply. As a result, consumption and investment were expected to remain lackluster in the near term. *See also* RUSSIAN FEDERATION.

TRUST FUND. The Trust Fund was established in 1976 as an intermediate agency to receive funds from the profits of sales of the Fund's **gold** holdings, transfers from some of the beneficiaries of direct distributions of **gold sales** profits, and income from **investment** of assets. These proceeds were then channeled to eligible **developing countries** in the form of concessionary loans, repayable in installments over a period beginning 5.5 years and ending 10 years after disbursement of the loan and bearing a rate of interest of 0.5 percent a year. During the 1976–1981 period, the Fund provided SDR 2.9 billion from the Trust Fund, in two successive periods of two years, to 61 eligible developing member countries, defined as those having a per capita income of SDR 300 or less in 1973 and SDR 520 or less in 1975. The Trust Fund made its final disbursements in March 1981. Thereafter, interest on and repayments of Trust Fund loans were transferred to the Fund's **Special Disbursement Account**.

U

UGANDA AND HIPC. Uganda was the first country to be declared eligible for assistance under the **heavily indebted poor countries (HIPC)** initiative in April 1997. On 8 April 1998, following the declaration of the country's eligibility, the Fund and the **World Bank** agreed that Uganda had met the requirements for receiving nearly $650 million in debt relief from its external creditors under the HIPC initiative.

Under the agreement, relief from all of Uganda's creditors would be worth $350 million (in terms of net present value), to which the World Bank would contribute about $160 million and the Fund $69 million. This total represented about 20 percent of Uganda's **external debt**. The Fund's portion of the debt relief was to be made available in the form of a grant to pay part of the debt falling due to it. To relieve the country's debt to the International Development Association, the World Bank's contribution was to be made in three ways—partly in the form of a grant, partly as the payment or cancellation of debt, and partly by payment of Uganda's debt service by means of a grant from the HIPC Trust Fund.

In making the joint announcement, the Fund and World Bank press release noted that Uganda was one of the strongest performing economies in Africa, with an average annual economic growth over the preceding 10 years of 6 percent. Inflation had been contained and the economy was becoming increasingly diversified. The country had regained its position as Africa's premier coffee producer, the tea industry was being revitalized, a small horticulture industry was emerging, and maize exports were expanding. In addition, the country's transportation system was being rehabilitated, a national grid system to connect all parts of the country was being worked on, and the government had begun a program to bring about universal primary education.

In November 1997, the Fund approved a three-year arrangement under the **enhanced structural adjustment facility (ESAF)** in a total amount equivalent to about $138 million, to be drawn semiannually over the three years. In November 1998, the Fund approved the second annual loan for Uganda under the ESAF arrangement, equivalent to about $46 million, in support of the government's economic program for 1998–1999. The loan is available in two annual installments, the first of which, equivalent to $23 million, was disbursed on 25 November 1998.

The Fund noted that macroeconomic performance in 1997–1998 was generally in line with the program. Real GDP, which was adversely affected by El Nino weather conditions in the first half of the year, recovered in the second half, rising by 5.5 percent for the year. Inflation had been low and **international reserves** had been rebuilt to a relatively comfortable level. Notable progress had been made in 1997–1998 in a number of structural areas, particularly trade liberalization, civil service reform, tax administration, and financial sector reform, although privatization targets had not been fully achieved.

UNIFORMITY OF TREATMENT. The **Executive Board** has at various times stressed the importance of maintaining the uniformity of treatment of member countries. This principle, which requires that members in similar circumstances be treated similarly, applies to all Fund activities.

UNITED NATIONS, RELATIONS WITH. The Fund works in collaboration with other agencies within the United Nations family of agencies. As noted in the 1947 agreement between the Fund and the United Nations, the Fund is an independent international organization. The responsibility for maintaining day-to-day contact with the United Nations rests with the Fund's Special Representative to the United Nations, who maintains an office in the headquarters of the United Nations and devotes his activities solely to sustaining the Fund's close relations with the United Nations.

The **Managing Director** of the Fund also participates in a number of functions of the United Nations and its specialized agencies. He attends the meetings of the Administrative Coordinating Committee of the United Nations, speaks at sessions of the Economic and Social Council, the Economic Commission for Latin America and the Caribbean, the United Nations Conference on Trade and Development, and, when invited, also addresses other meetings and conferences of the United Nations and its specialized agencies on matters of relevance to the Fund. *See also* WORLD BANK; WORLD TRADE ORGANIZATION.

URUGUAY ROUND. The Uruguay Round of Multilateral Trade Negotiations—the eighth in the series conducted under the **General Agreement on Tariffs and Trade (GATT)** since 1947—began in Punta del Este, Uruguay, in January 1986. Originally scheduled to be completed by 1990, the tortuous negotiations, frequently on the brink of a complete breakdown, dragged on for eight years. Completed at the end of 1993, it marked the biggest reform of international trade since 1948. In the end, the agreement succeeded in bridging great differences of opinion between Europe and the United States, as well as those among a number of other countries, especially on the question of agricultural subsidies. The issues included (1) a significant reduction in trade barriers; (2) restoring to GATT the responsibility for monitoring trade in certain items that had moved outside multilateral trade negotiations, such as textiles and clothing; (3) bringing discipline to the trade-related aspects of intellectual property; (4) improving the rules and dispute settlement system; and (5) providing a framework for trade in services. Other matters under discussion included trade-related investment measures and the relations of GATT with the Fund and the **World Bank**. In addition, and of most importance, the Uruguay Round approved a proposal to establish a new international trade organization, the **World Trade Organization**, based on international law and having wider responsibilities than GATT, which it replaced, effective 1 January 1995.

USE OF FUND RESOURCES. Use of the Fund's resources is defined by its **Articles of Agreement**, which state in Article I(iv) that the Fund is to make the "general **resources** of the Fund temporarily available to them [members] under adequate safeguards, thus providing them with an opportunity to correct maladjustments in their **balance of payments** without resorting to measures destructive of national or international prosperity." The essential provisions are first, a member may draw on the Fund only to meet a balance of payments need; and second, use of the Fund's resources must be temporary (i.e., **drawings** must be repaid within a reasonable time). It follows, then, that in making finance available, the Fund must be assured that the member will adopt **adjustment** policies to correct the imbalance in its payments and be able to repay the Fund over the medium term. Influenced by the discussions held at the **Bretton Woods Conference**, the Fund decided that repayments (**repurchases**) should be over three to five years, or earlier if warranted by an improvement in the country's balance of payments position.

Early in the 1950s, the Fund clarified the terms on which a member could use its resources by establishing the so-called tranche policies. These consist of a reserve tranche and four **credit tranches**, normally each tranche amounting to 25 percent of a member's **quota**. The reserve tranche is a floating tranche and can be used without challenge. Drawings in the credit tranches require safeguards in terms of policy adjustments; moderate safeguards for drawings in the first credit tranche, but more substantial ones for drawings in the upper credit tranches.

In 1952, the Fund devised the **stand-by arrangement**, an original instrument under which members make almost all their drawings from the Fund.

Nearly all stand-by arrangements in the upper credit tranches contain criteria linking performance under adjustment programs to phased disbursements under stand-by arrangements.

The simple schema for use of the Fund's resources soon became more complicated, however, as elements in the balance of payments were picked out for special treatment and as a deepening and structural imbalance in world payments required longer term adjustment programs, increased temporary resources through Fund **borrowings**, and enlarged **access limits**. The process began in 1963 with the establishment of the compensatory financing facility to provide financing to members, with little or no **conditionality** and in amounts over and above those available under credit tranche policies, to offset shortfalls in export earnings.

This was followed by a **buffer stock financing facility** in 1969; the **oil facilities**, financed by Fund borrowings, in 1974 and 1975; the **supplementary financing facility**, again financed by borrowings, in 1979; the **Enlarged Access Policy**, financed by a mix of ordinary and borrowed funds, in 1981; the **structural adjustment facility**, providing loans on concessional terms and financed from reflows from the **Trust Fund**, in 1986; the **enhanced structural adjustment facility**, also providing loans on concessional terms and funded in part from resources derived from the structural adjustment facility and partly from donations and loans, in 1987; the **compensatory and contingency financing facility**, combining the various elements of compensatory financing with contingency financing, in 1989; the **systemic transformation facility**, for use by countries in transition to a market-based economy, in 1993; and, finally, the **Emergency Financing Mechanism** in 1995.

The conditionality attached to use of the Fund's financial resources has been subjected to much public discussion and many periodic reviews within the Fund. In 1979, the **Executive Board** established a set of guidelines to clarify the standards for the drawing up of stand-by and extended arrangements. Although the guidelines largely codified existing practices, they gave **developing countries** an opportunity to define and express some of their concerns about Fund conditionality. One guideline, regarded as being of great importance by developing countries, is that in devising adjustment programs, the Fund will pay due regard to the domestic social and political objectives, the economic priorities, and the circumstances of members. Another is that performance criteria will normally be confined to macroeconomic variables. The guidelines have been reviewed by the Board several times since 1979, but have not undergone substantive change.

In general, these guidelines are intended to prevent Fund-supported adjustment programs from interfering with national policy objectives, such as consumer subsidies or military expenditures, adopted for social or national security purposes. Nevertheless, the preparation of a realistic adjustment program often poses difficult and unwanted choices for national policy makers, particularly if they approach the Fund as a last resort, when their economic and financial affairs are in an extreme state of disorder. When requested, the Fund's **staff** can help by providing optional scenarios showing the various means to attain the targeted macroeconomic variables. In the last analysis, however, member countries are responsible for accepting and implementing the details of their adjustment programs.

During the 1990s, the largest commitments of the Fund's resources—each over SDR 10 billion—were for **Russia**, **Mexico**, **Korea**, **Indonesia**, **Argentina**, and India, although not all the commitments were, in fact, disbursed.

UNION OF SOVIET SOCIALIST REPUBLICS (USSR) AND THE FUND. The USSR participated in the **Bretton Woods Conference** in July 1944 and was given a **quota** in the Fund, but ultimately decided against joining it. Thereafter, occasional and informal contacts between the Fund and the U.S.S.R. took place until July 1990, when the Fund was asked to convene a joint study on the Soviet economy for the **Group of Seven**, to be carried out in conjunction with the **World Bank**, the Organization for Economic Cooperation and Development, and the European Bank for Reconstruction and Development. The joint study's recommendations were made public in December 1990, and in the following October the Fund and the USSR entered into a Special Association. This enabled the Fund to develop closer links with the USSR, provide **technical assistance**, and prepare and publish economic studies of all 15 states of the former Soviet Union (FSU) in mid-1992. The Fund's **Executive Board** completed premembership economic reviews of the 15 states, announced the quota calculations, and submitted membership resolutions to the **Board of Governors**, which in May 1992 agreed to admit to **membership** all the countries of the FSU. The original quota for Russia was determined at SDR 2.9 billion, but has increased to SDR 5.9 billion as of 30 December 2009. Russia has the tenth largest quota in the Fund, after Canada. *See also* RUSSIAN FEDERATION.

V

VIENNA INSTITUTE. The Joint Vienna Institute opened in Vienna in October 1992 to train officials from former centrally planned economies in various aspects of public administration and economic management. The Institute is sponsored by the Fund, the **Bank for International Settlements**, the Commission of the European Communities, the European Bank for Reconstruction and Development, the **World Bank**, and the Organization for Economic Cooperation and Development. *See also* IMF INSTITUTE AND REGIONAL INSTITUTIONS; TECHNICAL ASSISTANCE AND TRAINING.

VOTING PROVISIONS IN THE FUND. The voting structure in the Fund is distinguished by the fact that, in contrast to the situation in the **United Nations**, voting power is not based on "one member, one vote," but is weighted according to a member's financial contribution (its **quota**) to the organization. Each member receives a basic allotment of 250 votes, and also receives one additional vote for each part of its quota equivalent to SDR 100,000. The basic allotment of 250 votes for each member was intended to ensure that all members, no matter how small, would have some weight in influencing the operations of the organization. Over the years, however, the basic allotment of votes per member did not change, although the number of total votes expanded significantly over the decades in the context of general and ad hoc quota increases and the addition of new members. For example, in 1958, when the Fund had 69 members with total quotas of $9.2 billion, the basic votes of all members amounted to nearly 16 percent of total votes. By 2008, the number of basic votes had risen through new memberships to 46,000, which represents 2.1 percent of the current total voting power in the Fund. Therefore, an integral part of the form of quota and voice adopted by the **Board of Governors** in April 2008 provided for at least a doubling of basic votes as well as measures to protect the relative share of basic votes in total votes in the future.

The Board of Governors is the senior organ of the Fund, and the Governor of each member is entitled to cast the votes of the member appointing him. He cannot cast fewer votes than he is entitled to, and must either cast all his votes or abstain. The Board of Governors has delegated most of its powers to the **Executive Board**, but a number of powers that have a special institutional importance are confined to the Board of Governors. Basically, the Board of Governors takes decisions by a simple majority of the votes cast, but there are many decisions that require special majorities of 70 percent or 85 percent. Allocation and cancellation of **Special Drawing Rights (SDRs)**, valuation of SDRs, rates of charge and **remuneration**, sale of **gold** holdings, increases or decreases in the number of **Executive Directors**, and compulsory withdrawal of members are a few of the decisions that require special majorities.

Executive Directors cast the votes of the members that appointed or elected them. They cannot split their votes, however, and must either abstain from voting or cast all the votes of their constituency as a whole for or against a decision. In practice, the Executive Board rarely votes and reaches a decision by a "sense of the meeting." On particularly controversial issues, Executive Directors may meet in informal sessions, in seminar form, or in groups with the **Managing Director** as a precursor to reaching a consensus at a formal Board meeting. A well-informed Executive Director presenting a solid and persuasive case can have an influence far beyond his or her formal voting power, and it has become a tradition in the Executive Board to seek to accommodate the interests of as many Directors as possible in the final decision. In practice, however, decisions tend to reflect the various statements made by each speaker at a formal meeting and the voting strengths they command.

The International Monetary and Financial Committee is an advisory body and its recommendations reflect a consensus view. The **Articles of Agreement** provide for the Committee to be succeeded by a Council (if voted into existence by an 85 percent majority of the Board of Governors), having the same structure and representation as the Committee, but with decision-making powers. Members of the Council would be able to split their votes, casting separately the number of votes allotted to each member in their constituencies.

W

WHITE, HARRY DEXTER (1892–1948). Harry Dexter White and **Lord John Maynard Keynes** were the men primarily concerned in founding the Fund. White joined the staff of the U.S. Treasury in 1934, becoming an Assistant Director in the Division of Research and Statistics in 1936, Director of the Division of Monetary Research in 1938, Assistant to the Secretary in 1941, and Assistant Secretary in 1945. He resigned that position the following year to take up the post of U.S. Executive Director of the Fund. Accused of being a communist, and even a spy (charges that were never proved), he resigned from the Fund in 1947 and died the following year. *See also* WHITE PLAN.

WHITE PLAN. Harry Dexter White began working on a plan for a comprehensive international agreement in the monetary field as early as 1941 and produced a first completed version in March 1942 entitled *Preliminary Draft Proposal for a United Nations Stabilization Fund and Bank for Reconstruction and Development of the United Nations and Associated Nations.* Unlike the **Keynes Plan**, White's Stabilization Fund required contributions from members and provided for members to be able to purchase **currencies** of other members. Foreseeing the disruption caused by the war, the plan called for the Stabilization Fund to accept blocked balances in return for usable currencies, to be repaid over time in units, called *Unitas.* Members were to eliminate within a year all restrictions and controls over **foreign exchange** transactions and to alter their exchange rate only to correct a fundamental disequilibrium in their **balance of payments**, and then only with the consent of the Stabilization Fund. These and other features were merged with Keynes' plan for a Clearing Union, as well as with other plans put forward later by other authorities. These plans were discussed for nearly two years and were finally negotiated as the **Articles of Agreement** of the International Monetary Fund at the International Monetary and Financial Conference of the United and Associated Nations at **Bretton Woods**, New Hampshire, in July 1944.

WITTEVEEN, H. JOHANNES (1921–). Johannes Witteveen, of the Netherlands, was the Fund's fifth **Managing Director** from September 1973 to June 1978. From 1948 to 1963, he had been Professor of Economics at the Rotterdam School of Economics; from 1963 to 1965, Minister of Finance; and from 1967 to 1971, he had been both Deputy Prime Minister and Finance Minister.

WORLD BANK. The World Bank, officially known as the International Bank for Reconstruction and Development, came into existence at the same time as the International Monetary Fund at the United Nations International Monetary Conference held at **Bretton Woods**, New Hampshire, in 1944. The Bank's primary responsibility is the financing of economic development. Its first loans were to finance the postwar reconstruction of Europe and other areas ravaged by the war. Since those days, the Bank has concentrated its efforts on assisting **developing countries** by financing the development of infrastructure (dams, bridges, roads, airports, hydroelectric supplies, education, sewage, water supply, telecommunications, population, and health care) and by promoting agriculture, urban development, and other sectors critical for economic development.

The World Bank comprises two major organizations: the International Bank for Reconstruction and Development and the International Development Association (IDA). Associated with the World Bank, but legally separate from it, are the International Finance Corporation (IFC), the International Center for Settlement of Investment Disputes (ICSID), and the Multilateral Investment Guarantee Agency (MIGA). Together, these five organizations are referred to as the World Bank Group.

The World Bank obtains most of the funds it lends to finance development by borrowing in world markets through the issuance of bonds (guaranteed by member governments) to individuals and private institutions. It lends to creditworthy governments of developing countries at an interest rate that is slightly above the market rate at which the Bank itself can borrow; its loans must generally be repaid in 12 to 15 years.

The IDA, on the other hand, obtains its funds largely by grants and donations from member governments. It lends only to governments of very poor developing countries, and its loans are interest free and have a maturity of 35 or 40 years.

The IFC mobilizes funds for private enterprises in developing countries, providing both loan and equity capital in partnership with commercial banks and private corporations.

The ICSID, as its name suggests, brings together parties that are in conflict in an attempt to settle investment disputes between them.

The MIGA, the newest member of the World Bank Group, offers insurance coverage against certain risks connected with foreign investment in developing countries. *See also* FUND–BANK RELATIONS; UNITED NATIONS.

***WORLD ECONOMIC OUTLOOK* (WEO).** The Fund's WEO exercise originated with an informal discussion by the **Executive Board** in 1969. It sprang to prominence in 1973, when the first oil price shock impacted the international payments system, creating imbalances between oil-exporting and oil-importing countries on a scale that had never been seen before. Within a few years it became a regular agenda item for both the **Executive Board** and the **Interim Committee** (later the **International Monetary and Financial Committee**), and much of its development was driven by the policy concerns of those governing bodies.

By the late 1970s, the WEO had become a major semiannual forecasting project, supplemented by analyses of trends and policy issues, evolving to include medium-term projections or "scenarios." By the mid-1980s, the role of the scenarios grew to the point where the primary focus of the WEO was no longer short-term scenarios in which cyclical fluctuations dominated, but rather the policy requirements for sustainable, noninflationary growth and for consistency between countries. The economic analysis underpinning the scenarios also evolved during the 1980s, from one based primarily on Keynsian models of aggregate demand to one that emphasized neoclassical macroeconomics and incorporated a systematic role for structural policies.

The **staff's** ability to prepare scenarios representing viable policy options hinged on the development of increasingly sophisticated econometric models. That process also began in the 1960s, with the specification of the **Multilateral Exchange Rate Model (MERM)**. Both the MERM and the later World Trade Model, however, were static representations with only limited applicability to policy analysis. The breakthrough came in 1986 with the emergence of MINIMOD, a scaled-down version of a dynamic multicountry model developed elsewhere. Not only was the Fund version smaller and more manageable, it also incorporated endogenous, forward-looking, model-consistent expectations. The credibility gained from that exercise paved the way for the development of MULTIMOD, the staff's first full-scale dynamic model. MULTIMOD, and a separate system of developing-country models, enabled the staff to develop more detailed scenarios within the short lead times required for the WEO. After its discussion by the Executive Board, the WEO is published twice a year, together with the staff's related analytical papers.

WORLD TRADE ORGANIZATION (WTO). The WTO came into existence on 1 January 1995, and took over, amended, and expanded the responsibilities of the **General Agreement on Tariffs and Trade (GATT)**, which were incorporated into the new WTO agreement. Whereas GATT dealt only with trade in goods, the WTO agreement covers services and intellectual property as well. In October 1997, the WTO had 132 members and 34 observer countries. The latter, which had all applied to join the WTO, included China (although not **Hong Kong SAR**, which was a founding member), the **Russian Federation**, and a large number of countries that were members of the former Soviet Union.

The Fund, which had a special relationship with GATT, signed a Cooperation Agreement with the WTO on 9 December 1996. The agreement seeks to formalize and build on the close, collaborative relationship that had evolved between the Fund and the contracting parties to GATT. It provides for the Fund to have observer status in the main bodies and committees of the WTO and for the two organizations to exchange an extensive range of their documents. *See also* UNITED NATIONS, RELATIONS WITH.

Statistical Appendix

Table 1. Managing Directors

Name	*Nationality*	*Term of Service*	
Camille Gutt	Belgium	6 May 1946	5 May 1951
Ivar Rooth	Sweden	3 August 1951	3 October 1956
Per Jacobsson	Sweden	21 November 1956	5 May 1963
Pierre-Paul Schweitzer	France	1 September 1963	31August 311973
H. Johannes Witteveen	Netherlands	1 September 1973	16 June 1978
Jacques de Larosière	France	17 June 1978	15 January 1987
Michel Camdessus	France	16 January 1987	14 February 2000
Horst Köhler	Germany	1 May 2000	4 March 2004
Rodrigo de Rato	Spain	7 June 2004	31 October 2007
Dominique Strauss-Kahn	France	1 November 2007	—

Table 2. Selected Financial Indicators during the Financial Year Ended April 30

(Millions of SDRs)

Disbursements

	2005	*2006*	*2007*	*2008*	*2009*
Total	2,379	2,559	2,806	1,952	17,082

Purchases by Facility[1]

	2005	*2006*	*2007*	*2008*	*2009*
GRA[2]	1,614	2,156	2,329	1,468	16,363
PRGF loans	771	403	477	484	719

GRA, General Resources Account; *PRGF*, poverty reduction and growth facility.

Repurchases and Repayments

	2005	*2006*	*2007*	*2008*	*2009*
Total	14,830	35,991	14,678	3,324	2,301
GRA	13,907	32,783	14,166	2,905	1,833
SAF/PGRF	923	3,208	512	419	468

GRA, General Resources Account; *PGRF*, poverty reduction and growth facility; *SAF*, structural adjustment facility.

Outstanding IMF Credit

	2005	*2006*	*2007*	*2008*	*2009*
Total	56,576	23,144	11,216	9,844	24,625

1. Includes reserve tranche purchases.

2. Includes first credit tranche drawings.

Source: Annual Report of the Executive Board, 2009.

Table 3. Members' Quotas and Voting Power as of 1 February 2010

Member	*Quota* *Million SDRs*	*Votes* *Percent*
Afghanistan, Islamic State of	161.9	0.08
Albania	48.7	0.03
Algeria	1,254.7	0.58
Angola	286.3	0.14
Antigua and Barbuda	13.5	0.02
Argentina	2,117.1	0.97
Armenia	92.0	0.05
Australia	3,236.4	1.47
Austria	1,872.3	0.86
Azerbaijan	160.9	0.08
Bahamas, The	130.3	0.07
Bahrain	135.0	0.07
Bangladesh	533.3	0.25
Barbados	67.5	0.04
Belarus	386.4	0.19
Belgium	4,605.2	2.09
Belize	18.8	0.02
Benin	61.9	0.04
Bhutan	6.3	0.01
Bolivia	171.5	0.09
Bosnia and Herzegovina	169.1	0.09
Botswana	63.0	0.04
Brazil	3,036.1	1.38
Brunei Darussalam	215.2	0.11
Bulgaria	640.2	0.30
Burkina Faso	60.2	0.04
Burundi	77.0	0.05
Cambodia	87.5	0.05
Cameroon	185.7	0.10
Canada	6,639.2	2.88
Cape Verde	9.6	0.02
Central African Republic	55.7	0.04
Chad	56.0	0.04
Chile	856.1	0.40
China	8,090.1	3.66
Colombia	774.0	0.36
Comoros	8.9	0.02
Congo, Dem. Rep. of	533.0	0.25
Congo, Republic of	84.6	0.05
Costa Rica	164.1	0.09
Côte d'Ivoire	325.2	0.16
Croatia	365.1	0.18
Cyprus	139.6	0.07
Czech Republic	819.3	0.38
Denmark	1,642.8	0.75
Djibouti	15.9	0.02
Dominica	8.2	0.01

(continued)

Member	Quota Million SDRs	Votes Percent
Dominican Republic	218.9	0.11
Ecuador	302.3	0.15
Egypt	943.7	0.44
El Salvador	171.3	0.09
Equatorial Guinea	32.6	0.03
Eritrea	15.9	0.02
Estonia	65.2	0.04
Ethiopia	133.7	0.07
Fiji	70.3	0.04
Finland	1,263.8	0.58
France	10,738.5	4.85
Gabon	154.3	0.08
Gambia, The	31.1	0.03
Georgia	150.3	0.08
Germany	13,008.2	5.88
Ghana	369.0	0.18
Greece	823.0	0.38
Grenada	11.7	0.02
Guatemala	210.2	0.11
Guinea	107.1	0.06
Guinea-Bissau	14.2	0.02
Guyana	90.9	0.05
Haiti	81.9	0.05
Honduras	129.5	0.07
Hungary	1,038.4	0.48
Iceland	117.6	0.06
India	4,158.2	1.89
Indonesia	2,079.3	0.95
Iran, Islamic Republic of	1,497.2	0.69
Iraq	1,188.4	0.55
Ireland	838.4	0.39
Israel	928.2	0.43
Italy	7,055.5	3.19
Jamaica	273.5	0.13
Japan	13,312.8	6.02
Jordan	170.5	0.09
Kazakhstan	365.7	0.18
Kenya	271.4	0.13
Kiribati	5.6	0.01
Korea	2,927.3	1.33
Kosovo	59.0	0.04
Kuwait	1,381.1	0.63
Kyrgyz Republic	88.8	0.05
Lao People's Democratic Republic	52.9	0.04
Latvia	126.8	0.07
Lebanon	203.0	0.10
Lesotho	34.9	0.03
Liberia	129.2	0.07

(continued)

Member	*Quota Million SDRs*	*Votes Percent*
Libya	1,123.7	0.52
Lithuania	144.2	0.08
Luxembourg	279.1	0.14
Macedonia, FYR	68.9	0.04
Madagascar	122.2	0.07
Malawi	69.4	0.04
Malaysia	1,486.6	0.68
Maldives	8.2	0.01
Mali	93.3	0.05
Malta	102.0	0.06
Marshall Islands	3.5	0.01
Mauritania	64.4	0.04
Mauritius	101.6	0.06
Mexico	3,152.8	1.43
Micronesia, Federal States of	5.1	0.01
Moldova	123.2	0.07
Mongolia	51.1	0.03
Montenegro	27.5	0.02
Morocco	588.2	0.28
Mozambique	113.6	0.06
Myanmar	258.4	0.13
Namibia	136.5	0.07
Nepal	71.3	0.04
Netherlands, The	5,162.4	2.34
New Zealand	894.6	0.41
Nicaragua	130.0	0.07
Niger	65.8	0.04
Nigeria	1,753.2	0.80
Norway	1,671.7	0.77
Oman	194.0	0.10
Pakistan	1,033.7	0.48
Palau	3.1	0.01
Panama	206.6	0.10
Papua New Guinea	131.6	0.07
Paraguay	99.9	0.06
Peru	638.4	0.30
Philippines	879.9	0.41
Poland	1,369.0	0.63
Portugal	867.4	0.40
Qatar	263.8	0.13
Romania	1,030.2	0.48
Russia	5,945.4	2.69
Rwanda	80.1	0.05
Samoa	11.6	0.02
San Marino	17.0	0.02
São Tomé and Principe	7.4	0.01
Saudi Arabia	6,985.5	3.16
Senegal	161.8	0.08

(continued)

Member	*Quota Million SDRs*	*Votes Percent*
Serbia	467.7	0.22
Seychelles	8.8	0.02
Sierra Leone	103.7	0.06
Singapore	862.5	0.40
Slovak Republic	357.5	0.17
Slovenia	231.7	0.12
Solomon Islands	10.4	0.02
Somalia	44.2	0.03
South Africa	1,868.5	0.85
Spain	3,048.9	1.39
Sri Lanka	413.4	0.20
St. Kitts and Nevis	8.9	0.02
St. Lucia	15.3	0.02
St. Vincent and the Grenadines	8.3	0.02
Sudan	169.7	0.09
Suriname	92.1	0.05
Swaziland	50.7	0.03
Sweden	2,395.5	1.09
Switzerland	3,458.5	1.57
Syrian Arab Republic	293.6	0.14
Tajikistan	87.0	0.05
Tanzania	198.9	0.10
Thailand	1,081.9	0.50
Timor-Leste	8.2	0.01
Togo	73.4	0.04
Tonga	6.9	0.01
Trinidad and Tobago	335.6	0.16
Tunisia	286.5	0.14
Turkey	1,191.3	0.55
Turkmenistan	75.2	0.05
Uganda	180.5	0.09
Ukraine	1,372.0	0.63
United Arab Emirates	611.7	0.29
United Kingdom	10,738.5	4.85
United States	37,149.3	16.77
Uruguay	306.5	0.15
Uzbekistan	275.6	0.14
Vanuatu	17.0	0.02
Venezuela, República Bolivariana de	2,659.1	1.21
Vietnam	329.1	0.16
Yemen, Republic of	243.5	0.12
Zambia	489.1	0.23
Zimbabwe	353.4	0.00
Total	217,431.7	100.00

Note: No increase in quotas can take effect before the date on which the Fund determines that members having not less than 85 percent of the total quotas on 23 December 1997 have consented to the increase in their quotas. A member's quota cannot be increased until it has consented to the increase and paid the subscription.

Source: *Annual Report of the Executive Board*

Table 4a. Stand-by and Other Arrangements Approved in the Financial Years Ended April 30, 1953–2009

Stand-bys	*EFF*	*SAF*	*PRGF*	*Total*	*Millions*	*Number of Arrangement*	*SDRs*
1953–1957	20					20	1,368
1958–1962	65					65	4,558
1963–1967	108					108	7,016
1968–1972	110					110	6,090
1973–1977	73	5				78	8,931
1978	19	3				18	5,877
1979	15	5				20	2,643
1980	22	7				29	3,803
1981	22	15				37	10,795
1982	23	12				35	16,206
1983	30	9				39	25,035
1984	30	5				35	18,569
1985	27	3				30	11,675
1986	24	2				26	4,907
1987	23	1	10		34	5,391	
1988	18	2	25		45	4,540	
1989	14	2	23	7	46	6,608	

EFF, Extended Fund facility; *PRGF,* poverty reduction and growth facility; *SAF,* structural adjustment facility.

Table 4b. Stand-by and Other Arrangements (concluded)

Stand-bys	*EFF*	*SAF*	*FCL*	*ESAF/ PRGF*	*Total Millions*	*Number of Arrangements*	*SDRs*
1990	19	4		17		11 51	13,911
1991	14	5		12		14 45	14,652
1992	22	7		8		16 53	19,203
1993	15	6		4		20 45	15,279
1994	16	6		3		22 47	8,428
1995	19	9		1		27 56	23,385
1996	21	7		1		28 57	27,918
1997	14	11				35 60	17,996
1998	14	13				33 60	45,069
1999	5	4				10 19	29,413
2000	11	4				10 25	22,929
2001	11	1				14 26	14,333
2002	9					9 18	41,287
2003	10	2				10 22	30,571
2004	5					10 15	15,486
2005	6					8 14	1,713
2006	5	1				7 13	8,474
2007	2					10 12	60
2008	3	1				4 8	1,333
2009	14				1	13 28	66,736
Total 846	70		38		1	170 1125	562,728

EFF, Extended Fund facility; ESAF, enhanced structural adjustment facility; FCL, flexible credit line; SAF, structural adjustment facility.

Source: *Annual Reports of the Executive Board*

Bibliography

BIBLIOGRAPHY

Contents

Publications Issued by the Fund

General Bibliography

The following bibliography lists selective publications on the history and evolution of the International Monetary Fund. The Fund itself periodically published, from 1951 through 1985, comprehensive bibliographies in various issues of its quarterly economic journal, *Staff Papers*. Many of these bibliographies were compiled by Anne C. M. Salda, who on her retirement from the Joint Fund-Bank Library compiled an extensive and annotated bibliography, *International Monetary Fund*, which references publications on the Fund since its inception (*see under* General Bibliography).

The first section of this bibliography lists publications issued by the Fund. The second section concentrates on citing substantive material published outside the Fund dealing with its work and related matters. No attempt has been made to cover the many serious and interesting articles that have appeared in newspapers and news magazines.

The Fund's public website was opened in September 1996 at the address http://www.imf.org. From the home-page menu, hyperlinks lead to various submenus, including a catalogue of publications. A number of publications are also available in full text on the website.

The Fund issues annually a catalog of available publications.

PUBLICATIONS ISSUED BY THE FUND

Reports and Documents

Agreement between the United Nations and the International Monetary Fund, 1956.

Annual Report of the Executive Board, 1946 to date. Published also in French, German, and Spanish.

Annual Report on Exchange Arrangements and Exchange Restrictions, 1979 to date.

Annual Report on Exchange Restrictions, 1950 to date.

Articles of Agreement of the International Monetary Fund, Original Articles in 1946; as modified by the first amendment to the Articles, 1968; as modified by the second amendment to the Articles, 1978; and as modified by the third amendment to the Articles, 1992. Also in Arabic, French, Russian, and Spanish.

By-Laws, Rules and Regulations, issued periodically since 1947.

Establishment of a Facility Based on Special Drawing Rights in the International Monetary Fund and Modifications in the Rules and Practices of the Fund: A Report by the Executive Directors to the Board of Governors Proposing Amendment of the Articles of Agreement, 1968.

International Monetary Reform: Documents of the Committee of Twenty, 1974.

Proposed Third Amendment of the Articles of Agreement: A Report to the Board of Governors of the International Monetary Fund Containing the Managing Director's Proposal on the Allocation of Special Drawing Rights for the First Basic Period, 1969. Also in French and Spanish.

Schedule of Par Values, irregular, 1946 to 1971.

Selected Decisions of the International Monetary Fund and Selected Documents, irregular, 1st issue 1962, 23rd issue, 1998, 33rd issue, 2008.

Summary Proceedings of the . . . Annual Meetings of the Board of Governors, 1946 to date.

Books

A Better World for All: Progress Toward the International Development Goals, 2000.

Adjustment and Financing in the Developing World: The Role of the International Monetary Fund, papers presented at a seminar sponsored by the IMF and the Overseas Development Institute, London, England, edited by Tony Killick, 1982.

Adjustment, Conditionality, and International Financing, papers presented at a seminar in Viña del Mar, Chile, sponsored by the Central Bank of Chile, the Frederico Santa Maria University, and the IMF, edited by Joaquín Muns, 1983.

Adjustment Policies and Development Strategies in the Arab World, papers presented at a seminar in Abu Dhabi, United Arab Emirates, at a seminar sponsored by the Arab Monetary Fund and the IMF, edited by Said El-Naggar, 1987.

Africa and the International Monetary Fund, papers presented at a symposium sponsored by the Association of African Central Banks and the IMF, edited by G. K. Helleiner, 1987.

Analytical Issues in Debt, by Jacob A. Frenkel, Michael P. Dooley, and Peter Wickham, 1989.

Approaches to Exchange Rate Policy, papers presented at a seminar on exchange rate policy in developing and transitional economies held by the IMF Institute, edited by Richard Barth and Chorng-Huey Wong, 1994.

Balance of Payments Adjustment, 1945 to 1986: The IMF Experience, by Margaret Garritsen de Vries, 1987.

Balance of Payments Compilation Guide, a companion document to the fifth edition of the *Balance of Payments Manual*, 1995.

Balance of Payments Manual, the fifth edition of this manual, revised and updated, 2005.

Balance of Payments Textbook, a companion document to the *Balance of Payments Manual*, 1996.

Bank Restructuring and Resolution, edited by David S. Hoelscher, 2006.

Bank Soundness and Macroeconomic Policy, by Carl-Johan Lingren, Gillian Garcia, and Matthew I. Saal, 1996.

Banking Crises: Cases and Issues, edited by V. Sundarajan and Thomas J. T. Baliño, 1991.

Beyond Adjustment: The Asian Experience, edited by Paul Streeten, 1988.

Building Monetary and Financial Systems: Case Studies in Technical Assistance, edited by Marta de Castello Branco, Charles Enoch, and Karl Friedrich Habermeier, 2007.

Building Sound Finance in Emerging Market Economies, edited by Gerard Caprio, David Folkerts-Landau, and Timothy D. Lane, 1994.

The Caribbean: From Vulnerability to Sustained Growth, edited by Paul Cashin, David O. Robinson, and Ratna Sahay, 2006.

Central Bank Independence, Accountability, and Transparency—A Global Perspective, by Jean-François Segalotto, Marco Arnone, and Bernard Laurens, 2009.

Central and Eastern Europe: Roads to Growth, papers presented at a seminar moderated by George Winckler, organized by the IMF and the Austrian National Bank, 1992.

Central Banking Technical Assistance to Countries in Transition, proceeding of a joint meeting of central bank technical assistance held in St. Petersburg, Russia, in 1994, edited by J. B. Zulu, Ian S. McCarthy, Susan Almuiña, and Gabriel Sensenbrenner, 1994.

Central Bank Reform in Transition Economies, contains the background papers prepared for the second coordinating meeting of 23 participating central banks of the

Baltic States and the Commonwealth of Independent States, edited by V. Sundarajan, Arne B. Petersen, and Gabriel Sensenbrenner, 1997.

The CFA Franc Zone: Common Currency, Uncommon Challenges, edited by Charalambos G. Tsangarides, and Anne Marie Gulde, 2008.

Choosing an Exchange Rate Regime: The Challenge for Smaller Industrial Countries, edited by Victor Argy and Paul de Grauwe, 1990.

Coordinated Portfolio Investment Survey Guide, a guide for balance of payments compilers in conducting an internationally coordinated survey of security holdings under the auspices of the IMF, 1996.

Coordinating Public Debt and Monetary Management: Institutional and Operational Arrangements, edited by V. Sundarajan, Peter Dattels, and Hans Blommestein, 1997.

Coordinating Stabilization and Structural Reform, papers presented in an IMF Institute seminar covering four case studies—China, Poland, Argentina, and The Gambia, edited by Richard C. Barth, Alan R. Roe, and Chorng-Huey Wong, 1994.

Current Legal Issues Affecting Central Banks, Vols. I, II, III, and IV, papers presented at four biennial seminars sponsored by the IMF for central banks, edited by Robert C. Effros, 1992, 1994, 1995, and 1997.

Deepening Structural Reform in Africa: Lessons from East Asia, the proceedings of a seminar involving policymakers and senior government officials from Africa and East Asia and senior staff of international organizations, edited by Laura Wallace, 1997.

Debt Stocks, Debt Flows and the Balance of Payments, prepared jointly by the Bank for International Settlements, the International Monetary Fund, the Organization for Economic Cooperation and Development, and World Bank, 1994.

Economic Adjustment: Policies and Problems, proceedings of a seminar held in Wellington, New Zealand, concentrating on economic adjustment problems in the South Pacific, edited by Sir Frank Holmes, 1987.

Economic Policy Coordination, the proceedings of a seminar held in Hamburg, Germany, moderated by Wilfred Guth, 1988.

Economic Adjustment: Policies and Problems, papers presented at a seminar sponsored by the IMF in Wellington, New Zealand, edited by Sir Frank Holmes, 1987.

Economic Policy Coordination, papers presented at a seminar sponsored by the IMF in Hamburg, Germany, 1988.

Effective Government Accounting, by A. Premchand, 1995.

Emerging Financial Centers: Legal and Institutional Framework, edited by Robert C. Effros, 1982.

EMU and the International Monetary System, the proceedings of a seminar held in Washington, sponsored by the IMF and the Fondation Camille Gutt, 1997.

Evolving Role of Central Banks, papers presented at a seminar sponsored by the IMF at the Fund's headquarters, edited by Patrick Downes and Reza Vaez-Zadeh, 1991.

Exchange Rate Analysis in Support of IMF Surveillance: A Collection of Empirical Studies, by Charalambos G. Tsangarides, Carlo Cottarelli, Atish R. Ghosh, and Gian Maria Milesi-Ferretti, 2008.

External Debt: Definition, Statistical Coverage and Methodology, a comparative description of statistics collected by the Bank for International Settlements, the International Monetary Fund, the Organization for Economic Cooperation and Development, and the World Bank, 1998.

External Debt Management, papers presented at a seminar sponsored by the IMF, Washington, D.C., edited by Hassanali Mehran, 1985.

External Debt, Savings, and Growth in Latin America, papers presented at a seminar sponsored by the Instituto Torcuato di Tella and the IMF in Don Torcuato, Argentina, edited by Ana María Martirena-Mantel, 1987.

Fifty Years after Bretton Woods: The Future of the IMF and the World Bank, the proceedings of a conference held in Madrid, Spain, sponsored by the IMF and the World Bank to commemorate the fiftieth anniversary of the two institutions, edited by James M. Boughton and K. Sarwar Lateef, 1994.

Financial Globalization: The Impact on Trade, Policy, Labor, and Capital, compilation of articles published over the period 1999 to 2007, 2007.

Financial Policies and Capital Markets in Arab Countries, the proceedings of a seminar held in Abu Dhabi, edited by Said El-Naggar, 1994.

Financial Programming and Policy: The Case of Hungary, edited by Karen A. Swiderski, 1992.

Fiscal Federalism in Theory and Practice, papers on a number of countries examining the relationships among central, state, and local governments in respect to their spending and revenue-raising responsibilities, edited by Teresa Ter-Minassian, 1997.

Fiscal Policies in Economies in Transition, edited by Vito Tanzi, 1992.

Fiscal Policy, Economic Adjustment, and Financial Markets, papers presented at a seminar sponsored by the Centre for Financial and Monetary Economics, Università Luigi Bocconi, in Milan, Italy, and the IMF, edited by Mario Monti, 1989.

Fiscal Policy Formulation and Implementation in Oil-Producing Countries, by Jeffrey M. Davis, Annalisa Fedelino, and Rolando Ossowski, 2003.

Fiscal Policy in Open Developing Economies, papers presented at the 44th Congress of the International Institute of Public Finance, edited by Vito Tanzi, 1990.

Fiscal Policy, Stabilization, and Growth in Developing Countries, edited by Mario I. Blejer and Ke-young Chu, 1992.

Foreign Direct Investment Statistics: How Countries Measure FDI 2001, 2003.

Foreign and Inter-Trade Policies of Arab Countries, papers presented at a seminar sponsored by the IMF in Abu Dhabi, United Arab Emirates, edited by Said El-Naggar, 1992.

Framework for Monetary Stability: Policy Issues and Country Experience, edited by Tomás J. T. Baliño and Carlo Cottarelli, 1994.

The Functioning of the International Monetary System, Vols. I and II, 30 analytical papers on the system as it functioned in 1987–1991, edited by Jacob A. Frenkel and Morris Goldstein, 1996.

The Future of the SDR in Light of Changes in the International Monetary System, proceedings of a seminar held at the IMF, edited by Michael Mussa, James Boughton, and Peter Isard, 1996.

Government Financial Management: Issues and Country Studies, edited by A. Premchand, 1990.
Growth-Oriented Adjustment Programs, papers presented at a symposium sponsored by the IMF and the World Bank in Washington, D.C., edited by Vittorio Corbo, Morris Goldstein, and Mohsin Khan, 1987.
Helping Countries Develop: The Role of Fiscal Policy, by Benedict J. Clements, Sanjeev Gupta, and Gabriela Inchauste, 2004.
How to Measure the Fiscal Deficit: Analytical and Methodological Issues, edited by Mario I. Blejer and Adrienne Cheasty, 1992.
IMF Glossary, English–French–Arabic, by the IMF Bureau of Language Services, 1996.
IMF Glossary, English–French–Spanish, by the IMF Bureau of Language Services, 1997.
IMF Glossary, English–French–Russian, by the IMF Bureau of Language Services, 1998.
The IMF's Data Dissemination Initiative after Ten Years, by John Cady, Jesus Gonzalez-Garcia, and William E. Alexander, 2007,
The IMF's Statistical Systems in Context of Revision of the United Nations' "A System of National Accounts," edited by Vicente Galbis, 1991.
Improving Tax Administration in Developing Countries, edited by Richard M. Bird and Milka Casanegra de Jantscher, 1992.
Inflation and Growth in China, proceedings of a conference, edited by Manuel Guitián and Robert Mundell, 1996.
Integrating Europe's Financial Markets: Beyond and Through the Crisis, by Wim Fonteyne, Jörg Decressin, and Hamid Faruqee, 2009.
Interest Rate Liberalization and Money Market Development, papers presented at a seminar held in Beijing, China, sponsored by the IMF and the People's Bank of China, edited by Hassanali Mehran, Bernard Laurens, and Marc Quintyn, 1995.
International Financial Policy: Essays in Honor of Jacques J. Polak, papers presented at a conference sponsored by the Netherlands Bank and the IMF in Washington, D.C., edited by Jacob A. Frenkel and Morris Goldstein, 1991.
International Monetary Cooperation since Bretton Woods, a comprehensive history written by Harold James and published jointly by the IMF and Oxford University Press, 1996.
The International Monetary Fund, 1945–1965: Twenty Years of International Monetary Cooperation. Vol. I, *Chronicle*, by J. Keith Horsefield; Vol. II, *Analysis*, by Margaret G. de Vries and J. Keith Horsefield with the collaboration of Joseph Gold, Mary H. Gumbart, Gertrude Lovasy, and Emil G. Spitzer; and Vol. III, *Documents*, edited by J. Keith Horsefield, 1969.
The International Monetary Fund, 1966–1971: The System under Stress. Vol. I, *Narrative*, by Margaret Garritsen de Vries; Vol II, *Documents*, edited by Margaret Garritsen de Vries, 1976.
The International Monetary Fund, 1972–1978: Cooperation on Trial. Vols. I and II, *Narrative and Analysis*, by Margaret Garritsen de Vries; and Vol. III, *Documents*, edited by Margaret Garritsen de Vries, 1985.

International Reserves: Needs and Availability, papers presented by a number of scholars and Fund staff members at a seminar convened at the Fund's headquarters, 1970.

Legal and Institutional Aspects of the International Monetary System: Selected Essays, Vols. I and II, by Joseph Gold, 1984.

Legal Effects of Fluctuating Exchange Rates, by Joseph Gold, 1990.

Macroeconomic Accounting and Analysis in Transition Economies, by Abdessatar Ouanes and Subhash Thakur, 1997.

Macroeconomic Adjustment: Policy Instruments and Issues, edited by Jeffrey M. Davis, 1992.

Macroeconomic Issues Facing ASEAN Countries, papers prepared for the ASEAN conference held in Jakarta, edited by John Hicklin, David Robinson, and Anoop Singh, 1997.

Macroeconomic Models for Adjustment in Developing Countries, edited by Mohsin S. Khan, Peter J. Montiel, and Nadeem U. Haque, 1991.

Macroeconomic Policies in an Interdependent World, edited by Ralph Bryant, David Currie, Jacob A. Frenkel, Paul Masson, and Richard Portes, 1989.

Macroeconomics and the Environment, the proceedings of a seminar held at the IMF at which experts from academic and research institutions, nongovernmental organizations, and staff from the IMF and World Bank shared their views on macroeconomic policies and the environment, edited by Ved P. Gandhi, 1996.

The Macroeconomics of HIV/AIDS, by Markus Haacker, 2004.

The Macroeconomy of Central America, by Robert Rennhack and Erik Offerdal, 2004.

Manual on Government Finance Statistics, 1986.

The Modern VAT, by Jean-Paul Bodin, Liam P. Ebrill, Michael Keen, and Victoria P. Summers, 2001.

The Monetary Approach to the Balance of Payments, edited by Rudolf R. Rhomberg, 1977.

Optimum Currency Areas: New Analytical and Policy Developments, a revisit to Robert Mundell's pioneering theory of optimum currency areas, with an update by Robert Mundell himself, edited by Mario I. Blejer, Jacob A. Frankel, Leonard Leiderman, and Assaf Razin, 1997.

Pacific Island Economies, by Christopher Browne, 2006.

The Payment System: Design, Management and Supervision, 12 papers by central bank experts from around the world, edited by Bruce J. Summers, 1994.

Payment System, Monetary Policy, and the Role of the Central Bank, by Otomunde E. G. Johnson, Richard K. Abrams, Jean-Marc Destresse, Tony Lybek, Nicholas Roberts, and Mark Swinburne, 1997.

Performance Budgeting: Linking Funding and Results, by Marc Robinson, 2007.

Policies for African Development: From the 1980s to the 1990s, a collection of papers presented at a seminar in Gaborone, Botswana, edited by I. G. Patel, 1992.

Policies for Growth: The Latin American Experience, papers presented at a seminar in Rio de Janeiro, Brazil, moderated by André Lara Resende, 1995.

Post-Stabilization Economics in Sub-Saharan Africa: Lessons from Mozambique, by Shanaka J. Peiris and Jean A. P. Clément, 2008.

Poverty and Social Impact Analysis by the IMF: Review of Methodology and Selected Evidence, edited by Robert Gillingham, 2008.

Privatization and Structural Adjustment in the Arab Countries, papers presented at a seminar sponsored by the IMF in Washington, D.C., edited by Said El-Naggar, 1989.

Promoting Fiscal Discipline, by Manmohan S. Kumar and Teresa Ter-Minassian, 2007.

Public Expenditure Handbook: A Guide to Public Policy Issues in Developing Countries, edited by Ke-young Chu and Richard Hemming, 1991.

Public Expenditure Management, by A. Premchand, 1993.

Public Investment and Public-Private Partnerships: Addressing Infrastructure Challenges and Managing Fiscal Risks, proceedings from a high-level international seminar for government officials, edited by Ana Corbacho, Katja Funke, and Gerd Schwartz, 2008.

Reforming China's Public Finances, the proceedings of a conference held in Shanghai, China, with supplemental papers, edited by Ehtisham Ahmad, Gao Qiang, and Vito Tanzi, 1995.

Report on the Measurement of International Capital Flows and Background Papers, 1992.

Report on the World Current Account Discrepancy, by the IMF and other international organizations, 1987.

Safeguarding Financial Stability: Theory and Practice, by Garry J. Schinasi, 2005.

Silent Revolution: The International Monetary Fund, 1979–89, the fourth in a series of narrative histories of the Fund, written by James Boughton, 2000.

The Social Effects of Economic Adjustment on Arab Countries, papers presented in a seminar sponsored by the Arab Fund for Economic and Social Development, the Arab Monetary Fund, the IMF, and the World Bank, edited by Taher H. Kanaan, 1997.

Strategies for Structural Adjustment: The Experience of Southeast Asia, papers presented at a seminar sponsored by the IMF in Kuala Lumpur, Malaysia, moderated by Ungku A. Aziz, 1990.

Structural Adjustment and Macroeconomic Policy Issues, papers presented at a conference in Lahore, Pakistan, moderated by V. A. Jafarey, 1992.

Supply-Side Tax Policy: Its Relevance to Developing Countries, by Ved P. Gandhi, Liam P. Ebrill, George A. Mackenzie, Luis Mañas-Anton, Jitendra R. Modi, Somchai Richupan, Fernando Sanchez-Ugarte, and Parthasarathi Shome, 1987.

System of National Accounts, prepared by the Joint Commission of the European Communities, the International Monetary Fund, the Organization for Economic Cooperation and Development, the United Nations, and World Bank, 1993.

Systemic Bank Restructuring and Macroeconomic Policy, sets out cross-country restructuring experiences, edited by William E. Alexander, Jeffrey M. Davis, Liam P. Ebrill, and Carl-Johan Lindgren, 1997.

Tackling Japan's Fiscal Challenges: Strategies to Cope with High Public Debt and Population Aging, by Anne O. Krueger and Keimeir Kaizuka, 2006.
Tax Law Design and Drafting, Vol. I and II, edited by Victor Thuronyi, 1996.
Tax Policy Handbook, edited by Parthasarathi Shome, 1995.
Taxing the Financial Sector: Concepts, Issues, and Practice, by Howell H. Zee, 2004.
Trade Policy Issues, papers presented in a seminar sponsored by the IMF, edited by Chorng-Huey Wong, 1997.
Transition to Market Studies in Fiscal Reform, edited by Vito Tanzi, 1993.
The Uruguay Round and the Arab Countries, papers presented at a seminar sponsored by the IMF, the Arab Fund for Economic and Social Development, the Arab Monetary Fund, and the World Bank, edited by Said El-Naggar, 1996.
Using the Balance Sheet Approach in Surveillance: Framework and Data Sources and Availability, by Johan Mathisen and Anthony J. Pellechio, 2007.
Value-Added Tax: International Practice and Problems, by Alan A. Tait, 1988.
Who Will Pay? Coping with Aging Societies, Climate Change, and Other Long-Term Fiscal Challenges, by Peter S. Heller, 2003.

Periodicals

Finance & Development, jointly published by the Fund and the World Bank up to June 1998, when the IMF became the sole publisher. The magazine contains articles in nontechnical language explaining the financial and development issues. Published quarterly, 1964 to date. In Arabic, Chinese, English, French, German, Portuguese, Spanish, and Russian (*free*).
IMF Economic Reviews, a triennial collection of public information notices issued in the preceding trimester.
IMF Survey, maintains a running record of the Fund's policies, decisions, and activities, as well as country and world economic developments. Issued twice a month, 1972 to date. Also in French and Spanish.
Staff Papers, quarterly, 1950 to date. In 2010, *Staff Papers* is expected to be replaced by a new journal. The following are selected articles:

"Analysis of Proposals for Using Objective Indicators as a Guide to Exchange Rate Changes," by Trevor G. Underwood, Vol. 20 (Mar. 1973), pp. 100–17.
"The Appropriate Use of Monetary and Fiscal Policy for Internal and External Stability," by Robert A. Mundell, Vol. 9 (Mar. 1962), pp. 70–79.
"Are Debt Crises Adequately Defined?" by Andrea Pescatori and Amadou N. R. Sy, Vol. 54 (June 2007), pp. 306–37.
"Are Exchange Rates Excessively Volatile? And What Does 'Excessively Volatile' Mean, Anyway?" by Leonardo Bartolini and Gordon M. Bodnar, Vol. 43 (Mar. 1996), pp. 72–96.
"Asset Prices and Current Account Fluctuations in G-7 Economies," by Marcel Fratzscher and Roland Straub Vol. 56 (Aug. 2009), pp. 633–54.
"Balance of Payments Adjustment among Developed Countries," by Anne Romanis Braun, Vol. 12 (Mar. 1965), pp. 17–34.

"Bankruptcy Procedures for Sovereigns: A History of Ideas, 1976–2001," by Kenneth Rogoff and Jeromin Zettelmeyer, Vol. 49 (Sept. 2002), pp. 470–507.

"Can We Predict the Next Capital Account Crisis?" by Marcos Chamon, Paolo Manasse, and Alessandro Prati, Vol. 54 (June 2007), pp. 270–305.

"Capital Account Liberalization and Economic Performance: Survey and Synthesis," by Hali J. Edison, Michael W. Klein, Luca Antonio Ricci, and Torsten Sløk, Vol. 51 (Aug. 2004), pp. 220–56.

"Competitive Depreciation," by Walter Gardner and S. C. Tsiang, Vol. 2 (1951–1952), pp. 399–406.

"Conditionality: Past, Present, Future," by Manuel Guitían, Vol. 42 (Dec. 1995), pp. 792–835.

"Consumption. Income, and International Capital Market Integration," by Tamim Bayoumi and Ronald MacDonald, Vol. 42 (Sept. 1995), pp. 552–76.

"Crises, Contagion, and the Closed-End Country Fund Puzzle," by Eduardo Levy-Yeyati and Angel Ubide, Vol. 47 (Nov. 2000), pp. 54–89.

"Currency Unions, Economic Fluctuations, and Adjustment," by Tamim Bayoumi and Eswar Prasad, Vol. 44 (Mar. 1997), pp. 36–58.

"Corruption around the World: Causes, Consequences, Scope, and Cures," by Vito Tanzi, Vol. 45 (Dec. 1998), pp. 559–54.

"The Determinants of Banking Crises in Developing Contraries," by Asli Demirgüç-Kunt and Enrica Detragiache, Vol. 45 (Mar. 1998), pp. 81–109.

"Devaluation Versus Import Restriction as an Instrument for Improving Foreign Trade Balance," by Sidney S. Alexander, Vol. 1 (1950–51), pp. 379–96.

"Developments in the International Payments System," by J. Marcus Fleming, Vol. 10 (Nov. 1963), pp. 461–84.

"Does Monetary Policy Stabilize the Exchange Rate Following a Currency Crisis?" by Ilan Goldfajn and Poonam Gupta, Vol. 50 (Apr. 2003), pp. 90–114.

"Domestic Financial Policies under Fixed and Floating Exchange Rates," by J. Marcus Fleming, Vol. 9 (Nov. 1962), pp. 369–80.

"Effectiveness of Exchange Rate Policy for Trade Account Adjustment," by Alfred Steinherr, Vol. 28 (Mar. 1981), pp. 199–224.

"Effects of a Devaluation on a Trade Balance," by Sydney S. Alexander, Vol. 2 (Apr. 1952), pp. 263–78.

"Effects of Various Types of Reserve Creation on Fund Liquidity," by J. Marcus Fleming, Vol. 12 (July 1965), pp. 163–88.

"An Evaluation of the World Economic Outlook Forecasts," by Allan Timmermann, Vol. 54 (May 2007), pp. 1–33.

"Exchange Market Pressure and Monetary Policy: Asia and Latin America in the 1990s," by Evan Tanner, Vol. 20 (Sept. 2000), pp. 310–33.

"The Exchange Rate Regime: An Analysis and a Possible Scheme," by Fred Hirsch, Vol. 19 (July 1972), pp. 259–85.

"Exchange Rates, Inflation, and Vicious Circles," by John F. O. Bilton, Vol. 27 (Dec. 1980), pp. 679–711.

"Extreme Contagion in Equity Markets," Jorge A. Chan-Lau, Donald J. Mathieson, and James Y. Yao, Vol. 51 (Aug. 2004), pp. 386–408.

"Fifty Years of Exchange Policy and Research at the International Monetary Fund," by Jacques V. Polak, Vol. 42 (Dec. 1995), pp. 734–61.
"Fiscal Policy and Long-Run Growth," by Vito Tanzi and Howell H. Zee, Vol. 44, (June 1997), pp. 179–209.
"Fixed and Flexible Exchange Rates: A Renewal of the Debate," by Jacques Artus and John H. Young, Vol. 26 (Dec. 1979), pp. 654–98.
"Fluctuating Exchange Rates in Countries with Relatively Stable Economies: Some European Experiences after World War I," by S. C. Tsiang, Vol. 7 (Oct. 1959), pp. 244–73.
"From Centrally-Planned to Market Economies: The Road from CPE to PCPE," by Guillermo A. Calvo and Jacob A. Frenkel, Vol. 38. (June 1991), pp. 268–99.
"The Fund and International Liquidity," by J. Marcus Fleming, Vol. 11 (July 1964), pp. 177–215.
"Fund Members' Adherence to the Par Value Regime: Empirical Evidence," by Margaret G. de Vries, Vol. 13 (1966), pp. 504–32.
"Global Dispersion of Current Accounts: Is the Universe Expanding?" by Hamid Faruqee and Jaewoo Lee, Vol. 56 (Aug. 2009), pp. 574–95.
"Government Spending, Taxes, and Economic Growth" by Paul Cashin, Vol. 42 (June 1995), pp. 237–69.
"Herd Behavior in Financial Markets," by Sushil Bikhchandani and Sunil Sharma, Vol. 20 (Sept. 2000), pp. 280–310.
"The Historical Development of the Principle of Surveillance" by Harold James, Vol. 42 (Dec. 1995), pp. 762–91.
"How Does the Global Economic Environment Influence the Demand for IMF Resources?" by Selim Elekda, Vol. 55 (Dec. 2008), pp. 624-653.
"How Long Can the Unsustainable U.S. Current Account Deficit Be Sustained?" by Carol C. Bertaut, Steven B. Kamin, and Charles P. Thomas, Vol. 56 (Aug. 2009), pp. 596-632.
"Improving the Demand for Money Function in Moderate Inflation," by William H. White, Vol. 25 (Sept. 1978), pp. 564–607.
"In Finance, Size Matters," by Biagio Bossone and Jong-Kun Lee, Vol. 51 (Apr. 2004), pp. 19–46.
"Indexation of Wages and Salaries in Developed Economies," by Anne Romanis Braun, Vol. 23 (Mar. 1976), pp. 226–71.
"An Indicator of Effective Exchange Rates," by Fred Hirsch and Ilse Higgins, Vol. 17 (Nov. 1970), pp. 453–84.
"Indices of Effective Exchange Rates," by Rudolf R. Rhomberg, Vol. 23 (Mar. 1976), pp. 88–112.
"Interest Rate Differences, Forward Exchange Mechanism, Scope for Short-Term Capital Movements," by William H. White, Vol. 10 (Nov. 1963), pp. 485–503.
"International Financial Integration and the Real Economy," by Martin D. D. Evans and Viktoria V. Hnatkovska Vol. 54 (June 2007), pp. 220–69.
"International Liquidity and the Role of the SDR in the International Monetary System," by Peter B. Clark and Jacques J. Polak, Vol. 51 (Apr. 2004), pp. 49–71.
"International Monetary Fund: A Selected Bibliography," by Martin Loftus and Anne C. M. Salda, Vol. 1 (1951)–Vol. 25 (Dec. 1985), various issues.

"Is Housing Wealth an 'ATM'? The Relationship between Household Wealth, Home Equity Withdrawal, and Saving Rates," by Vladimir Klyuev and Paul Mills, Vol. 54 (July 2007), pp. 539–61

"Liberalization and the Behavior of Output during Transition from Plan to Market," by Ernesto Hernández-Catá, Vol. 44 (Dec. 1997), pp. 405–29.

"The Long-Run Relationship between Real Exchange Rates and Real Interest Rate Differentials: A Panel Study," by Ronald MacDonald and Jun Nagayasu, Vol. 47 (Nov. 2000), pp. 116–28.

"The Macroeconomic Impact of Privatization," by G. A. Mackenzie, Vol. 45 (June 1998), pp. 363–400.

"The Management of International Liquidity," by Oscar L. Altman, Vol. 13 (July 1966), pp. 216–47.

"The Missing Globalization Puzzle: Evidence of the Declining Importance of Distance," by David T. Coe, Arvind Subramanian, and Natalia T. Tamirisa, Vol. 54 (May 2007), pp. 34–58.

"Monetary Analysis of Income Formation and Payments Problems," by Jacques J. Polak, Vol. 6 (Nov. 1957), pp. 1–50.

"The Monetary Approach to the Exchange Rate: Some Empirical Evidence," by John F. O. Bilson, Vol. 25 (Mar. 1978), pp. 48–75.

"A Multilateral Exchange Rate Model," by Jacques Artus and Rudolf R. Rhomberg, Vol. 20 (Nov. 1973), pp. 591–611.

"Mundell-Fleming Lecture: Exchange Rate Systems, Surveillance, and Advice," by Stanley Fischer, Vol. 55 (July 2008), pp. 367–83.

"Northwest of Suez: The 1956 Crisis and the IMF," by James Boughton, Vol. 48 (Jan. 2002), pp. 425–46.

"Official Intervention in the Forward Exchange Market: A Simplified Analysis," by J. Marcus Fleming and Robert A. Mundell, Vol. 11 (Mar. 1964), pp. 1–9.

"On the Origins of the Fleming-Mundell Model," by James M. Boughton, Vol. 50 (Apr. 2003), pp. 1–9.

"Openness, Human Development, and Fiscal Policies: Effects of Economic Growth and Speed of Adjustment" by Delano Villanueva, 41 (March 1994), pp. 1–29.

"A Panic-Prone Pack? The Behavior of Emerging Market Mutual Funds," by Eduardo Borensztein and R. Gaston Gelos, Vol. 50 (Apr. 2003), pp. 43–63.

"The Peace Dividend: Military Spending Cuts and Economic Growth," by Malcolm Knight, Norman Loayza, and Delano Villanueva, Vol. 43 (Mar. 1996), pp. 1–37.

"The Persistence of Corruption and Slow Economic Growth," by Paolo Mauro, Vol. 51 (Apr. 2004), pp. 1–18.

"Portfolio Diversification, Leverage, and Financial Contagion," by Garry J. Schinasi and R. Todd Smith, Vol. 47 (Dec. 2000), pp. 159–70.

"The Present System of Reserve Creation in the Fund," by Hannan Ezekiel, Vol. 13 (Nov. 1966), pp. 398–420.

"The Productivity Bias in Purchasing Power Parity: An Econometric Investigation," by Lawrence H. Officer, Vol. 23 (Nov. 1976), pp. 545–75.

"Professor Triffin on International Liquidity and the Role of the Fund," by Oscar L. Altman, Vol. 8 (May 1961), pp. 151–92.

"The Purchasing-Power-Parity Theory of Exchange Rates: A Review Article," by Lawrence H. Officer, Vol. 23 (Mar. 1976), pp. 1–60.
"Restraining Yourself: The Implications of Fiscal Rules for Economic Stabilization," by Tamim Bayoumi and Barry Eichengreen, Vol. 42 (Mar. 1995), pp. 32–48.
"A Revised Version of the Multilateral Exchange Rate Model," by Jacques Artus and Anne Kenny McQuirk, Vol. 28 (June 1981), pp. 275–309.
"Rhyme or Reason: What Explains the Easy Financing of the U.S. Current Account Deficit?" by Ravi Balakrishnan, Tamim Bayoumi, and Volodymyr Tulin, Vol. 56 (June 2009), pp. 410–45.
"The Role of Incomes Policy in Industrial Countries since World War II," by Anne Romanis Braun, Vol. 22 (Mar. 1975), pp. 1–6.
"The Role of the International Monetary Fund in Promoting Price Stability," by Walter Gardner, Vol. 7 (Apr. 1960), pp. 319–26.
"Safety from Currency Crashes," by Kent Osband and Caroline Van Rijckeghem, Vol. 47 (Dec. 2000), pp. 238–58.
"The SDR as a Basket of Currencies," by Jacques J. Polak, Vol. 26 (Dec. 1979), pp. 627–53.
"The SDR: Some Problems and Possibilities," by J. Marcus Fleming, Vol. 18 (Mar. 1971), pp. 25–47.
"SDRs and the Working of the Gold Exchange Standard," by Fred Hirsch, Vol. 18 (July 1971), pp. 221–53.
"Separate Exchange Markets for Current and Capital Transactions," by Anthony Lanyi, Vol. 22 (Nov. 1975), pp. 714–49.
"Some Economic Aspects of Multiple Exchange Rates," by Edward M. Bernstein, Vol. 1 (1950–51), pp. 224–37.
"Special Drawing Rights: Renaming the Infant Asset," by Joseph Gold, Vol. 23 (July 1976), pp. 295–311.
"Stabilization Programs in Developing Countries: A Formal Framework," by Mohsin S. Khan and Malcolm D. Knight, Vol. 28 (Mar. 1981), pp. 1–53.
"Strategic Factors in Balance of Payments Adjustment," by Edward M. Bernstein, Vol. 5 (Aug. 1956), pp. 205–49.
"A Survey of Literature on Controls over International Capital Transactions," by Michael Dooley, Vol. 43 (Dec. 1996), pp. 639–87.
"The Vicious Circle Hypothesis," by John F. O. Bilson, Vol. 26 (Mar. 1979), pp. 1–37.
"Warning: Inflation May Be Harmful to Your Growth," by Atish Ghosh and Steven Philips, Vol. 45 (Dec. 1998), pp. 672–715.
"Why is China Growing So Fast?" by Zului F. Hu and Mohsin S. Khan, Vol. 44 (Mar. 1997), pp. 103–31.

Statistical Publications

(All four statistical publications are available on tape.)
Balance of Payments Statistics Yearbook, 1948 to date.
Direction of Trade Statistics, quarterly and yearbook issues, 1986 to date.

Government Finance Statistics Yearbook, 1977 to date.
International Financial Statistics, monthly and yearbook issues, 1948 to date.

World Economic and Financial Surveys

Developments in International Exchange and Payments Systems, by a staff team, 1991.
Developments in International Exchange and Trade Systems, by a staff team, 1989.
Global Financial Stability Report, by a staff team (This publication replaced the regular International Capital Markets: Developments and Prospects in August 2001).
International Capital Markets: Developments and Prospects, annually, 1981 to 2001. Issues from 1981–1985 were issued in the *Occasional Papers* series.
Issues and Developments in International Trade Policy, by a staff team headed by Margaret Kelly and Anne Kenny McQuirk, 1992.
Issues in International Exchange and Payments, by an IMF staff team, issued in 1989, 1992, and 1995.
Multilateral Official Debt Rescheduling: Recent Experience, by a staff team, 1987, 1988, and 1990.
Officially Supported Export Credits: Development and Prospects, by a staff team, 1986, 1988, 1989, 1990, and 1995.
Primary Commodity Markets, staff studies, annually from 1986 through 1990.
Private Market Financing for Developing Countries, staff study, 1991, 1992, 1993, and 1995.
Staff Studies for the World Economic Outlook. Supporting material for the analysis and scenarios depicted in *World Economic Outlook.*
World Economic Outlook: A Survey by the Staff of the IMF, from 1980 to date, biannually. Also in French, Spanish, and Arabic.

Occasional Papers (series)

International Capital Markets: Recent Developments and Short-Term Prospects, by a staff team headed by R. C. Williams, 1980. No. 1.
External Indebtedness of Developing Countries, by a staff team headed by Bahram Nowzad and Richard Williams, 1981. No. 3.
The Multilateral System of Payments: Keynes, Convertibility, and the International Monetary Fund's Articles of Agreement, by Joseph Gold, 1981. No. 6.
International Comparisons of Government Expenditure, by Alan A. Tait and Peter S. Heller, 1982. No. 10.
Effects of Slowdown in Industrial Countries on Growth in Non-Oil Developing Countries, by Morris Goldstein and Mohsin S. Khan, 1982. No. 12.
Currency Convertibility in the Economic Community of West African States, by John B. McLenaghan, Saleh M. Nsouli, and Klaus-Walter Riechel, 1982. No. 13.
Developments in International Trade Policy, by S. J. Anjaria, Z. Iqbal, N. Kirmani, and L. L. Perez, 1982. No. 16.

Aspects of the International Banking Safety Net, by G. G. Johnson, with Richard K. Abrams, 1983. No. 17.
Alternatives to the Central Bank in the Developing World, by Charles Collyns, 1983. No. 20.
Interest Rate Policies in Developing Countries, a study by the Research Department, 1983. No. 22.
Recent Multilateral Debt Restructuring with Official and Bank Creditors, by a staff team headed by E. Brau and R. C. Williams, with P. M. Keller and M. Nowak, 1983. No. 25.
The Fund, Commercial Banks, and Member Countries, by Paul Mentré, 1984. No. 26.
Exchange Rate Volatility and World Trade, a study by the Research Department, 1984. No. 28.
Issues in the Assessment of the Exchange Rates of Industrial Countries, a study by the Research Department, 1984. No. 29.
The Exchange Rate System—Lessons of the Past and Options for the Future, a study by the Research Department, 1984. No. 30.
Foreign Private Investment in Developing Countries, a study by the Research Department, 1985. No. 33.
Adjustment Programs in Africa: The Recent Experience, by Justin B. Zulu and Saleh M. Nsouli, 1985. No. 34.
The West African Monetary Union: An Analytical Review, by Rattan J. Bhatia, 1985. No. 35.
Formulation of Exchange Rate Policies in Adjustment Programs, by a staff team headed by G. G. Johnson, 1985. No. 36.
Export Credit Cover Policies and Payment Difficulties, by Eduard H. Brau and Champen Puckahtikom, 1985. No. 37.
A Case of Successful Adjustment: Korea's Experience during 1980–84, by Bijan B. Aghevli and Jorge Márquez-Ruarte, 1985. No. 39.
Recent Developments in External Debt Restructuring, by K. Burke Dillon, C. Maxwell Watson, G. Russell Kincaid, and Champen Puckahtikom, 1985. No. 40.
Fund-Supported Adjustment Programs and Economic Growth, by Mohsin S. Khan and Malcolm D. Knight, 1985. No. 41.
Global Effects of Fund-Supported Adjustment Programs, by Morris Goldstein, 1986. No. 42.
A Review of the Fiscal Impulse Measure, by Peter S. Heller, Richard D. Haas, and Ahsan H. Mansur, 1986. No. 44.
Switzerland's Role as an International Financial Center, by Benedicte Vibe Christensen, 1986. No. 45.
Fund-Supported Programs, Fiscal Policy, and Income Distribution, a study by the Fiscal Affairs Department, 1986. No. 46.
Strengthening the International Monetary System: Exchange Rates, Surveillance, and Objective Indicators, by Andrew Crockett and Morris Goldstein, 1987. No. 50.
The Role of the SDR in the International Monetary System, by the Research and Treasurer's Departments, 1987. No. 51.

Floating Exchange Rates in Developing Countries: Experience with Auction and Interbank Markets, by Peter J. Quirk, Benedicte Vibe Christensen, Kyung-Mo Huh, and Toshihiko Sasaki, 1987. No. 53.

Protection and Liberalization: A Review of Analytical Issues, by Max Corden, 1987. No. 54.

Theoretical Aspects of the Design of Fund-Supported Adjustment Programs, a study by the Research Department, 1987. No. 55.

Privatization and Public Enterprises, by Richard Hemming and Ali M. Mansoor, 1988. No. 56.

The Implications of Fund-Supported Adjustment Programs for Poverty: Experiences in Selected Countries, by Peter S. Heller, A. Lans Bovenberg, Thanos Catsambas, Ke-young Chu, and Parthasarathi Shome, 1988. No. 58.

Policies for Developing Forward Foreign Exchange Markets, by Peter J. Quirk, Graham Hacche, Viktor Schoofs, and Lothar Weniger, 1988. No. 60.

Policy Coordination in the European Monetary System, by Manuel Guitián, Maximo Russo, and Giuseppe Tullio, 1988. No. 61.

Common Agricultural Policy of the European Community: Principles and Consequences, by the European Department, 1988. No. 62.

Managing Financial Risks in Indebted Developing Countries, by Donald J. Mathieson, David Folkerts-Landau, Timothy Lane, and Iqbal Zaidi, 1989. No. 65.

The European Monetary System in the Context of the Integration of European Financial Markets, by David Folkerts-Landau and Donald Mathieson, 1989. No. 66.

The Role of National Saving in the World Economy: Recent Trends and Prospects, by Bijan B. Aghevli, James M. Boughton, Peter J. Montiel, Delano Villanueva, and Geoffrey Woglom, 1990. No. 67.

Debt Reduction and Economic Activity, by Michael P. Dooley, David Folkerts-Landau, Richard D. Haas, Steven A. Symansky, and Ralph W. Tryon, 1990. No. 68.

International Comparisons of Government Expenditure Revisited: The Developing Countries, by Peter S. Heller and Jack Drummond, 1990. No. 69.

The Conduct of Monetary Policy in the Major Industrial Countries: Instruments and Operating Procedures, by Dallas S. Batten, Michael P. Blackwell, In-Su Kim, Simon E. Nocera, and Yuzuru Ozeki, 1990. No. 70.

MULTIMOD Mark II: A Revised and Extended Model, by Paul Masson, Steven Symansky, and Guy Meredith, 1990. No. 71.

The Czech and Slovak Federal Republic: An Economy in Transition, by Jim Prust and an IMF staff team, 1990. No. 72.

German Unification: Economic Issues, by Leslie Lipschitz and Donogh McDonald, 1991. No. 75.

China: Economic Reform and Macroeconomic Management, by Mario Blejer, David Burton, Steven Dunaway, and Gyorgy Szapary, 1991. No. 76.

The Determinants and Systemic Consequences of International Capital Flows, by Morris Goldstein, Donald J. Mathieson, David Folkerts-Landau, Timothy Lane, J. Saul Lizondo, and Liliana Rojas-Suarez, 1991. No. 77.

Exchange Rate Policy in Developing Countries: Some Analytical Issues, by Bijan Aghevli, Mohsin Khan, and Peter J. Montiel, 1991. No. 78.

Domestic Public Debt of Externally Indebted Countries, by Pablo E. Guidotti and Manmohan S. Kumar, 1991. No. 80.

Currency Convertibility and the Transformation of Centrally Planned Economies, by Joshua E. Greene and Peter Isard, 1991. No. 81.

Characteristics of a Successful Exchange Rate System, by Jacob A. Frenkel, Morris Goldstein, and Paul R. Masson, 1991. No. 82.

Value-Added Tax: Administrative and Policy Issues, edited by Alan A. Tait, 1991. No. 88.

The Internationalization of Currencies: An Appraisal of the Japanese Yen, by George S. Tavlas and Yuzuru Ozeki, 1991. No. 90.

Economic Policies for a New South Africa, edited by Desmond Lachman and Kenneth Bercuson, 1991. No. 91.

Regional Trade Arrangements, by Augusto de la Torre and Margaret R. Kelly, 1991. No. 93.

Tax Harmonization in the European Community: Policy Issues and Analysis, by George Kopits, 1992. No. 94.

The Fiscal Dimensions of Adjustment in Low-Income Countries, by Karim Nashashibi, Sanjee Gupta, Claire Liuksila, Henri Lorie, and Walter Mahler, 1992. No. 95.

Policy Issues in the Evolving International Monetary System, by Morris Goldstein, Peter Isard, Paul R. Masson, and Mark P. Taylor, 1992. No. 96.

Rules and Discretion in International Economic Policy, by Manuel Guitián, 1992. No. 97.

Financial Sector Reforms and Exchange Arrangements in Eastern Europe, by Guillermo A. Calvo, Manmohan S. Kumar, Eduardo Borensztein, and Paul R. Masson, 1993. No. 102.

The Structure and Operation of the World Gold Market, by Gary O'Callaghan, 1993. No. 105.

Economic Adjustment in Low-Income Countries: Experience under the Enhanced Structural Adjustment Facility, by Susan Schadler, Franek Rozwadowski, Siddarth Tiwari, and David O. Robinson, 1993. No. 106.

Recent Experiences with Surges in Capital Inflows, by Susan Schadler, Maria Carkovic, Adam Bennett, and Robert Kahn, 1993. No. 108.

Limiting Central Bank Credit to the Government: Theory and Practice, by Carlo Cottarelli, 1993. No. 110.

The Russian Federation in Transition: External Developments, by Benedicte Vibe Christensen, 1994. No. 111.

The Behavior of Non-Oil Commodity Prices, by Eduardo Borensztein, Mohsin Khan, Carneb M. Reinhart, and Peter Wickham, 1994. No. 112.

Exchange Rates and Economic Fundamentals: A Framework for Analysis, by Peter B. Clark, Leonardo Bartolini, Tamim Bayoumi, and Steven Symansky, 1994. No. 115.

Improving the International Monetary System: Constraints and Possibilities, by Michael Mussa, Morris Goldstein, Peter B. Clark, Donald J. Mathieson, and Tamim Bayoumi, 1994, No. 116.

Uganda: Adjustment with Growth, 1987–94, by Robert L. Sharer, Hema R. De Zoysa, and Calvin A. McDonald, 1995. No. 121.

Capital Flows in the APEC Region, edited by Mohsin S. Khan and Carmen M. Reinhart, 1995. No. 122.

Saving Behavior and the Asset Price "Bubble" in Japan: Analytical Studies, edited by Ulrich Baumgartner and Guy Meredith, 1995. No. 124.

The Adoption of Indirect Instruments of Monetary Policy, by a staff team headed by William E. Alexander, Tómas J. T. Baliño, and Charles Ecoch, 1995. No. 126.

Road Maps of the Transition: The Baltics, the Czech Republic, Hungary, and Russia, by Biswajit Banerjee, Vincent Koen, Thomas Krueger, Mark S. Lutz, Michael Marrese, and Tapio O. Saavalainen, 1995, No. 127.

IMF Conditionality: Experience under Stand-by and Extended Arrangements, Part I: Key Issues and Findings, by Susan Schadler, Adam Bennett, Maria Carkovic, Louis Dicks-Mireaux, Mauro Mecagni, James H. J. Morsink, and Miguel A. Savastano, 1995. No. 128.

IMF Conditionality: Experience under Stand-By and Extended Arrangements, Part II: Background Papers, by Susan Schadler, ed., Adam Bennett, Maria Carkovic, Louis Dicks-Mireaux, Mauro Mecagni, James H.J. Morsink, and Miguel A. Savastano, 1995. No. 129.

Capital Account Convertibility: Review of Experience and Implications for IMF Policies, by staff teams headed by Peter J. Quirk and Owen Evans, 1995. No. 131.

Financial Fragilities in Latin America: The 1980s and 1990s, by Liliana Rojas-Suárez and Steven R. Weisbrod, 1995. No. 132.

Policy Experiences and Issues in the Baltics, Russia, and Other Countries of the Former Soviet Union, edited by Daniel A. Citrin and Ashok K. Lahiri, 1995. No. 133.

India: Economic Reform and Growth, by Ajai Chopra, Charles Collyns, Richard Hemming, Karen Parker, with Woosik Chu and Oliver Fratzscher, 1995. No. 134.

Aftermath of the CFA Franc Devaluation, by Jean A. P. Clément, with Johannes Mueller, Stéphane Cossé, and Jean Le Dem, 1996. No. 138.

Reinvigorating Growth in Developing Countries: Lessons from Adjustment Policies in Eight Economies, by David Goldsbrough, Sharmini Coorey, Louis Dicks-Mireaux, Balazs Horvath, Kalpana Kochhar, Mauro Mecagni, Erik Offerdal, and Jianping Zhou, 1996. No. 139.

Monetary and Exchange System Reforms in China: An Experiment in Gradualism, Hassanali Mehran, Marc Quintyn, Tom Nordman, Bernard Laurens, 1996. No. 141.

Adjustment for Growth: The African Experience, by Michael Hadjimichael, Michael Nowak, Robert Sharer, and Amor Tahari, 1996. No. 143.

Exchange Rate Movements and Their Impact on Trade and Investment in the APEC Region, by Takatoshi Ito, Peter Isard, Steven Symansky, and Tamim Bayoumi, 1996. No. 145.

Thailand: The Road to Sustained Growth, by Kalpana Kochhar, Louis Dicks-Mireaux, Balazs Horvath, Mauro Mecagni, Erik Offerdal, and Jiamping Zhou, 1996. No. 146.

The Composition of Fiscal Adjustment and Growth: Lessons from Fiscal Reforms in Eight Economies, by G. A. Mackenzie, David W. H. Orsmond, and Philip R. Gerson, 1997. No. 149.

Currency Board Arrangements: Issues and Experiences, by D. Mihalke, 1997. No. 151.

Hong Kong, China: Growth, Structural Change, and Economic Stability during the Transition, by John Dodsworth and Dubravko Mihaljek, 1997. No. 152.

Credibility without Rules, by Carlo Cottarelli and C. Giannini, 1997. No. 154.

The ESAF at Ten Years: Economic Adjustment and Reform in Low-Income Countries, by the staff of the IMF, 1997. No. 156.

Central Bank Reforms in the Baltics, Russia, and the Other Countries of the Former Soviet Union, by a staff team headed by Malcom Knight, 1997. No. 157.

Transparency in Government Operations, by George Kopitz and Jon Craig, 1997. No. 158.

Fiscal Reforms in Low-Income Countries, by an IMF staff team headed by George Abed, 1998. No. 160.

Fiscal Policy Rules, by G. Kopits and S. Symansky, No. 162.

MULTIMOD Mark III: The Core Dynamic and Steady State Model, by David Laxton, Peter Isard, et al., 1998. No. 164.

Hedge Funds and Financial Market Dynamics, by B. Eichengreen and D. Mathieson, 1998. No 166.

Capital Account Liberalization: Theoretical and Practical Aspects, by a staff team led by Barry Eichengreen and Michael Mussa, with Giovanni Dell'Ariccia, Enrica Detragiache, Glan Maria Milesi-Ferretti, and Andrew Tweedie, No. 172.

Exchange Rate Regimes in an Increasingly Integrated World Economy, by Michael Mussa, Paul R. Masson, Alexander K. Swoboda, Esteban Jadresic, Paolo Mauro, and Andrew Berg, 2000. No. 193.

Modern Banking and OTC Derivatives Markets: The Transformation of Global Finance and Its Implications for Systemic Risk, by Garry J.Schinasi, R. Sean Craig, Burkhard Drees, Charles Frederick Kramer, 2001. No. 203.

Advanced Country Experiences with Capital Account Liberalization, by Age Bakker and Bryan Chapple, 2002. No. 214.

Managing Systemic Banking Crises, by David S. Hoelscher and Marc Quintyn, 2003. No. 224.

Effects on Financial Globalization on Developing Countries: Some Empirical Evidence, by Eswar Prasad, Kenneth Rogoff, Shang-Jin Wei, and M. Ayhan Kose, 2003. No. 220.

Monetary Union among Member Countries of the Gulf Cooperation Council, by Ugo Fasano-Filho and Andrea Schaechter, 2003. No. 223.

Evolution and Performance of Exchange Rate Regimes, by Kenneth Rogoff, Aasim M. Husain, Ashoka Mody, Robin Brooks, and Nienke Oomes, 2004. No. 229.

Sovereign Debt Structure for Crisis Prevention, by Eduardo Borensztein, Marcos Chamon, Olivier Jeanne, Paolo Mauro, and Jeromin Zettelmeyer, 2005. No. 237.

Debt-Related Vulnerabilities and Financial Crises, by Christoph B. Rosenberg, Ioannis Halikias, Brett E. House, Christian Keller, Jens Nystedt, Alexander Pitt, and Brad Setser, 2005. No. 240.

The Design of IMF-Supported Programs, by Atish R. Ghosh, Charalambos Christofides, Jun I. Kim, Laura Papi, Uma Ramakrishnan, Alun H. Thomas, Juan Zalduendo, 2005. No. 241.

Monetary Policy Implementation at Different Stages of Market Development, by Bernard Laurens, 2005. No. 244.

Sovereign Debt Restructuring and Debt Sustainability: An Analysis of Recent Cross-Country Experience, by Harald Finger and Mauro Mecagni, 2007. No. 255.

Moving to Greater Exchange Rate Flexibility: Operational Aspects Based on Lessons from Detailed Country Experiences, by Inci Ötker, 2007. No. 256.

IMF Support and Crisis Prevention, by Atish R. Ghosh, Bikas Joshi, Jun Il Kim, Uma Ramakrishnan; Alun H. Thomas and Juan Zalduendo, 2008. No. 262.

Reaping the Benefits of Financial Globalization, by Giovanni Dell'Ariccia, Julian di Giovanni, André Faria, M. Ayhan Kose, Paolo Mauro, Martin Schindler, Marco Terrones, Jonathan David Ostry, 2008. No. 264.

Developing Essential Financial Markets in Smaller Economies: Stylized Facts and Policy Options by Mark R. Stone, Seiichi Shimizu, Anna Nordstrom, and Hervé J. Ferhani, 2008. No. 265.

The Debt Sustainability Framework for Low-Income Countries, by Bergljot Barkbu, Christian H. Beddies, and Marie-Helene Le Manchec, 2009. No. 266.

Pamphlet Series

This series covers, in depth, various aspects of the Fund, its functions, policies, and legal concepts (*free*). The following is an incomplete listing.

1. *Introduction to the Fund*, by J. Keith Horsefield, 1964.
2. *The International Monetary Fund: Its Form and Function*, by J. Marcus Fleming, 1964.
3. *The International Monetary Fund and Private Business Transactions: Some Legal Effects of the Articles of Agreement*, by Joseph Gold, 1965.
4. *The International Monetary Fund and International Law: An Introduction*, by Joseph Gold, 1965.
6. *Maintenance of the Gold Value of the Fund's Assets*, by Joseph Gold, 1971.
7. *The Fund and Non-Member States; Some Legal Effects*, by Joseph Gold, 1971.
9. *Balance of Payments: Its Meaning and Uses*, by Poul Høst-Madsen, 1967.
10. *Balance of Payments Concepts and Definitions*, 1969.
12. *The Reform of the Fund*, by Joseph Gold, 1969.
13. *Special Drawing Rights: Character and Use*, by Joseph Gold, 1970.
14. *The Fund's Concepts of Convertibility*, by Joseph Gold, 1971.
16. *Some Reflections on the Nature of Special Drawing Rights*, by J. J. Polak, 1971.
18. *Valuation and Rate of Interest of the SDR*, by Jacques J. Polak, 1974.
19. *Floating Currencies, Gold, and SDRs: Some Recent Legal Developments*, by Joseph Gold, 1976.

20. *Voting Majorities in the Fund: Effects of the Second Amendment to the Articles*, by Joseph Gold, 1977.
21. *International Capital Movements under the Law of the International Monetary Fund*, by Joseph Gold, 1977.
22. *Floating Currencies, SDRs, and Gold: Further Legal Developments*, by Joseph Gold, 1977.
23. *Use, Conversion, and Exchange of Currency under the Second Amendment of the Fund's Articles*, by Joseph Gold, 1978.
25. *The Second Amendment of the Fund's Articles of Agreement*, by Joseph Gold, 1978.
26. *SDRs, Gold, and Currencies: Third Survey of New Legal Developments*, by Joseph Gold, 1979.
27. *Financial Assistance by the International Monetary Fund: Law and Practice*, by Joseph Gold, 1980.
28. *SDR*, by J. J. Polak, 1979.
31. *Conditionality*, by Joseph Gold, 1979.
32. *The Rule of Law in the International Monetary Fund*, by Joseph Gold, 1980.
33. *SDRs, Currencies, and Gold: Fourth Survey of New Legal Developments*, by Joseph Gold, 1980.
35. *The Legal Character of the Fund's Stand-By Arrangements and Why It Matters*, by Joseph Gold, 1980.
36. *SDRs, Currencies, and Gold: Fifth Survey of New Legal Developments*, by Joseph Gold, 1981.
37. *The International Monetary Fund: Its Evolution, Organization, and Activities*, by the staff, 1984.
38. *Fund Conditionality: Evolution of Principles and Practices*, by Manuel Guitián, 1981.
39. *Order in International Finance, the Promotion of IMF Stand-By Arrangements, and the Drafting of Private Loan Agreements*, by Joseph Gold, 1982.
40. *SDRs, Currencies, and Gold: Sixth Survey of New Legal Developments*, by Joseph Gold, 1983.
44. *SDRs, Currencies, and Gold: Seventh Survey of New Legal Developments*, by Joseph Gold, 1987.
45. *Financial Organization and Operations of the IMF*, by the Treasurer's Department, 1991.
46. *The Unique Nature of the Responsibilities of the International Monetary Fund*, by Manuel Guitián, 1992.
47. *Social Dimensions of the IMF's Policy Dialogue*, by the staff of the IMF, 1995.
48. *Unproductive Public Expenditures: A Pragmatic Approach to Policy Analysis*, by the Fiscal Affairs Department, 1995.
49. *Guidelines for Fiscal Adjustment*, by the Fiscal Affairs Department, 1995.
50. *The Role of the IMF: Financing and Its Interactions with Adjustment and Surveillance*, by Paul Masson and Michael Mussa, 1995.
51 *Debt Relief for Low-Income Countries: The HIPC Initiative*, by Anthony R. Boote and Kamau Thugge, 1997.

52. *The IMF and the Poor*, by the Fiscal Affairs Department, 1998.
53. *Governance of the International Monetary Fund (IMF) Decision Making, Institutional Oversight, Transparency and Accountability*, by Leo van Houtven, 2002.
54. *Fiscal Dimensions of Sustainable Development*, by Michael Keen, Benedict J. Clements, Kevin Fletcher, Luiz de Mello, Luiz, and Mathukumara Mani, 2002.
55. *Fiscal Adjustment for Stability and Growth*, by Daniel James and the Fiscal Affairs Department, 2006.

Booklets

This new series, which was launched in 1996, is designed to make available to a readership of nonspecialists some of the economic research being carried out in the Fund. The papers are written in nontechnical language.

1. *Growth in East Asia: What We Can and What We Cannot Infer*, by Michael Sarel, 1996.
2. *Does the Exchange Rate Regime Matter for Inflation and Growth*, by Atish R. Ghosh, Ann-Marie Gulde, Jonathan D. Ostry, and Holger Wolf, 1996.
3. *Confronting Budget Deficits*, by Rozlyn Coleman, prepared from a working paper by Paul R. Masson and Michael Mussa, 1996.
4. *Fiscal Reforms That Work*, by C. John McDermott and Robert F. Wescott, 1996.
5. *Transformation to Open Market Operations: Developing Economies and Emerging Markets*, by Stephen H. Axilrod, 1996.
6. *Why Worry About Corruption?* by Paolo Mauro, 1997.
7. *Sterilizing Capital Flows*, by Jang-Yung Lee, 1997.
8. *Why Is China Growing So Fast?* by Zuliu Hu and Moshin S. Khan, 1997.
9. *Protecting Bank Deposits*, by Gillian G. Garcia, 1997.
10. *Deindustrialization—Its Causes and Implications*, by Robert Rowthorn and Ramana Ramaswamy, 1997.
11. *Does Globalization Lower Wages and Export Jobs?* by Matthew J. Slaughter and Phillip Swagel, 1997.
12. *Roads to Nowhere: How Corruption in Public Investment Hurts Growth*, by Vito Tanzi and Hamid Davoodi, 1998.
13. *Fixed or Flexible: Getting the Exchange Right in the 1990s*, by Francescp Caramazza and Jahangir Aziz, 1998.
14. *Lessons from Systemic Bank Reconstructing*, by Claudia Dziobek and Ceyla Pazarbasioglu, 1998.
15. *Inflation Targeting as a Framework for Monetary Policy*, by Guy Debelle, Paul Masson, Miguel Savastano, and Suni Sharma, 1998.

Papers on Policy Analysis and Assessment

Beginning in January 1999, this series was renamed *Policy Discussion Papers* (PDP). The series comprises staff studies in the area of policy design and research. They are aimed primarily at operational staff involved in mission work and economists elsewhere interested in policy issues. The following is a selective listing.

Japan's Corporate Groups and Imports, by Daniel A. Citrin, 1992. PPAA/92/2
The Operation of the Estonian Currency Board, by Adam G. G. Bennmett, 1992. PPAA/92/3
Real Exchange Rate Targeting in Developing Countries, by Peter J. Montiel and Jonathan D. Ostry, 1993. PPAA/93/2
Adjusting to Development: The IMF and the Poor, by James Boughton, 1993. PPAA/93/4
A Cautionary Note on the Use of Exchange Rate Indicators, by Peter Wickham, 1993. PPAA/93/5
The Strategy of Reform in the Previously Centrally Planned Economies of Eastern Europe: Lessons and Challenges, by Eduardo Borensztein, 1993. PPAA/93/6
The Capital Inflows Problem: Concepts and Issues, by Guillermo A. Calvo, Leonardo Leiderman, and Carmen Reinhart, 1993. PPAA/93/10
Options for Monetary and Exchange Arrangements in Transition Economies, by Delano Villanueva, 1993. PPAA/93/12
Aspects of the Design of Financial Programs with the Adoption of Indirect Monetary Controls, by Barry Johnston, 1993. PPAA/93/16
The Taxation of High Income Earners, by Parthasarathi Shome, 1993. PPAA/93/19
International Capital Transactions: Should They Be Restricted? by Norman S. Fieleke, 1993. PPAA/93/20
On the Political Sustainability of Economic Reform, by Carlos M. Asilis and Gian Maria Milesi-Ferretti, 1994. PPAA/94/3
The New Protectionism in Industrial Countries: Beyond the Uruguay Round, by Douglas A. Irwin, 1994. PPAA/94/5
Asset Prices, Monetary Policy, and the Business Cycle, by Garry J. Schinasi, 1994. PPAA/94/6
Emerging Equity Market: Growth, Benefits, and Policy Concerns, by Robert A. Feldman and Mammohan S. Kumar, 1994. PPAA/94/7
Establishing Monetary Control in Financial Systems With Insolvent Institutions, by Donald Mathieson and Richard D. Haas, 1994. PPAA/94/10
Use of Central Bank Credit Auctions in Economies in Transition, by Matthew I. Saal and Lorena M. Zamalloa, 1994. PPAA/94/11
Macroeconomic Management with Informal Financial Markets, by Pierre-Richard Agénor and Nadeem U. Haque, 1994. PPAA/94/12
Currency Arrangements in the Countries of the Former Ruble Area and Conditions for Sound Monetary Policy, by Thomas A. Wolf, 1994. PPAA/94/15
Currency Board: Issues and Experiences, by Adam G. G. Bennett, 1994. PPAA/94/18
Structural Policies in Developing Countries, by Eduardo Borensztein, 1994. PPAA/94/19
Russia and the IMF: The Political Economy of Macro-Stabilization, by Ernesto Hernández-Catá, 1994. PPAA/94/20
The IMF and the Latin American Debt Crisis: Seven Common Criticisms, by James M. Boughton, 1994. PPAA/94/23
The Speed of Financial Sector Reform: Risks and Strategies, by R. Barry Johnston, 1994. PPAA/94/26

Social Safety Nets for Economic Transition: Options and Recent Experiences, by the Expenditure Policy Division Staff, 1995. PPAA/95/3

Non-G-10 Countries and the Basle Capital Rules: How Tough a Challenge Is It to Join the Basel Club? by Claudia Dziobek, Olivier Frécaut, and Maria Nieto, 1995. PPAA/95/5

Discretion with Rules? Lessons from the Currency Board Arrangement in Lithuania, by Wayne Camard, 1996. PPAA/96/1

Borrowing by Subnational Governments: Issues and Selected International Experiences, by Teresa Ter-Minassian, 1996. PPAA/96/4

Social Protection in Transition Countries: Emerging Issues, by Ke-young Chu and Sanjeev Gupta, 1996. PPAA/96/5

Fiscal Dimensions of EMU, by Paul R. Masdson, 1996. PPAA/96/7

The Definition of Reserve Money: Does It Matter for Financial Programs? by Kalpana Kochhar, 1996. PPAA/96/10

Conditionality as an Instrument of Borrower Credibility, by Pierre Dhonte, 1997. PPAA/97/2

The Macroeconomic Impact of Privatization, by G. A. Mackenzie, 1997. PPAA/97/9

Making a Currency Board Operation, by Charles Enoch and Anne-Marie Gulde, 1997. PPAA/97/10

Bank Soundness and Currency Board Arrangements Issues and Experience, by Veerathai Santiprabhob, 1997. PPAA/97/11

Transparency in Central Bank Operations in the Foreign Exchange Markets, by Charles Enoch, 1998. PPAA/98/2

The Payment System and Monetary Policy, by Omotunde E. G. Jouhnson, 1998. PPAA/98/4

Sequencing Capital Account Liberalization and Financial Sector Reform, by R. Barry Hohnston, 1998. PPAA/98/8

Systemic Banking Distress: The Need for an Enhanced Monetary Survey, by Olivier Frécaut and Eric Sidgwick, 1998. PPAA/98/9

Working Papers, 1997

This series is designed to make Fund staff research available to a wide audience. The series began in 1991, and about 180 working papers are released each year. In many cases the papers are subject to ongoing work and revision. Many will eventually be published by the Fund as articles in one of the Fund's serial publications. The series is available on a subscription basis.

Staff Country Reports

The IMF releases Staff Country Reports on about 150 member countries each year. The reports contain comprehensive background material on economic developments as part of the annual consultations that the IMF conducts with most member countries.

GENERAL BIBLIOGRAPHY

General

Bank for International Settlements. *Annual Reports*. Basel, Switzerland, 1931 to date.

Harrod, R. F. *The Life of John Maynard Keynes*, Harcourt, Brace (Princeton, New Jersey, 1951).

Howell, Kristin. "The Role of the Bank for International Settlements in Central Bank Cooperation," *Journal of European Economic History*, Vol. 22, No. 2 (Fall 1993).

Jacobsson, Erin E. *A Life for Sound Money: Per Jacobsson; His Biography*, Clarendon Press (Oxford, 1979).

Keynes, John Maynard. *The Collected Writings of John Maynard Keynes*, Vols. 24, 25, and 26, ed. Donald Moggridge, Macmillan (London and New York, 1982).

Odell, John S. *U.S. International Monetary Policy: Markets, Power, and Ideas as Sources of Change*, Princeton University Press (Princeton, New Jersey, 1982).

Rees, David. *Harry Dexter White: A Study in Paradox*, Coward, McCann and Geoghenan (New York, 1973).

Salda, Anne C. M. *International Monetary Fund: A Selected Bibliography*, International Organizations Series, Vol. 4, Transaction Publishers (New Brunswick, New Jersey, 1992).

Skidelski, Robert. *John Maynard Keynes: The Economist as Saviour*, Macmillan (London, 1992).

Background of the Bretton Woods System

Bernanke, Ben, and Harold James. "The Gold Standard, Deflation, and Financial Crisis in the Great Depression: An International Comparison," in *Financial Markets and Financial Crises*, ed. R. Glenn Hubbard, University of Chicago Press (Chicago, 1991).

Bernstein, Edward M. "The Adequacy of United States Gold Reserves," *American Economic Review* (Papers and Proceedings of the Seventy-Third Annual Meeting of the American Economic Association), Vol. 51 (1961), pp. 439–46.

Bloomfield, Arthur I. *Monetary Policy under the Gold Standard: 1880–1914*, Federal Reserve Bank of New York (New York, 1959).

Brown, William Adams, Jr. *The International Gold Standard Reinterpreted 1914–1934*, National Bureau of Economic Research (New York, 1940).

Cassel, Gustav. *The Downfall of the Gold Standard*, Clarendon Press (Oxford, 1936).

Clarke, Stephen V. O. *The Reconstruction of the International Monetary System: The Attempts of 1922 and 1933*, Princeton Studies in International Finance No. 33, Princeton University Press (Princeton, 1973).

———. *Exchange-Rate Stabilization in the Mid-1930s: Negotiating the Tripartite Agreement*, Princeton Studies in International Finance No. 41, Princeton University Press (Princeton, New Jersey, 1977).

Clavin, Patricia. "The World Economic Conference 1933: The Failure of British Internationalism," *Journal of European Economic History*, Vol. 20, No. 3 (Winter, 1991).

Cooper, Richard N. *Gold Standard: Historical Fact and Future Prospects*, Brookings Papers on Economic Activity (Washington, D.C., 1982).

De Cecco, Marcello. *The International Gold Standard: Money and Empire*, St. Martin's Press (New York, 1984).

Eichengreen, Barry J. "The Gold Standard and the Great Depression," *NBER Reporter*, National Bureau of Economic Research (Spring 1991).

———. *Golden Fetters: The Gold Standard and the Great Depression, 1919–1939*, Oxford University Press (New York, 1992).

Eichengreen, Barry J., and Jeffery Sachs. "Exchange Rates and Economic Recovery in the 1930s," *Journal of Economic History*, Vol. 45 (1985).

Palyi, Melchior. *The Twilight of Gold 1914–1936: Myths and Realities*, Henry Regnery (Chicago, 1972).

Schubert, Aurel. *The Credit-Anstalt Crisis of 1931*, Cambridge University Press (Cambridge, England, 1991).

Establishing the Bretton Woods System

Argy, Victor. *The Postwar International Money Crisis: An Analysis*, Allen & Unwin (London, 1981).

Black, Stanley W. *A Levite among the Priests: Edward M. Bernstein and the Origins of the Bretton Woods System*, Westview Press (Boulder, Colorado, 1991).

Bordo, Michael D. "The Bretton Woods System: A Historical Overview," in *A Retrospective on the Bretton Woods System: Lessons for International Monetary Reform*, ed. Michael D. Bordo and Barry Eichengreen, University of Chicago Press (Chicago, 1993).

Bordo, Michael D., and Barry Eichengreen, eds. *A Retrospective on the Bretton Woods System: Lesson for International Monetary Reform*, University of Chicago Press (Chicago, 1993).

Bordo, Michael D., Dominique Simard, and Eugene White. "France and the Bretton Woods International Monetary System, 1960 to 1968," NBER Working Paper No. 4642, National Bureau of Economic Research (Cambridge, Massachusetts, 1994).

Dormael, Armand van. *Bretton Woods: Birth of a Monetary Order*, Holmes and Meier (New York, 1978).

Ebke, Werner F., et al., eds. *Festschrift in Honor of Sir Joseph Gold*, Verlag Recht und Wirtschaft (Heidelberg, Germany, 1990).

Feis, Herbert. "Restoring Trade after the War," *Foreign Affairs* (New York), Vol. 20 (1941–1942).

Gardner, Richard N. *Sterling-Dollar Diplomacy*, Columbia University Press (New York, 1969).

Mikesell, Raymond F. "Negotiating at Bretton Woods, 1944," in *Negotiating with the Russians*, ed. Raymond Dennett and Joseph E. Johnson, World Peace Foundation (Boston, 1951), pp. 101–16.

Mikesell, Raymond F. *The Bretton Woods Debates: A Memoir*, Essays in International Finance No. 192, Princeton University Press (Princeton, New Jersey, 1994).
Mossé, Robert. *Le système monétaire de Bretton Woods et les grands problèmes de l'après guerre*, Recueil Sirey (Paris, 1948).
Officer, Lawrence H. "Are International Monetary Fund Quotas Unfavorable to Less-Developed Countries? A Normative Historical Analysis," *Journal of International Money and Finance*, Vol. 10, No. 2 (June 1991).
Robertson, Dennis H. "The Post-War Monetary Plans," *The Economic Journal* (London), Vol. 53 (1943), pp. 352–60.
——. *Utility and All That*, Allen and Unwin (London, 1952).
Robinson, Joan. "The International Currency Plans," *The Economic Journal* (London), Vol. 53 (1943), pp. 161–75.
Southard, Frank. *The Evolution of the International Monetary Fund*, Essays in International Finance, No. 135, Princeton University Press (Princeton, New Jersey, 1979).
United Nations Monetary and Financial Conference, Bretton Woods, New Hampshire, 1944. *Proceedings and Documents*, 2 vols., U.S. Government Printing Office (Washington, D.C., 1944).
[U.S.] Board of Governors of the Federal Reserve System. *Bretton Woods Agreements: A Bibliography, April 1943–December 1945* (Washington, D.C., 1946).
[U.S.] Department of State. *Proceedings and Documents of United Nations Monetary and Financial Conference, Bretton Woods, New Hampshire, July 1–22, 1944* (Washington, D.C., 1948).
[U.S.] Treasury Department. *Questions and Answers on the International Monetary Fund* (Washington, D.C., June 1944).
Van Dormael, Armand. *Bretton Woods: Birth of a Monetary System*, Holmes and Meier (New York, 1978).
Viner, Jacob. "Two Plans for International Monetary Stabilization," *Yale Review* (New Haven), Vol. 33 (1943–1944).
White, Harry D. "Post-War Currency Stabilization," *The American Economic Review*, Vol. 33 (1943), Supplement.
Williams, John. H. *Postwar Monetary Plans and Other Essays*, Wilkins (New York, 1947).
Young, John Parke. "Developing Plans for an International Monetary Fund and a World Bank," *Department of State Bulletin* (Washington, D.C.), Vol. 23 (1950).

Macroeconomic and Structural Adjustment and Fund Conditionality

Acheson, A. L. K., J. F. Chant, and M. F. J. Prachowny, eds. *Bretton Woods Revisited: Evaluations of the International Monetary Fund and the International Bank for Reconstruction and Development*, University of Toronto Press (Toronto, 1972).
Aliber, Robert Z. *The International Money Game*, Basic Books (New York, 1987).
Bangura, Yusuf. "IMF/World Bank Conditionality and Nigeria's Structural Adjustment Programme," in *The IMF and the World Bank in Africa: Conditionality,*

Impact and Alternatives, ed. Kjell J. Havnevik, Scandinavian Institute of African Studies (Uppsala, 1987).

——. "Crisis and Adjustment: The Experience of Nigerian Workers," in *The IMF, the World Bank and African Debt*, Vol. 2, *The Social and Political Impact*, ed. Bade Onimode, Institute for African Alternatives and Zed Books (London, 1989).

Battaile, Bill, et al. *The Poverty Reduction Strategy Initiative: An Independent Evaluation of the World Bank's Support through 2003*, World Bank (Washington, DC, 2004).

Bazdresch, Carlos, and Santiago Levy. "Populism and Economic Policy in Mexico 1970–1982," in *Macroecomics of Populism in Latin America*, ed. Rudiger Dornbusch and Sebastian Edwards, University of Chicago Press (Chicago, 1991).

Bergsten, C. Fred. *International Adjustment and Financing: The Lessons from 1985–1991*, Institute for International Economics (Washington, D.C., 1991).

Bourguignon, François, and Cristian Morrison. *Adjustment and Equity in Developing Countries: A New Approach*, Organization of Economic Cooperation and Development (Paris, 1992).

Bruno, Michael. "Stabilization and the Macroeconomics of Transition: How Different Is Eastern Europe?" *Economics of Transition*, Vol. 1 (1993).

Callaghy, Thomas M. "Lost between State and Market: The Politics of Economic Adjustment in Ghana, Zambia, and Nigeria," in *Economic Crisis and Policy Choice: The Politics of Adjustment in the Third World*, ed. Joan Nelson, Princeton University Press (Princeton, New Jersey, 1990).

Campbell, Horace. *Tanzania and the IMF: The Dynamics of Liberalization*, Westview (Boulder, Colorado, 1992).

Campbell, K., and John Loxley, eds. *Structural Adjustment in Africa*, St. Martin's Press (New York, 1989).

Campos, Roberto de Oliveiro. "Inflation and Balanced Growth," in *Economic Development in Latin America: Proceedings of a Conference Held by the International Economic Association*, ed. Howard S. Ellis, St. Martin's Press (New York, 1961).

Cline, William R., and Sidney Weintraub, eds. *Economic Stabilization in Developing Countries*, Brookings Institution (Washington, 1981).

Cornia, Andrea, Richard Jolly, and Francis Stewart, eds. *Adjustment with a Human Face*, 2 vols., Oxford University Press (Oxford, 1987).

Cotés Conde, Roberto. "Growth and Stagnation in Argentina," in *Towards a Development Strategy for Latin America: Pathways from Hirschman's Thought*, ed. Simón Teitel, Inter-American Bank (Washington, 1992).

David, Wilfrid L. *The IMF Policy Paradigm: The Macroeconomics of Stabilization, Structural Adjustment and Economic Development*, Praeger (New York, 1985).

Demekas, Dimitri G., et. al. *Building Peace in South East Europe: Macroeconomic Policies and Structural Reforms Since the Kosovo Conflict*, The World Bank (Washington, D.C., 2002).

De Vries, Rimmer. "The Limited Role of the IMF," *World Financial Markets*, Morgan Guarantee Trust Company, Apr. 1982.

Dell, Sidney. "The Question of Cross-Conditionality," *World Development*, Vol. 16, No. 5 (May 1988).

——. *On Being Grandmotherly: The Evolution of IMF Conditionality*, Essays in International Finance, No. 144, Princeton University Press (Princeton, New Jersey, 1981).

——. "Balance of Payments Adjustment in the 1980s," *World Development*, Vol. 14, No. 8, (Aug. 1986), pp. 873–1105.

Dell, Sidney, and Roger Lawrence. *The Balance of Payments Adjustment Process in Developing Countries*, Pergamon Press (New York, 1980).

Dornbusch, Rudiger. *Structural Adjustment in Latin America*, Woodrow Wilson Center (Washington, 1991).

Edwards, Sebastian. "The International Monetary Fund and the Developing Countries: A Critical Evaluation," *Carnegie-Rochester Conference Series on Public Policy*, Vol. 31 (Fall 1989), pp. 7–68.

Feinberg, Richard E. "The Changing Relationship between the World Bank and the International Monetary Fund," *International Organization*, Vol. 42, No. 3 (Summer 1988), pp. 545–60.

Finch, David. *The Record and the Prospect*, Essays in International Finance, No. 175, Princeton University Press (Princeton, New Jersey, 1989).

——. "Let the IMF be the IMF," *The International Economy*, Jan./Feb. 1988.

Frenkel, Jeffrey A., and Harry G. Johnson, eds. *The Monetary Approach to the Balance of Payments*, Allen and Unwin (London, 1976).

Goode, Richard B. *Economic Assistance to Developing Countries through the IMF*, Brookings Institution (Washington, D.C., 1985).

Gwin, Catherine. "Financing India's Adjustment: The Role of the Fund," in *IMF Conditionality*, ed. John Williamson, Institute for International Economics (Washington, D.C., 1983).

Haggard, Stephan, Richard N. Cooper, and Chung-in-Moon. "Policy Reform in Korea," in *Political and Economic Interactions in Economic Policy Reform: Evidence from Eight Countries*, ed. Robert H. Bates and Anne O. Krueger, Basil Blackwell (Oxford, 1993).

Hawkins, Jeffrey J. "Understanding the Failure of IMF Reform: The Zambian Case," *World Development*, Vol. 19, No. 7 (July 1991).

Herbst, Jeffrey. "The Structural Adjustment of Politics in Africa," *World Development*, Vol. 18, No. 7 (July 1990).

Johnson, Harry G. "Economic Policies for Less Developed Countries," in *International Monetary Reform*, Brookings Institution (Washington, D.C., 1967), pp. 212-36.

Kenen, Peter B. *Financing, Adjustment and the International Monetary Fund*, Brookings Institution, (Washington, D.C., 1986).

Killick, Tony. "Kenya, the IMF, and the Unsuccessful Quest for Stabilization." In *IMF Conditionality*, ed. John Wiliamson, Institute for International Economics (Washington, D.C., 1983).

——. ed. *The Quest for Economic Stabilization: The IMF and the Third World*, St. Martin's Press (Washington, D.C., 1984).

Krueger, Anne O. *Liberalization Attempts and Consequences*, Ballinger for National Bureau of Economic Research (New York, 1978).

——. *Political Economy of Policy Reform in Developing Countries*, MIT Press (Cambridge, Massachusetts, 1993).

Lancaster, Carol. *African Economic Reform: The External Dimension*, Institute for International Economics (Washington, D.C., 1991).

Leith, J. Clark, and Michael F. Lofchie. "The Political Economy of Structural Adjustment in Ghana," in *Political and Economic Interactions in Economic Policy Reform: Evidence from Eight Countries*, ed. Robert H. Bates and Anne O. Krueger, Basil Blackwell (Oxford, 1993).

Levitt, Kari. "Stabilisation and Structural Adjustment: Rhetoric and Reality," *Caribbean Affairs*, Vol. 3, No. 1 (Jan./Mar. 1990).

Loxley, John. "Structural Adjustment in Africa: Reflections on Ghana and Zambia," *Review of African Political Economy*, No. 47 (Spring 1990).

Manzetti, Luigi. *The International Monetary Fund and Economic Stabilization: The Argentine Case*, Praeger (New York, 1991).

Matin, K. M. "Structural Adjustment under the Extended Fund Facility: The Case of Bangladesh," *World Development*, Vol. 16, No. 6 (June 1990).

Mikesell, Raymand F. "Appraising IMF Conditionality: "Too Loose, Too Tight, or Just Right," in *IMF Conditionality*, ed. John Williamson, Institute for International Economics (Washington, D.C., 1983).

Moore, Will H., and James R. Scarritt. "IMF Conditionality and Policy Characteristics in Black Africa: An Exploratory Analysis," *Africa Today*, Vol. 37 (4th quarter, 1990).

Myers, Robert J., ed. "The Political Morality of the International Monetary Fund," *Ethics and Foreign Policy*, Vol. 3, Transaction Books (New Brunswick, New Jersey, 1987).

Ncube, P. D., M. Sakala, and M. Ndulo. "The International Monetary Fund and the Zambian Economy: A Case," in *The IMF and the World Bank in Africa: Conditionality, Impact and Alternatives*, ed. Kjell J. Havnevik, Scandinavian Institute of African Studies (Uppsala, 1987).

Nelson, Joan M., and contributors. *Fragile Conditions: The Politics of Economic Adjustment*, Transaction Books (New Brunswick, New Jersey, 1989).

Nelson, Joan M., ed. *Economic Crisis and Policy Choice: The Politics of Adjustment in Developing Countries*, Princeton University Press (Princeton, New Jersey, 1990).

Obstfeld, Maurice, and Kenneth Rogoffs. *Foundations of International Macroecomics*, MIT Press (Cambridge, Massachusetts, 1996).

Pauly, Lewis W. *Who Elected the Bankers? Surveillance and Control in the World Economy*, Cornell University Press (Ithaca, New York, 1997).

Plumptre, A. F. W. *Three Decades of Decision: Canada and the World Monetary System, 1944–75*, McClelland and Stewart (Toronto, 1977).

Pöhl, Karl Otto. "You Can't Robotize Policymaking," *The International Economy*, Oct./Nov. 1987.

Polak, Jacques J. *The Changing Nature of IMF Conditionality*, Essays in International Finance, No. 184, Princeton University Press (Princeton, New Jersey, 1991).

Sachs, Jeffrey D. "The Current Account and Macroeconomic Adjustment in the 1970s," *Brookings Papers on Economic Activity*, Brookings Institution (Washington, D.C., 1981).

Seddon, David. "The Politics of Adjustment: Egypt and the IMF, 1987–1990," *Review of African Political Economy*, No. 47 (Spring, 1990).

Sidell, Scott R. *The IMF and Third-World Political Instability: Is There a Connection?* St. Martin's Press (New York, 1988).

Spraos, John. *IMF Conditionality: Ineffectual, Inefficient, Mistargeted*, Essays in International Finance, No. 166, Princeton University Press (Princeton, New Jersey, 1986).

Taylor, Lance. *Varieties of Stabilization Experience: Towards Sensible Macroeconomics in the Third World*, prepared for the World Institute for Development Economic Research of the United Nations University, Clarendon Press (Oxford, 1988).

Thirwell, A. P. *Growth and Development, with Special Reference to Developing Economies*, Macmillan (Basingstoke, Hampshire, England, 1989).

Vera, Leonardo, *Stabilization and Growth in Latin America: A Critique and Reconstruction from Post-Keynesian and Structuralist Perspectives*, Palgrave (New York, 2001).

Williamson, John. "On Judging the Success of IMF Policy Advice," in *IMF Conditionality*, ed. Williamson, Institute for International Economics (Washington, D.C., 1984).

——. ed. *IMF Conditionality*, Institute for International Economics (Washington, D.C., 1983).

Wohlmuth, Karl, ed. *Structural Adjustment in the World Economy and East-West-South Economic Cooperation*, Institute for World Economics and International Management, University of Bremen (Bremen, Germany, 1989).

Wulf, Jürgen. "Zambia under the IMF Regime," *African Affairs*, Vol. 87 (Oct. 1988).

Exchange Rate Systems and Markets

Approaches to Greater Flexibility of Exchange Rates: The Bürgenstock Papers, arranged by C. Fred Bergsten, George N. Halm, Fritz Machlup, and Robert V. Roosa, and edited by George N. Halm, Princeton University Press (Princeton, New Jersey, 1970).

Artus, Jacques R., and Andrew D. Crockett. *Floating Exchange Rates and the Need for Surveillance*, Essays in International Finance, No. 127, Princeton University Press (Princeton, New Jersey, 1978).

Balassa, Bela. "The Purchasing-Power Parity Doctrine: A Reappraisal," *Journal of Political Economy*, Vol. 72 (Dec. 1964).

Balassa, Bela, and John Williamson. *Adjusting to Success: Balance of Payments Policy in the East Asian NICs*, Institute for International Economics (Washington, D.C., 1987).

Barr, Michael S., Anjali Kumar, and Robert E. Litan, eds. *Building Inclusive Financial Systems: A Framework for Financial Access*, Brookings Institution Press (Washington, D.C. 2007).

Branson, William H., Jacob A. Frenkel, and Morris Goldstein, eds. *International Policy Coordination and Exchange Rate Fluctuations*, University of Chicago Press (Chicago, 1990).

Bürgenstock Papers. See *Approaches to Greater Flexibility of Exchange Rates.*

Catte, Pietro Giampaulo Gali, and Salvatore Rebecchini. "Concerted Interventions and the Dollar: An Analysis of Daily Data," in *The International Monetary System*, ed. Peter Kenen, Cambridge University Press (Cambridge, 1994).

Cooper, Richard N., et al. *The International Monetary System under Flexible Exchange Rates, Global, Regional, and National: Essays in Honor of Robert Triffin*, Ballinger (Cambridge, Massachusetts, 1982).

Council on [U.S.] Foreign Relations. *Smithsonian Agreement and Its Aftermath: Several Views*, The Council (New York, 1972).

De Grauwe, Paul, Hans Dewachter, and Marc Embrechts. *Exchange Rate Theory: Chaotic Models of Foreign Exchange Markets*, Basil Blackwell (Oxford, 1993).

Destler, I. M., and C. Randall Henning. *Dollar Politics: Exchange Rate Policymaking in the United States*, Institute for International Economics (Washington, D.C., 1989).

Dominguez, Kathryn, and Jeffrey A. Frankel. *Does Foreign Exchange Intervention Work?* Institute for International Economics (Washington, D.C., 1993).

Edwards, Sebastian. *Real Exchange Rates, Devaluation and Adjustment: Exchange Rate Policy in Developing Countries*, MIT Press (Cambridge, Massachusetts, 1989).

Funabashi, Yoichi. *Managing the Dollar: From the Plaza to the Louvre*, 2nd ed. Institute for International Economics (Washington, D.C., 1989).

Kenen, Peter B. *EMU After Maastricht*, Group of Thirty (Washington, D.C., 1992). *Managing Exchange Rates*, Routledge (London, 1988).

———. "The Coordination of Macroeconomic Policies," in *International Policy Coordination and Exchange Rate Fluctuations*, ed. William Branson, Jacob A. Frenkel, and Morris Goldstein, University of Chicago Press (Chicago, 1990).

League of Nations. *International Currency Experience: Lessons of the Inter-War Period*, League of Nations (Geneva, 1944).

———. *Report on Exchange Control*, League of Nations (Geneva, 1938).

Litan, Robert. E. Paul Masson, and Michael Pomerleano. *Open Doors: Foreign Participation in Financial Systems in Developing Countries*, Brookings Institution Press (Washington, D.C., 2001).

Mikesell, Raymond F. *Foreign Exchange in the Post-War World*, 20th Century (New York, 1954).

Pauls, B. Dianne. "U.S. Exchange Rate Policy: Bretton Woods to Present," *Federal Reserve Bulletin*, Board of Governors of the Federal Reserve System, Vol. 76, No. 11 (November 1990).

Ungerer, Horst. *A Concise History of European Monetary Integration: From EPU to EMU*, Quorum Books (Westport, Connecticut, 1997).

Williamson, John. *The Crawling Peg*, Essays in International Finance, No. 50, Princeton University Press (Princeton, New Jersey, 1965).

Williamson, John. *Currency Convertibility in Eastern Europe*, Institute for International Economics (Washington, D.C., 1991).
———. *The Exchange Rate System*, Institute for International Economics (Washington, D.C., 1983; 2nd ed. 1985).
Williamson, John, and Marcus H. Miller. *Targets and Indicators: A Blueprint for International Coordination of Economic Policy*, Institute for International Economics (Washington, D.C., 1987).

International Currencies, Liquidity, and the SDR

Balogh, Thomas. *The Dollar Crisis: Causes and Cure, A Report to the Fabian Society*, Basil Blackwell (Oxford, 1949).
Bell, Geoffrey. *The Euro-Dollar Market and the International Financial System*, Wiley (New York, 1973).
Bergsten, C. Fred. *The Dilemmas of the Dollar: The Economics and Politics of United States International Monetary Policy*, New York University Press (New York, 1975).
Bernstein, Edward M. "The Dollar Is the Problem of the International Monetary System," *Quarterly Review and Investment Survey*, Model, Roland & Co. (New York, Second Quarter, 1971).
———. "Further Evolution of the International Monetary System," *Moorgate and Wall Street* (London, Summer 1965).
———. "A Practical Program for International Monetary Reserves," *Quarterly Review and Investment Survey*, Model, Roland & Co. (New York, Fourth Quarter, 1963).
———. "Statement: The Problem of International Monetary Reserves," in *International Payments Imbalances and Need for Strengthening International Financial Arrangements*, U.S. Congress, Joint Economic Committee, Hearings before the Subcommittee on International Exchange and Payments, 87th Cong., 1st sess., May 16–June 21, 1961 (Washington, 1961).
———. "The U.S. Balance of Payments and International Liquidity" (June 18, 1965), "Changes in the International Monetary System" (Oct. 27, 1964), "Two Reports on International Liquidity" (Aug. 19, 1964), and "The Underdeveloped Countries and Monetary Reserves" (Mar. 24, 1965), in *Guidelines for International Monetary Reform*, U.S. Congress, Joint Economic Committee, Hearings before the Subcommittee on International Exchange and Payments, 89th Cong., 1st sess., Part 2, Supplement (Washington, D.C., 1965).
Bolton, Sir George. "Background and Emergence of the Eurodollar Market," in *The Eurodollar*, ed. Herbert V, Prochnow, Rand McNally (Chicago, 1970).
Bryant, Ralph C., *Crisis Prevention and Prosperity Management for the World Economy*, Brookings Institution Press (Washington, D.C., 2004).
———. *Turbulent Waters: Cross-Border Finance and International Governance*, Brookings Institution Press (Washington, D.C., 2003).
Cairncross, Alec, and Barry Eichengreen. *Sterling in Decline: The Devaluations of 1931, 1949, and 1976*, Basil Blackwell (Oxford, 1983).

Chrystal, K. Alec. *International Money and the Future of the SDR*, Essays in International Finance, No. 128, Princeton University Press (Princeton, New Jersey, 1978).

Coats, Warren L. "Enhancing the Attractiveness of the SDR," *World Development*, Vol. 18, No. 7 (July 1990).

Despres, Emile, Charles Kindleberger, and Walter S. Salant. "The Dollar and World Liquidity: A Minority View," *Economist*, Feb. 11, 1966.

Feaveryear, Sir Albert. *The Pound Sterling: A History of English Money*, 2nd ed. Oxford University Press (Oxford, 1963).

Feldstein, Martin, ed. *Economic and Financial Crises in Emerging Market Economies*, University of Chicago Press (Chicago, 2003).

Goodhart, Charles A. E. "Monetary Policy in the United Kingdom," in *Monetary Policy in Twelve Industrial Countries*, ed. Karel Holbik, Federal Reserve Bank of Boston (Boston 1973).

Haberler, Gottfried. "How Important Is Control over International Reserves?" (1977) in *Selected Essays of Gottfried Haberler*, ed. Anthony Y. C. Koo, MIT Press (Cambridge, Massachusetts, 1985).

Harrod, R. F. *Reforming the World's Money*, Macmillan (London, 1965).

Hirsch, Fred. *The Pound Sterling: A Polemic*, Victor Gallancz (London, 1965).

Hoffmeyer, Erik. *Dollar Shortage and the Structure of U.S. Foreign Trade*, Ejnar Munksguard (Copenhagen, 1958).

Kindelberger, Charles P. *The Dollar Shortage*, MIT Press (Cambridge, Massachusetts, 1950).

———. "The Price of Gold and the N-1 Problem," in Kindleberger, *International Money: A Collection of Essays*, Allen and Unwin (London, 1981).

———. "International Monetary Stabilization," in *Postwar Economic Problems*, ed. S. E. Harris, McGraw-Hill (New York, 1943).

Park, Y. S. *The Link between Special Drawing Rights and Development Finance*, Essays in International Finance, No. 100, Princeton University Press (Princeton, New Jersey, 1973).

Patel, I. G. *The Link between the Creation of International Liquidity and the Provision of Development Finance*, United Nations Conference on Trade and Development (Geneva, 1967).

Polk, Judd. *Sterling: Its Meaning in World Finance*, Harper (New York, 1956).

Schott, Paul Allan, *Reference Guide to Anti-Money Laundering and Combating the Financing of Terrorism*, The World Bank (Washington, D.C., 2006).

Strange, Susan. *Sterling and British Policy: A Political Study of an International Currency in Decline*, Oxford University Press (Oxford, 1971).

Swoboda, Alexander K. *The Euro-Dollar Market: An Interpretation*, Essays in International Finance, No. 64, Princeton University Press (Princeton, New Jersey, 1968).

Tavlas, George S. *On the International Use of Currencies: The Case of the Deutschemark*, Essays in International Finance No. 181, Princeton University Press (Princeton, New Jersey, 1991).

Triffin, Robert. *Gold and the Dollar Crisis: The Future of Convertibility*, Yale University Press (New Haven, Connecticut, 1960).

——. *Gold and the Dollar Crisis: Yesterday and Tomorrow*, Essays in International Finance, No. 132, Princeton University Press (Princeton, New Jersey, 1961).

——. "The Return to Convertibility: 1926–1931 and 1958– ? or, Convertibility and the Morning After," *Quarterly Review*, Banca Nazionale del Lavoro (Rome), Mar. 1959.

——. "Tomorrow's Convertibility: Aims and Means of International Monetary Policy," *Quarterly Review*, Banca Nazionale del Lavoro (Rome), June 1959.

——. *The World Money Maze: National Currencies in International Payments*, Yale University Press (New Haven, Connecticut, and London, 1966).

Walters, Alan. *Sterling in Danger: The Economic Consequences of Pegged Exchange Rates*, Fontana (London, 1990).

Williams, David. "The Evolution of the Sterling System," in *Essays in Money and Banking in Honour of R.S. Sayers*, ed. C. R. Whittlesay and J. S. G. Wilson, Clarendon Press (Oxford, 1968).

Williamson, John. *A New SDR Allocation*, Institute for International Economics (Washington, D.C., 1984).

International Trade and Payments

Bacha, Edmar Lisboa, and Carlos F. Díaz-Alejandro. "Tropical Reflections on the History and Theory of International Financial Markets," in *For Good or Evil: Economic Theory and North-South Negotiations*, ed. Gerald K. Helleiner, University Press of Toronto, (Toronto, 1982).

Bergsten, C. Fred. *America in the World Economy: A Strategy for the 1990s*. Institute for International Economics (Washington, D.C., 1988).

——. "Economic Imbalances and World Politics," *Foreign Affairs*, Vol. 65, No. 4 (Spring 1987).

Bhagwati, Jagdish N. "Export Market Disruption, Compensation and GATT Reform," in *The New International Economic Order: The North-South Debate*, ed. Bhagwati, MIT Press (Cambridge, Massachusetts, 1977).

——. *Anatomy and Consequence of Exchange Control Regimes*, Ballinger for National Bureau for Economic Research (New York, 1978).

Bruno, Michael. "Inflation and Growth in Recent History and Policy: Applications of an Integrated Approach," in *Understanding Interdependence: The Macroeconomics of the Open Economy*, ed. Peter Kenen, Princeton University Press (Princeton, 1995).

Bryant, Ralph C., *International Financial Intermediation*, Brookings Institution (Washington, D.C., 1987).

Bryant, Ralph C. et al., eds. *Macroeconomic Policies in an Interdependent World*, Brookings Institution (Washington, D.C., 1989).

Coombs, Charles A. *The Arena of International Finance*, Wiley (New York, 1976).

Cooper, Richard N. et al. *Can Nations Agree? Issues in International Economic Cooperation*, Brookings Institution (Washington, D.C., 1989).

Crockett, Andrew. *International Money: Issues and Analysis*, Nelson (Sunbury-on-Thames, Surrey, England, 1977).

——. "Strengthening International Economic Cooperation: The Role of Indicators in Multilateral Surveillance," in *The Quest for National and Global Economic Stabillity*, ed. Wietze Eizenga, E. Frans Limburg, and Jacques J. Polak, Kluwer (Dordrecht, 1988).

Day, C. C. L. "The World's Payments System," in *International Payments Imbalances and Need for Strengthening International Financial Arrangements*, U.S. Congress, Joint Economic Committee, Hearings before the Subcommittee on International Exchange and Payments, 87th Cong., 1st sess., May 16–June 21, 1961 (Washington, D.C., 1961).

Diaz-Alejandro, Carlos. "Some Economic Lessons of the Early 1980s," in *Power, Passion, and Purpose: Prospects for North South Negotiations*, ed. Jagdish N. Bhagwati and John Ruggie, MIT Press (Cambridge, Massachusetts, 1984).

Dobson, Wendy. *Economic Policy Coordination: Requiem or Prologue?* Institute for International Economics (Washington, D.C., 1991).

Dornbusch, Rudiger. "Discussion," in Federal Reserve Bank of Boston, *Key Issues in International Banking*, Federal Reserve Bank of Boston (Boston 1977).

Ellis, Howard S. *Bilateralism and the Future of International Trade*, Essays in International Finance, No. 5, Princeton University Press (Princeton, New Jersey, 1945).

Feldstein, Martin, ed. *International Economic Cooperation*, Chicago University Press (Chicago, 1988).

Fellner, William, et al. *Maintaining and Restoring Balance in International Payments*, Princeton University Press (Princeton, New Jersey, 1966).

Fleming, J. Marcus. *Essays in International Economics*, Allen and Unwin (London, 1971).

Frankel, Jeffrey A., and Kathrine C. Rockett. "International Macroeconomic Policy Coordination When Policymakers Do Not Agree on the True Model," *American Economic Review*, Vol. 78 (June 1988).

Ghai, Dharam, ed. *The IMF and the South: The Social Impact of Crisis and Adjustment*, Zed Books (London, 1991).

Gilbert, Milton. *Quest for World Monetary Order: The Gold-Dollar System and Its Aftermath*, Wiley (New York, 1980).

Gwin, Catherine, and Richard E. Feinberg, eds. *Pulling Together: The International Monetary Fund in a Multipolar World*, Transaction Books (New Brunswick, New Jersey, 1989).

Hewitt, Adrian P. "Stabex and Commodity Export Compensation Schemes: Prospects for Globalization," *World Development*, Vol. 15, No. 5 (May 1987).

Hoffmeyer, Erik. *The International Monetary System: As Essay in Interpretation*, North Holland (Amsterdam, 1992).

Jacobson, Harold Karan, and Michel Oksenberg. *China's Participation in the IMF, the World Bank and GATT: Toward a Global Economic Order*, University of Michigan Press (Ann Arbor, Michigan, 1990).

Johnson, Harry G. *Money, Balance of Payments Theory, and the International Monetary Problem*, Essays in International Finance, No. 124, Princeton University Press (Princeton, New Jersey, 1977).

Karns, Margaret P., and Karen A. Mingst, eds. *The United States and Multilateral Institutions: Patterns of Changing Instrumentality and Influence*, Unwin Hyman (Boston, Massachusetts, 1990).

Kenen, Peter B. "Capital Controls, the EMS and EMU," *Economic Journal*, Vol. 105 (Jan., 1995).

Kindelberger, Charles P. *International Money: A Collection of Essays*, Allen & Unwin (London and Boston, Massachusetts, 1981).

Lim, David. *Export Instability and Compensatory Financing*, Routledge (New York, 1991).

Meade, J. E. "International Economics," in the *Collected Papers of James Meade*, Vol. IV, ed. Susan Howson, Allen & Unwin (London, 1988).

Meier, Gerald M. *Problems of a World Monetary Order*, Oxford University Press (New York, 1982).

Mossé, Robert. *Les Problèmes monétaires internationaux*, Payot (Paris, 1967).

Mundell, Robert A., and Alexander K. Swoboda, eds., *Monetary Problems of the International Economy*, University of Chicago Press (Chicago, 1969).

Mundell, Robert. "A Theory of Optimal Currency Areas," *American Economic Review*, Vol. 51 (Sep. 1961).

Patterson, Gardner. *Discrimination in International Trade: The Policy Issues, 1945–1965*, Princeton University Press (Princeton, New Jersey, 1966).

Penrose, Edith. "The Development of Crisis," in *The Oil Crisis*, ed. Raymond Vernon, W. W. Norton (New York, 1976).

Polak, Jacques J. *Financial Policies and Development*, Development Centre of the Organisation for Economic Co-operation and Development (Paris, 1989).

Polk, Judd, and Gardner Patterson. "The Emerging Pattern of Bilateralism," *Quarterly Journal of Economics*, Vol. 62 (1947–1948).

Fried, Edward R., and Philip H. Trezise. *The Third World Debt: The Next Phase*, Brookings Institution (Washington, D.C.,1989).

Scammell, William McConnell. *The Stability of the International Monetary System*, Macmillan (Basingstoke, Hampshire, England, 1987).

Shonfield, Andrew, ed. *International Economic Relations of the Western World, 1959–1971*, 2 vols., Oxford University Press for the Royal Institute of International Affairs (London and New York, 1976).

Soloman, Robert. *The International Monetary System, 1945–1981*, Harper & Row (New York, 1982).

U.S. Commission on International Trade and Investment Policy, *United States International Economic Policy in an Interdependent World: Report to the President* (Washington, D.C., 1971).

U.S. Congress, Joint Economic Committee. "Action Now to Strengthen the U.S. Dollar," *Report of the Subcommittee on International Exchange and Payments*, 92d Cong., 1st sess., (Washington, D.C., 1971).

Van Meerhaeghe, M. A. G. *International Economic Institutions*, Longman (London, 1971).

Volker, Paul A., and Toyoo Gyohten. *Changing Fortunes: The World's Money and the Decline of American Supremacy*, Times Books (New York, 1992).

Williamson, John. *The Economic Opening of Eastern Europe*, Institute for International Economics (Washington, D.C., 1991).
[Radcliffe] Committee on the Working of the Monetary System, *Report*, Cmnd. 827, HMSO (London, 1959).

International Debt Problems

Arruda, Marcos, *External Debt: Brazil and the International Financial Crisis*, Pluto Press (Sterling, Va., in association with Christian Aid, 2000).
Aspe Armello, Pedro. "The Renegotiation of Mexico's External Debt," Institute of Development Studies, *IDS Bulletin*, Vol. 21, No. 2 (1990).
——. *Economic Transformation: The Mexican Way*, MIT Press (Cambridge, Massachusetts, 1993).
Aubon, Roger. *The Bank for International Settlements, 1930–1955*, Essays in International Finance No. 22, Princeton University Press (Princeton, New Jersey, 1955).
Avery, William P. "Origins of Debt Accumulation among LDCs in the World Political Economy," *Journal of Developing Areas*, Vol. 24 (July 1990).
Bird, Graham, ed. *Third World Debt: The Search for a Solution*, E. Elgar (Aldershot, Hampshire, England, 1989).
Grown, Richard P. C. *Public Debt and Private Wealth: Debt, Capital Flight and the IMF in Sudan*, Macmillan (London, 1992).
Clark, John, and Caroline Allison. *Zambia: Debt & Poverty*, Oxfam (Oxford, 1989).
Claudon, Michael P., ed. *World Debt Crisis: International Lending on Trial*, Ballinger (Cambridge, Massachusetts, 1986).
Cline, William R. "International Debt: Analysis, Experience and Prospects," *Journal of Development Planning*, No. 16 (1985).
——. "The Baker Plan and Brady Reformulation: An Evaluation," in *Dealing with the Debt Crisis*, ed. Ishrat Husain and Ishac Diwan, World Bank (Washington, D.C., 1989).
Cohen, Benjamin J. *Developing-Country Debt: A Middle Way*, Essays in International Finance, No. 173, Princeton University Press (Princeton, New Jersey, 1989).
Commonwealth Secretariat. *The Debt Crisis and the World Economy: Report by a Commonwealth Group of Experts*, Commonwealth Secretariat (London, 1984).
Congdon, Tim. *The Debt Threat: The Dangers of High Real Interest Rates for the World Economy*, Basil Blackwell (Oxford, 1988).
Conway, Patrick. "Baker Plan and International Indebtedness," *World Economy*, Vol. 10, No. 2 (June 1987).
Diaz-Alejandro, Carlos F. *Some Aspects of the 1982–83 Brazilian Payments Crisis*, Brookings Papers on Economic Activity, No. 2, Brookings Institution (Washington, D.C., 1983).
——. *Exchange-Rate Devaluation in a Semi-Industrialized Country: The Experience of Argentina 1955–1961*, MIT Press (Cambridge, Massachusetts, 1965).
Dornbusch, Rudiger. "Overborrowing: Three Case Studies," in *Dollars, Debts and Deficits*, by Dornbusch, MIT Press and Leuven University Press (Cambridge, Massachusetts, and Leuven, Belgium, 1986).

——. Mexico: Stabilization, Debt and Growth," *Economic Policy*, No. 7 (October 1988).

——. "The World Debt Problem: 1980–84 and Beyond," in Dornbusch, *Dollars, Debts and Deficits*, MIT Press and Leuven University Press (Cambridge, Massachusetts and Leuven, Belgium, 1986).

Felix, David. "Latin America's Debt Crisis," *World Policy Journal*, Vol. 7, No. 4 (Fall 1990).

Fried, Edward R., and Charles L. Shultze, *Higher Oil Prices and the World Economy: The Adjustment Problem*, Brookings Institution (Washington, D.C., 1975).

George, Susan. *A Fate Worse Than Debt*, Penguin Books (London, 1988).

Ghosh, Jayati. "Foreign Debt and Economic Development: The Case of Zaire," *Development and Change*, Vol. 17 (1986).

Griffith-Jones, Stephany, ed. *Managing World Debt*, Harvester-Wheatsheaf (Hemel Hempstead, Hertfordshire, England, 1988) and St. Martin's Press (New York, 1988).

Helleiner, Gerald K. "International Policy Issues Posed by Sub-Saharan African Debt," *World Economy*, Vol. 12, No. 3 (Sept. 1989).

Kenen, Peter B. "Organizing Debt Relief: The Need for a New Institution," *Journal of Economic Perspectives*, Vol. 4 (Winter 1990).

Knox, David. *Latin American Debt: Facing Facts*, Oxford International Institute (Oxford, 1990).

Kraft, Joseph. *The Mexican Rescue, Group of Thirty* (New York, 1984).

Lancaster, Carol, and John Williamson, eds. *African Debt and Financing*, Institute for International Economics (Washington, D.C., 1986).

Lissakers, Karin. *Banks, Borrowers, and the Establishment: A Revisionist Account of the International Debt Crisis*, Basic Books (New York, 1991).

Lomax, David F. *The Developing Country Debt Crisis*, St. Martin's Press (New York, 1986).

Lustig, Nora. *Mexico, The Remaking of an Economy*, Brookings Institution (Washington, D.C., 1992).

MacDonald, Scott B., Margie Lindsay, and David Crum. *The Global Debt Crisis: Forecasting for the Future*, Pinter (London and New York, 1990).

Miller, Morris. *Coping Is Not Enough! The International Debt Crisis and the Roles of the World Bank and International Monetary Fund*, Dow Jones-Irwin (Homewood, Illinois, 1986).

Nafziger, E. Wayne. *The Debt Crisis in Africa*, Johns Hopkins University Press (Baltimore, 1993).

Onimode, Bade, ed. *The IMF, the World Bank and African Debt*, 2 vols., Zed Books (London and Atlantic Highlands, New Jersey, 1989).

Parfitt, Trevor W., and Stephen P. Riley. *The African Debt Crisis*, Routledge (London, 1989).

Rieffel, Alexis. *The Role of the Paris Club in Managing Debt Problems*, Essays in International Finance, No. 161, Princeton University Press (Princeton, New Jersey, 1985).

Rieke, Wolfgang. "The Development of the Deutschemark as a Reserve Currency, in *Reserve Currencies in Transition*, Group of Thirty (New York, 1982).

Roll, Eric. "Behind Bretton Woods: The Climate Then and Today," in *International Capital Movements, Debt and Monetary System*, ed. Wolfram Engels, Armin Gutowski, and Heny C. Wallich, v. Hase & Koehler (Mainz, 1984).
Sampson, Anthony. *The Money Lenders: Bankers in a Dangerous World*, Hodder & Stoughton (London, 1988).
Singer, H. W., and Soumitra Sharma, eds. *Economic Development and World Debt*, Macmillan (London, 1989).
Stiles, Kendall Wayne. *Negotiating Debt: The IMF Lending Process*, Westview Press (Boston, Massachusetts, 1991).
World Institute for Development Economics Research. *Debt Reduction: Report of a Study Group of the World Institute for Development Economics Research*, World Institute for Development Economics Research of the United Nations University, Study Group Series, No. 3 (Helsinki, 1989).

Reform of the International Monetary System

Bhagwati, Jagdish N., ed. *The New International Economic Order: The North–South Debate*, MIT Press (Cambridge, Massachusetts, 1977).
Bird, Graham. *World Finance and Adjustment: An Agenda for Reform*, Macmillan (London, 1985).
Bretton Woods Commission. "Commission Report," in *Bretton Woods: Looking to the Future*, Bretton Woods Committee (Washington, D.C., 1994).
Carin, Barry and Angela Wood. *Accountability of the International Monetary Fund*, Ashgate. (Burlington, Vermont, 2005).
Cline, William R. *International Monetary Reform and the Developing Countries*, Brookings Institution (Washington, D.C., 1976).
Cooper, Richard N. "A Monetary System for the Future," *Foreign Affairs*, Vol. 63, No. 1 (Fall 1984).
———. "What Future for the International Monetary System?" in *International Financial Policy: Essays in Honor of Jacques J. Polak*, ed. Jacob A. Frenkel and Morris Goldstein, International Monetary Fund and De Nederlandsche Bank (Washington, D.C., 1991).
———. The Evolution of the International Monetary Fund toward a World Central Bank," in *The International Monetary System: Essays in World Economics*, ed. Cooper, MIT Press (Cambridge, Massachusetts, 1987, originally published in 1983).
———. *The International Monetary System*: Essays in World Economics, MIT Press (Cambridge, Massachusetts,1987).
Crockett, Andrew. "The International Monetary Fund in the 1990s," *Government and Opposition*, Vol. 27, No. 3 (1992).
Dam, Kenneth W. *The Rules of the Game: Reform and Evolution in the International Monetary System*, University of Chicago Press (Chicago, 1982).
de Grauwe, Paul. *International Money: Post-War Trends and Theories*, Clarendon Press (Oxford, 1989).
de Vries, Tom. "Jamaica, or the Non-reform of the International Monetary System," *Foreign Affairs*, Vol. 54, No. 3 (April 1976).

Dell, Sydney, ed. *The International Monetary System and Its Reform: Papers Prepared for the Group of Twenty-four by a United Nations Project directed by Sidney Dell*, North Holland (New York, 1987).

Dornbusch, Rudiger. *Economic Performance*, Vol. 1, *The International Financial System*, ed. Jeffrey D. Sachs, University of Chicago Press (Chicago, 1989).

Edwards, Richard W. *International Monetary Collaboration*, Transnational Publishers (Dobbs Ferry, New York, 1985).

Expert Group on International Monetary Issues (UNCTAD). *International Monetary Issues and the Developing Countries*, UN document TD/B/32 and TD/B/C. 3/6 (New York, 1965).

Frantianni, Michele, Paolo Savona, and John J. Kirton eds. *Sustaining Global Growth and Development: G7 and IMF Governance*, Ashgate (Burlington, Vermont, 2003).

Friedman, Irving S. *Toward World Prosperity: Reshaping the Global Money System*, Lexington Books (Lexington, Massachusetts, 1986).

German Council of Economic Experts. *Toward a New Basis for International Monetary Policy*, Princeton Essays in International Finance, No. 31, Princeton University Press (Princeton, New Jersey, 1972).

Gowa, Joanne S. "Hegemons, IOs, and Markets: The Case of the Substitution Account," *International Organization*, Vol. 38, No. 4 (Autumn 1984).

———. *Closing the Gold Window: Domestic Politics and the End of Bretton Woods*, Cornell University Press (Ithaca, New York, 1983).

Group of Thirty. *Towards a Less Unstable International Monetary System: Reserve Assets and a Substitution Account*, Reserve Asset Study Group, Group of Thirty (New York, 1980).

Grubel, George N. *Jamaica and the Par-Value System*, Essays in International Finance, No. 20, Princeton University Press (Princeton, New Jersey, 1977).

Grubel, Herbert G. *The International Monetary System: Efficiency and Practical Alternatives*, Penguin Books (Harmondsworth, Greater London, England, 1984).

———. ed. *World Monetary Reform: Plans and Issues*, Stanford University Press (Stanford, California, 1963).

Hamouda, Omar F., Robin Rowley, and Bernard M. Wolf, eds. *The Future of the International Monetary System: Change, Coordination or Instability?* E. Elgar (Aldershot, Hampshire, England, 1989).

Houthakker, Hendrik S. "The Breakdown of Bretton Woods," in *Economic Advice and Executive Policy: Recommendations from Past Members of the Council of Economic Advisers*, ed. Werner Sichel, Praeger (New York, 1978).

Independent Commission on International Development Issues. *North–South: A Programme for Survival: A Report of the Independent Commission on International Development Issues under the Chairmanship of Willy Brandt*, MIT Press (Cambridge, Massachusetts, 1980).

International Institute of International Finance. *Financial Crises in Emerging Markets*, by a working group chaired by William Cline (Washington D.C., 1999).

Khatkhate, Deena, ed. "The Evolving International Monetary System," *World Development*, Vol. 15, No. 12 (Dec. 1987).

Machlup, Fritz. *Plans for Reform of the International Monetary System*, Special Papers in International Economics, No. 3, Princeton University Press (Princeton, New Jersey, 1962 and 1964).

——. *Remaking the International Monetary System: The Rio Agreement and Beyond*, Committee for Economic Development, Supplementary Paper, No. 24, Johns Hopkins Press (Baltimore, 1968).

Machlup, Fritz, and Burton G. Malkiel, eds. *International Monetary Arrangements: The Problem of Choice*, Study Group of 32 Economists (Princeton, New Jersey, 1964).

McKinnon, Ronald I. *An International Standard for Monetary Stabilization*, Institute for International Economics (Washington, D.C., 1984).

——. "The Rules of the Game: International Money in Historical Perspective," *Journal of Economic Literature*, Vol. 31 (March 1993).

Mozhin, Alexei V. "Russia's Negotiations with the IMF," in *Changing the Economic System in Russia*, ed. Anders Åslund and Richard Layard, Pinter Publishers (London, 1993).

Mundell, Robert A., and Jacques J. Polak, eds. *The New International Monetary System*, Columbia University Press (New York, 1977).

Narasimham, M. *Bretton Woods—Forty Years On*, Forum of Free Enterprise (Bombay, 1984).

O'Brien, Robert, et. al. *Contesting Global Governance: Multilateral Economic Institutions and Global Social Movements*, Cambridge University Press (Cambridge, U.K., 2000).

Ossola, Rinaldo. *Towards New Monetary Relationships*, Essays in International Finance, No. 87, Princeton University Press (Princeton, New Jersey, 1971).

Palyi, Melchior. *Managed Money at the Crossroads: The European Experience*, University of Notre Dame Press (Notre Dame, Indiana, 1958).

Polak, Jacques. J. *The World Bank and the International Monetary Fund: A Changing Relationship*, Brookings Institution (Washington, D.C., 1994).

Putnam, Robert D., and Nicholas Bayne. *Hanging Together: The Seven-Power Summits*, Harvard University Press (Cambridge, Massachusetts, 1984).

Rasminski, Louis. "Canadian Views," in *Bretton Woods Revisited*, ed. A. L. K. Acheson, J. F. Chant, and M. F. J. Prachowny, University of Toronto Press (Toronto, 1972).

Roosa, Robert V. *Monetary Reform for the World Economy*, The Elihu Root Lectures, 1964–1965 (New York, 1965).

Soloman, Robert. "International Monetary Reform: The Future Is Not What It Used to Be!" in *The Future of the International Monetary System: Change, Coordination or Instability*, ed. Omar F. Hamouda, Robin Rowley, and Bernard M. Wolf, M. E. Sharpe (Armonk, New York, 1989).

Soros, George. *The Crisis of Global Capitalism*, American Public Affairs (Washington D.C., 1998).

Suzuki, Yoshio, Junichi Miyake, and Mitsuaki Okabe, eds. *The Evolution of the International Monetary System: How Can Efficiency and Stability Be Maintained?* University of Tokyo Press (Tokyo, 1990).

Tinbergen, Jan. *Reshaping the International Order: A Report to the Club of Rome*, E. P. Dutton (New York, 1976).

Triffin, Robert. "The European Monetary System: Tombstone or Cornerstone," in Federal Reserve Bank of Boston, *The International Monetary System: Forty Years After Bretton Woods*, Conference Series, No. 28, Federal Bank of Boston (Boston, 1984).

Truman, Edwin M., *A Strategy for IMF Reform*, Institute for International Economics. (Washington, D.C. 2006).

Tsoukalis, Loukas, ed., *The Political Economy of International Money: In Search of a New Order*, Royal Institute of International Affairs, Sage Publications (London, 1985).

United Nations Conference on Trade and Development (UNCTAD). *Compendium of Selected Studies on International Monetary and Financial Issues for the Developing Countries*, United Nations (New York, 1987).

[U.S.] Federal Reserve Bank of Boston. *The International Monetary System: Forty Years after Bretton Woods*. Proceedings of a Conference Sponsored by the Federal Reserve Bank of Boston in May 1984, Conference Series, No. 28 (Boston, 1984).

U.S. Senate Foreign Relations Committee. *The Meltzer Commission: The Future of the IMF and World Bank*, U.S. G.P.O. (Washington, D.C., 2000).

Williamson, John. *The Failure of World Monetary Reform, 1971–74*, New York University Press (New York, 1977).

About the Authors

Norman K. Humphreys was a member of the staff of the International Monetary Fund, holding the post of chief editor for 23 years before retiring in 1986. Born in the United Kingdom, he graduated from the London School of Economics and Political Science with a BSc (econ), specializing in banking and currency. For many years, he worked in London as an economist in the Research Department of an international bank, and for two years was the resident economist for that bank in Brazil. While in Brazil, he was the Rio de Janeiro correspondent of the London *Financial Times*. He has contributed articles to a number of financial journals and newspapers. He moved to Washington, D.C., in 1963, first joining the staff of the World Bank and then the staff of the International Monetary Fund, where he had overall responsibility for the Fund's extensive publications program.

Sarah Tenney also served as a staff member of the International Monetary Fund from 1987 to 2003. During this period, she held positions of increasing responsibility in the Secretary's Department, the Human Resources Department, and the Technology and General Services Department. Born in the United States, she was educated at Marietta College (U.S.) and the University of Kent at Canterbury (U.K.), receiving a master's degree in international relations. Prior to joining the staff of the International Monetary Fund, she was a news analyst for a private consulting firm in Washington, D.C. She received a PhD from the University of Mississippi, specializing in international relations and comparative politics, in 2007. She is now an assistant professor in the Political Science and Criminal Justice Department at The Citadel in Charleston, South Carolina.

www.ingramcontent.com/pod-product-compliance
Ingram Content Group UK Ltd.
Pitfield, Milton Keynes, MK11 3LW, UK
UKHW041634031026
15587UKWH00001B/291

9 780810 867901